To Marlene,
With best wishes

Angus HShaw.

Is There Any Scandal?

A Brief History of the People of the Howe of Fife Parish Church

Angus H. Shaw

All profits from the sale of this book go to
Howe of Fife Parish Church Development Fund

First published in the United Kingdom by Angus H. Shaw in 2016

Paradise, Craigrothie, Cupar Fife KY15 5PH

shawangus3@gmail.com

ISBN 978-0-9954887-0-0

A catalogue record for this book is available from the British Library

Cover photograph: The Lomonds overlooking the Howe of Fife

Copy-editing and layout: Daisy Editorial (daisyeditorial.co.uk)

For my wife Ann

~

Without whose patience and support this book would not have been completed

Contents

~

Illustration credits

Acknowledgements

~

In preparing this volume I have been supported by many people in the parish and beyond. They have been so generous with their time and making available to me information and photographs, books and memories. While all deserve recognition, I can name only some here: Rev. Malcolm Aldcroft; Marjory Anderson; David Beveridge; Marion Calley; Baron Cochrane of Cults; Leslie Cook; Ruth Forbes; Elder and Karen Garland; Ella Kinnear; Marianna Lines; Mary Loudon; Dennis McInnes; Fay Neilson; Nell and Will Nicholson; Norma Nicol; Ann Page; Helen Paterson; Rev. Marion Paton; Edwina Proudfoot; Sandy Scott; John Stark; Mr and Mrs David Wood; Rev. Ian Wotherspoon and members of Ladybank Mission. There are also those who are, sadly, no longer with us but whose contribution has been invaluable: Jean Bradbury; Rev. Iain Forbes; John Ronaldson; Harry Sangster; James Stark. I also wish to acknowledge the assistance of the staff of St Andrews University Library Special Collections Department and Fife Council Archive Centre. Have I forgotten to mention you? If so I am very sorry because without the help of each one of you this would never have reached completion. I must also recognise the Rev. Gordon McCracken, who first planted the idea of this book into my head, Rev. Bill Hunter, who has been helpful and encouraging, and my wife Ann for support, proofreading and giving me the backing I needed.

Introduction

∼

The title of this book, *Is There Any Scandal?*, may surprise some modern folk. Today the word scandal is used when someone's behaviour is considered outrageous or offensive. As a result, seeking scandal is to seek the worst in others and is tantamount to gossiping, which in itself is nasty and outrageous. It certainly is not very Christian, in that it does not reflect the love of God and a readiness to major on what is good in our fellow travellers through life.

I have adopted this title here not for any nefarious purposes but because generations of ministers of the Church of Scotland opened Kirk Session meetings with that question. What they wanted to know was if anything might be happening that could lead their people away from God.

Those were the days when the moral probity of parishioners was believed to be the concern of the Kirk Session. Many things that we take for granted today would have been considered to be leading people away from God and so be 'scandal': working on Sunday, swearing, joining religious groups that did not conform to the national church, playing cards, attending theatres or public houses on Sunday. Today they pass without comment. It is important to remember that, in the past, people did things differently. It is very tempting to judge them, but we must not do that. They lived according to their circumstances and the norms of their time. We do the same in the 21st century. Judgement is not helpful. Learning from the people of the past, their strengths and their weaknesses, and their coping mechanisms, is helpful, and that is the point of history. The past teaches us how to live in the present and prepare for the future.

It is the aim of this book to look at the lives of the folk who inhabited the place we now call the Parish of the Howe of Fife. It is a history of the ancient churches that have been here for more than a thousand years. Throughout all of that time the parishioners had to cope with the political, religious and social influences of the world around them. Each generation had to adapt to suit the circumstances in which they lived. It is their story that is being told here.

I hope you find this book informative and entertaining. No doubt there are things omitted that the reader may think should have been included and things included that some may think would have been better left out. The book is as it is. If someone is inspired to research in greater depth something I have only touched upon then it has fulfilled its purpose.

HIRTHA

MARE DEVCALIDONIVM

Rona

SCHIA LEVISSA

HEBRIDES INSVLAE
XLIII

Dungisbeput

Kirkualia
Renonia
ORCA

Renolse

Cathenesia

MVLA

IONA

ILA

CVMBRA

ARGADIA

Arana

HVLTONIA

na metrop:

Boisdail

SOTHERLANDIA

ROS-
SIA

MORA
VIA

Elgon

Strauagrin

Dorno
DOH

Lindarnan
Tardus.f.

Comoria
Sinus salutis

Emernes

Spca.f.

Roxmai

Stermaggi

Dea.f.

Banf
NIA Buzham
Slanis

BVTHA

Buthuana prom.

DI

MARIA

Aberdonia

Coue

Dononer

Lorogton

LOVAERTA

GRAM
PIVS

Nafs.f.

AI DAC

Tayf.

Erna.f.

DON

S.Ioanes

MARNI
A

Dunkel

Brechin

ANGV

Dombram
Lacus leuinu
Dode
SIA

Abbroth prn.

Monros

Porthea

Donfermilg FIFA

Lacus
Air

Dombroton
Glafco
Lizhco

Sterling

Hamelton

Kinghorn

S.Andreas
Xetropolis

Dumbar

Du:
Kelson

GAL
ALOVI
DIA

Paslci

Edinburg

B.gt

Sinus
Siliniauns

Tr.
Wigton

Galeis

Ken.

Kirtolbro

Tueda.f.

Dunfras

Norham

Peruicum

Insula Sacra

Bambrog

Anwik

mule prom. PARTE

Agrement

CVM
BRIA Coker
Carleolum

month

Tina.f.

Tini.f.

Tinmouth D. INGHILTERRA

20

The Mists of Time

~

As the English clergyman and poet John Donne said in his Meditation XVII, 'No man is an Island, entire of itself; every man is a piece of the Continent, a part of the main'. The truth of this becomes very clear as we examine our past and the people who have through their great endeavours carved the world we have inherited. They were influenced by great national and international events that occurred before and during the times in which they lived. We too find that the past, as well as current affairs, influences every part of our daily lives. Yet sometimes it is only with the benefit of hindsight that we can appreciate how the 'bigger picture' shaped the detail. This chapter is a brief flight through the development of Christianity in Scotland. It aims to put into context the events that were taking place in Fife, Scotland and the world and their effect on the lives of the people who, over the centuries, formed the communities and the churches that lie within the bounds of the modern Parish of the Howe of Fife.

There are records of the remains of ancient peoples being found at Kettle and Collessie, but often valuable clues to the lives and beliefs of the earliest inhabitants were removed and destroyed in the process in the days before archaeological techniques were developed and the value of the finds was not properly understood. More recently, excavation work for the new Queensferry Crossing has unearthed the remains, on the south side of the Forth, of a Mesolithic home believed to be over 10,000 years old.[1] This shows us that people settled in the area within a few hundred years of the retreat of the last great ice sheet that covered Scotland. These were largely hunter–gatherers and evidence of their settlements and burial sites has been identified by archaeologists across the area we now know as the Howe of Fife. About 4000 BC the first farms were established, and it is understood that the climate was warmer and drier than it is today. These early people left behind cists and cairns containing the remains of their loved ones and artefacts that give evidence of their belief in an afterlife. Around 79 AD the Romans arrived and built camps throughout the county at St Andrews, Newburgh, Auchtermuchty and Boarhills.[2] The Romans appear not to have lingered but the fertility of the land

---

[1] http://www.bbc.co.uk/news/uk-scotland-edinburgh-east-fife-20376243
[2] http://www.historic-scotland.gov.uk/prehistoric-settlement.pdf

retained communities in the Howe of Fife. One well-known relic of these ancient times is the standing stone called Collessie Man, which can be found just outside the village of Collessie. Being dated to about 500 AD, it is in fact comparatively modern and lies within the period when Christianity was beginning to develop in Scotland.

Early Christianity in Scotland

St Colmcille (Columba) Heritage Centre, Garten, Co. Donegal

Ninian is normally recognised as Scotland's earliest saint, but was he in fact a northern English saint? Was the *Book of Kells* the product of the Irish monastery of Iona, or was it the work of Pictish scribes? While this seems unlikely, there is a question mark over its origin. In these early days, Ireland, England and Scotland, as we know them, did not exist. We can trace Columba (or Colum Cille as he is also known) back to his birthplace at Garten in County Donegal. We can also follow his mission across the sea to western Scotland and Iona. The story of St Columba is well documented. Adamnan, the seventh-century Abbot of Iona, wrote his biography.

The Kingdom of Dalriada, which originated in County Antrim in Northern Ireland, eventually extended across the sea to Argyll and north to include Mull and Iona. When the Kings of Dalriada decided to leave Ireland, a new centre was created at Dunadd in Kilmartin, Argyllshire. It is believed that a castle, similar to the motte and bailey castles introduced by the Normans following their invasion of England in 1066, stood on the now unimpressive rocky outcrop of Dunadd from about 500–850 AD. The capital of this ancient kingdom was run by a people known as the Scoti, a people who were to give Scotland its name. There were many battles between the Scots and the Picts, who occupied much of Scotland. On the other hand, they faced a common enemy in the form of the Vikings. In one raid against the Picts their King, Nechtan, was killed.

This left a power vacuum that had to be filled. The Gael Kenneth MacAlpin was said to have a Pictish mother and so he became a unifying force bringing Gaels and Picts together against the Vikings. The raids by the Norsemen were terrible and Dalriada disappeared from the map. In its place Alba, which was to become Scotland, emerged with Kenneth MacAlpin as King.

Much of what we read about the earliest times relies upon Bede, who was a Northumbrian monk, and it may have been in his interests to see Whithorn and Iona from a Northumbrian perspective. So it is that the 'Venerable' gentleman relates the importance of Ninian's training in Rome and, as Whithorn came under the control of the Northumbrian Church at that time, he was included in Bede's *History of the English Church and People* written in AD 731. It mattered to Bede that Ninian was seen to have Roman and not Celtic roots, for he reports that there was a dispute about the calculation of Easter between Roman and Celtic Churches. It has been suggested that he may have made more of this dispute than it deserved, but then Bede was in the 'Roman camp'.

Ninian, about whom we know very little, is closely associated with Whithorn, which was for centuries a centre for pilgrims who sought to visit his shrine. Whithorn has long been part of the northern kingdom, and Ninian, who is believed to have started his first Christian mission in Whithorn, is now generally accepted as Scotland's first saint. Archaeological evidence dates the settlement in the area to about the fifth century and some of the earliest Christian relics found in Scotland belong to this area. According to Bede, Ninian was responsible for Christianising the southern Picts. While this may well be so, the extent of his work is unknown. What is known is that when he returned to Whithorn he built a church in what was once a pagan cemetery and it was known as the Candida Casa – the White House. From these beginnings in the extreme south-west of the country other traditions developed and were spread by people whose names are familiar but who are otherwise mysterious. Such people include St Serf, who was associated with Loch Leven and Culross, and St Kentigern or Cantigernus, popularly called St Mungo (probably from a notable Cumbrian or Welsh lineage). Mungo is associated with Glasgow and is credited with bringing Christianity to the area. He is believed to have been a contemporary of St Columba, dying about AD 614.[3]

Columba too was an important figure in bringing Christianity to Scotland and northern England, but it is clear that the spread of Christianity here did not originate with him. Following the Synod of Whitby in 664 when the Roman Church emerged victorious in its dispute with the Picts about the date of Easter and other matters of discipline, northern Britain soon fell into line. Nechtan, King of the Picts, and the centres of Iona and Whithorn accepted Roman authority and so the influence of Iona contracted. The eighth century brought the Scandinavian invasion into northern Scotland and central England. Scotland was effectively isolated from Ireland, southern England and the continent of Europe including Rome.

---

[3]   www.undiscoveredscotland.co.uk/

It appears to be about this time that the Culdees or Celedi (Servants of God) came to the fore. Their origins are problematic and, with so many conflicting accounts, the Culdees are shrouded in mystery. Some have claimed they originated in Jerusalem, that they were among the earliest followers of Christ and that they fled to Britain when Jesus was crucified, but there is little evidence to support this. In his book on early Scotland, W. Croft Dickson sees the Culdees as having their origins among a hermitic movement in the Celtic Church, and this seems to agree with those who see them as the inheritors of Columban Christianity.[4] In fact, there seems to be a great deal of imagination but little evidence to support any theory of their beginnings. Nevertheless, we know that they existed and were found mainly in eastern Scotland, though some claim they were also to be found in south-west Scotland, Ireland and England around York. Dr Oliver O'Grady defines his use of the term Culdee as referring to 'pre-reformed monastic clergy in Scotland' and this, he says, is in keeping with the Later Medieval general tradition. It would probably be best if we too think of the Culdees in these terms as we consider their importance in Fife and the East of Scotland.[5]

Dr O'Grady maintains that much of the early missionary work that emanated from Iona affected the peoples of southern Pictland. By the 12th century in Fife there is evidence of two important houses, one at Loch Leven and the other at St Andrews, where the Culdees built a chapel close to the remains of the collegiate church of St Mary on the Rock. The first mention of an Abbey at Kilrymont (St Andrews) was in the mid 8th century. Others were at Scone, Dunkeld, Abernethy, Brechin and Monymusk in Aberdeenshire as well as Iona. Each was an independent establishment with its own abbot. Their position in St Andrews allowed them to claim involvement in the election of bishops up to the middle of the 13th century. In 1273 Rome stripped them of their long-standing privileges. It was not only the Church that sought their demise, for the Crown too saw advantages in maintaining a close relationship with Rome. Margaret, the Saxon queen of Malcolm III (1057–93), was unimpressed with Culdee ways and worked successfully to eradicate them. Indeed, Margaret sought assistance from the Benedictines in Canterbury to establish a priory at Dunfermline, and she is also credited with founding a Benedictine Abbey on Iona. So it was that these once influential people disappeared from the pages of history. It can be assumed, however, that not all chapels were associated with great Christian centres and there were many smaller Culdee chapels in Fife and elsewhere, suitable for only small numbers of worshippers.

Church and State between 1060 and 1560

People are complex and, despite Margaret's attempt to draw the Scottish Church into line with the rest of Europe, she and Malcolm made gifts to the Culdee community on Loch Leven. She appears to have been concerned with some things like the date of

---

4   W. Croft Dickinson, *Scotland: From the Earliest Times to 1603*, rev. and ed. Archibald Duncan (Oxford, The Clarendon Press, 1977)

5   O. O'Grady, 'Culdee Archaeology Project – lecture notes', Iona Workshop 11th April 2012, www.ionahistory.org. uk/iona-conf-ogrady-revised-2.pdf

the beginning of Lent and the way the mass was conducted. She seems to have been less concerned with the celibacy of the priesthood or the granting of high office in the church to laymen. Ethelred, her son, was made abbot of Dunfermline, although he was not ordained or in any way a clergyman. Nevertheless, she initiated sufficient change to bring European practices into the Scottish Church.

At a Church Council at Windsor in 1072, which lacked any representation from the Scottish Church, it was declared that the province of York should stretch from the Humber to the northernmost shores of Scotland. Some historians point out that the Scottish bishops were poorly funded and this was a reason for their exclusion. They also point out that they tended to be in the pocket of the monarch, but this was also true of the English bishops. The division between Church and State was not always well defined in either kingdom. Whatever the reasons for the exclusion of Scottish representation at the Council, this decision gave no consideration to the wishes of the King or the people of the northern kingdom. It might be interpreted as the English King extending his control over his Scottish neighbour through the Church.

This inevitably led to a dispute regarding the suitability of the Archbishop of York to consecrate the primate of Scotland. By the time of Alexander I and David I it became an issue of the independence of the Scottish Church, and by implication the independence of the Scottish nation. An appeal to the Pope was rejected because of English opposition to Scotland being declared a metropolitan see. Behind the whole affair were English claims over Scotland, and much politicking ensued. In 1176 Pope Alexander III wrote to the bishops of Scotland telling them York had no authority over them. In 1192 Pope Celestine made the Scottish Church a 'special daughter' of Rome. As a result, when Bishop David de Bernham was elected Bishop of St Andrews in 1239, the papal mandate reveals that the approval of the Scottish King, not the Archbishop of York, had been sought. York could never again claim any authority over the Scottish Church.[6]

The Church in Medieval Scotland

By the end of the 12th century the country was divided into 11 effective bishoprics. Cathedral churches were erected and these were monuments to the power and wealth of the Church of Rome. A renewed missionary zeal swept the land and monasteries were being built and financed by the religious enthusiasm of the rich and powerful Anglo-Normans from the south.

Initially the Scottish earls north of the Forth were suspicious of the infiltration of monastic establishments on the English lines and populated by monks from Canterbury, Pontefract and Rievaulx. In time, however, the feelings of distrust wore off and in the 12th century both St Andrews Cathedral (1158) and the Abbey of Lindores (1195) were built and they exercised great influence in the history of the parishes within the Howe of Fife and the nation as a whole.

---

[6]   Croft Dickinson, *Scotland*

It was at this time that the influential Arbroath Abbey was founded, as well as St Machar's Cathedral in Aberdeen and St Magnus Cathedral in Orkney and many others. St Andrews Cathedral became the principal establishment in Scotland with its bishops acting as primates of the whole country.

All of this was being achieved with the blessing of the King (Robert the Bruce attended the consecration of St Andrews Cathedral in 1318)[7] as well as that of the Pope. The Anglo-Norman influence entered Scotland with English settlers and Norman knights. They crowded into Scotland in the reigns of Alexander and David and exercised a tremendous influence on these Kings.

One important family in the early stories of both Collessie and Lathrisk is that of the first Earl of Winchester, Saer de Quincy. It would appear they arrived in England from France with the Norman Conquest. By the 12th century they were cousins to the Scottish Kings Malcolm and William the Lion and the de Quincy name appears as a witness in charters of King Malcolm IV. This connection brought the family lands at Forfar and Haddington. The royal link may also have been influential in de Quincy's choice of wife, Orabilis, daughter of Ness. She was her father's heir and so through marriage de Quincy found himself inheritor of lands at Leuchars, Lathrisk and Beath in Fife, as well as Gask and Deuglie near Glenfarg in Perthshire and Trenent in Lothian. There is also a tradition that the lands of Kinloch were in the possession of David, Earl of Huntingdon, brother of William the Lion, and it was he who granted the lands to de Quincy.[8] By the time of Alexander III (1249–86) de Quincy's descendant had given a charter for part of the lands of Kinloch to John de Kyndeloch.

Bishop de Bernham

A special year in the history of the three churches that now constitute most of the Parish of the Howe of Fife is 1243. This date is special due to the activities of Bishop David de Bernham who, as we see in the *Proceedings of the Society of Antiquaries of Scotland*, was elected Bishop of St Andrews on 2nd June 1239 with the approval of the King, Alexander II.[9] David de Bernham was born around 1200 in Berwick-upon-Tweed when the town lay in Scotland. We first hear of David as a sub-deacon attached to the court of Alexander II. In time he was elevated to the position of chamberlain. Clearly he was known to the King when Alexander II approved of his election as bishop. We find de Bernham's signature witnessing a charter granting teinds (tithes) to the church of Kinglassie in 1234, prior to his elevation to the bishopric, and his signature as bishop appears on various other charters and deeds.

David de Bernham was not the favourite to follow in the footsteps of Bishop William de Malvoisin, who died in 1237. It was a monk, Galfrius Liverance, a Red Friar and Bishop of Dunkeld, who was the popular option. Apparently he was not the King's

---

7   J. Dowden (ed.) 'Chartulary of the Abbey of Lindores' (Edinburgh University Press for the Scottish History Society, 1903, p. xvi)
8   C.P. Collins Jr, *Royal Ancestors of Magna Charta Barons* (Dallas, Carr P. Collins Jr, 1959) pp. 208–09
9   *Proceedings of the Society of Antiquaries of Scotland*, 86: VIII (1885), p. 198

choice, however. He wanted David de Bernham to succeed and, being King, he got his way.[10]

The elevation of David de Bernham to Bishop occurred soon after the period of dispute involving King William I, the Pope and the Archbishop of York. By 1239, when the Pope was elected, we learn that he confirmed that the King's approval had been sought and granted. The position in which de Bernham found himself was extremely prestigious in Scotland. While there was no archbishop in the country until the 15th century, St Andrews was nevertheless considered an important see.

It was Bishop David de Bernham who single-handedly, between 1240 and 1249, initiated and performed the rededication services in his enormous diocese, which stretched from Aberdeen to the English Border. It was he too who chaired a diocesan Synod in Musselburgh in 1242 where a series of 26 decrees were approved. These decrees give us some idea of the standard every church was expected to attain.

Included in the list we find: the enclosure of the churchyard to protect it from wild animals; the responsibility placed on the rector and parishioners to keep the chancel in good repair; and the provision of a silver chalice 'and other necessary furniture' at the rector's expense. The clergy had to wear a large tonsure (which distinguished them as Roman as opposed to Celtic clerics) and they had to refrain from attending taverns, except when on a journey. The local priest also had to refrain from playing dice and lead a chaste life. Another rule that will sound strange to modern ears is that women were not to give confession between the chancel-screen and the altar 'but in some other part of the church and out of hearing but not out of sight of the faithful'.[11]

His work began in the summer of 1240 and continued to the autumn of 1249. In that period he reconsecrated 140 of the 234 churches in his diocese. The list of dedications is contained in a pontifical and includes churches in Kincardineshire, Clackmannanshire, Berwickshire, Fife, Angus, Edinburgh and many others. This was a great feat of endurance for it meant travelling great distances at a time when transport was difficult. The services themselves were lengthy and involved the mass. This great endeavour brought praise from many of his contemporaries.

The reason for this mass consecration was clearly to Romanise the Church in Scotland, and there is no doubt that it succeeded in its purpose. It also ensured that every church was 'fit for purpose'. Among the churches reconsecrated were Lathrisk (recorded Losserech but to become Kettle in 1636), dedicated to St John the Evangelist and St Athernase on 28th July 1243, Collessie (recorded Callesyn) on 30th July 1243 and Cults (recorded Cuilte) on 8th August 1243. The fact of this reconsecration suggests that these churches already existed, that their structures were sound, that vestments for the priests were present and that they contained the means of administering the sacraments of baptism and holy communion.

---

[10]   W. Lockhart, *The Church of Scotland in the Thirteenth Century: The Life and Times of David de Bernham of St Andrews (Bishop) AD 1239–1253* (Edinburgh and London, William Blackwood and Sons, 1899)

[11]   Lockhart, *Life and Times of David de Bernham*

On 13th July 1249 Bishop de Bernham crowned Alexander III at Scone, and in 1250 he took part in a ceremony at Dunfermline in honour of Queen Margaret, who had died in 1093. David de Bernham died in 1253. There is no doubt that he is a significant figure, intellectually and physically strong. He played an important part in the history of Scotland and also in the history of the Howe of Fife. That importance is now less clear for the passage of time and the effect of the Reformation has confined him to the shadows of the past.[12]

Life in Pre-Reformation Scotland

Life in pre-Reformation Scotland was very different from what is familiar to us today. It was not only that it was a pre-industrial society lacking the wonders of modern technology; it was also different in how people viewed life and death. The fundamental question facing everyone was, 'How do I enter the Kingdom of Heaven?' At the heart of this question was fear of suffering the eternal damnation that was expected to be delivered on Judgement Day. Theologians in places of learning, like the universities, tried to create a division between reason and faith, claiming that, while parts of the religion depended on faith, other parts depended upon reason. There were those, like John Wycliffe, the English dissident who died in 1384, who could not agree with this division and were condemned for it. The problem for the ordinary folk was that the question they urgently needed to be answered was not being addressed. They required real, meaningful spiritual guidance but did not receive it. The University of St Andrews was established in order to fight such heresies as Wycliffe's, but only two people in Scotland were executed for sharing his belief. Meantime ordinary folk continued to fear a Devil that was just as real as the God whom they longed for. Churches held pictures of Heaven and Hell on roodscreens and on the walls, reminding the devout of the inevitability of their fate.

Come the 15th century things were changing. Tensions broke out between Crown and Pope concerning the authority to provide bishops and also the money taken by Rome from a hard-pressed people. The Crown felt its authority and its financial resources were being threatened. By the time James V came to the throne in 1488 the relationship was very difficult, for the King saw it as acceptable for his sons to hold high office in the great abbeys of the land. His eleven-year-old son, Alexander, was made Archbishop of St Andrews, and others found themselves at Melrose and Kelso. At this time the Pope was feeling at a disadvantage because Henry VIII, who ascended to the English throne in 1491, had broken with the Church of Rome and the Pontiff was anxious to ensure that Scotland did not go down the same path.[13] Rome was prepared to approve anyone that James put forward as a bishop, no matter how unsuitable the choice was. This resulted in the illegitimate sons of the Royal House controlling the great abbeys and the substantial incomes from these establishments being used to support the nobility.

---

[12]   Lockhart, *Life and Times of David de Bernham*
[13]   Croft Dickinson, *Scotland*

Those running these ecclesiastic centres had little regard for the spiritual or material welfare of the people, for their only interest was to lay their hands on the money to use it for their own ends. In short, the Church had become corrupt at the highest level in the land. There is no doubt that this was a major reason for the Reformation in Scotland because the Church, though not the faith, had lost all credibility in the eyes of the people.

At the time Henry VIII was dissolving monasteries in England, James V achieved the same end by a different route. In 1532, in order to 'preserve Catholicism', he required monasteries to raise large sums of money. The only way the tens of thousands of pounds could be raised was for these great religious houses to sell their land. In St Andrews, Cardinal Beaton called a meeting, which decided to raise £10,000 by taxing prelacies and beneficiaries in order to 'maintain the liberty of the Church and preserve the State'. The structure of the Church was in decline, for it had become the provider of jobs for the children of the Crown who were born out of wedlock. They used the great religious houses as milch cows for the Crown. These men were incompetent to fulfil any pastoral role and rule the Church as priests, for priests they most certainly were not! In order to escape eternal damnation, or at least reduce time spent in purgatory, gifts were made to the Church and people bought relics of the saints. In truth these were often just pigs' bones passed off as part of the skeletons of the saints and any old splinter of wood might be sold as a fragment of the cross. The relationship between Church and State, so closely linked for so long, was in a bad way. Reform was inevitable. This is perceived to have been the state of the Church not only in Scotland but across Europe, but the extent to which this perception accurately portrays the situation is open to debate. In the end the Reformers won the battle and so the version of history we are familiar with is, as always, that provided by the victors.

Whatever the whole truth may be, the public perception of the time was of a corrupt Church and this led to a great revolution against the old order. Many, like the German Reformer Martin Luther, who was an Augustinian monk, found the corruption indefensible. As a result, he nailed his famous protest to the door of the church at Wittenberg in 1517. This started a movement that swept through Europe, turning the society of the day upside down.

The Reformation

The seeds of the Scottish Reformation were sown in 1528 when Cardinal Beaton had Patrick Hamilton, the Reformation's first martyr, executed in St Andrews. The Scottish Parliament passed acts in 1525 and in 1535 which tried to prevent the spread of Martin Luther's 'heresies'. Hamilton had been educated on the continent and became a follower of Luther's cause. W. Croft Dickinson tells us that Luther declared, 'If a Christian has faith he has everything', while Hamilton preached that faith brought 'Man and God together'.[14] This reliance on faith was the 'heresy' that Church and Parliament wanted to crush. So it was that on February 29th 1528 Patrick Hamilton was burned at the stake. A monogram of the letters 'PH' on the pavement in St Andrews marks the place of his execution.

With the death of James V in 1542, politics and religion once again became confused. The infant queen, Mary, was being raised a Catholic by her mother Mary of Guise. Inevitably there was a battle for control of the regency with the Earl of Arran, who declared himself a Protestant, coming to the fore having seen off the competition in the form of Cardinal Beaton of St Andrews. This arrangement suited Henry VIII of England because he wanted his son Edward to marry the infant Scottish Queen, so giving the English Crown control over Scotland. Treaties were signed at Greenwich on July 21st 1543. The two were to marry when they were 10 years of age, and a treaty of peace was also signed that would last until a year after the death of either monarch.

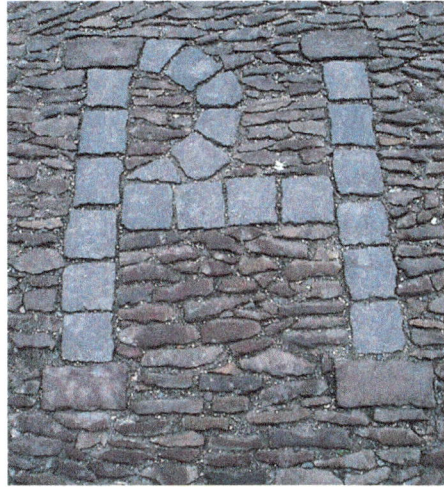

Memorial to Patrick Hamilton marking the place of his execution at St Salvator's Chapel and College

In Scotland this was far from popular among those who remembered the Auld Alliance with France. Nor was it popular in Catholic France or with the Pope. As a result of this opposition the Scottish Parliament annulled the Greenwich treaties in December of that year. Henry was furious and responded as one would expect of such a man, by bullying the Scots: destroying the great churches in the Borders and attacking Edinburgh. This did nothing to change the mind of the Scots. Arran then decided he was no longer a Protestant and embraced the Catholic faith again, much to the displeasure of the King of England. Consequently, when Cardinal Beaton had George Wishart martyred in St Andrews, it was as much for political as for religious reasons. Protestantism was associated with forming an alliance with England, the 'Auld Enemy', while Catholicism was supporting the Auld Alliance with France. This in effect became a choice between English and French domination. The Protestants were inflamed by the execution of Wishart in March 1546 and in May of the same year Beaton was assassinated.

A meeting of the Provincial Council of Scotland took place in Edinburgh in 1549. The last Catholic Archbishop of St Andrews, John Hamilton, presided and the meeting comprised the senior churchmen of the country. It was their intention to identify the causes of the troubles facing the Church and to address them. The causes were identified as 'the corruption of morals and profane lewdness of life in churchmen of almost all

---

[14]   Croft Dickinson, *Scotland*

ranks, together with crass ignorance of literature and of all the liberal arts – and from these two sources principally spring many abuses'.[15] In naming the Church as the cause of the problem it reached a popular conclusion, and it was creating the circumstances for the Reformation to gain momentum. Through the requisition of parish churches by the Crown and the nobility, the parishes and their people were neglected. Incomes of the clergy were depleted and consequently parishes were often filled with illiterate men who were popularly considered needy and greedy. The poor were left to go hungry and buildings left to suffer from poor maintenance. The lack of respect for the clergy went hand in hand with an absence of respect for the Pope. Morality plays, ballads and books all fed the already widespread contempt for churchmen.

Not all of the criticism levied by the Provincial Council was valid, and in any case the attitudes and accusations being made had been in circulation long before the 16th century, so this alone does not justify the Reformation. St Andrews Cathedral was involved in training prospective priests, so the staff were hardly illiterate. Once the Reformed Church was in place many of the Catholic clergy of the old parishes were considered fit and good men to continue in their charges. Nevertheless, attempts to address the criticisms that had been growing, and which found voice in Martin Luther and Patrick Hamilton, were too late. The Church was mistaken to think it would calm the crowds by burning the critics. For too long the churchmen had denied their parishioners what they were crying out for: access to the Gospels in their own tongue; the preaching of the Reformers; belief in justification through faith; the priesthood of all believers; and direct access to the grace of God without the priest acting as mediator. This motivated the Reformers in their desire for change. They wanted a Church that would preach the faith free from man-made ceremonies and rituals. Most of all they rejected the mass that was delivered in a tongue that common folk could not understand. The mood for change was unstoppable and was supported by many churchmen, as well as by people of all ranks of society. It was indeed a popular revolt!

The Troubles of Queen Mary

With Henry VIII pursuing his Rough Wooing of the infant Queen, Catholic France came to Scotland's rescue after the battle of Pinkie when Henry's forces prevailed. This help came with the condition that Mary would marry the future King of France. Indeed, the French King, Henry II, wanted Mary to be raised in the French court. In 1553, following much wheeling and dealing by the Queen's mother, Mary of Guise took over from Arran as regent. This resulted in an increase in control by the continental allies. French influence grew and, only a few weeks before Mary was to marry Francis, the heir to the French throne, she signed a secret agreement granting the French King full control over Scotland and also granting him her rights to the English throne in the

---

[15] *Statutes of the Scottish Church 1225–1559*, being a translation of 'Concilia Scotiae: Ecclesiae Scoticanae Statuta Tam Provincialia Quam Synodalia Quae Supersunt', ed. David Patrick, Scottish History Society, vol. 54 (Edinburgh, 1907)

event of her death. All of this came to nothing, however, for when Francis II of France and King of Scots died in December 1560, Mary returned to Scotland a widow and the link with France was weakened. The Reformers confronted the regent, Mary of Guise, who was defeated and with her the influence of France.

Throughout her brief reign as sole monarch of her kingdom, Mary maintained her Catholic faith but had no intention of imposing it upon her Protestant people. This was difficult for the Reformers because they were out to establish the only Church in Scotland and Mary's insistence on following her own separate faith challenged this. The sorry story of her battles with the Church, especially John Knox, and her life and loves is well documented and we need not go into it here. Her reign came to an end in 1567 when Mary was forced to abdicate the Scottish Crown in favour of her one-year-old son, James VI. Her imprisonment, fleeing to England and eventual execution were the tragic conclusion to a tragic life.

With Mary now out of the way, the Reformation Settlement of 1560 was confirmed. James was raised a Protestant under the tutorage of George Buchanan and a succession of regents – Moray, Mar and Morton. The future of the Protestant faith as envisaged by the leaders of the new Church appeared secure.

John Knox

John Knox Preaching at St Andrews, by Sir David Wilkie

The martyrdom of Patrick Hamilton marked the beginning of a movement that proved to be unstoppable. On 1st March 1546 George Wishart, a schoolteacher from Angus and a preacher of Lutheran doctrine, like Patrick Hamilton before him, was martyred in St Andrews on the instructions of Cardinal Beaton. John Knox knew Wishart and wrote a moving description of his friend's cruel death.[16] He also described the murder three months later of Cardinal Beaton, who was seen to be the chief villain behind the martyrdom of both Wishart and Hamilton.[17]

St Andrew's Castle

Following Beaton's murder, St Andrews Castle was in the hands of the Reformers, including Knox. Catholic France, still an ally of Scotland, set about retrieving the castle from the rebels. As a result of this, Knox was made a prisoner of the French and sent to the galleys, and he later spent several years in England and on the Continent. He became a minister in English churches at Berwick and Newcastle when Henry VIII's son, Edward VI, was England's King. Indeed, he became royal chaplain at the court of Edward and made a contribution to his second prayer book. On the monarch's untimely death, Edward's Catholic half-sister Mary became Queen and Knox fled to Switzerland, where he came under the influence of John Calvin.[18] He described Calvin's Geneva as 'the most perfect school of Christ that was ever on earth since the days of the Apostles'.

On his return to Scotland in 1559, Knox became recognised as a powerful preacher of the reformed religion and so he came to lead the Protestant Reformation in association with sympathetic members of the nobility. Some historians see Knox as a great Reformer, while others consider him a great man; still others have a different view of him. These were violent times in a cruel and unforgiving age. Leading the movement for religious change was no job for a shrinking violet. Love him or hate him, John Knox cannot

---

[16]   R. Goring (ed.) *Scotland: The Autobiography* (Penguin, 2008, p. 52)
[17]   Goring, *Scotland: The Autobiography*, pp. 53–54
[18]   P. Lorimer, *John Knox and the Church of England: His Work in Her Pulpit and His Influence Upon Her Liturgy, Articles, and Parties* (London, Forgotten Books, 2013; original work published 1875)

be ignored in the history of Scotland.[19] Important though he was, he could not have achieved all that was gained by the new Kirk on his own, for Knox was one of many who were responsible for the events which took place in Scotland at this time.

Knox's followers were determined to eradicate all vestiges of Roman Catholicism and in 1558 nine outbreaks of iconoclasm (the destruction of religious images) occurred in the religious houses at St Andrews, Arbroath, Lindores, Holyrood and Elgin among others. Some survived, particularly Aberdeen, Glasgow, Dundee and St Giles, Edinburgh.

Though stripped of their treasures, these were not lost to the world, for some were hidden away until more favourable times returned. Many of the buildings that were destroyed became quarries to build the surrounding towns and villages. There are many examples of this in Newburgh, St Andrews and Arbroath. Whatever our feelings about the justification for the Reformation and the perceived need to see the Church of Rome replaced or reformed, it is difficult not to see this as an act of unbelievable vandalism. Had this not taken place, modern Scotland could have boasted cathedrals to match those of any country in Europe. As it is, we have survivors like Glasgow Cathedral, St Giles in Edinburgh, St Machar's Cathedral and the Church of St Nicholas in Aberdeen, as well as St Magnus in Orkney and Dunfermline Abbey, which are now shadows of their former selves. Others are ruins that are cared for so that future generations can see what grandeur once graced our land. Through Henry VIII, the Reformers and later Oliver Cromwell, Scotland's medieval ecclesiastical architecture has been badly treated.

St Andrews Cathedral

---

19 A. Lang, *John Knox and the Reformation* (Project Gutenberg, 2004; original work published 1905), www.gutenberg. org/files/14016/14016-h/14016-h.htm

The detailed story of the Reformation is too complicated to record here, yet its influence on the people of the Parishes that were to form the Howe of Fife was great. In August 1560 the Scottish Parliament received a petition signed by all ranks in society seeking the abolition of papal authority over Scotland and the legal recognition of the reformed faith. As a result of this, Parliament asked the reformed ministers to draw up a confession defining the country's new religion. Four days later, Knox and his colleagues delivered a list of 25 articles which, after examination, were approved by Parliament. Thus Scotland became a Protestant country.

Those leading the Reformation included the Kirk's first lay Moderator, George Buchanan, and they developed a form of government for the Kirk that reflected his democratic principles. Buchanan, one-time tutor to King James VI, was considered one of the most influential thinkers in Europe in his day. His far-seeing theories of democracy are embodied in *A Dialogue on the Law and Government Among the Scots*, which he published in 1579.[20] Here Buchanan said that the people have the right to confer royal authority upon whomever they wish.[21] Aidan O'Neill QC points out that, 'The law and customs of the Scots in relation to Kings was therefore said to be one of a limited constitutional monarchy involving subordination of the Crown to the law, the Crown's answerability before the courts, and the people's right of revolt against a monarch in fundamental breach of his or her duties.'[22] So, it would appear that Buchanan was simply restating what was already accepted thinking in Scotland at that time.

The General Assembly of 1562 approved Knox's Book of Common Order, which provided the liturgy for public worship. The First Book of Discipline (1560) set out the organisation of both the Church and national life. It envisaged the establishment of reformed ministers, a national system of education and poor relief. Ministers were to be elected by their congregation and 'readers' were to be appointed to satisfy the short-term shortage of suitably qualified ministers. Education was to be provided at primary and secondary level with schools in every parish, and they and the universities, also controlled by the Kirk, were to be inspected and examined. Poor relief was envisaged on a scale unique in Europe. Kirk Sessions were to exist in every parish and they had become very much part of local church life by 1559. Moderators were introduced in 1563. The earliest form of the General Assembly mirrored the Scottish Parliament, which consisted of the 'Three Estates': Church (bishops and abbots), nobility and burgh commissioners (representatives of the royal burghs). The earliest General Assembly, which met in 1560, consisted of ministers and elders from the Kirk Sessions and members of the nobility. The General Assembly met twice each year during Queen Mary's reign until her abdication in 1567.

The authors of the First Book of Discipline envisaged superintendents to oversee large areas with many parishes and they were to refer directly to the General Assembly.

---

[20] *De Iure Regni apud Scotos Dialogus*
[21] A. Herman, *How the Scots Invented the Modern World* (New York, Three Rivers Press, 2002, p. 19)
[22] A. O'Neill QC, 'Some Reflections on the Scottish Constitution and the Role of the UK Supreme Court', 21st September 2011, available from http://ukscblog.com/we-need-to-talk-about-the-referendum/

Many considered these superintendents as bishops by another name, making it more agreeable to some when the Crown wanted to reintroduce bishops. Funding would be made available from the income of the old Church. The whole tone of the document was compassionate and democratic. It was also truly revolutionary in a world where the notion of democracy was novel if not seditious. On the other hand, the teaching contained in the First Book of Discipline envisaged the General Assembly acting as the conscience of the nation. Everyone, from the highest to the lowest in the land, had to perform their duties in accordance with the word of God. If they failed, it was the duty of the Kirk to 'teach' them how to carry out their duties in accordance with its doctrine. To modern ears this sounds like indoctrination. When James VI ascended to the throne it sounded to him like an attempt to grab his authority.

With the emergence of Presbyteries in 1580, the foundation of the modern Church of Scotland was laid. Achieving all of its great aims would inevitably take time. In addition, persuading the King and the ruling class to be sympathetic also took a great deal of time and money. Much to the annoyance of the Reformers, the new Church received only one sixth of the income of the pre-reformed Church, with much of the remainder going to the nobility. Nevertheless, the effect of this great movement has been felt, not only in Scotland, but also around the world in the succeeding centuries. With justification the Presbyterian Church has been severely criticised for its brutal excesses in promoting the faith. However, there is much that we can be proud of, for in the 16th century we see God's people being guided towards the light of a compassionate and democratic society. It would take several centuries before the turmoil that these ideas released would be resolved. Indeed, it could well be argued that the godly society they envisaged never materialised. Nevertheless, through the influence of Calvin on Knox and his compatriots, a beginning had been made.

The Roman Catholic Church and the Reformation

The supremacy of the Roman Catholic Church came to an end with the death of Archbishop Beaton on 28th May 1546. It was not until August 1560 that the authority of the Pope was repealed, but the direction in which events were travelling could not have been a surprise. Half-hearted attempts were made to reform the old Kirk, but there were too many vested interests in the income the Church and its property generated for this to gain momentum. There was also the political involvement of Protestant England, which wanted to fan the flames of reform in Scotland in order to alienate the northern kingdom from Catholic France. When Henry VIII started his Rough Wooing of Mary in the 1540s, this encouraged the Scots to see their future with France. When the demand for cutting the ties with the Pope gained popularity, Protestant England looked like a more promising ally than France. The revolt of the Reformers took place in 1559, the year that Mary married the Catholic Dauphine in Paris and her mother was removed from her position in government. So it was that in 1560 Scotland ceased to be a Catholic country, even although it had a Catholic monarch.

The effect on the Catholic Church had been developing for some time. The dioceses and hierarchy of the Church in Scotland were abandoned. In 1653 the whole of Scotland was placed under the authority of the Prefecture Apostolic, which effectively meant that Scotland was now viewed by the Vatican as a missionary area. Some growth must have been sustained as in 1694 it was elevated to the Vicariate Apostolic of Scotland. This meant that there was enough support for the Catholic Church in Scotland for the Vatican to hope that, in time, there would be sufficient Catholics for a Catholic Diocese to be established.

Clearly the hopes of the Vatican were not in vain, for in 1727 Scotland was divided into two Vicariates Apostolic, the Lowland District and the Highland District. This remained the case for 100 years when Scotland was divided into three Vicariates Apostolic, the Eastern District, the Western District, and the Northern District. Fife was included in the Eastern District until 1878 when Pope Leo XIII restored the Scottish Hierarchy and the Eastern District was elevated to the Archdiocese of St Andrews and Edinburgh.[23]

Andrew Melville

Two years after the death of John Knox in 1572, another strong figure arrived in Scotland. Born in Angus, Andrew Melville was educated first at Montrose before attending university at St Andrews and Lausanne. He then went to Geneva where he worked as a teacher and was greatly influenced by Theodore Beza. Beza was the successor of Calvin in Geneva and he held strong Presbyterian convictions. When Andrew Melville returned to Scotland in 1574 it was as principal of University College, Glasgow. He then went on to St Andrews where he continued to reform university education and establish a school of Protestant theology, which gained international recognition.

First and foremost, Melville was a Presbyterian and an opponent of any form of Episcopacy. Furthermore, it was his belief that in Scotland there were two kingdoms, one belonging to God and the other to the people of Scotland and their King. In the former, James was but a member like anyone else and he had no authority whatsoever. When he became Moderator of the General Assembly (in 1578, 1582, 1587 and 1594) he had a good platform from which to spread his views. He gained some influence and soon became a thorn in the flesh of the King James VI. In 1584 he was imprisoned at Blackness Castle for broadcasting his views as the King was determined to retain bishops. Eventually James forbade Melville from preaching.

It was the Reformer's firm conviction that what he referred to as 'the two kingdoms', temporal and ecclesiastic, were distinct from one another and that the temporal should not interfere with the ecclesiastic because the latter was superior. In addition, he considered the hierarchy inherent in the Episcopal form of church government to be unscriptural. He accepted, however, that ministers had to be answerable to the Church

---

[23] http://www.archdiocese-edinburgh.com/index.php?option=com_content&view=article&id=267&Itemid=158

and so he concurred with Knox's First Book of Discipline, which embodied the courts of the Church comprising ministers and elders.

James felt threatened and would never accept this. Melville was barred by royal command from attending the General Assemblies at Dundee and Montrose. The King confined him to St Andrews and then imprisoned him at Hampton Court. Eventually in 1611 he was exiled to France and died there in 1622. Andrew Melville's influence on the development of the Church of Scotland was not realised in his lifetime but its importance would be revealed as the 17th century developed.

Kirk and Crown

The King's dispute with Andrew Melville was rooted in his belief in the divine right of Kings: that is, that God had bestowed all political authority on himself as King. To Andrew Melville this was anathema and he was not alone in his desire to curtail the power of the monarchy.

James VI came to the throne in 1567 at the age of 11 as a result of the forced abdication of his mother. In 1584 the King called Parliament and had all previous legislation concerning the Kirk rescinded. He also forbade the Kirk to meet without his permission. Breaking the new laws would be considered a treasonable offence. This legislation became known as the 'Black Acts'.

By 1592 James had thought again and decided to cancel the Black Acts and to reinstate the most important parts of the Second Book of Discipline. Sadly, these measures had two defects. First, they maintained the authority of patrons, instead of the members of the congregation, to choose the minister. Second, the General Assembly was not allowed to meet without the King's permission.

By 1600 James decided to reimpose bishops on the Church. With the notion of superintendents embodied in the First Book of Discipline, this was not universally condemned, for it could be argued that they acted as bishops. Once in London, following the Union of the Crowns in 1603, James set about to make himself head of the Church of Scotland, just as he was head of the Church of England. He discontinued the 1605 General Assembly, and when the ministers decided to set the date for the 1606 Assembly, James expressed his anger by having 19 ministers imprisoned and six exiled to France.

An Act of 1607 reinstated the bishops who were nominated by the King, but there seemed to be little stomach for confrontation. The General Assembly accepted these measures and Parliament proved to be too submissive to oppose them. In 1618 a puppet assembly met at Perth and passed what has become known as the Five Articles of Perth instructing bishops to take part in confirmation, private baptism and private communion; worshippers had to kneel when receiving communion and the important points of the Christian calendar had to be observed.

In truth not everyone disliked the bishops and there were those who were prepared to adhere to James's wishes, but not everyone knelt when taking communion and some ministers were prosecuted for encouraging them. On the other hand, James is seen by many as having secured the position of Protestantism in Scotland. He promoted the idea that everyone should have their own Bible. He supervised the payment of ministers and founded Edinburgh University to address the shortage of qualified ministers. James also funded and promoted the catechisms, which were designed to instruct in true Protestant beliefs. When James addressed a congregation in St Giles in Edinburgh in 1603, before his departure for London, many in the congregation wept.[24] So James was certainly not universally unpopular in Scotland; yet his belief in the divine right of Kings laid the seeds of destruction for his son Charles. By the time Charles I succeeded his father in 1625, the principles that led to conflict between Crown and Kirk were well established.

The Covenanters

With the succession of Charles I the troubles between the people of Scotland and their King were about to get worse. Like his father, Charles wanted an Episcopal Church in Scotland but he was prepared to pursue his demands with even greater vigour. The Anglican coronation of Charles I in Edinburgh in 1633 and the election of a committee of the Lords of the Articles, which relied on the vote of the King's bishops, led to the confirmation of the King's ecclesiastical policies. As a result, all Kirks were to be rearranged to follow the English pattern and the communion table became an altar. Confession was to be heard by the ministers and in 1635 the Kirk was ordered to use the new Prayer Book that had been prepared without any contribution from a Church of Scotland minister.

There was much resentment against the King's determination to impose his will on the Scottish Church and people. As a result, in 1638 thousands of adult Scottish men gathered at Greyfriars Kirkyard in Edinburgh to sign, some with their own blood, the National Covenant. This was a solemn affirmation of their loyalty to the King but also of their commitment to the Scottish Presbyterian tradition, in defiance of the religious policy of Charles I. Among the leaders of this movement was Alexander Henderson, minister of the Fife church of St Athernase in Leuchars. Later that year at a General Assembly in Glasgow, with Mr Henderson as Moderator, bishops were deposed and with them Episcopacy.[25]

This action by the Covenanters, as they were known, was supported by the Scottish Parliament and acted as a warning shot across the bows of the monarchy. It heralded a furious retaliation from the King. In the spring of 1639 the King marched north at the head of an army. It was his intention to defeat the Scots and impose his own political and ecclesiastical will north of the border. In fact, no battle was fought and a treaty known as the Pacification of Berwick took place when the King accepted the Scots' right to free church assembly and a free parliament. Later the General Assembly not only

---

[24] J. Prebble, *The Lion in the North* (New York, Taylor & Francis, 1971, p. 231)
[25] J.H.S. Burleigh, *A Church History of Scotland* (Oxford University Press, 1961)

ratified its decision to abolish the bishops but went further, declaring such authority to be contrary to scripture. The Scottish Parliament then abolished the idea of absolute royal authority.

This decision by the Scottish Parliament angered Charles, for it was contrary to his belief in the divine right of Kings. Once again he decided to lead an army north and teach the Scots a lesson, but he received no support from the English Parliament when he tried to raise funds for this. Nevertheless, he gathered forces and pursued his attack on his northern kingdom, only to be defeated at the Battle of Newburn. The Scots then occupied Newcastle and cut off coal supplies to London. Once again Charles tried to reach a treaty with the Scots, but they refused to reach agreement with him unless that agreement was approved by the English Parliament. Charles was forced to call what became known as the Long Parliament, which eventually brought about his downfall.

It was as a result of this that in 1642 civil war broke out in England. Both sides sought the support of the Scots and it was the Roundheads who won the day. They were more sympathetic to the Presbyterian form of church government. In 1643 both Parliaments of the United Kingdom entered into a Solemn League and Covenant that the churches in Scotland, England and Ireland would be governed by Presbytery. When Charles was defeated at Naseby in 1646, it was to the Scots that he surrendered but, refusing his captors' terms, Charles was handed over to Cromwell's men. It was for this reason that the Scots reacted so badly to the execution of the King in 1649, as that was never part of their plan. They were shocked and appalled and great feelings of guilt arose for the support given to the parliamentarians.

The Scots wanted to put things right and Charles II, who agreed to sign both the 1638 and 1643 Covenants, was crowned at Scone on January 1st 1651. This infuriated Cromwell, who invaded Scotland and absorbed it by force into his Commonwealth. There followed austere times, much of the misery being created in Scotland by a leading extreme faction in the Church. With the restoration of the monarchy in 1660, things were going to get a lot worse for both the Kirk and the ordinary folk.[26]

The restoration saw the return of a King who wished to impose an Episcopal Church on the people of Scotland. He had no intention of honouring the Covenants he had signed prior to his Scottish coronation in 1651 and he soon set about imposing bishops on the Scottish Church. This form of Episcopacy was different from the English model in numerous ways, yet it failed to satisfy many in the Scottish Kirk. Those who adhered to the Covenant were bitterly persecuted. It did not take the King long to have legislation passed by Parliament requiring all ministers appointed after 1649 to resign and offer themselves for reinstatement by lay patrons of their parishes. This was not just about patronage; it was, in Charles' eyes, about loyalty to the Crown. With the retention of Synods and Presbyteries, some ministers provided little opposition to the introduction of bishops. In 1661 the Scottish Parliament revoked every law passed since 1633, thus

---

[26] Prebble, *The Lion in the North*, pp. 256–258

restoring the powers won by the Covenanters to the King in London. Once again the Covenanters gathered, creating a strong defiant voice. To Charles, these Dissenters were too closely attached to the ideas of Andrew Melville, who believed the King's authority to be inferior to the spiritual authority of the Church. As King he was convinced that he ruled by divine right and would never accept that his position was inferior to any other, spiritual or secular.

About 274 ministers chose expulsion from their parishes in the winter of 1662 rather than submit to the King's demands. There were 900 parishes in Scotland at that time and 97 became vacant through death and retirement of ministers. This meant that more than one third of charges became vacant at the same time. This was also a time when the number of candidates entering university was relatively small and so the acute shortage of qualified men caused a serious problem. The bishops addressed this by ordaining men who would otherwise have been considered unsuitable. This gave rise to great anger, especially in the south-west where Presbyterianism rained strong and where most of the vacancies were. Accusations were made against the curates about intellectual and moral suitablility for the role they held and the predictable response of anger and stubborn defiance against the Episcopalians.[27] The equally predictable response of the King's supporters, especially Sir Thomas Dalziel of Binns, was suppression with such cruelty that many, including members of the Episcopal clergy, reacted with abhorrence.

In 1681 another Act, known as the Test Act, was passed whereby anyone seeking to hold office in Scotland had to swear an oath to the King. This mirrored a similar Act passed by the English Parliament in 1673 but in Scotland it alienated large parts of the population, including many clergymen.

During the remainder of Charles II's reign the Covenanters held services, or 'conventicles', in the open air, on hillsides and wherever they felt safe. Further rebellion and cruel suppression of folk throughout Scotland, including folk in the Howe of Fife, took place until the King died in 1685. On his deathbed Charles was converted to Roman Catholicism. His brother James VII came to the throne as one who had converted to the Roman Catholic faith some time previously. It was not long before both Scotland and England rebelled against James as they were unhappy at the prospect of having a Catholic monarch on the throne. So it was that in 1688 James fled the country and was replaced by William of Orange.

The departure of James was met with great rejoicing and in 1690 the Settlement of the Revolution ensured that the Church of Scotland would be Presbyterian.[28] While the establishment of William and Mary on the throne brought an end to the terrible persecution of those ministers who refused to comply with the demands of Charles II and his brother James, it did not end the troubles of the Kirk.

---

[27] M.L. Mirabello, 'Dissent and the Church of Scotland 1660—1690' (PhD dissertation, University of Glasgow, January 1988)

[28] C. Michie, *The Covenanters: The Historical Background to their Struggle* (Lochgoin and Fenwick Covenanters Trust, 1991)

A New Monarchy

From the outset it was clear that William intended to ignore the Solemn League and Covenant that had brought Scotland into the so-called English Civil War on the side of the English Parliament. Nor did William reverse Charles's decision to repeal the 1649 Act which had granted freedom of General Assemblies and abolished patronage. The weaknesses inherent in James VI's 1592 Act of the Scottish Parliament therefore remained. Nevertheless, the Church of Scotland was re-established as a Presbyterian Church and it spawned Presbyterian churches throughout the English-speaking world. Indeed, it still holds an important place in the Communion of Reformed Churches.

The 60 ministers and 120 elders who comprised the General Assembly of 1690 had all been involved in the bitter struggle to uphold their principles. As a result, when the King urged them to advance 'a calm and peaceable procedure', they found it hard advice to follow. There were some, more extreme in their views than the majority, who presented a petition. They were three ministers of the group dubbed Cameronians. This group followed Richard Cameron, who had been trained as a preacher in Holland. Cameron was killed fighting for his beliefs in 1680 but many of his followers remained in the Church. They held more fundamental Presbyterian principles than their compatriots and were unwilling to comply with their brethren who, they felt, were too ready to succumb to the terms laid down by the Crown. The Covenanters, especially the Cameronians, were considered by many to be fundamentalist radicals, though some believe they fought for freedom of religious principles and democracy. The Cameronians continued to be a minority group until 1843 when they were constituted as the Reformed Presbyterian Church. Most joined the Free Church in 1876 but a minority maintained their independence and fostered connections with similar churches overseas.[29]

The Revolution Settlement, which placed the right to choose a minister in the hands of the Kirk Session acting together with the local patron, was repealed in 1712. It was then that the Tory advisers to Queen Anne had the Act of Toleration passed by Parliament. This not only allowed Episcopalian Dissenters to use the English liturgy, itself the cause of bitter controversy, but the same Parliament also restored lay patronage in Scotland. Many believed this act to be in violation of the terms of the Treaty of Union and against which the Church had always protested. The issue of patronage was now to dominate the concerns of churchmen in Scotland for the next 200 years. The first breach came in 1733 when four ministers felt they could not conform to the agreement between the Crown and the Church of Scotland and left the Church, though they continued to minister in their parishes with the support of the members. This became known as the First Secession.

Initially the new order seemed to operate without difficulty. The patron presented a preacher to the parish; the Presbytery approved his qualifications; and if the congregation were willing to call him, the Presbytery proceeded to form the pastoral tie. But as time

---

29   Burleigh, *A Church History of Scotland*

went on, another division emerged in the Church. Two parties appeared, with the moderates upholding the rights of the patrons, while the more Calvinist Evangelicals supported the rights of the congregation. The distinction between the parties was reinforced by the difference in styles of preaching. In 1752 another group of dissenting ministers were expelled. They went on to form the Relief Church in 1761.[30]

Throughout the 18th and into the 19th century, other groups seceded from the national Church. In time some of these also split, creating a very complex church structure. Clearly the Established Church was having difficulty in holding its members together. Its authority was being challenged and many see these schisms as unnecessary: disharmony among petulant men resulting in a very weakened Church. On the other hand, these divisions may be seen as a struggle for a form of democracy that was not available to ordinary folk in any other sector of society at that time. Here was the struggle of the farm workers, the spinners and weavers to have a voice in matters that affected their lives. As we shall see, the Howe of Fife was not immune from these events and secessionist churches were established in Pitlessie and Kettle.

A Wind of Change Across Scotland

The 1700s was an eventful time for the development of Christianity in Scotland as a whole as well as for the Church of Scotland. In 1732, John Glas, a minister from Tealing, near Dundee, was one of those to secede from the Church of Scotland. He believed that the Church ought to be purely spiritual in its organisation with no connection with the state. This teaching was totally opposed to the existence of an Established Church. As the Church of Scotland is the 'Church by law established', his teaching brought him into conflict with it. He became founder of a sect known as the Glassites. In time they were to be the Sandemanians as the Glassites saw common cause with the movement founded by Robert Sandeman, who also seceded in 1732. These groups had much in common with the Baptists and in 1750 William Sinclair brought them together to form a church at Keiss in Caithness north of Wick. It was not until the 1760s, however, that a Baptist Church was formed in Edinburgh.[31]

There was at this time an enthusiastic Evangelical movement within the Kirk as well as in wider society. John Erskine, the minister of Old Greyfriars Church in Edinburgh and who participated in a Cambuslang revival in 1742, was such a man. He was greatly influenced by the publications of an American theologian called Johnathan Edwards.

As the 18th century wore on, others with influence like Robert and James Haldane arose. They were sons of a wealthy noble family with a seat at Airthrey Castle near Stirling (where Stirling University stands today). Robert had a distinguished career in the Royal Navy before he retired. Once home he began to study the scriptures. This led in time to his determination to pursue the path to which his faith led him. His brother James was initially less involved in his brother's mission. It was his attendance at the

---

30   T.M. Divine, *The Scottish Nation 1700–2000* (Penguin Books, 2000, p. 89)
31   H.L. McBeth, *The Baptist Heritage* (B&H Publishing Group, 1987)

General Assembly of the Church of Scotland and its decision to defeat a motion 'That it is the duty of Christians to send the gospel to the heathen world' that changed his mind. He felt this decision displayed a 'smug self-righteousness and lack of concern for the unsaved'. As a result, he joined his brother in studying the Bible in 'childlike spirit, without seeking any interpretation that would agree with his own ideas'.[32] Believing the ministers of northern Scotland to be cold and immoral, they held open-air meetings and distributed tracts. Although not ordained, they saw it as their duty as Christians to preach. It was not the intention of the Haldane brothers to create a new denomination, so for a time they had an association with the Congregational Church in England. Before long this link was broken, for they rejected infant baptism, believing that only total immersion was in accordance with scripture.

The brothers spent much of their time and great wealth promoting the Society for Propagating the Gospel at Home (SPGH), which they had been involved in establishing in 1797. This organisation was instrumental in establishing 85 Scottish churches within 10 years of its foundation.

The Church of Scotland did not welcome this missionary organisation and in 1799 the Moderator, William Moodie, warned against the disorder and anarchy of the SPGH. Nevertheless, the popularity of the Haldanes continued. An early meeting place was a converted theatre in Edinburgh known as The Circus. In 1801 a new building, seating 3,000 and known as The Tabernacle, was erected on Leith Walk. It was at the end of the 18th century that James Haldane was ordained the pastor of The Circus and the decision was made that authority within the Church should be in the hands of the congregation and not a Presbytery.

It was into this land of spiritual controversy and turmoil that an English Baptist, Andrew Fuller, first descended in 1799. He was invited by Charles Stuart of Dunearn in Fife. Stuart was a Baptist and a physician. He was an important man in these days, having influenced Erskine and Chalmers as well as the Haldane brothers.

Fuller was known as a man who spoke his mind plainly, rejecting superficial politeness, and this gained some enemies. To his friends his forthrightness and lack of self-importance endeared him to them. In return Fuller never failed to express his appreciation of their friendship. He was known as one of the most widely read authors of religious works in the United Kingdom and America between the 1770s and his death in 1815. Through Stewart he met Erskine and the Haldane brothers. On each of his visits to Scotland he travelled widely and led six or eight meetings each week, every one packed with congregations numbering in the thousands. Fuller soon found that he was even more popular in Scotland than in England. Kettering was his home and it was from there that he continued to lead the Baptist Church. During his last visit to Scotland in 1813 Fuller met Rev. Thomas Chalmers. Chalmers himself was to become renowned not only as a preacher but also as the one to lead the Disruption in 1843.

---

[32]   J.D. Murch, *The Free Church: A Treatise on Church Polity with Special Relevance to Doctrine and Practice in Christian Churches and Churches of Christ* (Restoration Press, 1966)

At the time of the meeting, Chalmers was minister of Kilmany Church and afterwards he wrote, 'I felt my humble country manse greatly honoured by harbouring him for a day and two nights within its walls.' Chalmers continued to speak most highly of Fuller and his fellow Baptists as a community of ministers, even though neither Fuller nor the others had any formal theological training.[33]

Before Fuller died he wanted to pass responsibility for the fledgling Baptist Church to the theologian Christopher Anderson, with whom he had a long association. Anderson was very much engaged in Edinburgh establishing the Gaelic School Society and the Bible Society. He felt he was already fully employed in these tasks. In addition, the London leadership seemed to be unwilling to have a Scotsman at the helm. Fuller was afraid that London financiers would take over the Church and try to run it as a business. In fact, after his death the London leadership did take over, and in 1828 division within the Church took place. Anderson became an important player in repairing the breach, so perhaps, in the end, Fuller got his way.

Worship in the Church of Scotland in the Early 1800s

Un-numbered Cults communion token from 1839

The Presbyterian manse was simple and lacking in anything that might be construed as unnecessary adornment. Similarly, the places of worship were simple to the point of being austere. The walls were either undecorated, leaving the stone visible, or whitewashed. The pews were simple wooden seats with straight backs and no opportunity to get so comfortable that the worshipper might snooze during the very long sermon. Many post-Reformation churches had the pulpit on the long wall and the pews arranged so that the congregation was gathered around the minister. In some churches a long communion table was set against a wall when not in use. In others the wooden partition separating the front pews from the aisle could be converted into the communion table.

This harks back to the days when the communicants had a token with a number on it. They would enter the church by the east door and sit around the table. Those not called would remain outside and be 'catechised' until they were called. Each group called around the Lord's Table had a full service, including a sermon that could last an hour. After the service came to a close the congregation would leave by the west door, making way for the next group to be called. Communion tended to last all day. It is not surprising that it took place only twice each year. Another reason for occasional communions is that in the early days the Kirk was short of ordained ministers. Communion was one of only two sacraments that would be practised; the other, also

---

33   M.A.G. Haykin, 'Andrew Fuller and his Scottish Friends', *History Scotland*, vol. 15(6) 2015

instituted by Christ, was baptism. While normal Sunday worship could be conducted by a layman, the sacraments required the services of one divinely appointed. So it was that ministers often travelled around those parishes where no minister had been called. In these days congregations would have been familiar with the psalms, which they sang while seated. For prayers the congregation stood. There was no organ and singing was led by a precentor who sang each line, which was then sung by the congregation. This was called 'lining'.

The pews were rented out. This was to raise money for the minister's stipend as well as for general maintenance of the building. Pews were priced according to their position in the church. Those who could afford it got the best seats. Those who could pay nothing had to sit in the less convenient places like behind pillars or in a dark corner. It was this that gave the Kirk the reputation for being unfriendly, for if a visitor sat in a well-positioned pew, the one paying rent would probably object and insist the usurper move. This arrangement meant that one's wealth and therefore social class was evident for all to see and the stigma of being behind a pillar would also be noted.

The Minister's Man, by H.W. Kerr 1892

It was not until the second half of the 19th century that change came about. It was Rev. Robert Lee of Greyfriars Church in Edinburgh who led a movement to improve both the buildings and services of worship that took place in them. In 1867 a book of prayers was published offering ministers a selection of liturgies to follow. Ministers started to read their services from written notes and they were shortened to about 30 minutes. Congregational hymn singing replaced the traditional psalms only slowly and there was much opposition to the introduction of the 'kist fu' o' whistles' (the organ). While the first organs appeared in 1807, they were soon removed because they were condemned by both the courts of the Kirk and the worshippers. It was not until 1866, and following a bitter struggle, that organs were allowed in Church of Scotland churches. It took another 17 years to persuade the Free Kirk of their value. Hymns had been sung in the Free Kirk in the 1850s and the Established Church in the 1870s, with the adoption of the Scottish Hymnal, which contained 200 hymns, in the same year.

Ministers would not have celebrated either Christmas or Easter as the Kirk considered these to be pagan survivals adopted by the Roman Catholic Church and regarded them as both idolatrous and frivolous. Moreover, the observance of the Scottish Sabbath was strict and few would dare to break it by fishing, getting drunk, playing cards or other 'silly games'. All public places like public parks, museums, public houses and restaurants were closed and families were expected to stay at home. Walking was for the purpose of going to or from the church. Some housewives refrained from cooking on the Sabbath, dishing up cold meals that had been prepared the day before. Sunday was a day to read the Bible and reflect upon it. Many people found the Sabbath day a trial and it is not surprising that succeeding generations have come to reject this austere discipline.[34]

1843 An' A' That!

Octavius Hill's famous picture recording the signing of the Act of Separation 1843

The events of 1843 are well known and affected every parish in Scotland. It was a continuation of the struggle for the spiritual independence of the Church of Scotland over its own affairs. This had some recognition in the Claim of Right of 1689 that was

---

[34] T. Griffiths and G. Morton (eds), *A History of Everyday Life in Scotland, 1800 to 1900* (Edinburgh University Press, 2010)

ratified by the Act of Union in 1707. However, the right of a wealthy patron to install a minister of his or her choice continued to be a point of contention. There were those who regarded this as an infringement of the spiritual independence of the Church, and others who thought it was a matter of property under the state's jurisdiction. The dispute, having rumbled away between the two sides for over a century, came to a head when the Evangelical party gained a majority at the General Assembly in 1834. They were able to use their majority to pass the Veto Act, which gave congregations the right to reject a nominee presented by the patron.

In 1839 a case was brought before the Court of Session when the congregation of the Established Church of Auchterarder objected to a minister presented by their patron, the Earl of Kinnoull. The Court found in favour of the patron, declaring the Veto Act passed by the General Assembly as unlawful because it conflicted with the law of Parliament. When the House of Lords supported this decision, it was clear to the Evangelicals in the Church that the matter could not be left as it was.[35]

Several legal confrontations took place culminating in the Evangelicals, following a meeting of November 1842, presenting to Prime Minister Sir Robert Peel and his cabinet a Claim, Declaration and Protest anent the Encroachments of the Court of Session. The Claim of Rights accompanied this document. This paper recognised the jurisdiction of the civil courts over the endowment given by the state to the Established Church, but resolved to renounce these privileges rather than see the spiritual independence of the Church compromised. In January 1843 Sir James Graham, the Home Secretary, wrote on the Claim the word 'Unreasonable'. As a result of this, at the General Assembly of May 1843, over 450 ministers walked out. At a later meeting on May 23rd the ministers signed the Act of Separation and the Free Church of Scotland came into being.

The result of this was that ministers found themselves without a living. In one day, with that signature, they lost their churches, their homes and their incomes. It was now the responsibility of each Dissenter to found and finance a national Church from scratch. With the distance of time it is easy to underestimate the effect of this revolt on the families of the ministers and parishioners involved. A casual glance through Rev. Thomas Brown's *Annals of the Disruption* published in 1884 gives ample evidence of the difficulties faced by many ministers and lay people alike. Some faced a great deal of hostility, especially from landowners. In Aberdeen, for example, women who worked in a cotton factory were threatened with redundancy if they supported the Free Kirk. There is another account of an elderly couple being threatened with expulsion from their home if the woman did not cease her adherence to the Free Kirk.[36] In *The Cruise of the Betsey* Hugh Miller,[37] himself a key figure in the Disruption, tells us that some lairds had the right, under feudal law, to forbid the construction of Free churches on

---

[35] T.C. Smout, *A Century of the Scottish People 1830–1950* (Fontana Press, 2010)
[36] T. Brown, *Annals of the Disruption, with Extracts from the Narratives of Ministers Who Left the Scottish Establishment in 1843*, vol. II (MacNiven & Wallace, 1884, pp. 148 ff.)
[37] H. Miller, *The Cruise of the Betsey, with Rambles of a Geologist* (facsimile edition, National Museums of Scotland, 2003; original published 1856, p. 98)

their land. Miller recounts the experience of his friend Rev. John Swanson, Minister of Small Isles, who was forced to use a boat, the *Betsey*, to act as church and manse. He travelled from island to island preaching the word. His family suffered greatly and his small son pleaded with his father to take him back to the manse which they had been forced to leave and which he knew as home. Congregations without a minister or a church frequently found themselves dispirited, wondering how they would ever be able to raise sufficient funds to replace the churches, manses and schools they had left. The 450 ministers who walked out of the Assembly in May 1843 were brave men indeed and relied on God alone to provide for them and their families. When they were attached to a congregation it was often they who were expected to lead the flock to find the physical resources necessary to erect the buildings that were so desperately needed.

The Free Kirk's Integrity Brought into Question

The lack of money can lead us all into having strange bedfellows. This was true of the Free Kirk when it appealed to Presbyterians in America for funding. This was soon after the Disruption and a time when they wondered how they were to raise enough money to fulfil their vision of an alternative national Church. Towards the end of 1843 Rev. Dr Cunningham and Mr Henry Fergusson, an elder from Dundee, crossed the Atlantic to hold a series of meetings with their 'American brethren'. They found themselves being welcomed not only by Presbyterians but also by Methodists, Congregationalists and Baptists.[38] Their journey took them to the Deep South, the area where slavery was most widespread. The deputation was well received and a considerable amount of money (about £3,000) was raised.

When word of this broke out in Scotland, and indeed across the UK, there was outrage. Thomas Chalmers was asked to address the criticism. In a letter to Rev. Dr Smyth, Charlestown, South Carolina, which was published in many newspapers, Dr Chalmers attempted to defend his position. While condemning slavery he felt it was wrong to 'unchristianize part of the American churches'. He also lacked sympathy with those who 'felt unable to maintain any fellowship or interchange of good offices … with its churches or its ministers'.[39] As the controversy raged, Rev. Dr Candlish's contribution that, while slavery was a sin, slaveholding was not, did little to calm the situation.[40]

An African American named Frederick Douglass visited the UK and Scotland about that time. Frederick had started life as a slave but, by the time he entered the debate, he was recognised as a leading abolitionist of the slave trade, a writer, orator, social reformer and statesman. He asked the Free Church to discuss the matter with him and a date, time and place were agreed, but the Free Kirk representatives did not turn up. Soon he found himself at the centre of a movement to 'send back the money'. The Kirk's way of handling this sort of situation was to bury it. A committee was set up at the 1847

---

[38]   Brown, *Annals of the Disruption*, part III, p. 138
[39]   *Glasgow Herald* Monday 30th December 1844
[40]   *Dumfries & Galloway Standard* 8th January 1845

General Assembly and debate closed. The Glasgow Emancipation Society, which was backing the movement, went bust and the whole issue died.

In a recent radio interview with opera singer Andrea Baker, David Robertson, Moderator of the United Free Church, said that Frederick Douglass failed in his efforts. He believes the Free Kirk did not attend the proposed meeting because they knew that the Established Church was using this issue to discredit them and Douglass was being used to embarrass the fledgling Kirk. This was not, he admits, the Free Kirk's finest moment. The money should have been sent back and the issue of slavery should have remained on the agenda.[41]

The only positive thing that emerges from this sorry saga is that the mass of the people in Scotland, and the UK as a whole, were clearly totally opposed to slavery.

The Effect of the Disruption on the Kirk

Up to 1843 the Kirk could, with justification, call itself a national Church. Those who did not conform were a growing minority. This minority consisted mainly of groups who seceded during the 18th century, a few Baptists, Episcopalians and Catholics. The majority of Catholics were to be found in Aberdeenshire and the Western Isles. Episcopalians were by and large members of the aristocracy.

With 40 per cent of the Kirk walking out in 1843, one would expect the influence of the Church to be diminished. This was not the case. Thomas Chalmers, one-time minister of Kilmany, had, in his early ministry, very conservative views on the Church. He changed dramatically following an illness, and perhaps through the influence of Andrew Fuller, and became the voice of the Evangelicals from 1832 onwards. He saw the way forward as being a partnership between Church and State. His preaching was said to be magnetic and he gained the respect of his peers for his pastoral work, first in Fife and later in Glasgow. His experience in working with the poor made him a leading light in discussions on such matters as the Poor Law and education. By the time he became Moderator of the Church of Scotland in 1832, Thomas Chalmers was so respected that he was said to be the voice of the Church in Scotland. Between 1833 and 1843 there were many clashes between the Kirk and the State. When the Disruption finally took place it was Thomas Chalmers who led the Dissenters out of the General Assembly. He was to become the first Moderator of the Free Kirk, clearly expecting the state to recognise that the extent of the dissention from the Old Kirk justified it being recognised as the Established Church.[42]

It was not long after 1843 before the Free Kirk came to depend upon the financial generosity of the wealthy middle class. This had the effect of alienating many ordinary folk who had formed the grass-roots support that brought it into being. Chalmers was so disappointed at the way things turned out that he retired from his role of leadership within the Free Kirk.

[41] BBC Radio Scotland, 'A Man's a Man for a' That: Frederick Douglass in Scotland', Sunday 3rd January 2016
[42] Brown, *Annals of the Disruption*, pp. 470 ff.

As the 19th century drew to a close a schism took place in 1892, with the Free Presbyterians breaking away from the Free Church. This conservative group was protesting against what it perceived as the lowering of confessional standards within the Free Kirk. This body is still active, with its stronghold in the highlands and western islands of Scotland. Eight years later, the United Presbyterians and the Free Church came together to form the United Free Church. When this body agreed to unite with the Established Church in 1930, one group, which was opposed to any connection between Church and State and believed that churches should have greater theological liberty, wished to retained its independence, and it is this group that continues to be known as the United Free Church. Today this body claims to have over 100 practising congregations and a membership of over 13,000.

The Rise of the Secular Society

Others too were engaged in the national debate about matters of concern including reforming housing and sanitation. Before the Disruption in 1833, Kirk leaders were very vocal in their opposition to slavery and this continued up to 1865 and the end of the American Civil War. Oddly, many of the reforms that took place involved taking traditional responsibilities away from the Church and putting them into the hands of the secular society. The Poor Law after 1845, for example, removed the responsibility for the poor from the Churches (a responsibility they had shouldered since before the Reformation) and placed it with the democratically elected Poor Law Board. Similarly, the Education Act of 1872, when the Churches handed their schools over to local School Boards without charge, put universal education into the hands of the Scottish Education Department, again relieving the Church of this responsibility. There were still strong Christian influences during the 19th century and many great reforming leaders arose like William Quarrier, who established the children's homes, and William Collins, the Glasgow publisher, who was influential in the temperance movement. Nevertheless, the foundation of a more secular society was being laid, even though there is little evidence that it was being viewed that way by the churchmen of the day.

The secular institutions responsible for social welfare were run by elected members who were almost exclusively from either the Church of Scotland or the Free Kirk, many of them elders or clergy. As a result, the influence of the Church continued to dominate society throughout the 19th century and so there was no concern about the Church losing influence. It had not occurred to the many ministers who supported and encouraged the Education Act of 1872 that one day they may not have right of entry into schools. They did not foresee a time when they would have to seek an invitation from the head teacher. This showed a lack of awareness, for the Church of Scotland had been losing its influence over educating the young for some time. While some parochial schools were highly thought of, other denominations were also very effective in this area. Secularisation was further advanced when laws were enacted to allow registrars to perform weddings, record deaths and register the birth of children. A law passed in

1854 removed the long-held responsibility of ministers to maintain records of births, deaths and marriages and placed this in the hands of the Registrar General, a new office centred in Edinburgh.

The effect of all this was a growing disconnect between the Church and many working folk in Scotland. A class consciousness between the minister and the people developed which spawned resentment against the Kirk. The General Assembly of 1896 stated, 'No reflection is more sad than the apparent inability of the regular ministry of the Church to reach the lower depths of the population.' Reference to the working folk as 'the lower depths of the population' in itself reflects the attitude of the ministry that underpinned the problem. If the ordinary working folk of the parish were viewed in this way by the Church, there is little wonder a great chasm opened up that alienated many of God's people from those there to serve them. The wonder is that the damage done was not even greater. In the 18th century the minister, like the gentry, embodied the parish. By the end of the 19th century, the minister was seen as middle class and alien from the folk who worked in the mill or ploughed the field.

It is popular to see the various divisions and sub-divisions that took place in the Church of Scotland in the 18th and 19th centuries as the petulant behaviour of self-righteous religious bigots. There is no doubt that Scotland's national Church was weakened, but perhaps it deserved that fate. As indicated above, the problem seems to have been rooted in the establishment within the Church of Scotland being out of step with the people of the time. The clergy had become too ready to identify with and accommodate the great and the good of the land and unwilling to address the needs of the ordinary folk. After all, it was the ordinary folk who were their flock. The events that were dividing the Kirk need to be seen against the backdrop of an emerging desire for self-determination by the working classes, not only in Scotland but across Western European society. The 18th century saw the widely unpopular Union of 1707, the American War of Independence and the French Revolution, the last causing fear and uncertainty in the British nobility. The 19th century saw the Tolpuddle Martyrs, the rise of the Chartist movement, Karl Marx and Communism and the American Civil War. It also saw the growth of the cities as well as the industrialisation and overcrowding that went with it. This was accompanied by rural depopulation and the notorious Highland Clearances. These were times of great social, political and economic change. The Church could not be immune from these influences in wider society. People who wanted political democracy also wanted equality in their Kirk. After all, through Knox and Melville the Kirk was founded on that very principle.

The 20th Century

In spite of this the Church maintained its influence on Victorian society. Membership remained strong at the turn of the century. Even after the First World War, superficially, the Church appeared in good heart. The 'war to end wars' did, however, have a marked effect on the beliefs of ordinary folk. In 1914 there had been a tendency to portray it as a holy war and many ministers and their sons joined up. It was not long before the full barbarity of the trenches became clear and this resulted in many turning away from the Kirk.

Yet in 1930 the influential minister The Very Rev. John White noted that throughout his ministry there had been a widespread change in attitude. No longer was the Church and the Christian faith accepted without question. There was abroad what he described as 'a secular rationalism, Hedonism and New Psychology'. While John White seems to have been largely correct in this assessment of the situation, his contribution to Catholic/Protestant sectarianism in the 1930s has, in the eyes of many, contaminated his reputation.[43]

In the 1930s, following the union of the Established Church and the United Presbyterian Church, there was a resurgence in the influence of the General Assembly as the voice of Scotland. This was not entirely justified as the Catholic, Episcopalian and Baptist Churches, together with other smaller denominations, were growing in popularity. But the Church of Scotland was holding its own and by 1961 church membership had increased in the 30 years since 1931, and this was largely due to successful outreach in the post-war housing schemes. The Catholic Church seemed to do well in the 1930s as Kirk ministers with sectarian views condemned it from their pulpits. In the fullness of time Catholic congregations too would feel the effect of a growing secularisation in the country. In spite of its growth up to the mid 1960s, which many commentators now see as matching the rise of Scottish nationalism, the congregations and the influence of the Kirk continued to decline throughout the 60s, 70s and 80s. Nevertheless, the importance of the General Assembly was widely recognised until the 1990s and the establishment of the Scottish Parliament. It was this that encouraged Margaret Thatcher, UK Prime Minister during the 1980s, to address this body. Having said that, the influence of the Church and Nation Committee, which is responsible for promoting Christian teaching on the moral life of the country, found its opinions on almost any part of national life – economic, educational or entertainment – largely unheeded. With declining membership and the emergence of the Holyrood Parliament, the General Assembly was no longer seen as voicing the will of the Scottish people. As a result, any lingering influence the General Assembly may have had nationally diminished.

By the end of the 20th century the Kirk was becoming a leaner body. Congregations were uniting and churches, many dating back to the days of the Free Kirk, were closing. This trend has continued into the 21st century. Attempts have been made to reverse the trend by adopting new theologies and new ways of leading worship. Church buildings are becoming more open places seeking to welcome people of any or no faith, not only for worship but also for recreation. Parish centres are clearly vibrant community facilities replacing the old sanctuaries that lay cold and empty for much of the week.

---

[43]   H. Reid, *Outside Verdict: An Old Kirk in a New Scotland* (Edinburgh, Saint Andrew Press, 2002)

A New Century and New Challenges

The Kirk cannot insulate itself from changes in society. The General Assembly agreed to the ordination of women as elders in 1966 and two years later it also agreed to the ordination of women as ministers. Despite the intentions of the General Assembly, progress was slow and many Kirk Sessions were unwilling to ordain women as elders, and even more reluctant to call them as ministers. Indeed, Inverness had its first female minister, Rev. Fiona Smith, in 2012, although it must be recognised that women have now been playing important leadership roles in the Kirk for several decades.

Time was clearly against male chauvinism and in the new century the Kirk inducted its first female Moderator, Dr Alison Elliot, an elder, in 2004. Dr Elliot was not only the first woman to hold this office but the first lay person in 400 years. By 2007 the second female Moderator was appointed, The Very Rev. Dr Sheilagh Kesting, and in 2013 the third, The Very Rev. Dr Lorna Hood. While the new century is still young, changes in the Kirk continue with the General Assembly's agreement to accept openly gay ministers. As with all change, this has not taken place without much soul-searching and pain. Some congregations have chosen to leave the Kirk, threatening a new schism; but while their loss has been felt, their numbers are low.

Styles of worship are also changing, with a move towards more participation by the congregation in worship and responses in prayers now widely accepted. The new hymn book, CH4 published in 2005, has assisted this modernisation of worship through using praise that expresses contemporary thoughts and music that is more easily accepted by the modern worshipper. The cry goes out that the Kirk is a reformed and reforming Kirk, so justifying the changes that have taken place, not only within itself but also in its relationships with those of other denominations. A hundred years ago it would have been inconceivable that the Parish Church would have worked with the local Episcopal, Catholic and Baptist Churches in providing ecumenical Christian centres where coffee, meals and bookshops serve communities. Today this is so normal that it goes without comment. Even some places of worship are shared by different denominations, and churches see it as their role to make their facilities available to all members of the community, whether church members or not.

So it is that in this more open and tolerant society the Kirk is still playing its part in providing facilities for all of God's people within the parish. Numerically, the membership of the Kirk is smaller than before. It has many challenges to face, not least the lack of available candidates to the ministry. In so many ways it is, however, rising to the challenges of the modern world, and through the leadership provided by men and women of faith, the Kirk will continue to serve God's people throughout Scotland and beyond.

James W Gillin. '79

CHAPTER TWO: FOUR KIRKS, ONE HISTORY
PART ONE: COLLESSIE

The Parish of Collessie:
An Ancient Place

∾

There is a great deal of archaeological evidence to tell us that Collessie and surrounding area have a very long history, with human habitation going back to very early times. It is a matter of regret that the further back we go the harder it is to discover details of the lives, hopes, fears and beliefs of the people who lived there. Their trials, hardships, pleasures, loves and faith have largely disappeared from the records. We do, however, find glimpses into that distant world that looks so very strange to modern eyes.

The parish of Collessie on John Adair's map of 1684

The earliest maps of Fife reveal a landscape in the parish of Collessie that was very different from the one we know today. Rossie Loch, covering some 300 acres, stretched north and west from where Kinloch House now stands and was filled with pike and eels.

There is a record of Douglas Turner of Ladybank excavating an Earth House in 1937,[44] near to where the shoreline of Rossie Loch would have lain. Apart from a yellow bead and an interesting primitive quern, little was found. A burial mound once lay to the south of Collessie and was known as Gask Hill. Swans and ducks visited this area and the village of Kinloch, the largest settlement in the parish, nestled at its head. In contrast to the tiny cruck houses of that village were the great houses of Rossie, Halhill and Kinloch. In the 1790s the Rev. Andrew Walker recorded in the Old Statistical Account[45] that the River Eden 'abounds with trout' but that it was prone to flooding at 'seed-time and harvest'. Rossie Loch had been drained earlier in the 18th century. In winter it was still given to flooding, yet it was able to produce sufficient hay and pasture for 120 head of cattle each year. By the end of the 1700s much of the land was arable and enclosed and there were only three flocks of sheep. With the enclosed fields, sheep, cattle and arable land, the parish had come to look more familiar to modern eyes.

Deer antlers and the remains of oak trees dating back to 9000 or 10000 BC have been found in land where once Rossie Loch would have provided natural drainage for the area and food for any nearby inhabitants. Ancient woodland once adorned this place and it would have been filled with deer and other game.

Both the Old and New Statistical Accounts[46] (1791 and 1836) refer to the remains of a feature known as the Maiden Castle, which lay to the west of Trafalgar, just opposite the entrance to Meadowells Farm. The Old Statistical Account of the parish provides us with a fanciful tale of the castle being under siege when the governor died. His daughter concealed his death and gave orders in his name that saved the castle. Archaeological investigations in 1933 and 1956 could find no evidence to substantiate this story and Dr K.A. Steer of RCAHMS concluded that it was not of any historical importance and was probably a plantation bank or stock enclosure.[47] George Calley, in his book *Collessie, A Parish Alphabet*, was not convinced about this and suggests it may be the remains of a former Kinloch House. This site, being higher than the surrounding area, would have been more suitable for habitation. The land around the present house was not drained until 1699.[48]

Rev. Andrew Walker also mentions another castle which was about 30 feet high and lying to the east of Trafalgar. He saw this and the Maiden Castle as being guardians of the pass that stretches past Lindores Loch to Newburgh. Rev. John McFarlane, writing the New Statistical Account in 1836, names the feature Agabatha Castle, which, he says, means 'marsh-field castle'.[49] Certainly, the two men agree that this feature, which they believed had a moat, lay in a very wet place. Mr McFarlane, in the New Statistical Account, tells us that around this structure several artefacts have been found – a quern

---

[44]   Royal Commission on the Ancient and Historical Monuments of Scotland (RCAHMS), https://canmore.org.uk/site/30161/rossie-house-tomb

[45]   J. Sinclair, *The Statistical Account of Scotland* (Edinburgh, William Creech, 1791–99) ('Old Statistical Account')

[46]   J. Sinclair, *The Statistical Account of Scotland* (Edinburgh, William Creech, 1834–45) ('New Statistical Account')

[47]   RCAHMS, https://canmore.org.uk/

[48]   G. Calley, *Collessie: A Parish Alphabet* (George Calley, 2000)

[49]   S. Taylor and G. Markus, *The Place-names of Fife*, vol. 4 (Donnington, Shaun Tyas, 2010, pp. 202 ff.)

of mica slate and a number of coins belonging to the period of Edward I of England. According to Mr McFarlane, the land between these two features has produced traces of human remains, stone coffins and urns providing evidence of early settlement in the area.[50] Today there is no evidence of Agabatha Castle.

Still very much in evidence today is a nine-foot standing stone in a field about half a mile to the south-east of the village. According to local artist and historian Marianna Lines, it is a Bronze Age standing stone with a much later Pictish carving of a naked warrior carrying a ball-weighted spear in his right hand and a shield in his left. This can be seen in the upper part of the stone, with a Pictish symbol known as the arch or horseshoe below to the right of the figure and positioned over a Pictish beast. This carving is one of only two such examples, the other being the Rhynie Man carving in Aberdeenshire. Marianna believes this to be the earliest representation of a human being in Fife and could date from the fourth century AD. The figure is possibly a representation of a god. She indicates a similarity to some of the East Wemyss cave carvings, which, she suggests, are dated about the fifth century AD.[51]

Left: Collessie Man from a painting by Marianna Lines. *Right*: Bronze stone with Pictish carving

It is not only archaeological remains that tell something of the past, for even the names of the places that are so familiar to us find their origins in a time before recorded history. The name of the village of Collessie, which was also given to the parish around it, is said to be of Gaelic origin. *Col* or *Cul* is understood to signify the back, corner or recess. The next syllable, *eas*, signifies a waterfall. While there is no waterfall in the village now, there is the Den Burn which flows from the Black Loch.[52]

---

50 https://canmore.org.uk/site/30169/agabatha-castle
51 M. Lines, *The Traveller's Guide to Sacred Scotland: A Guide to Scotland's Ancient Sites and Sacred Places* (Somerset, Gothic Image Publications, 2014)
52 Taylor, *The Place-names of Fife*, vol. 4, pp. 202 ff.

The Arrival of the Normans in Collessie

As we saw in Chapter 1, the Church of Collessie (recorded Callesyn) was rededicated by Bishop David de Bernham on 30th July 1243. Nineteen years later Collessie was granted to the Abbey of Lindores. This is recorded in the Chartulary of Lindores as a gift by Roger de Quincy, Earl of Winton and Constable of Scotland, whose main Scottish seat was at Leuchars. This land came to him as a result of the marriage between his grandfather Robert de Quincy and his grandmother Orabilis, who herself inherited the lands from her father, Ness, Lord of Leuchars. Robert de Quincy the younger, father of Roger, had also granted the monks of Lindores the right to gather broom, heather and moss and to graze their cattle and have right of way on his lands on the moor of Kyndeloch (Kinloch), Edyn and Monagrey. Roger, the patron of Collessie, added the church but at the time the grant was made a well-known man was already rector and this change in arrangement could not take place while he was in post. That man was Adam Malcarvaston, one-time envoy of King Alexander III to King Henry III of England. He was also the Pope's chaplain and provost of St Mary's Church in St Andrews. He resigned and so the transfer took place under Bishop Gamelin. The following year Master Malcarvaston became rector of Ceres.[53]

By the Late Medieval period Collessie was an agricultural centre with weaving as a secondary industry. According to legend, King James V would visit the area when in residence at Falkland Palace. It was his practice to meet his subjects in disguise, and many failed to recognise their King as he strolled along the shores of Rossie Loch. He would enter into conversation and find out how they viewed their King and government.

Life at this time was very much centred on the Church with its impressive abbeys and cathedrals, like those at St Andrews and Lindores. Yet the local Parish Church was also an important centre and all around there could be found shrines, altars, holy wells, religious relics, carved stone crosses and burial grounds. Beliefs were centred on fear of a very real and alive Devil and a very real Hell. In order to address their impending doom, some went to fight in the Crusades and others became pilgrims travelling vast distances to some holy shrine which contained the relic of a saint. Services were conducted in Latin and ordinary folk kept at a distance by a wooden rood screen decorated with paintings or carvings depicting Bible stories. Plays were acted out to tell the story of the cross and purgatory and local saints were prayed to. The Church was a very different place from what we are accustomed to today, and life tended to be much harder. Many folk were condemned to the brutality of serfdom. They were inclined to be shorter in stature than modern people and aged rapidly due to harsh working conditions, poor hygiene and widespread disease.[54] Surprisingly, the standard of living of ordinary folk improved in Scotland and the rest of Europe following the Black Death in 1350 because the plague brought about the death of about one third of the population, resulting in a shortage of workers everywhere, and so family incomes increased.

---

53   Dowden, *Chartulary of the Abbey of Lindores*, pp. lviii–lx
54   www.educationscotland.gov.uk/scotlandshistory/medievallife/religionfestivalsandbeliefs/index.asp

Kinloch

Throughout its history the parish of Collessie seems to have been connected with those who at one time would have been referred to as 'the highest in the land'. These notable parishioners can be traced back to the times when the Norman influence was becoming strong in Scotland, especially with the noble families. David, Earl of Huntingdon, brother of William I, the Lion, owned and hunted on the land now known as Lumquhat.[55] Another local name, Kinloch, belongs to one of the oldest families of Fife. It is first recorded in 1219 when one Murinus Kyndeloch bore witness to a charter granted by Saer de Quincy, Earl of Winchester. In 1296 William de Kyndeloch, like many other Scottish noblemen, swore fealty to Edward I of England. By 1452 the lands had come into the possession of the Crown and James II granted them to Alexander of Philde. At some time before 1527 the area around Collessie was divided into Easter and Wester Kinloch. Wester Kinloch was gifted as liferent holdings to a series of court dignitaries. Many noble families came and went. They included the Clerk of Justiciary Thomas Scott, David Balfour of Burleigh and, after Burleigh's death, the King's chief cook, Thomas Marschall.

James V died in 1542 and by 1566 the lands of Kinloch had returned to his grandson, James VI, who granted them to Michael Balfour of Burleigh, a descendant of David. The new Laird was the eldest son of James Balfour of Pittendreich, who had gained a reputation for himself which resulted in him being known by his contemporaries as 'Blak Ba'four'.

This family seems to have found it hard to avoid controversy, for Michael Balfour, the new incumbent of Kinloch, was said to have been involved in the murder of Darnley,[56] husband to Queen Mary. As a result of this, the land was confiscated and granted to John Ruthven, son of William, Lord Ruthven.

That was not, however, the end of the Balfours of Burleigh. The Historical Antiquities tell us that in 1677 John Balfour of Kinloch, a descendant of Michael Balfour and known as Captain Burleigh, refused to conform to King Charles II's Episcopal demands. Archbishop Sharp had decided to make life hard for those in north-east Fife who refused to conform. Captain Burleigh was a prominent Covenanter and he and a group of friends were forced to defend themselves against an attack by the Archbishop's man, Captain Carstairs. He, and about 12 others, arrived at the home of Balfour and started to shoot through the windows. Burleigh and his friends had no alternative but to defend themselves, but this resulted in him being branded an outlaw and he became the focus on which to condemn the whole Presbyterian cause.

As events unfolded, Burleigh became a prominent member of the group of assassins who killed Archbishop Sharp in 1679. In order to save himself from the authorities he fled to Holland. In Scotland he was condemned to death in his absence, while in

55 J.M. Leighton, *History of the County of Fife, From the Earliest Period to the Present Time*, vol. II (Glasgow, Joseph Swan, 1840)
56 A.H. Millar, *Fife: Pictorial and Historical, Its People, Burghs, Castles and Mansions*, vol. 1 (Cupar, A. Westwood & Son, 1885)

Holland he became highly respected and a commandant of the Dutch troops in the West Indies.[57]

Another in the parish who became noteworthy was Mr James Makgill of Rankeilour, who was Clerk Register at the end of the 17th century. In 1662 Makgill was fined £3,000 for nonconformity to Charles II's Scottish Church. The local Collessie nobility were not immune from the long hand of the Episcopal King, but nor were they ready to surrender their hard-won Presbyterian principles. Through these zealous Reformers, the folk of Collessie had a strong link with all that was going on during these turbulent years that have become known as the 'killing time'.

By the end of the 18th century, and having passed through the hands of many proprietors, the lands of Kinloch came to Charles Kinnear, a renowned agriculturalist who was responsible for draining much of the land. Charles Kinnear's son John Boyd Kinnear was a man of considerable ability and a very prominent member of the community, chairing and serving on the committees of many organisations in the county. He was born in 1828, graduated from the universities of Edinburgh and St Andrews, became a Scottish advocate and wrote many books on jurisprudence and women's rights. In 1885 he was elected Liberal MP for East Fife, but in 1886 he stood as a Liberal Unionist and was defeated by Asquith, the future prime minister. This larger-than-life figure was, no doubt, loved and hated in equal measure, for he was outspoken on the topics he believed to be important but he was also very generous.

The estate remained with the Kinnear family until 1920 when John Boyd Kinnear died aged 92 and Henry Hutchison of Kirkcaldy bought it. He died in 1937 and the estate was then purchased by his nephew John Key Hutchison and his wife, who lived there until 1953 when they moved to Little Kinloch House. During the war the Key Hutchisons took in evacuees from Edinburgh. These children were well treated and regularly taken to Collessie Church on Sundays. In 1954 the property was gifted to the Presbytery of St Andrews, which converted it into an Eventide Home until 1998 when it was closed by the Church of Scotland and once more became a private residence.[58]

The Village of Kinloch

One surprising fact that has emerged is that, according to the Old Statistical Account dated 1791, the largest settlement in the parish was the village of Kinloch. In that year it had a population of 191. The entry in Samuel Lewis's *A Topographical Dictionary of Scotland* dated 1846 reads:

> KINLOCH, a village, in the parish of Collessie, district of Cupar, county of Fife, 5 miles (W) from Cupar; containing 58 inhabitants. It is situated a little to the south of the road from Cupar to Auchtermuchty, and a short distance from the village of Collessie. Not many years since, it was the largest village in the parish, having nearly four times its present

---

[57]   J.W. Taylor, *Some Historical Antiquities, Chiefly Ecclesiastical, Connected with the North, the East and the Centre of Fife* (Cupar, William Robertson, 1868)
[58]   Calley, *Collessie: A Parish Alphabet*

amount of population; a number of families, however, who resided here, have removed to Monkton. The houses form a line, with an interval of twelve feet between every four. The lands around the village have latterly been much improved by draining.[59]

In fact, the population of Kinloch was removed not only to Monkstown but also to Edenstown and Giffordtown. The village was situated south of Little Kinloch House on the old New Inn to Newburgh Road, by Sheills Bridge and Easter Kilwhiss. The reason for the demise of the village, according to George Calley, is that Andrew Thomson, owner of Wester or Little Kinloch, wished to have the village removed so as to have a clear view from the house he built in 1805.

A plea was successfully brought before Lord Gifford (Chancellor in 1825) on behalf of Andrew Thomson to remove the residents of Kinloch. As a result of this the village of Kinloch was demolished and the hamlets of Giffordtown, Edenstown, Charlottetown and Monkstown were created. The new settlements comprised single-storey weavers' cottages. These buildings remain to this day, although they have been considerably changed through

Kinloch House

upgrading over the years. Giffordtown was named after the said Lord Gifford, while Edenstown got its name for its position on Edensmuir. Monkstown was named after the monks who came from Lindores to cut peat, while Charlottetown got its name from Charlotte Paterson who once owned the land in that area.[60]

Halhill

There is another important estate in the history of the parish, but this one no longer exists. It is the lands of Easter Collessie or Halhill. This property comes to our attention in 1477–78 when it was, like the lands of Kinloch, Crown property. King James III gifted the estate to a court official known only as Ross Herald. In 1507 James IV gifted the lands to the Marchmont Herald, William Cuming of Inverallochy. His son sold the estate in 1513 to Henry Balnavis, a self-made man coming from humble origins in Kirkcaldy. He studied law and quickly became recognised as a man of considerable ability. In 1538 he was appointed Ordinary Lord of Session. Part of his education took

---

59 S. Lewis, *A Topographical Dictionary of Scotland*, vol. 2 (London, 1846), www.british-history.ac.uk/topographical-dict/scotland

60 Calley, *Collessie: A Parish Alphabet*

place at St Andrews University and part in Cologne. It was while in Germany that his enthusiasm for religious reformation developed and when he returned home a close association developed with Knox. He is known to have been involved in the overthrow of Cardinal Beaton and is believed to have been part of the assassination plot. As a result he was imprisoned in France and deprived of his land at Halhill by James Hamilton, Regent of Scotland and Second Earl of Arran. By 1563, however, when Hamilton had lost his influence, Balnavis returned to his seat on the bench and the title Lord Halhill. He remained active, being involved in the trial of Bothwell for the murder of Darnley, and acted as a Commissioner at York when Queen Mary faced the same charge.[61]

Balnavis sold Halhill to Sir James Melville of Raith, the son of a prominent Reformer, also James Melville, who died for his cause. Sir James himself was a most interesting character. He was born in 1535 and at the age of 14 was sent to France by the Queen Regent to act as page to Monluc, Bishop of Valence. While in France he visited Queen Mary before she returned to Scotland, and as a result of this meeting he became a member of her court and served loyally throughout her eventful reign. Following Mary's abdication, James Melville became a noted courtier of James VI. His invitation to join him in London following the Union of the Crowns in 1603 was, however, declined. One reason Sir James Melville is widely remembered is that he wrote memoirs in which he described in some detail his life of service to Mary, Queen of Scots and her son James. He became the proprietor of Halhill, previously known as Easter Collessie, in about 1575. In 1675, some 58 years after Sir James's death, Halhill became part of the parkland around Melville House and the old house was demolished.[62]

Rossie

While Kinloch could be found at the eastern end of Rossie Loch, the lands of Rossie lay at the western end. Both places were named through their relationship to Rossie Loch: Kinloch referring to its place at the head of the Loch and Rossie coming from the Gaelic *ros* meaning promontory. Like Kinloch it has an ancient history, with some claiming that it was first recorded in the reign of the Roman Emperor Flavian, though I have failed to find sources to substantiate that.

There certainly is reference to Rossie during the reign of King David I (1083–1153) when a major building is recorded and the land belonged to Sir Henry Rossie of that Ilk. In 1160, however, Sir Henry's son Sir Alexander Rossie forfeited the lands to King Malcolm IV, who gave them to Duncan, Earl of Fife. Clearly it was the custom for men to find themselves either in favour with the King, when they received land, or out of favour, when they were forced to relinquish the land. So the Regent Albany gave Rossie to Sir John Sibbald of Balgony and he managed to retain it until 1172. It is recorded that the Hall of Rossie was in existence in 1488 and it is claimed that a stone staircase and the cellars of the present house date from that period.

---

61   Millar, *Fife Pictorial and Historical*
62   Taylor, *Some Historical Antiquities*

James II gave Rossie to William Bonar, Keeper of the Rolls, but his son James Bonar found himself on the wrong side at the Battle of Sauchieburn in 1488 when James III was defeated by his son James IV, and so James lost the lands of Easter Rossie, the Hall, the Loch and island. The King considered his support of his father, James III, as treason, so it was passed to George Hall of Ayton.

James Bonar regained part of the land in 1493 but his inheritance was not fully restored until 1509. A letter of 1531 confirms the right to fish in the loch with boats, nets and 'eil-ark' (eel traps). The hall was mentioned again in a charter, confirming William, son of John Bonar, as rightful inheritor of the land in 1541. One Robert Hardy gained possession of Wester Rossie in 1541, with permission to build a mansion house and garden. He could also plant trees and grow lint and hemp, giving us an idea of the cash crops that engaged local farmers in the 16th century. It must have been during the time when William was Laird that Queen Mary was recorded to have been engaged in hunting on these lands. On William's death in 1573 the inheritance was passed to the eldest of his three sons, John, who also acquired the lands of Lumquhat. It was in the time of John that a charter emerges containing the curious passage 'because of the zeal of the father and son for the propagation of the Gospel the presentation to the Parish Church of Collessie'.[63] The Bonars left Rossie for the last time in 1630. During the following years the lands passed through various hands including Sir James Scott.

In a plantation not far from Rossie House lies a partially ruined tomb. An excavation that took place there between 1933 and 1938 revealed two skeletons.[64] At the time it was decided that it was not possible to identify the sex of the skeletons. Further investigation revealed that one was male and the other female. It is thought that the female skeleton is that of Lady Rossie, who was buried on 27th May 1663, and the male is Sir James Scott, who died in 1669.

James Cheape of Ormiston bought Rossie from the Scott family in 1669. It was then to remain in the hands of this family until the 19th century. The Cheape family did much to improve the land including draining the Loch in 1740 and again in 1805. They may well also have been responsible for building the present Rossie House, which is

Rossie House

reckoned to be Georgian, although no date of its construction is recorded. The Cheape family are interred in Collessie Church graveyard in the family tomb just to the left of the churchyard gate as we enter.

Rankeilour

The fourth estate to be mentioned lies at the eastern boundary where Collessie, Springfield and Monimail parishes meet. It is the estate once known as Nether Rankeilour. Over

63 Millar, *Fife Pictorial and Historical*
64 RCAHMS, Archaeology Notes, https://canmore.org.uk/event/684756

Rankeilour, in the parish of Monimail, and Nether Rankeilour once belonged to the family that gave the estate its name. It is recorded that 'Johan Rankeilour de eodem' was a member of a jury in 1517 that settled a valuation of the County of Fife at the court in Cupar.[65] David, the last of the Rankeilour family, sold Nether Rankeilour to Sir James Makgill in 1553. Sir James was son of a provost of Edinburgh and trained in law, eventually taking his seat on the bench as Lord Rankeilour in 1554. In 1559 he found himself in sympathy with the Reformation and became a friend of John Knox. When Queen Mary returned from France, he was sworn to her Council in 1561. In time he was seen to have been one of those implicated in the murder of Rizzio and found it necessary to flee Edinburgh and take refuge in the highlands. In 1567 he was restored by the Regent Murray and was involved in negotiation with Queen Elizabeth of England concerning accusations against Mary Stewart, Queen of Scots. From 1571–72 he served as ambassador at the court of England's Queen.

During the period of dispute between Queen Mary's followers and the Reformers, Makgill seems to have suffered badly. He lost valuables worth about £1,000 to the Queen's supporters as they were transported by boat from Leith to Pinkie in 1571. The following year his 'Edinburgh house was pulled down and sold for firewood'.[66]

Towards the end of the 17th century Sir James Makgill married Janet Crichton, daughter of James, 1st Viscount of Frendraught. The family remained at Rankeilour until the death of the last male heir, also James. The estate then passed to his sister, Isabella Makgill. Isabella married a local Cupar minister, Rev. William Dick, in 1724. Their daughter Margaret, heiress to the estate, married the Hon. Fredrick Lewis Maitland, sixth son of the Earl of Lauderdale. They had a son, Charles Maitland, a captain in the Royal Navy, who distinguished himself in 1760 and again in 1778. He, in turn, had a son, also Charles, who joined the 17th Light Dragoons. He rose to the position of Colonel and fought in the West Indies in 1794. Charles's son, David, born in 1801, was known as David Maitland Makgill and was baptised in Collessie Church.[67] In 1837 his name was legally changed to David Maitland Makgill Crichton. This was because he served as heir in line of James Crichton of Frendraught as a result of the Makgill connection with the Crichton family in the 17th century.[68]

David was a highly respected advocate and was widely appreciated for his ability as an orator. He was a prominent supporter of the Free Church at the time of the Disruption. He also ensured that a bridge was built over the new railway at Cupar instead of the level crossing which the rail company had intended. Ill health forced him to give up his fight for religious and political causes when he was in his forties and he died in 1851 at the age of 50. A statue in memorial to Mr Makgill Crichton stands overlooking the bridge at Cupar station.

---

65 Leighton, *History of the County of Fife*
66 D. Dalrymple, *An Historical Account of the Senators of the College of Justice of Scotland from its Institution in 1532* (Edinburgh, James Stillie, 1849)
67 Leighton, *History of the County of Fife*
68 www.thepeerage.com/p3426.htm

The Rev. John McFarlane, minister of Collessie and author of the New Statistical Account of 1836, recounted a tale about Ballomill, which lies to the south of Nether Rankeilour, close to the River Eden. We are told that James IV had found himself in the vicinity of Ballomill roaming in disguise as a poor travelling man. It was evening and he knocked on the door of the miller's house and, after some persuasion, managed to gain lodging for the night. James was entertained round the fire by the family enjoying the friendship and hospitality. The miller was a kind and open man and the visitor found himself with a strong feeling of friendship towards him. In the morning the miller accompanied his guest to the boundary of the farm when they were approached by the royal guards. It was then that the identity of the stranger became evident to his host. As a reward for his hospitality the King told the miller that he could have either the fourth part, eighth part or sixteenth part of the land on which they stood. The miller was no mathematician and he thought to himself that a sixteenth part sounded greedy while a fourth part seemed to cheat himself, so he settled for an eighth part. As a result, an eighth part of the lands of Ballomill was measured and given to the miller's family. At the time of writing the 1836 Statistical Account, it was claimed that the description in the title deeds was 'All and whole the one eighth part of the lands of Ballomill'. According to Mr McFarlane, the Royal Charter was preserved in the parish.[69]

Building a New Church

In the New Statistical Account written in 1836 we find the following description of the church building that existed at that time:

> The church is an exceedingly uncomfortable and ill-adapted structure. It is one of the few remaining long and narrow buildings that seems to have been common in the country in Roman Catholic times. It is 75 feet long, by 25 broad. The pulpit is in the middle, and there are galleries to the right and left of it. Some of the old seats that remain bear the date of the fifteenth century. From its original situation, or by the accumulation of graves in the church-yard in which it stands, it is sunk some feet below the level of the ground, and is in the winter season cold and damp in the extreme. It cannot, at the utmost, be seated for more than 400 hearers; and, besides being too small for the population of the parish, it is irremediably defective in form, and can by no repair be rendered commodious or comfortable. There is no remedy but a new one, which, it is hoped, will be erected soon.

To 21st-century folk like me it sounds like a gem that would have been well worth preserving, but to the Rev. John MacFarlane, parish minister and author of the above, there was nothing to be done but tear it down and build a new church. While he was to get his way in the end, his plans did meet with opposition. On the other hand, it could be argued that the pragmatism of the minister ensured that the parishioners had a modern building 'fit for purpose'. His concern, after all, was preaching the Gospel

---

69 New Statistical Account (1836), p. 29

and not preserving old buildings – no matter how historic. The Heritors, the Cheapes of Rossie, did look into the matter of repairs on the old church in 1837 when an advertisement appeared in the *Fife Herald* appealing for contractors to visit Rossie House to view the specifications. Clearly this was considered uneconomic because the decision for a new build was made the following year. The *Fife News* of September 1838, in support of a new build, reports that 'the wonder is how such a building could so long have been in use'.

While there was no argument about the need for a new church, the parishioners wanted it built on new ground as the established site contained graves that would have to be disturbed for the erection of a larger building. The *Fife Herald* tells us that Presbytery inspected the site proposed for the new church and declared it 'a very handsome plan'. While Presbytery approved using 'another commodious site', it was pointed out that if unavailable then building should be on the existing site. Presumably alternative land was not available and so it was necessary to build on the ancient plot.

Despite a petition supporting the popular view of choosing an alternative location and the *Fife News* expressing sorrow that they were not 'removing the church from the territory of the dead',[70] work started on the new building on the site that had held a church since at least the 13th century. The last service took place in the old building on 31st March 1839. Soon it was demolished and the builders, Messrs T. Ireland and D. Smith of Cupar, started work. The headstones that had to be moved were incorporated into the church wall. During the day the building work progressed and at night members of the community, showing the strength of their feelings, demolished it. This happened three times and on each occurrence Baillie Honeyman of Auchtermuchty read the Riot Act. Finally, there was the threat of the involvement of the Cupar militia to keep the peace. This allowed building to progress and the new site was dedicated on Sunday 15th December 1839.[71] When the new church was opened for public worship the *Fifeshire Journal* gave the following account of events:

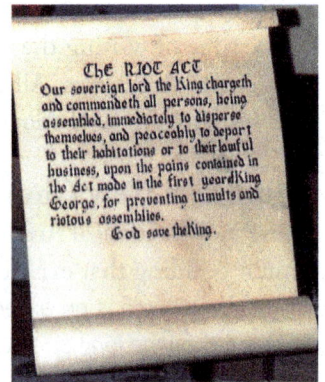

> On Friday 13th December the seats were divided by Sheriff Jameson. The Sheriff rejected the claim to two family seats in respect of Weddersbie and Rossie and William Johnston of Lathrisk on the ground that no heritor, however extensive his possessions, had a right to more than one family seat.

In the afternoon the Heritors entertained the Presbytery, the Sheriff and others at an excellent dinner in 'Mr Kinnimont's admirable hostelry at Trafalgar, the Earl of Leven and Melville in the chair. The dinner party broke up at eight'. Clearly the important

---

70   *Fife News* September **1838**
71   E.M. Gillin, D. Toulmin and I.G. Wotherspoon, *A Short History of Collessie Parish* (John & Reid, 1979)

people of the parish had to be entertained according to their rank and importance. Most of the congregation, being 'less important', were excluded from the festivities.

The new building met with wide approval and, according to the *Fife Herald*, Sir David Wilkie's comment on seeing it for the first time was, 'Nothing can be happier than the manner in which the sky-line is marked by the roof and tower of this church.' No doubt such an observation from the great man himself would have quietened any who wanted to nurse old grievances.[72]

The Graveyard

Prominently situated in the graveyard and next to the road is the Melville tomb. This was built by Sir James Melville in 1609, just eight years before his death. Recently restored, it is a fine building of its period with complex mouldings and a famous inscription on the wall facing the road.

The inscription is in Scots and reads:

> 1609 YE LOADIN PILGRIMS PASSING LANGS THIS WAY, PANS ON YOUR FALL AND YOUR OFFENCES PAST. HOW YOUR FRAIL FLESH FIRST FORMIT OF THE CLAY IN DUST MON BE DESOLVIT AT THE LAST. REPENT AMEND ON CHRIST HE BURDEN CAST OF YOUR SAD SINNES WHO CAN YOUR SAULS REFRESH. SYNE RAIS FROM GRAVE TO GLOIR. YOUR GRISLIE FLESH DEFYLE NOT CHRISTS KIRK WITH YOUR CARRION. A SOLEMNE SAIT FOR GODS SERVICE PREPARD FOR PRAIER PREACHING AND COMMUNION. YOUR BYRIAL SHOULD BE IN THE KIRKYAIRD. ON YOUR UPRYSING SET YOUR GREAT REGARD WHEN SAULL AND BODY JOYNES WITH JOY TO RING IN HEAVEN FOR AY WITH CHRIST OUR HEAD AND KING.

---

[72] *Fife Herald* 12th December 1839

Translation:

> *You laden pilgrims who have, for long, passed this way, concentrate on your fall and past offences. How your frail flesh that comes from clay will, in the end, dissolve into dust. Repent and seek amends in Christ where you must cast your sins so that your soul may be cleansed. In time you will rise from the grave to glory. Meantime, do not defile Christ's Kirk with your dead body. It is a place for worship, prayer and taking communion. Your burial should be in the churchyard. Think of your resurrection when your soul and body will join with joy to reign in heaven for ever with Christ our Head and King.*

While the inscription is not unique in its sentiment, it is more fulsome than others in its expression. The advice not to bury the dead within the church is designed to discourage folk from following the old Catholic practice and to embrace the new Presbyterian ways and inter their nearest and dearest in the graveyard. Although this has been a burial ground since the 12th century, the earliest recorded burial is of the interment of Sir James Melville of Halhill in his tomb in 1617. On the right of the graveyard entrance there is the Kinnear of Kinloch tomb, with Cheape of Rossie on the left and the Melville tomb just beyond it. Near the north-east corner of the church is the Bogie of Little Kinloch tomb.

The Melville tomb in Collessie churchyard

The churchyard covers an area of 2,938 square yards and was extended to the north and north-west in 1871. Henry Rae-Arnot recorded in 1912 that there were 140 tombstones.[73] The regulations governing the churchyard seem to have developed

---

[73]   H. Rae-Arnot, *Collessie Churchyard. To 31 Dec. 1911 (With a plan)* (Cupar, J. & G. Innes, 1912; part published by the Fife Family History Society in Publication 17, *Monumental Inscriptions*)

from 1840 to 1907, with the greatest number emerging in 1907. Under the Heritors' obligations we are told that 'the Churchyard belongs to the Heritors subject to the burden of interring the dead'. But it also declares that 'the Heritors are owners of the trees, but not of the grass'. Apparently, 'The people have no right to any particular piece of ground; a new grave has fulfilled its duty when it has reduced the body to dust, and it can then be used again.' Does the reduction to dust include the bones? This would not be possible in the timescale envisaged and so the regulation creates some rather gruesome mental images of what was going on in Collessie kirkyard!

In 1876 it was decided that no more than two lairs would be allowed to each new family. It would appear, however, that this rule was not always followed meticulously. 'Chains and kerbs are not to be allowed: the former interfere with free passage, the latter with grave digging.' When the new church was being built in 1839, instructions were given to the beadle, who was also the gravedigger, that 'no graves should be dug closer than of seven feet to the walls of the church'.

The quotations on the tombstones are normally of the sort one would expect. There are words of appreciation; 'gratitude, love and reverence by their surviving children', said the children of James Patrick and his wife Jessie Millar in 1906. There is the poignant 'Sleep on sweet babe, God called thee home. He thought it best' on the gravestone of William J.C. Brown, who was drowned at Kinloch in 1878 aged just 16 months. There are those who had been valued members of the community, like the surgeon Michael Malcolm who died in 1833: 'He was much valued in his profession and deeply regretted by all who knew him.' There is also the not to be misunderstood inscription on Rev. Andrew Walker's memorial where God is thanked 'for his unspeakable gift'.

Churchyards are always interesting places, for they reveal the changing community over the generations and include some who reached a great age and those – always far too many – who died in infancy. In this, Collessie churchyard is no different, but to do it justice it would deserve a dedicated volume.[74]

Ministers of Collessie: Our Earliest Records

We occasionally get glimpses of the Collessie clergy in the very early years, like when a certain **Johanne capellano de Cullessy** (John), chaplain of Collessie, attended the presentation of a silver chalice to John de Dundemor, knight, at Abdie (recorded Ebdyn) on 6th May 1253. **Adam Malcarston** was rector at the time de Quincy gifted the church to the Abbey of Lindores in 1262. This gift was confirmed by Bishop Gamlin of St Andrews in June of the same year. This left Collessie Church as a possession of Lindores Abbey according to the gift made by Sir Roger de Quincy in 1262. Elsewhere we learn that in 1276 the vicar of Collessie was **Boiamund** as it is recorded that he received 20s. from the Bishop of St Andrews.[75]

---

74   Rae-Arnot, *Collessie Churchyard*
75   Dowden, *Chartulary of Lindores*, pp. lviii–lx

1560–1579: A Shortage of Ministers

Following the Reformation in 1560 it was hard for the newly reformed Church to find suitably qualified men to minister to the people. So it is that we find in 1561 the pulpit at Collessie supplied by **John Wosbster**. He is described by the *Fasti Ecclesiae Scoticanae* first as an exhorter (and unordained lay preacher) and in 1567 as a reader (a trained but not ordained preacher). In 1574 **John Kilgour** filled this post and in 1576 it was **Thomas Robertson,** also a reader. In 1578 **Alexander Jarden** was removed from Monimail to Collessie, but he also had Auchtermuchty and Ebdie in his charge and he returned to Monimail a year later.[76] It is strange to think that the dearth of suitably qualified ministers in the 16th century necessitated a similar response to that of the modern Kirk to the shortage of ministers five centuries later with the use of readers and approved preachers.

1580–1968

Henry Balfour, a reader at Monimail from 1574 to 1579, was removed in 1580 to the charge of Collessie and on 11th August 1586 he was promoted to the vicarage by James VI. Mr Balfour served the parish for 48 years. Sadly, on 7th October 1628 the Presbytery resolved to 'inhibit him from preaching, because of his weakness, by reason of great age' and Mr Balfour died the following year.

In 1628 the inheritor of Mr Balfour's charge was **John Moncrieff**. A graduate of the University of St Andrews, he was to serve the parish for the next 11 years. In fact, Mr Moncrieff arrived in Collessie in 1626 to assist the failing Mr Balfour. Before Mr Balfour was 'inhibited from preaching', the congregation was informed by the Synod that Mr Moncrieff was 'to be removed unless the parishioners provide a competent provision'. Clearly the parish was able to meet its commitment to their minister, for he remained until he was translated to Kinghorn on 11th April 1639. But we will remember that these were difficult times, with King Charles I insisting on an Episcopal Church throughout his kingdoms. At first Mr Moncrieff appears to have complied with the King's demands, for he was presented to the Assembly by Charles I on 20th September 1629. But his liking for bishops was short-lived and in 1638 he became a member of the Assembly in Glasgow that swept Episcopacy away and deposed the bishops.

A period of vacancy ensued and it was not until 1641 that **John Littlejohn** arrived in the parish. Another graduate of St Andrews University, Mr Littlejohn had been 'on the exercise' in Kirkcaldy in 1631 and a reader in Dysart in 1633. He was admitted to Collessie some time prior to 6th April 1641. Little is said of his ministry during the years of Civil War and Cromwell's Commonwealth when he, like all other ministers, was obliged to be a Presbyterian. Shortly after Mr Littlejohn arrived troubled times hit the Presbytery, and indeed all of Fife, with an outbreak of plague.

---

[76]   H. Scott, *Fasti Ecclesiae Scoticanae, Volume 5: Synods of Fife and of Angus and Mearns: The Succession of Ministers in the Church of Scotland from the Reformation* (Edinburgh, Oliver & Boyd, 1925, pp. 133 ff.)

Plague

In the records of the Presbytery of Cupar of June 1647 we find several references to this terrible and much feared infection. The effect was immediate and it was given as the reason for delaying a planned visitation to some kirks in the Presbytery in June of that year. The great concern was the danger of spreading infection, which would, in the opinion of Presbytery, have the effect of reducing the memberships of the various parishes under its authority. At first sight this may seem an insular and unfeeling sentiment until we remember that in 1647 it included virtually everyone in the parish. Their fear was great and genuine and we can only imagine the feelings of those who issued the following guidelines, for each one of them and their loved ones were directly under the threat of a terrible death. Their understanding of disease was so limited as to be virtually non-existent and cure was impossible. A very few survived infection but no one knew why. Their ignorance inhibited their ability to have any meaningful control of the situation. With that background we can understand why the Committee of the Shire asked Sir James Arnott of Fernie, a member of Cupar Presbytery, to raise the issue of preventing the spread of infection in Fife. Presbytery concluded that it was its duty to support the committee in its endeavours by:

- seeking the agreement of other Presbyteries in the county in the measures to be adopted;
- sending two ministers and one elder, all members of Presbytery, to represent Cupar Presbytery on the Committee of the Shire;
- proposing that the movement of people in the towns and country parishes should be restricted by the use of both civil passes and 'spiritual testimonials', with severe punishment meted out to anyone who issued counterfeit passes;
- asking Presbytery to use its powers to support the Committee of the Shire in the measures it deemed necessary, with violation of the measures employed resulting in the Sessions imposing the severest penalties, including public repentance before the pulpit, noting that social status would not protect the offender.

The seriousness of the situation is underlined in the same minute when we learn that the house of Mr David Allerdice of Falkland was burned down 'for avoiding the plague'. Presbytery was, however, generous and sought the support of Sessions in the Presbytery to rebuild his house.[77] The last major outbreak of plague in Scotland was in 1644–1649. Even Aberdeen was affected, a town that, despite its size and importance, was normally shielded by its remoteness from the centres of population in the central belt.

The Killing Times

These were indeed difficult times. Following the Scottish reaction of horror to the execution of Charles I in 1649, Oliver Cromwell sent his troops north and there was invasion into Fife at Inverkeithing and Dunfermline. With the restoration of the

---

[77] *Ecclesiastical Records: Selections from the Minutes of the Presbyteries of St Andrews and Cupar* (Edinburgh, printed for the Abbotsford Club, 1837, p. 114)

monarchy in 1660, the troubles for the Kirk were only just beginning, for with Charles II came the Killing Times. For nearly 30 years the Episcopal monarch waged war on Presbyterianism, and in particular on the Covenanters.

It was under these circumstances that in 1662 Mr Littlejohn nailed his colours to the mast and, when so many clergymen had left their charges in revolt against the King's demands, he is recorded as having 'conformed to Episcopacy'. It would have been interesting to have had a record of any conversation between the Rev. Littlejohn and Mr James Makgill of Rankeilour, who, as we have seen, was fined £3,000 in the same year 'for Nonconformity'. Of course, the extent to which Mr Littlejohn's apparent changing of sides was according to conviction or convenience is difficult to say. It is also difficult to judge how we would have behaved had we lived through such troublesome times. Nevertheless, he must have been happy in Collessie as he remained there for 42 years.[78]

Perhaps Messrs Littlejohn and Makgill were not on such bad terms as one might expect. According to Presbytery minutes, Mr John Makgill, elder, and Mr David Orme, minister of Monimail, were appointed to visit Collessie to ensure that the minister was receiving the appropriate remuneration as laid down by Parliament. They were content that indeed the Heritors were meeting their obligations to Mr Littlejohn in stipend, manse, glebe, communion elements, grass and foggish (winter grazing). They did recommend, however, that the minister receive 500 merks 'for re-edifying the manse'.

Following the death of Mr Littlejohn in 1680 there was a period of vacancy. Then in 1683 **John Ogilvie**, son of Mr George Ogilvie, a minister in Kirkcaldy, arrived at Collessie. He had studied at St Salvator's College, and gained his degree from the University of St Andrews on the 19th of July 1664. It was George, Bishop of Edinburgh who licensed him on 8th March 1667. He was admitted to the charge of Collessie around the 4th of April 1683, but was then removed by the Privy Council on the 3rd of September 1689 for not reading the Proclamation of the Estates, and not praying for their Majesties William and Mary. This suggests he had Jacobite sympathies, supporting those who wanted the return of James VII and II to the throne. He retired to Edinburgh, where he was accused on 20th March 1706 of celebrating 'irregular marriages' and he died on 30th July 1708, aged about 64. For over 120 years there had been controversy in Church politics. It was set to continue throughout the 18th, 19th and 20th centuries.

Mr Ogilvie's successor was **William Pitcairn**, another graduate from St Andrews University, who gained his degree of MA on 14th July 1694 and was licensed by the Presbytery of Cupar on 17th March 1696. He was a young man, aged just 23, when he was called to Collessie Kirk on the 4th of June of that year and on September 9th he was ordained. Twice married, his first wife Jean, daughter of Thomas Mitchell, minister of Kilmarnock, died on 30th January 1704. There does not appear to be a marked grave in the graveyard for Mrs Pitcairn. The record of interments for Collessie churchyard by Henry Rae-Arnot records simply that she is presumed to have been buried there.[79]

---

[78]   Taylor, *Some Historical Antiquities*
[79]   Rae-Arnot, *Collessie Churchyard*

Mr Pitcairn then married Mary, daughter of John Bethune of Blebo. She had two sons, John and Harry, who died before 30th May 1730, and four daughters, but on 14th May 1722 Mr Pitcairn died at the age of just 49.

Mr Pitcairn's successor, **Thomas Thomson**, arrived in 1723. Another young man of 23 he was licensed by the Presbytery of Kirkcaldy on 20th October 1720. It was on 11th April 1723 that he was called to Collessie and then ordained on 17th September of that year. Sadly, Mr Thomson died only a few weeks after his wife, Katherine. The cause of death was said to have been the 'ague' caught at Rossie Loch. Mr Thomson's death on 9th May 1728 followed only five years of ministry and he was only 28 years of age. Clearly there is a tragic tale behind these events, which are recorded on a tablet on the north wall of the church.

On 13th November 1728 **Rev. John Ballingall** was called and he was ordained on 29th March 1729. He remained until he was translated to Cupar in August 1738.

Mr Ballingall was followed by **George Kay**, who was called on 7th June 1739 and ordained on 13th September of that year. On 23rd October 1741 he was translated to Minto. The next minister to arrive at Collessie was **Hugh Blair**, called on the 28th May 1742 and ordained on 23rd September in the same year. He too stayed only a short time before being translated to Canongate, Edinburgh, on 14th July 1743. But this gentleman was to gain a considerable reputation in Edinburgh, being appointed Professor of Belles Lettres and Rhetoric at the University. As a result we have come to know more about him than many of his contemporaries.

At Canongate Mr Blair gained a reputation as a preacher and in 1745 he preached a memorable sermon in favour of the Hanoverian monarchy; this at the time of Bonnie Prince Charlie and the rebellion of 1745. He found himself under the patronage of Lord Kames and became known to Dr Johnson. Among his friends he counted David Hume, Alexander Carlyle, Adam Ferguson, Adam Smith, William Robertson and James McPherson. All were eminent men of the 18th century and leaders of the Scottish Enlightenment.[80]

Rev. Dr Hugh Blair by John Kay 1798

Another who became a friend was Robert Burns, who had this to say of the man who was so many years his senior: 'I never respect him with humble veneration; but when he kindly interests himself in my welfare, or, still more, when he descends from his pinnacle and meets me on equal ground, my heart overflows with what is called *liking*', and again, 'He has a heart, not of the finest water, but far from being an ordinary one. In short, he is truly a worthy and most respectable character.' When Burns left Edinburgh he wrote to Mr Blair on 3rd May 1787. He addressed him as 'Reverend and much respected Sir' and

---

80   *A Series of Original Portraits and Caricature Etchings by the Late John Kay, Miniature Painter, Edinburgh*, vol. 1 (Edinburgh, Adam and Charles Black, 1877, pp. 120 ff.)

thanked him for 'kindness, patronage and friendship' and enclosed a portrait of himself after Naysmyth.[81]

Blair's friendship with Macpherson led him to extol his attempts to recover 'traditional Highland poetry' and he was the first to bring his friend to the attention of the world through a critical dissertation of the soon to be discredited *Poems of Ossian*. This man, who was a moderate in the church politics of his day, was widely considered to be vain, susceptible to flattery and a bit of a dandy in his dress. Nevertheless, he clearly gained the affection and respect of Robbie Burns, a man with a keen eye for hypocrisy and a pen that was ready to expose it. Blair married his cousin Katherine Bannatyne in 1748 and they had a son who died in infancy and a daughter who died at the age of 21. Rev. Dr Hugh Blair's life came to an end on 27th December 1800 at the age of 83, five years after his wife.[82]

When ministers come and go quickly it can be demoralising for a congregation, so when **John Mathie** (or Mathew) was called on 31st January 1744 and ordained on 13th October of that year, he seemed set to stay for some time. He had been licensed by the Presbytery of Haddington in 1739 so had some experience before he arrived. Sadly, he died, unmarried, on 11th April 1755 and was buried in Collessie graveyard. Two years later, on 22nd September 1757, **James Ballingall** was ordained, but he was translated to Dundee on 22nd November 1759.

Collessie certainly was not doing very well at keeping its ministers and this lack of good fortune continued with the **Rev. William Walker**, who was ordained on 24th September 1760. Yet this young man, only 24 when he arrived, was to become noteworthy. The youngest son of Alexander Walker of St Fort, he was, like many of his predecessors, educated at St Andrews. On 2nd November 1762 he married Margaret Manderston and they had a son Alexander of Bowland. Alexander created a notable collection of Oriental manuscripts, which his son, Sir William Walker, presented to the Bodleian Library, Oxford. Their second son became Lieutenant-Colonel, HEICS (Honourable East India Company Service). The third son, William, was an attorney in Jamaica. They also had two daughters, Magdalen, who married William Walker of Pitlair, and Isobel, who married Paul Stevens Samuels, MD, Jamaica. Sadly, their father died on 14th November 1771. His burial place was under a seat he built in the graveyard. In spite of the illustrious future awaiting his children, it is recorded in the Collessie graveyard record that his friends gave 'one half guinea for the mortcloth'.

The next minister to come, also with the surname Walker, was Andrew and he was to be with the kirk to the end of the century and beyond. **Andrew Walker** hailed from Heggie Castle in Kennoway and graduated from St Andrews University with an MA in 1761. He had spent time as an assistant in the parish before being ordained on 24th September 1772. On 14th June 1781 he married Sophia Duddingston of St Fort and

---

81 *The Complete Works of Robert Burns. Including his Correspondence etc. With a Memoir by William Gunnyon* (Edinburgh, William P. Nimmo, 1873)
82 Scott, *Fasti Ecclesiae Scoticanae*, pp. 133 ff.

they had a large family: Margaret, Helen, Sophia, Andrew, Elizabeth, Fanny, James, Ann and Mary. Mr Walker died 'much lamented' on 16th May 1820 and his wife Sophia died on 13th November of the same year. According to *Fasti Ecclesiae Scoticanae*, Andrew was 78 when he died and his wife was 62. During his ministry he was responsible for the Collessie entry in the Old Statistical Account. It was also during his ministry that an entry in the Session minute of 14th May 1769 records that Mr Walker received a letter from Robert Miller, a wright at Kinloch. Through ill health neither he nor his wife were able to work and so could not earn sufficient money to live. They did not want to depend on charity but asked the Kirk Session for a loan of 40 shillings for one year. Robert's son Francis was to stand surety for the loan. The Session agreed to the request as it had been made clear that Robert was a highly respected man in the congregation.[83]

Up to the ordination of John Mathie (or Mathew) each minister had been called. From John Ballingall in 1757 onwards, however, the ministers were presented. David Hay of Leys presented James Ballingall and William Walker, and John Hay Balfour of Leys presented Andrew Walker. By 1821 the privilege of presenting ministers to Collessie Church had passed from the Hay family of Leys to William Johnston of Lathrisk. This is rather a strange transfer, for Lathrisk is in the parish of Kettle, not Collessie.

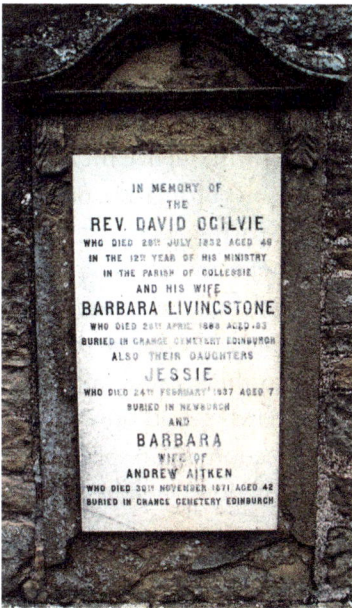

Ogilvie headstone

So it was that in December 1820 **David Ogilvie** was presented to the folk of Collessie and ordained on 9th May 1821. He married Barbara Livingstone and had two daughters, Barbara and Jessie. David was a local man, son of Philip Ogilvie of Auchtermuchty, and, like so many before him, was educated at St Andrews University. There was a very sad incident reported in the *Fife Herald* in 1831 that reflected badly on Collessie Kirk and its minister. It concerned the suicide of a young man 'of otherwise respectable character'. The insertion of these words alone tells us a lot about people's attitude to suicide at that time. An application by the family to have the body buried in Collessie churchyard was turned down, unless they agreed to the coffin being passed over the church wall, 'because, forsooth, should it have been carried through the porch in the usual way, the first child who should be brought through the same door to be baptised, would come to the same fate'. The article concludes, 'The unfeeling proposal was treated with the contempt which it merited; and the remains of the defunct were interred in the church-yard of Cults, where, it seems, the people are either more enlightened or less selfish than the wise acres of Collessie.'[84]

---

83   Minutes of the Kirk Session of Collessie Church, National Archives of Scotland Ref: CH2/765/1,2,3
84   *Fife Herald* 11th June 1831

One year after this unfortunate incident Mr Ogilvie died on 26th July 1832. According to the record of Collessie churchyard he was only 46 years of age and had been the parish minister for 11 years.

The next minister to be presented to the parish by William Johnston of Lathrisk was a man we encountered in the first chapter of this volume, **Rev. Dr John McFarlane**. He was an Edinburgh man, born and educated there. He was licensed at Linlithgow on 26th December 1821 and ordained at Ardoch at the age of 23. When he was admitted to Collessie on 15th March 1833 he brought with him more than a little experience. He was responsible for writing the New Statistical Account for Collessie and for building the present church in 1839. John MacFarlane joined the Dissenters in 1843 and was instrumental in establishing the Free Kirk at Giffordtown. Rev. John McFarlane was admitted to the Free Church in Dalkeith on 19th January 1844. His intellectual abilities became evident in the fullness of time and he gained a DD doctorate of divinity at Princeton University in 1853 and had several books published. Dr McFarlane was married twice, first to Janet Marshall in 1826 and their children were John, Catherine, Balfour, George, Jane, Jessy, Robina, William and Margaret. Sadly, Janet died on 20th January 1852. Two years later John married Louisa Cecilia.

Dr McFarlane leaving for the Free Kirk created a vacancy in the Parish Kirk and so Mr Johnston of Lathrisk had to present another minister. This time it was **Rev. Dr Robert Williamson**. An Anstruther man born in 1803, he was educated at St Andrews University and licensed by the Presbytery of St Andrews. His first position was as tutor to the families of Sir Robert Calder and William Johnston of Lathrisk, hence the reason he was known to the superior of Collessie Kirk. Robert Williamson's ordination on 27th September 1843 heralded a long and successful ministry in the parish.

In 1862 Dr Williamson was awarded a DD (St Andrews University) and was highly respected by the people of the parish. He was very much involved in the excavation of the burial cairn known as Gask Hill, just south of the village. No doubt this was fuelled by Dr Williamson's interest in education. In addition to this he took a leading role in the erection of the Parish Church of Ladybank and donated £2,000 towards it. There can be no doubt that Dr Williamson truly earned the affection and respect of his parishioners, and there was great sadness throughout the congregation when he died on 6th November 1887 aged 84.

The following was mentioned in the school log for that year as a tribute to Dr Williamson, who had at one time been chairman of the School Board: 'Throughout his long and useful life he did much to promote the cause of education and always took the deepest interest in the education and welfare of the young.' The school was closed on the day of his funeral as a mark of respect.

Scandal

Dr Williamson's health had been deteriorating for some time and he was clearly finding it increasingly difficult to pursue his duties as parish minister. It was, therefore, agreed with the Kirk Session and Presbytery that someone should be appointed as assistant and successor to Dr Williamson. Such an arrangement would ensure the smooth transfer of pastoral provision from the much-loved minister to one who was to follow him.

On 1st October 1883 the **Rev. John Anderson Black** was inducted to Collessie. Following a service in the church a large party of about 50 people gathered at the Royal Hotel in Ladybank. At that gathering speeches were made indicating the impressive credentials of this man. He had been dux of Madras College St Andrews where he also gained the Tullis Gold Medal for proficiency in mathematics. He then attended the University of St Andrews where he gained a prize awarded by the late Dean Stanley, Lord Rector of the University. In 1877 he was licensed to preach by the Presbytery of Dundee and four years later, also in Dundee, he became assistant to the minister of St John's (Cross) Church. During this time he gained the respect of many as a preacher and was transferred to Newington Parish Church in Edinburgh where he acted as assistant to Dr Allison. The Reverend Gentleman clearly gained a high opinion of Mr Black, giving him an excellent reference regarding his character and abilities as a preacher. There can be no doubt about it, Mr Black came to Collessie in a blaze of glory and was seen to be a fitting successor to the beloved and highly respected Dr Williamson. In his thanks for the welcome Mr Black alluded to his awareness of 'his own weakness' but said he would endeavour to ensure that the trust placed in him would not be misplaced.[85]

At first Mr Black appears to have lived up to all expectations. In February 1885 it is recorded that he had presided over the winter communion 'to the satisfaction of the congregation, who were edified and impressed by the solemnity and ability with which he conducted the service'. In June 1885 we learn that he acted as Moderator of Presbytery. Yet in January the following year a letter from Presbytery is recorded where 'Rev. John Anderson Black, assistant and successor Collessie, is deposed from the office of holy ministry and prohibited and discharged from exercising the same in all time coming'.

The charges levelled against him were of the most serious kind. In the first place, he was seen to be drunk at a farm in the parish and, even more seriously, he was accused of indecency with a local boy. This is something that had exercised not only the Presbytery and local press, but also Mr Boyd Kinnear of Kinloch and, no doubt, the people of the parish. We clearly lack sufficient facts to draw any conclusions on the affair because no criminal proceedings took place and so the charges made against him were never tested in court. Mr Black was confronted with these charges by members of Presbytery and, while he accepted his guilt of the lesser charge of drunkenness, he denied the more serious charge. Mr Black was then called to face the accusations in front of the full Court of the Presbytery, but he did not appear. Instead, he wrote to Presbytery resigning his position as assistant and successor to Dr Williamson. Presbytery concluded that he had deserted his charge and proceeded to depose him of the office of holy ministry.

---

85   *Fife Herald* 8th October 1883

This sad tale illustrates to us that human frailty is not new and that it brings with it so much pain. At worst there was a child who carried the memory of abuse throughout his life, and we may never know how that affected his faith and his ability to trust others, including the Kirk and its ministers. At the very least we find a man of such great promise, loved and respected, falling from the pedestal on which he had been placed with a terrible crash. While we do expect more from our spiritual leaders than from ourselves, we must never forget that they are people and subject to all the frailties that haunt all of humanity, yet the trust placed in them must be respected. So, as the disgraced Mr Black scuttles off into the mists of the closing decades of the 19th century, we are left to reflect upon the sadness of the situation for the boy in question, the congregation and for John Anderson Black. He left Collessie and a promising career in a hurry – an ignominious end to one who, like us all, is loved by Christ.[86]

With the death of Mr Williamson in the summer of 1887, the vacancy was filled by **Rev. John Henderson**, who had acted as assistant in the parish since 1885, and he was ordained there in 1888. He was born in Leven on 24th November 1863. Educated at Scoonie Parish and Leven Sunday Schools, he graduated from the University of St Andrews with an MA in 1882 and a BD in 1885. The Presbytery of Kirkcaldy licensed him to preach on 24th May 1885 and he acted as assistant first at Inverkeilor from May to July of that year, then in Collessie parish from November 1885 to November 1887, serving as minister until 1925.

One would have thought that with the trauma of the sudden departure of Mr Black the parish would have been free from scandal. This was not to be, for on 29th July 1902 the *Edinburgh Evening News* reported on correspondence between Mr J. Boyd Kinnear of Kinloch and the minister. Mr Kinnear claimed that 'for many years past Mr Henderson held only one short service of devotional worship during the week in the parish of Collessie' and there was 'no Bible Class and no meeting for prayer or Scriptural instruction or meditation during the week'.

A COLLESSIE BIBLE CLASS.

Evening Post 30th July 1902

In reply Mr Henderson said that since the Disruption there had been only one service held in Collessie. He did not agree it was a short one – it lasted one and a half hours: 'Mr Kinnear had no grounds for complaint for the simple reason that on the few occasions when he came to church he was always late. He admitted there had been no Bible Class since 1896, but that was not his fault, as he had done all that he could to secure one.'[87]

---

[86]   Minutes of the Kirk Session of Collessie Church, National Archives of Scotland Ref: CH2/765/ 3
[87]   *Edinburgh Evening News* 29th July 1902

The matter rumbled on throughout 1902 and into 1903. Indeed, it got as far as the General Assembly in May of that year. Mr Boyd Kinnear was clearly not one to give up easily, but in the end the Assembly decided that Mr Henderson had no charge to answer. The remainder of his time at Collessie must have been happy, for his ministry was to last 37 years until he retired on 20th June 1925, when he was replaced by **Rev. John Taylor**.

Rev. John Taylor

When Mr Henderson died, the September edition of *The Presbytery of Cupar Magazine* carried an obituary. He was described as being of a 'quiet and unassuming nature' and was 'respected by all who knew him'. The funeral was taken by Rev. W.M. Tocher, minister of Dunbog, and in the tribute he spoke of Mr Henderson's great love for Collessie Church and its people. He was, by all accounts, one who felt for the sorrows of his parishioners and he also loved children and cared deeply for them. He was knowledgeable in Church law and so made great contributions to Presbytery.

Mr Taylor was translated from Golspie on 10th December 1925. There is a plaque in the church commemorating his ministry, which lasted until 1968 when he died at the age of 77. It also commemorates his wife Margaret, who was three years his junior but who also died in 1968.[88] It was shortly after his arrival at Collessie that he had reason to raise questions regarding his stipend. The method of calculation, which involved the market value of bere, once common in the Kirk, was complicated, as can be seen in the correspondence in the Appendix. Thankfully, the process of calculating the stipend was soon adjusted to a more orthodox method. Throughout his long ministry in Collessie, Mr Taylor was well supported by people of the parish. The photograph below shows Mr Taylor in the pulpit in the 1930s on harvest thanksgiving Sunday.

[88]   Scott, *Fasti Ecclesiae Scoticanae*, vol. 8

It was during his time at Collessie, in the winter of 1961–62, that the ancient coke boiler, which had supplied heating in the church, failed and it was a severe winter. Mr Taylor wrote to the General Trustees in Edinburgh seeking their urgent agreement to the installation of electric heating. The cost was to be £276 6s. 1d. not including installation of the underground cable needed to carry the power. Mr Taylor's letter also pled poverty, for he asked for a grant to meet the cost for his 172 parishioners, who were unable to raise the funds. The Home Board of the Church of Scotland provided a loan of £150 and a grant of £125 and so the electric heating was installed in the church making it a more comfortable place for worshippers to attend.[89]

Mr Taylor was the last minister of Collessie Church before the union with Ladybank in 1968. Mr Taylor died in hospital on 10th May just four months after the union, and Mrs Taylor died on 1st October of the same year. Both he and his wife were much loved and respected by many in the parish and missed greatly when they died. A plaque was presented to the church by Mrs King, daughter of Rev and Mrs Taylor. It was dedicated by Rev. Sandy Philp in 1972.

The Disruption of 1843 and Collessie

The Disruption of 1843 had a profound effect on the church at Collessie. The minister, **Mr John McFarlane**, had been responsible for the new building. He now felt compelled to leave the church and the manse that had become the home of his family and move into uncharted waters by supporting the 450 ministers who severed their connection with the Established Church. This was the cause of personal trauma for most of the ministers, who found themselves turning against the patron who had supported their admission to the charge they were now leaving. Rev. John MacFarlane found himself in just such a position, for he had been well supported by the local patron Mr Johnston of Lathrisk. Clearly the two had become friends, for Mr MacFarlane wrote the following letter in order to try to build a bridge where a great chasm had opened up between them. Happily, on this occasion the friendship appears to have survived.

Manse of Collessie, May, 1843. Dear Sir, You have already received, I have no doubt, official notice of the vacancy in the parish of Collessie, and the cause of that vacancy. I think it, however, only an expression of due respect to you as the patron of that parish, and by whom I have been so much obliged, to communicate with you directly on the subject. I shall not trouble you by an attempt to detail the reasons that have influenced me, along with so many of my brethren in the ministry, to resign my connection with the Establishment. Suffice it to say, that we are acting on a clear, deep, and conscientious conviction that the Established Church of Scotland, as defined by recent decisions of the Civil Courts – decisions virtually approved and ratified by the Legislature of the country – convert it into a kind of institution which we did not understand it to be when we became ministers of that Church; and that the only course that remained for us, as honest men

---

89   *Fife Herald* February 1962

and ministers of the Gospel, was to retire from an Establishment, the constitution of which, as so explained, we could no longer approve. Allow me, however, to say that I do not on that account feel the less indebted to you, as patron of the parish of Collessie, for the very handsome and disinterested manner in which you presented me to that charge. You acted, I believe, on public grounds alone, with exclusive reference to the interests of the parish in making that appointment, and I can only desire that during the period of my incumbency I had, by the blessing of God, been enabled more fully to justify your choice. You will believe me, that it is not any want of gratitude to you, or any feeling of dissatisfaction with a situation in every respect so very desirable, that influenced me in coming to the resolution I have taken. So far from it, the greatest sacrifice I have ever been called upon to make is that which I have made in resigning my place as a minister of the Establishment. Nothing but a deep sense of duty could have induced, or indeed would have warranted, our taking the step we have done. The course we have felt ourselves bound to adopt you may not think was called for, you may not approve. But you will allow me to express a hope that those mutual feelings of personal respect and goodwill which should universally prevail, will not be extinguished, or even diminished, by the distressing circumstances which, in the course of a wise but inscrutable providence, have been permitted to arise.[90]

On 4th June 1843, the Rev. John MacFarlane found himself preaching in a tent on Edensmuir near Giffordtown to an estimated congregation of about 500 people. They came from all around, many out of curiosity, to hear a conventicle service. No doubt David Maitland Makgill Crichton of Rankeilour, who had been baptised in Collessie Church, would have been included among those in attendance. This must have been a difficult time for Mr Makgill Crichton because, while his heart clearly lay with the Free Church, he was related to Mr Johnston of Lathrisk, patron of Collessie. On the other hand, among his many friends was Thomas Chalmers, one-time minister of Kilmany, and the journalist and geologist Hugh Miller, who was also influential among the Dissenters.[91] Within a few weeks John MacFarlane was also preaching at Pitlessie and in Annfield Den, finding support from Kettle as well as Pitlessie.

Giffordtown and Balmalcolm

As early as June 1843 a church was at the planning stage, with a site at Giffordtown having been acquired from Mr James Bogie of Little Kinloch. Soon it was cleared for building and before long a church, manse and schoolmaster's house with the beadle's house attached were built. It would be another 10 years before the school was constructed and until then the pupils were taught in the church. The opening service of the church took place on 19th February 1844 and worship was led by the new minister, **Rev. William Reid**. The previous December Mr Macfarlane had received a call from the Free Kirk in Dalkeith and, as there was no manse at that time, the congregation agreed to his

---

90 Brown, *Annals of the Disruption*, vol. III
91 Brown, *Annals of the Disruption*, vol. III

translation. The kirk cost £360 3*s*. The manse cost £250 plus £20 for a stable and £50 for a horse to transport the minister around the parish. While gifts were gratefully received (£95 from Rev. John MacFarlane and £200 from an elder and his brother) there was also a loan of £300, to be repaid with 3 per cent interest. Nevertheless, this showed the remarkable readiness of local folk to give to the future of their church. The whole episode was also a remarkable act of faith.

The surviving south wall of the Free Kirk in Giffordtown

The Kirk Session met on 12th November 1843 and consisted of 10 elders including Mr D.M.M. Crichton of Rankeilour; Mr Thomas Shaw of the farm of Wester Rossie; Mr Robert Millar, Collessie; Mr John Petrie, Ladybank (showing the name existed at that time); Captain James Maitland of Rossie; and others from Collessie and Letham.[92] In 1847 a bell was purchased and its distinctive ring announced the time of public worship at Giffordtown Free Kirk every Sunday for the next 19 years.[93] Today that bell remains in the belfry of St Mary's Church, Ladybank, now the Ladybank Church of the Howe of Fife Parish Church. It has remained silent for many years since the bell of the Kerr Memorial Church took over its function. Among the worshippers there was Charles Kinnear of Kinloch, whose two sons were John Boyd Kinnear and Charles Kinnear. They never became elders, no doubt because they were Heritors and supported the Free Church cause with great liberality.

In 1846 the school at Charlottetown was opened with Mr Officer as *domini*. Girls and boys attended, though the girls' education would have involved needlework, sewing and knitting. The school closed in 1875 with Mr Officer still in charge. The pupils then went either to Collessie or Ladybank schools. It was then that the building became Giffordtown Village Hall, a service it continues to provide for the community to this day.

The Free Kirk manse at Giffordtown

---

92   Free Church of Collessie 5th November 1843
93   Calley, *Collessie: A Parish Alphabet*

A Changing Place

With the draining of Rossie Loch, by 1775 Kinloch village, which consisted of poor-quality cruck houses, remained but it belied its name as there was no loch to overlook. Collessie's minister Rev. Andrew Walker, in the Old Statistical Account of 1791, tells us that the village of Kinloch had a population of 191 and was the principal village of the parish. The draining of the loch was only partially successful because the reclaimed land tended to flood in the winter, and it was not until Mr Cheape of Rossie improved the drainage early in the 19th century that reclamation was completely successful.[94]

The most fertile areas lay in the northern parts of the parish. This was reflected in the importance of the lairds of Rossie, Lochiehead, Kinloch, Pitlair and Rankeilour. Prior to 1675, we would have had to include Halhill, but these lands were absorbed by the Melville estate and the mansion house demolished. The south is bounded by the River Eden, which was given to flooding before defences were created in the late 18th century by Mr Johnston of Lathrisk. The central part, Monks Muir, was predominantly moss and heather in the early years.[95] By the time the New Statistical Account was written in 1836, the main crop was timber from plantations of fir trees, which was either being used locally for building materials or transported to Newburgh and on to Newcastle to be converted into pit props. There was, of course, no Ladybank until 1847, and the villages of Edenstown, Giffordtown and Monkstown did not appear until 1815 when the village of Kinloch was demolished.

According to the census of 1821, the population of Collessie parish was 1,030. This was an increase on the 949 recorded in the Old Statistical Account 30 years earlier. By 1836 and the New Statistical Account the population had increased further to 1,162. In 1821 one new house was being built and three stood empty, so there was room for further expansion. As we see, that expansion took place; not at a great rate but evidence of steady growth that reflected economic comfort for the people. Mr MacFarlane reached the same conclusion, for he said, 'The increase is to be referred to the steadily advancing prosperity and improvement of the country.' The 1,030 people of the 1821 census comprised 213 families, with the smallest number (64) employed in agriculture. The main employment came under the heading 'Trade, manufactures or handicraft' with 78 families involved mainly in handloom weaving. The weavers received the raw materials from an agent who then took the finished article to be sold in the cities of Glasgow, Dundee and Aberdeen. We are told that it takes a lot of work to earn just nine shillings (45p) per week, and the men and women got even less for their labour. The remaining 71 families were categorised under the heading 'All other families not comprised in the two preceding classes'. Apparently, each of the 213 families had their own house, which suggests that there was an acceptable standard of living for the inhabitants.[96]

---

94   New Statistical Account, vol. 9
95   Old Statistical Account, vol. 2
96   New Statistical Account, vol. 9

The Wee Hoose

The 'Wee Hoose'

Standing in the garden of Cedar Cottage in Collessie is a small white thatched cottage. This building was examined by the architect Tom Morton in 1998. According to his report, it is probably the oldest building in the village. Its construction has led him to the conclusion that it dates from the 16th century.

Over the years successive improvements have taken place. The lower part was built using large stones and lots of mortar. This suggests to Mr Morton that originally the wall, above the base, was of turf, which was replaced with masonry at some unknown date in its history. The windows and chimneys belong to the 19th century. The south gable has been constructed at an angle and, to Mr Morton, this suggests that it was built close to the old road to Monimail. The road stretched past the church gates and this house.

The road was moved to its present position around the time of the construction of Melville House in 1692, soon after Sir James Melville's Halhill was demolished in 1675. Evidence of the remains of the old road can be found in the 1855 OS map, which shows the road providing access to the fields. Further alterations have removed all evidence of it. The relevance of the road is that it shows us that this building once stood on the main thoroughfare through the village, past the very public inscription on Sir James Melville's tomb and on to the larger white thatched cottage that still stands just beyond the railway bridge where the road joins the modern Monimail road.

One interesting fact about this tiny house is that it has been reliably stated that it was a home as recently as the 1950s when it was occupied by a family of 13. The man who made that claim had been born in the house.

The Wash House

The Wash House

When we walk down the hill, past the church gate and the row of terraced houses at right angles to the road, we come to a quaint, curious building on our right. The current owner, Marianna Lines, believes that at one time it was an agricultural building or weaving shed. The date above the door is 1662 but the walls are constructed in such a way as to suggest that its height was increased in the 18th century, and this may coincide with it being converted into a community wash house. It was then that the upper floor would have been installed where, it is said, there was a bath house for the men of the village. The facilities for the ladies remain a mystery. Water from the nearby burn was heated in the old boiler and was used for washing clothes or carried up the external staircase to the bath house above. This wash house was in use until 1955 when a water supply reached the village and was piped to most of the houses, rendering it obsolete.

Marianna Lines took possession of the building in the mid 1990s. The old thatch roof was removed and replaced with a new one using reeds from the beds on the River Tay at Errol. She then went about clearing the inside of all sorts of accumulated bits and pieces from its days as a wash house, including washing boards, and set about creating a fascinating studio. A mezzanine floor provides her with a work space and an old lean-to at the back has been converted into a kitchen and toilet. Here Marianna works as an artist. She is an expert in standing stones and their symbols and has written a number of books on the subject.

Agriculture
Both the Old and New Statistical Accounts acknowledge the great fertility of the soil and throughout the 45 years between these documents agricultural improvement

continued. In 1836 fields with stone dykes or thorn hedges were common. The favourite stock was the Fifeshire black cattle. Always at the centre of life in Collessie parish throughout the 19th century was the Trafalgar Inn. The road from Cupar to Kinross was completed in 1805 – the year of the Battle of Trafalgar. George Calley attributes the naming of the inn to Grizel or Girsie Read who built the inn in 1803 at the crossroads. Initially, it had no name but, two years later when she heard of the victory at Trafalgar, she decided to give it that name. You will notice the picture depicting the Battle of Trafalgar on the wall in the photograph. So it is that the name remained for the inn until its demolition in 1926 when the name was transferred to the junction itself.[97]

Matthew Kidd, van man, with the Letham Bakers van outside Trafalgar Inn c. 1900

A popular agricultural show took place near the inn on October 21st each year commemorating the Battle of Trafalgar. The show was regularly reported in the *Fife Herald*, as in this example from October 1846, which informs us that 'The annual meeting of this society was held at Trafalgar Inn on Wednesday 21st inst.'. The weather that day was not good but it did not deter the contestants from farms with familiar names: Orchie, Nisbetfield, Hilton, Ramornie, Rossie, Kinloch, Rathillet, Kilwhiss and Kettle. Afterwards, about 39 members sat down 'to a most excellent dinner, furnished by Mr Willecot of the inn'. After the meal there was a talk by a certain Mr Buist on the 'application of chemistry to agriculture'.

While no doubt it was an occasion for socialising with neighbours, the purpose of the gathering was not pleasure alone. There was a willingness to learn of the agricultural advancements that were taking place and a readiness to share knowledge and experience. This was illustrated in the decision that 'next year the essay should be made to bear on

---

[97] Calley, *Collessie: A Parish Alphabet*

some practical subjects in which the members would require to give their opinion and experience'.[98] The farmers who gathered at Trafalgar each year did not want to be left out of the 'agricultural revolution' that was taking place within their time. The Trafalgar Agricultural Show took place as usual in October 1851, when there were 'few cattle on the ground, but a goodly number of young horses that promise to set their shoulders resolutely, along with their masters, to the first rate, both for quality and quantity'.[99] It all sounds quite idyllic.

In addition to the inn at Trafalgar there was in 1861 a joiner and a blacksmith located at that junction.

An early view of the Trafalgar Inn

Education

As we know, education has always been very important within the Presbyterian psyche. In the 16th century only the wealthiest families would educate their sons by using private tutors. In his First Book of Discipline Knox set out a structure which could deliver a national system of education. Critics often point out that the whole purpose of this was to ensure that the young were knowledgeable in the Christian faith and its scriptures. While it is true that the motivation of the Kirk's system of national education with schools in every parish was the propagation of the fundamental tenets of the faith, the idea of education for all was revolutionary. Once a person can read they are free to read whatever they want to and to be exposed to a variety of beliefs and standards.

In 1633 an Act had been passed by Parliament to establish a school in every parish, but it required the agreement of those paying the taxes or members of the congregation and the money was not always forthcoming. It did, however, have a limited success.

---

98 *Fife Herald* Thursday 29th October 1846
99 *Fife Herald* Thursday 23rd October 1851

In 1646 a more rigorous Act was passed and it made the following provision: 'A school in every parish with a schoolmaster approved by Presbytery. The Heritors in each Parish must provide suitable accommodation and a stipend for the schoolmaster of 100–200 merks.' A new tax on land and property was to be created to pay for this. 'Penalties will be inflicted on anyone refusing to comply.'[100]

The Presbytery of Cupar in June 1647 did its best to ensure that the folk in this part of Fife put the 1646 Act into effect and asked the membership to ascertain whether schools were being provided according to its provisions. Again on 9th September 1647 the meeting was concerned about the raising of 100 merks to pay for schoolmasters in the parishes. It is clear that education was a concern within the Presbytery and hence within the parish. This was a troubled time as the country was in the midst of a civil war and the use of Presbyteries rather than bishops to accommodate the Act inflamed an Episcopal opposition. As a result the law was never really enforced and it was rescinded in 1661 when Charles II came to the throne. It was not, therefore, until 1696 that the Act was reinstated and so laid the foundation of our modern education system.

By the end of the 18th century the Old Statistical Account records that there were 40 pupils in the local school. In 1836 this had increased to 65 in Collessie and 25 in Monkstown. Also, the Melville family had established a girls' school in a converted cottage where 50 girls not only received the general education of the day but were also taught knitting and needlework and were 'trained to habits of order and exactness'.

Thus 140 parish children were in receipt of education. There were also well-attended Sabbath Schools at Collessie, Rankeilour and Monkstown. Mr McFarlane records there was also a 'parochial Juvenile and Adult Library containing 370 well-selected volumes'.[101]

In 1874 the Education Act transferred responsibility for denominational schools to School Boards. Collessie's Rev. Williamson was a keen protagonist for the new Education Act and he is reported as having addressed a meeting on the subject at Collessie School on 10th April 1873.[102] In the first entry in the school log for the year 1874, Mr Williamson is recorded as being a member of the School Board. It was through his interest in education that he also came to be a founder of the school at Ladybank.

There are many interesting entries in the log for Collessie School, which was 'procured at the expense of the School Board', including a report that 8 boys and 15 girls had given 'satisfactory evidence of having been taught drawing'. We also learn that there were two pupil teachers, Alexander Scott and Robert Somers. HM Inspectors noted that they were not paid. Eighty-five pupils were presented for an examination in religious knowledge, which included 'portions of the Old and New Testaments and the Shorter Catechism'. Geography was taught as well as grammar and grammatical analysis. There was even a 'junior French class', which shows how forward-thinking the local education aims were. A report by HM Inspector was satisfied with ornamental drawing, though

---

[100] Ecclesiastical Records St Andrews and Cupar
[101] New Statistical Account, vol. 9
[102] *Fife Herald* 10th April 1873

penmanship was poor and there were 'too many failures in spelling'. Arithmetic, on the other hand, was good. One entry concerns a severe snowstorm that affected attendance on December 19th and 26th. A half-day holiday took place on Christmas Day.

Perhaps tucked away in the family archives of local folk there are photographs of the youngsters who attended in 1874. The photograph below is roughly of that date and is believed to show Collessie School pupils. Here we see something of the poverty of the time with four children without shoes. The faces look so earnest and sombre, but then it was the custom not to smile when a photograph was being taken because folk thought a grin would make them look foolish.

Life in the Parish

Life in the parish of Collessie at the end of the 18th century and into the 19th century was comparatively good and getting better. Even the poor were well catered for with a regular collection at the church generating £58 per annum. This allowed the dispersal of between four and ten shillings per month. In addition, about 30 cartloads of coal were distributed each year, with the farmers providing transport free of charge. The *Fife Herald* of 20th February 1873 reported that the Free Church of Collessie was adding to the generosity of the Established Church. Apparently, several tons of coal were distributed among the poor and, it was pointed out, denominational allegiance was not a qualification for receiving the gift.[103]

Concern for the poor is evident in the Kirk Session records that go back to 1696. Indeed, the initial records were concerned almost entirely with the accounts, including payments to the minister, Synod and the poor. We frequently hear criticism of the Kirk Sessions of the past for pulling some hapless couple before them and publicly humiliating and condemning them for perceived moral waywardness. This, however, is only one side of the picture, because the concern for the poor, and the care and the

---

[103] *Fife Herald* Thursday 20th February **1873**

generosity towards them, was a high priority in congregations throughout their history. It was also important to establish the paternity of a child conceived out of wedlock in order to ensure the mother received proper financial support.

One problem that faced the people of the parish in 1836 was transport. People had to travel three miles to get any form of public transport. A carrier operated between Cupar and Auchtermuchty twice each week. A runner carried letters and parcels between these centres each day, but travelling to Edinburgh, Dundee or Aberdeen meant covering the six miles to New Inn in order to get a carriage. Mr McFarlane looked forward to the proposed coming of the railway which would traverse the parish. It would take another 10 years for that to happen and, as we now know, it was to bring tremendous change to the folk in the parish of Collessie and communities everywhere. Not least among the benefits that were to be enjoyed was well-paid employment in constructing the line. In August of 1846 the *Fife Herald* reports that the railway lines 'in the vicinity of Cupar are progressing rapidly'. Of the 4,598 men working on the line from Kinghorn, 206 were on the stretch from Kettle to Collessie.[104] Of course, we are not aware of how many of these men were local. Most were probably 'navvies' who were employed to build railways all over the country.

People of Bygone Collessie

Either people of the past, and particularly those of the 16th and 17th centuries, were more sinful than modern people or social attitudes of the time provided a longer list of vices, making sin a more likely occurrence. When we look at the plight of poor James Wilkie, who found himself before Presbytery in April 1647, when Rev. John Littlejohn was minister, it becomes clear that it is the social attitudes that have changed. Mr Wilkie was found guilty of breaking the Sabbath. We do not have details but presumably he had performed some forbidden task. He exacerbated his crime by getting others to cover up for him. All of this was bad enough but he was an elder of the Kirk at Collessie and this made his 'great fault' greater still. For the next three Sundays he was to 'appear before the Session of Collessie' and 'humbly upon his knees acknowledge his fault'. After the first of these displays of humiliation he was to be 'deposed of his eldership by the Session'. One cannot but feel sympathy for Mr Wilkie, and perhaps many of his contemporaries would have shared our sentiments.[105]

A newspaper report in 1814 shows the Kirk in a more positive light. It concerns a curling match on the Loch of Lindores between the parishes of Cupar and a united team from Collessie and Monimail. The prize for the winners (which turned out to be the united team) was a 'quantity of meal for distribution amongst the poor of their respective parishes'. The winter of 1814 must have been a very cold one if they could curl on the loch. No doubt the poor greatly appreciated the selflessness of the participants.[106]

---

[104] *Fife Herald* Thursday 6th August 1846
[105] Ecclesiastical Records St Andrews and Cupar
[106] *Caledonian Mercury* Monday 21st February 1814

In 1836 Mr McFarlane pointed out that £58 was given annually for the poor but only £12–£15 given for the support of the institutions of the Established Church. It is clear that the local folk felt their first duty was to the poor. The needs of the poor were great and on 7th May 1843 the Kirk Session received a letter dated January of that year from the former minister, Mr McFarlane (who had joined the Dissenters at the Disruption at the General Assembly), expressing concern that the poor fund was exhausted. Clearly the needs were greater than the generosity of the congregation.[107]

Rev. Andrew Walker in the Old Statistical Account (1791) tells of Thomas Garrick who 'from best information that can be got' was 108 years of age. He had been a soldier in the Duke of Argyle's regiment in 1715 and had never been known to be confined to bed by sickness, but he was very deaf. He was described as of 'short stature, thin make, wears his own hair'. He was healthy and had married his third wife at the age of 99! Sadly, Mr Garrick survived only two years after his minister had mentioned him for posterity in the Old Statistical Account and he was buried in Collessie graveyard. Yet Mr Walker tells us he was not alone among those who lived a long life in the parish at that time. There were a number over the age of 80 and one or two over 90.[108]

Mr MacFarlane was of the opinion that life for the ordinary folk of his parish was improving in the 19th century and this can largely be borne out by the facts. That is not to say there weren't scoundrels around then but, while the Kirk Session still opened with a request for notification of 'any scandal in the parish', much of the responsibility for maintaining law and order had been removed from the shoulders of the Kirk Session. We also find newspapers like the *Fife Herald*, *Courier* and *Evening Telegraph* keeping the good folk of the village informed of the goings-on in the parish and outlying area. One event that would have exercised the congregation is reported in an issue of the *Courier* in 1897. A Mr J. Oliphant Watt, solicitor in Ladybank, who had absconded with 'considerable sums of monies belonging to Collessie Parish Council and private Trusts', had died. Apparently he had absconded with the money in January of that year.[109]

While the coming of the railway was seen as a great benefit to the whole community, it also brought with it personal tragedies that touched the lives of the folk. On Thursday 16th January 1873, the *Fife Herald* reported the death of a Collessie man who worked on the railway. The unfortunate man was William Crawford, an employee of the North British Railway. The newspaper reported that he had been on his way to repair a joint chair on a sleeper about a mile north of Collessie when he was knocked down by a passing train.[110] According to the record of Collessie churchyard he died at Abdie at the age of 61. By all accounts this man was highly respected by his fellow workmen and there was a large funeral which included among the mourners his wife and 'grown up family'.[111]

---

[107] Minutes of the Kirk Session of Collessie Church, National Archives of Scotland Ref: CH2/765/1,2,3
[108] Old Statistical Account, vol. 2
[109] *Dundee Courier* Wednesday 7th April 1897
[110] *Fife Herald* Thursday 10th April 1873
[111] Rae-Arnot, *Collessie Churchyard*

The *Fife Herald* of Thursday 16th December 1847 reported that Collessie had its own Co-operative. It had been started only 15 months previously and the AGM was held in the schoolroom the previous day. Apparently it was a very successful Co-operative as it had a turnover of £1,715 12*s.* over the previous 12-month period. This left a profit of £31 15*s.* 8*d.* raising the share from 3*s.* to 11*s.* 3½ *d.*[112] Not everything was positive and we discover that on Tuesday the 6th of October 1885 the railway bridge had burned down and some of the rails were found lying on the road. It was thought that a spark from a passing train may have started the fire.[113]

But all was not serious, for fun and entertainment took place. In July 1846 there was a very successful soirée at Giffordtown. The chairman provided 'humorous and quaint remarks' and the company danced to fiddle music until the early morning. It was reported that there were 'about one hundred persons of both sexes and all ages' present but 'no drunken bacchanalian reeled – reason reigned o'er all'.[114]

As the 19th century drew to a close, people were continuing to become richer and standards of living were improving. This is evident when we look at more school photographs. The one above was probably taken about 1880 and the one on the next page about 10 or 20 years later. By the beginning of the 20th century things had improved tremendously. Clearly children were better dressed and better fed and there are no bare feet to be seen. Many children are wearing fashionable clothes of the day, one girl with a brooch at the neck, a boy has a hat and all are looking very well off compared with the children in the earliest photograph. These youngsters are the ones referred to in the Collessie Public School log book.[115] Much of what it contains describes life in the parish at the end of the 19th century. In December 1874, for example, snowstorms affected the attendance at school, and no doubt the lives of the folk in the village. In 1877 there was an outbreak of whooping cough in January and scarlet fever in July.

112   *Fife Herald* Thursday 16th December 1847
113   *Fife Herald* Wednesday 7th October 1885
114   *Fife Herald* Thursday 16th July 1846
115   Collessie Public School Log Book (Extracts) 1874–1940

On June 24th 1887 the community celebrated Queen Victoria's Golden Jubilee. At school the children were given 'refreshments' by Dr Williamson the minister. Mr Hill, a member of the School Board, issued two new pennies to pupils of years IV, V and VI and he gave one new penny to the infants and pupils of years I, II and III. Mr Boyd Kinnear of Kinloch House opened the grounds to the whole community and provided tea. A band played for those who wished to dance. We are also told that 'Thursday and Friday were granted as holidays in honour of the occasion'.

The Diamond Jubilee 10 years later seemed to have attracted less attention, with only the following mentioned: 'There was no meeting of the school on Tuesday 22nd it being the Royal Diamond Jubilee of Her Majesty. The pupils were entertained to tea in Kinloch through the kindness of a number of the Heritors.' In April 1892 the Inspector complained that 'The Upper classes are inclined to be noisy'.

Clearly children were no more perfect then than they are today. One does wonder, however, if the Inspector's idea of a noisy class would be the same as that of a modern-day teacher.

There are many faces that were once as much part of the Kirk as the stones themselves. Yet, while the stones remain, the faces have gone. One such family, the Woods at Birns Farm, is pictured on the right about the turn of the century.

Standing: William, Ann, Andrew
Seated: John, John Senior (Father), Mary (Mother), George

The 20th Century

The first half of the 20th century was to be a troubled time for the world. Collessie did not escape the tribulation that followed the turn of the century nor all the social consequences of two world wars. The minister of the time was Rev. John Henderson who, as we have seen, was ordained to the charge in 1888 and remained there until his death in 1925. His ministry covered one of the most devastating events in world history, World War I.

Again we find the school log an important source of information about life in Collessie during the early years of the 20th century. January 1901 was another severe winter with school attendance affected by snow storms. In 1902 the girls' playground was fenced off from the boys' area. In 1910 the school closed because of the funeral of King Edward VII, and in 1911 Mr Coates of Paisley, the cotton manufacturer, wanted to present each child with a school bag. Little seems to be said about World War I except that in 1914 farmers were short-handed and in September children were employed to help.

The year 1911 was memorable for the parish. The church was renovated with work on heating and the ceiling, and the pews and pulpit were upholstered. There were new carpets and blinds and it all cost a total of £304 14s. 6½d. It was also the year of the coronation of King George V and Queen Mary. Many joined a celebration in the village on 22nd June with a service at the Parish Church, tea at Kinloch, evening refreshments, dancing and sports. It was rounded off with 'God Save the King' at 8 p.m.

Ella Kinnear provided the following memory of her father, who was a pupil of Collessie School in the early years of the 20th century:

> My father Andrew Wood was born at Cunnique Mill farm. I do not know when the family came to stay at Kinloch but Andrew went to Collessie School and I think the headmaster at that time was Mr Penman. The pupils were taught Latin and Euclid and they were tested on Religion. My father got a prize at school. My father told of how children got out to the playground to see the first car pass Trafalgar in 1900 and the pupils and teachers walked to Melville Gates to see Queen Victoria pass.[116]

A Collessie Golden Wedding

The Golden Wedding of Mr and Mrs John Duncan was recorded in the local press in August 1913. According to the *Dundee Courier* there was quite a party, with a large number of friends and neighbours attending at the farmhouse. The minister, John Henderson, presided at the lunch and William Robb of Braeside proposed the toast. This was replied to by Mr John Duncan Jr, who

---

[116] Personal communication

was also a farmer and resided at Cairneyhall. We are told that Mr J. Boyd Kinnear of Kinloch, who lived in the local 'big house', presented them with an antique fruit stand. The following background accompanied the photograph in another publication:

> Mr & Mrs John Duncan, Cornhill, Collessie, celebrated their golden wedding on 12th August 1913. Mr Duncan was born at Denmylne Farm, Newburgh, in 1836, and when he was eight years of age, his father leased Cornhill from Mr Kinnear. Mr Duncan had, therefore, spent the long period of 69 years at Cornhill. At the celebration of their golden wedding Mr and Mrs Duncan received many valuable gifts. The garden seat which appears in the photo was gifted to the old couple at their silver wedding by 'the Laird', Mr Boyd Kinnear of Kinloch.

Such was the happiness of the days that preceded the First World War – 'the war to end wars'.

The Great War

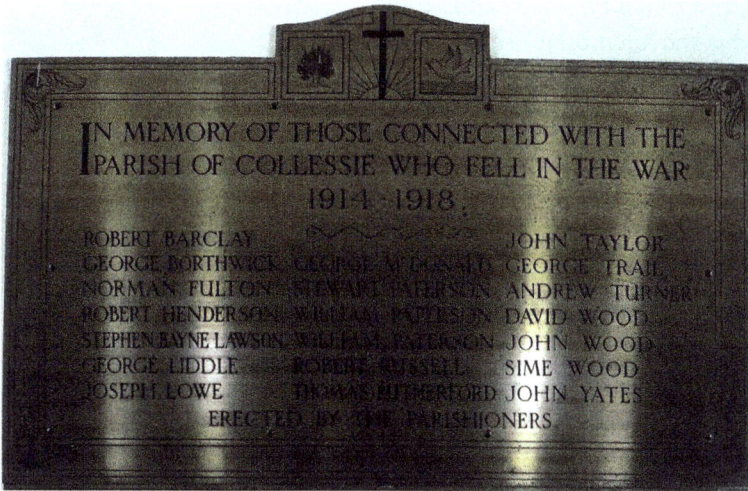

The First World War changed the lives of so many forever. A total of 91 local men entered the armed services from the parish. Three entered before 1914, including Field Marshall Douglas Haig, who was Commander in Chief of the British Army in France, and Lieutenant-Colonel Oliver Haig of Ramornie. One hesitates to single out any of the 88 conscripts for special mention, for each was a brave man in his own right. They came from places with familiar local names: Giffordtown, Innerleith, Charleston, Jeaniestown, Ladybank, Rossie, Trafalgar and, of course, Collessie itself.

It was on 30th April 1922 that a large congregation gathered and filled the church. Three ministers led the service, Revs Fyfe Scott of Creich, Alex Allison of Abdie and John Henderson of Collessie. Mr Scott, who gave the address, had lost both legs while serving as a lieutenant in the Highland Light Infantry. He spoke of the importance of the memorial as an aid to remember the war they once thought they would never forget, and the solemn vows to which they had committed themselves to create a better life for the sake of the fallen. Mr Henderson and Mr Allison led the Kirk Session to the memorial and the Union flag covering it was removed by Miss Walker of Pitlair. Mr Henderson read the names and Mr Scott led the congregation in prayer.

Collessie lost 19 of its young men between 1914 and 1919. Five are recorded as having died of their wounds. Another 16 were wounded some two, three or four times. Four were decorated; there were three military medals and one Belgian Croix de Guerre.[117] The names of the dead are recorded on the war memorial within the church, pictured on the previous page.

1918 – The Beginning of a New Era

When the war ended, the folk of the parish wanted a permanent memorial to be built. To this end a committee was established. A split occurred between those who wanted a Victory Hall and those who wanted a war memorial. The split fell between representatives of Collessie and those of Giffordtown and, as a result, the one committee became two. So it is that we find the war memorial outside the hall at Giffordtown and the Victory Hall at Collessie, with the memorial plaque in the church.

It was the parishioners who erected the memorial to their own young men. Not only did it keep their names at the centre of the parish but it reminds us, 100 years later, of the terrible sacrifice made by this small community. The photograph was taken when the war memorial at Giffordtown was unveiled.

Clearly Rev. Mr Henderson had served the parish well during these troubled times. He remained in post for another seven years after the war until he retired on 20th June 1925. In that year Cupar Presbytery published a book entitled *Church and Parish*, edited by Rev. George Walker, minister of Ceres. In it Mr Walker pays tribute to the recently retired Mr Henderson, who 'ministered to an attached people' for 37 years. Just the year before he died Mr Henderson dedicated Collessie's Victory Hall. He was much loved by his congregation.

---

117 Roll of Service in the Great War

The Victory Hall

Wedding slum yown babies 1934

On 15th March 1924 Mrs Milbank Leslie Melville of Melville House opened the Victory Hall. Her husband, the Earl of Leven and Melville, had donated the land on which it was built but the £1,000 needed had been raised through the efforts of the local people. According to the report in the local paper the hall provided accommodation for over 200 people. There is no doubt that it quickly became a popular venue for all sorts of activities. The oil lamps, which can be seen in the photographs here, were the only form of lighting in the hall.

Fancy dress party 1934

In 1919 Collessie, like many villages in the area, established a WRI (Women's Rural Institute). As there was no hall at that time, they met in the village school. Once the

Victory Hall was finished it became an important venue in the interwar years. In 1979 the WRI celebrated its Diamond Jubilee and the sole remaining founder member, Mrs Wood, pictured right, cut a cake.

The sadness at the loss of local folk did not end in 1918. In the church we find a plaque to the memory of Colonel Henry Oliphant Hutchison of Kinloch, who served at Meerut from 1932 to 1935. Colonel Hutchison, only son and heir to the Kinloch estate, died in 1935 aged just 52.

The Village School

In June 1920 there was an inter-school sports day at Ladybank and two years later the school closed to celebrate the marriage of Princess Mary (Princess Royal until her death in 1965) to Viscount Lascelles, sixth Earl of Harewood. For the visit of Queen Mary to Melville House in August 1923 the children were required to be at Melville Gates at 2.30 p.m. to welcome her.[118]

Collessie pupils on parade celebrating the Jubilee of George V in 1935

The number of pupils attending the school had always varied considerably due to some families moving into the parish and others moving out. Attendance, though a constant concern, was normally good. In 1932 it was decided that the provision of flush toilets would be too costly and so the pupils had to put up with dry toilets instead. This, of course, was the norm in the homes of folk throughout the parish up to the 1950s.

---

[118]   Collessie Public School Log Book (Extracts) 1874–1940

In 1935 there was another Jubilee to celebrate 25 years of the reign of King George V and Queen Mary. Jubilee shillings were distributed among the children. Within a few short years the mood changed and on 4th September 1939 the school was closed until further notice 'during evacuation'. This was concerning evacuees coming into the area; 92 arrived at the school on the Saturday and were 'allocated to billets within a short time'. We know that several of these children would have been taken to Kinloch House by the Hutchison family. The school nurse examined the new arrivals and, finding 'several with verminous heads', had them kept away from school for treatment.

The final entry in the school log in 1940 speaks volumes about wartime life in Collessie: 'February 6th – The Headmaster was out of school for part of the afternoon when an aeroplane crashed in a field at Hall-hill at 2.30 p.m. As Head Warden, the Headmaster went to investigate and report. Fortunately none of the occupants were hurt. The weather was rather misty at the time of the accident.'

Hard Times

The interwar years were austere times for the whole country and the folk of Collessie suffered hardship with everyone else. This is clear in the memories of Ella Kinnear, who recalls these difficult days when she was a child.[119]

My father was a tenant farmer and life was hard in the 1930s. There was unemployment and on the farm little profit in calves, lambs, grain or potatoes. If my memory is correct I think it was difficult to get 10s. for a hundred weight of potatoes – 50p today. There was one ploughman's cottage on the farm and we needed two men so a father and son were employed and lived there together. They got milk, meal and potatoes as part of their wages but I don't know what they got in cash. I do know I used to take a pitcher of milk to them in the evening. They had a wireless and would tell me to tell my father the latest news. It was near the end of the war before we got a wireless, which was brought by a relative from Greenock. My father had to take the accumulator to Ladybank to get it charged for there was no electricity or gas so we used paraffin lamps. Water was pumped to the house from a well by a petrol pump. Cooking was done on paraffin stove or in an oven over the fire in the living room.

Because we had no wireless news was slow in arriving. The postman, who originally had a motorbike and sidecar but did eventually have a van, brought the Courier every day. He always got a cup of tea and bread and jam for his piece. After the war started we got a Fordson tractor but I do not remember when we got the phone. When it did arrive our number was Ladybank 58. The Williamsons who manned the exchange at Ladybank would always take messages or tell us who was at home.

At the end of the 1930s war broke out and Ella remembers that day very clearly:

---

[119] Personal communication

The Second World War started 3rd September 1939 when I was 9 years old. As usual on a Sunday morning my father and I walked along the railway to the bridge at Cairnfield. There was a path up the bank to the road and we walked to Leslie Cottage where my father's parents and his sister lived. That day there was adult talk and worry if there was to be a war. My grandparents had a wireless and by 11 a.m. there was news that Britain had declared war against Germany. My thoughts were very troubled. There was talk of air raids and shelters which I could not understand. We had no safe place on the farm and there was talk of using the sheep dipper, which was a concrete hole with a sloping end for the sheep getting in. It only had a tin roof so would not have been much protection.

Between 1939 and 1945 a new generation had to undergo a similar trauma as their predecessors had endured 20 years before. Again Ella's memories give us a glimpse into these days.

Things changed with the war – evacuees, tank traps, roadblocks, identity cards, ration books, gas masks, and coupons. Farmers were given better prices because imported food was at risk of submarine attack and we were encouraged to produce as much as possible. Soldiers were billeted at the farm. Many local men were reported missing or dead. We knitted for the soldiers. It was only after the war started that we were allowed to knit or read on a Sunday and because of the need for food, farm work in the fields was allowed on the Sabbath Day.

Among the evacuees Ella mentioned was a group who lived with the Hutchisons at Kinloch. There were a number from Edinburgh staying with them and they were taken to Collessie Church every Sunday and sat in the Kinloch pew. Mr and Mrs Hutchison, who owned the flour mill in Kirkcaldy, were people of great faith and very active in the church.

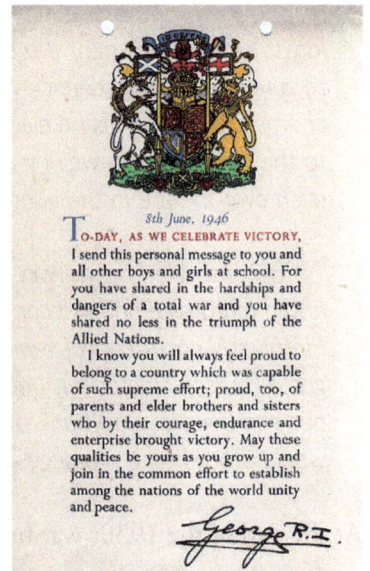

8th June, 1946

To-DAY, AS WE CELEBRATE VICTORY, I send this personal message to you and all other boys and girls at school. For you have shared in the hardships and dangers of a total war and you have shared no less in the triumph of the Allied Nations.

I know you will always feel proud to belong to a country which was capable of such supreme effort; proud, too, of parents and elder brothers and sisters who by their courage, endurance and enterprise brought victory. May these qualities be yours as you grow up and join in the common effort to establish among the nations of the world unity and peace.

George R.I.

Just as World War I changed the world so World War II changed it again. Once more there were casualties and the names above were added to the war memorial at Collessie Kirk. At the end of the war the King recognised the part played by the younger generation over the previous six years. A personal message from the King was sent to the young.

Peacetime Again

Once the war was over rationing continued into the 1950s and life continued to be hard for many. In Collessie and Giffordtown houses were of a poor standard compared with many in the towns. In 1955 when George and Marion Calley bought Rose Neuk in Giffordtown there was no mains water, sewage or electricity. Water was pumped into the house from a well in the garden and the sanitary facilities comprised a dry toilet in the garden. Their new home had been built in 1831 as a weaver's cottage to relocate a family from Kinloch. It was arranged so that the largest room, where the weaver would have worked, had a double window in order to take full advantage of available daylight.

Things were not very different in Collessie. The village has long been seen as distinctive with its thatched cottages, though it was not always admired. Nor were the thatched cottages always an asset. A group of three houses, including a joiner's shop, was burned down when a spark from a traction engine ignited a roof. An article in the *Evening Telegraph* of Tuesday 22nd May 1900 finds a contributor relating a cycle run from Cupar to Kinross describing Collessie as 'the tumble-down village of Collessie'. This is not a description that would be welcomed by modern inhabitants of what is now seen as a most desirable, quaint hamlet. The reputation the village had earned in 1900 remained into the mid 20th century and in 1965 an article in *The Scotsman* drew to public attention the lack of amenity in the village.

The picture below shows Mrs Robina Leitch emptying her dishwater into the village burn, just as she had always done. Mr Taylor the minister was also quoted in the same article as telling reporters that the village, with a population of about 60, lacked street lighting and drainage and that half the houses were unfit for habitation with no toilets, electricity or piped water. For most of his 40 years as parish minister, Mr Taylor and his family lit the manse with paraffin. By 1965, however, electricity had been introduced to the village, though not to every home.

Left: Mrs Leitch emptying dishwater into the village burn. *Right*: The 'well'

John Stark, one-time Session Clerk of the Howe of Fife, and his twin brother James were raised in the village and have many happy memories of their childhood there in the 1950s. There was a real sense of community as people met at the 'well' – actually a water tap – opposite Shuttle Cottage to collect all the water for the household needs. Wireless was powered by battery and lighting was by Tilley lamp. The schoolteacher, Mr Combs, was also Cub and Scout master. When the time came for the school report he would come knocking on the door of the family home and give the report to the parents of his pupils at their own fireside.

At one time there were two shops in the village but John remembers only one, the Post Office, where lemonade was sold as well as the very necessary paraffin for the Tilley lamps. The baker, butcher and fish man came round with vans ensuring that every necessity was provided for the folk of the village. The last postmistress was Miss Mary Coupar, who had been postmistress for 63 years when she retired in 1974.

POST OFFICE, COLLESSIE. 91308

There was no play park and so the children gathered on the biggest piece of available land to play games. They would also 'guddle for fish' and John remembers catching eels in the burn. At one time his uncle caught eels and sold them. The same uncle trapped rabbits and sold coal in the village. It was not uncommon for folk to have more than one occupation in order to improve their income. There still stands a pill box in the garden of the house opposite the church gates and there John and his friends would play. There were also tank traps and concrete blocks, all part of the wartime defence line from Dysart to Newburgh, and they made excellent places for post-war children to play.

Central to life in Collessie was the railway station. Everything came and went by rail. Papers were delivered in the morning and at weekends the sport edition arrived in the evening. John collected the papers and distributed them around the village. On one occasion he and his brother James received bicycles for Christmas from a cousin in England and they arrived at the station on Christmas Day. Farmers loaded their produce onto the trains and coal for the locals arrived. John even remembers being taken by his father to Ladybank by train to get a haircut. The station also became a great place for the children to play hide and seek, no doubt with the porter, who was also ticket clerk, turning a blind eye.

The station was so very important to the folk of the community, providing employment, communication and independence. Change was inevitable and with the changes came the demise of old Collessie. When electricity arrived the shop that sold the paraffin for the Tilley lamps was no longer needed and so it closed. With water and drainage being supplied to every home people no longer had the need to meet at 'the well'. In 1955 the station closed to passenger trains and in 1960 it closed to freight.

The Church

For many the church remained the only centre in the village community. Some drifted off to churches in Bow of Fife, Auchtermuchty and Ladybank, although many found comfort and spiritual leadership in Rev. John Taylor. John and James Stark have very good memories of Mr Taylor, whose son-in-law was a science teacher. He built a TV for Mr Taylor and John and James were

Sunday School prize winners of 1967

frequently invited round to the manse to watch the sport on Saturday afternoon, a rare treat for boys raised in a village where only a very few houses had electricity. Sunday worship was part of the weekly cycle of life for the Starks and John and James had Jenny Harwood as their Sunday School teacher. Jenny was a wonderful and much-loved lady both in the community and in the church. She served the Kirk throughout the Howe of Fife right up to her illness in 2010.

On Remembrance Sunday Mr Taylor would read each of the names on the war memorial in the church, and then he would add another. When John asked him why he added the other name, Mr Taylor explained that the serviceman in question had died of his injuries after the war memorial was erected.

In 1956 the memorial windows were installed at either side of the pulpit. The artist who made them, Douglas Hamilton, also made the window at Cults. This man gained quite a reputation and the windows attracted the attention of a minister in Melton Mowbray who was doing an MPhil in stained glass. John remembers the roof of the shed in his garden being used to assemble the windows before they were installed. Those who are familiar with the topography of Collessie will know that the house to the south of the church had a footpath at a higher level than the garden making this a feasible proposition. The window pictured on the left was installed in memory of local farmer John Duncan of Cornhill, while the one on the right is in memory of Francis Malcolm Watt and his wife Alice Kinnear.

Inevitable Changes

As we have seen, Collessie Parish Church has had a long and illustrious past. It has been the centre of the community for many generations. Its pulpit has been graced by notable men and its pews filled with high-ranking folk of principle as well as with hardworking ordinary folk. Ladybank already had strong connections with Collessie through the development of the Free Kirk, first in Giffordtown and then in Ladybank. In 1880 the Parish Church found a generous patron in Rev. Mr Williamson of Collessie, who donated £2,000 towards its construction. So, Ladybank was not a strange place with which to unite. Rather it was the natural inheritor of the great legacy that Collessie brought into that union in 1968. When the first meeting to arrange the union with the parish of Ladybank took place in the small hall of the Kerr Memorial Church, the atmosphere was happy and accepting of the situation. Much of the credit for the success of the union must go to Rev. Sandy Philp, who became the much-loved first minister of the united parish of Ladybank and Collessie.

In 1968 there was a terrible storm which caused one of the spires of the church to fall through the roof and land inside. Mr Taylor went to inspect the damage. In doing so he had an accident which broke his leg. Complications arose and, sadly, Mr Taylor died having been minister of the parish for 43 years. Mrs Taylor died in the same year. Collessie Kirk is still a centre of worship for folk in the village and surrounding area. It is also much loved by its parishioners.

In 1978, when the minister of the united charge of Ladybank and Collessie was Rev. Ian Wotherspoon, new furnishings, a font and communion table were added to the church through the dedication of loyal folk of the parish. The font is a large and impressive object made of marble and the communion table acts as a memorial to the fallen in the First World War. The story of their installation is told in a plaque that is positioned on a pillar by the font. The very grand marble font was a gift from Mr and Mrs John Reid. The communion table was part of that gift and they came from Cowlairs Sommerville Church in Springburn, Glasgow. They were dedicated by Rev. Ian Wotherspoon on 29th October 1978.

The congregation gathered for a flower show at Collessie Kirk in 1979; note the very young Rev. Ian Wotherspoon on the extreme left

Collessie in the 21st Century

Collessie Kirk, now part of the Parish of the Howe of Fife, still conducts regular services on the first Sunday each month. There are also remembrance, communion and special services throughout the year. While the Sunday School is very active, it varies in size according to the availability of children in the area. The folk of the parish also show their love of their Kirk through supporting the Friends of Collessie Church, which contributes significantly to its upkeep.

So it is that Collessie Kirk, which is now part of a larger family of churches in the Howe of Fife, is still very much at the centre of the village, not just physically but in the hearts of the people.

CHAPTER TWO: FOUR KIRKS, ONE HISTORY
PART TWO: LADYBANK

Ladybank:
A Product of the Industrial
Revolution?

~

It is tempting to think of Ladybank as a relatively modern creation compared with Collessie, Lathrisk, Kettle and Cults. This, however, is far from the case. While it is true that the name is a relatively recent invention, like the rest of the Howe of Fife its history stretches back to when settlers first reached the shores of Scotland.

An Ancient Place

This was a marshy area with extensive peat bogs, whins and heathers. The archaeological remains unearthed in the historic parishes of Kettle, Collessie and Cults reveal evidence of settled communities across the whole area from the times of the earliest settlers. It is hard to imagine that those folk from the distant past chose the ancient peat bog that has become the area where modern Ladybank stands as a place to build their communities. On the other hand, there can be little doubt that these early inhabitants knew the area well as they searched for fuel for the fires that warmed their homes. Up to 1836 when Rev. Mr McFarlane, minister of Collessie, contributed to the New Statistical Account, Edensmuir contained marshes and was subject to flooding in winter and heather was still found near Ramornie. Having said that, extensive drainage and the canalisation of the River Eden in the 18th century claimed much of the land for forestry and some agriculture.

Our earliest written records of people using the produce of the land comes from the medieval period. In the Chartulary of the Abbey of Lindores[120] in Newburgh, we read that on 8th March 1247 Roger de Quincy granted to Lindores Abbey 200 cartloads

---

[120] Dowden, Chartulary of Lindores

of heather from 'Kyndeloch' and permission to dig as much peat as was needed in his peat moss, which was called 'Monegro' or 'Monagrey'. They were also granted a free road through the wood of Kyndeloch 'as far as the moor of Eden' for heather. Roger had inherited this land from his grandfather Robert, the first de Quincy mentioned in Scotland. The land of Monagrey, which lay in the moor of Edyne (Eden), was rich in peat, broom and heather. It was here that the monks came to cut fuel to stoke the ovens of the Abbey. While Roger de Quincy may, or may not, have seen this gift to the church as his insurance for free passage into the hereafter, we see the record as providing a valuable insight into the medieval landscape of the part of the Howe of Fife where Ladybank and Edenstown lie today. The names 'Monksmoss', 'Monkston' or 'Monkstown' and 'Our Lady Bog' developed as a result of the gift. The last referred to the place where the monks cut peat and the dedication of Lindores Abbey to the Virgin Mary. The moor of Edyne and the land of Monagrey lay in the parish of Culessin (Collessie) and no doubt the locals would have sought the spiritual support of the priest there. So we find that the relationship between Collessie and the area around modern Ladybank is a very ancient one. Collessie Church, at that time, belonged to the Abbey of Lindores, in Newburgh.[121]

Ladybank – A Modern Invention

The popular belief is that the name 'Ladybank' is a product of the coming of the railway and of the local lairds who did not want a railway junction on their land. As a result, Pitlessie was bypassed and Kettle denied the status of being an important railway junction, with all of the benefits that would have accrued through employment and enlargement. So it is that the lands where once the monks of Lindores cut peat – their Lady Bog – was bought by the railways in 1847 and renamed Ladybank to suit the marketing sensibilities of the railway company. While it may be true that the railway preferred the name to Lady Bog, to suggest they invented it fails to recognise that the name was already in circulation. Evidence of this can be found in Collessie churchyard and from the elders of the Free Church at Giffordtown in 1843.

In 1810 Andrew Thomson of Wester Kinloch had a row of 24 cottages built on the land of Edensmuir which belonged to him. It was he who named this tiny settlement Monkstown in memory of the monks of Lindores. They were stone-built, single-storied weavers' cottages arranged in four blocks of six. Access to the rear of the buildings

---

121 Scott, *Fasti Ecclesiae Scoticanae*, vol. 5

was created between each block and residents are known to have kept pigs and grown vegetables there. Among the houses was a school. It was fee-paying and the first teacher was Mr Bannerman. No doubt the inhabitants found these houses a great improvement on the cruck houses they were familiar with in Kinloch. There certainly seem to have been no complaints from residents forced to move. The cottages were built along the road from the main Collessie/New Inn road to Kettle and Pitlessie. At this time there were no other houses and, of course, the railway had not been built.[122]

The Railway

If the canals were the great transport innovation that encouraged the industrial revolution in the 18th century, it was the railway that took over that role in the 19th century. Railways had long been used for horse-drawn transportation of heavy goods like coal. The advantages of rail were well known before the railway line was opened from Stockton to Darlington. At this time locomotives were still relatively limited and they were used on this line for short, level distances. Plans had been afoot as early as 1804 to build a steel railway track with horse-drawn carriages to transport coal from Lochore to Perth. Perth Council had been asked to provide 50 per cent of the cost. They were unable or unwilling to do this and so the project failed. Fife had long been a leader in the development of railways and so it is not surprising that in 1819 Robert Stevenson (builder of lighthouses and father to his more famous son, the author Robert Louis Stevenson) proposed a rail link between Edinburgh and Dundee through Fife. The aim was to transport coal from the rich coalfields of Fife to Dundee.

When the Stockton–Darlington line was opened in 1825, much of the work was carried out by stationary engines and horses. It was not until Stephenson's *Rocket* proved its advantage over its competitors in 1829 that steam locomotion 'took off'.[123] Initially, its primary purpose was to transport goods and it was not until 1833 that passenger carriages were added. News of the advantages of this new mode of transport travelled quickly as on 18th June 1835 we read of plans drawn up by John Geddes to construct a railway through Fife to Perth. In 1836 Robert Stevenson submitted another plan and Granger and Millar followed later that year. All the proposed routes were similar to the one eventually built. They stretched from the ferry at Burntisland through Kirkcaldy to a point north of Kettle (where Ladybank now stands) then divided to Perth and Newport. While these plans were not realised at that time, the advantages of transporting more than coal and lime were becoming clear. A Fife railway was now being seen as part of a network connecting the central belt with newly approved rail systems in Angus and, looking to the future, to creating a through route from Aberdeen to London.

The Collessie minister recorded in the New Statistical Account of 1836 his eager anticipation of the coming of this railway. The advantages for Fife, with a fast, efficient

---

122 Calley, *Collessie: A Parish Alphabet*
123 P. Mathias, *The First Industrial Nation: An Economic History of Britain 1700–1914* (London, Methuen & Co Ltd, 1969)

connection to Perth and Dundee, were extolled in the local press, where they were equated with the advantages gained by the coalfields of northern England and the manufacturing industries of Manchester and Sheffield. The transportation of coal and lime principally, but also ironstone, crockery, bricks and tiles, was seen as the main motivation for the venture. The author also mentions lead and silver in the Lomonds. The significance of the Howe of Fife was emphasised as the author proposed a line from Newburgh terminating at the 'foot of the Cult Lime Hill'. It could also transport coal from Burntuk, as well as other centres in Fife. The author was so enthusiastic about the project that he declared, 'in this view the amount of capital required to start with, would be so very inconsiderable, that we would be libelling the public spirit of our countrymen for a moment to suppose that the execution of so important an undertaking could remain one month in abeyance from such a cause'.[124] In April 1836 a prospectus was authorised to raise £450,000 in 9,000 shares of £50 for the Forth and Tay Railway Company. We are told that the distance from Burntisland to Newport is 34 miles and the route would include Kinghorn, Seafield, Kirkcaldy and Cupar.

The author was so enthusiastic that he would have arranged for the project to be completed immediately. In Victorian times, however, just like today, delays were inevitable. It was to be another 10 years before work on the new line would commence.

It took until 15th October 1840 until definite plans were becoming clear. By this time the country was plunging into a severe financial depression. There was also the problem of crossing the Forth from Granton in the south to Burntisland. Both ports had low-water piers and as a result they could not operate for much of the day. In any case it was believed by many that it would be quicker for freight and passengers alike to take the longer route through Stirling and Perth. It was for very sound economic reasons that it began to look as if Fife would be bypassed by the railway companies.

The Duke of Buccleuch, owner of the port at Granton, saved the day by investing in the harbour. It was his hope that he would be able to make it more profitable by building a new pier that would allow the port to remain open whatever the level of the tide. He also managed to get support from Sir John Gladstone of Fasque, who carried out similar work in Burntisland. The projects were completed in 1844 and, with their decision to run a steam ferry service across the Forth, building a railway through the 'Kingdom' became practical. Gladstone continued to show a commitment to a railway in Fife and he was influential in the Edinburgh and Northern Railway Company.[125] As the potential of the project was realised, interest grew. Soon it was intimated that the Corporation of St Andrews would subscribe for 10 shares. By now Fife was seen as an important artery not only to Perth and Dundee but also to Arbroath, Montrose and Aberdeen. A new committee had been formed and it was to head the future Forth and Tay Railway Company.[126]

---

124 *Fife Herald and Kinross, Strathearn and Clackmannan Advertiser* 18th June 1835
125 C. Robertson, *The Origins of the Scottish Railway System 1722–1844* (Edinburgh, John Donald Publishers Ltd, 1983, pp. 133 ff.)
126 *Fife Herald and Kinross, Strathearn and Clackmannan Advertiser* 15th October 1840

In October 1844 the *Fife Herald* had a notice of intention to apply to Parliament for leave to bring in a Bill for building the railway between Burntisland and Perth. The route outlined passed through the Howe of Fife, including Falkland, Kettle and Collessie, before going on to Abdie and Newburgh. The notice then goes on to indicate a branch off the main railway: 'a Branch Railway diverging from or out of the said intended main Railway at or near to the Farm-House called Heatherinch or at or near to the Village of Ladybank, both in the said Parish of Collessie, and terminating at a point at, in, or near to the Royal Burgh of Cupar.' Clearly Ladybank was already 'on the map'![127]

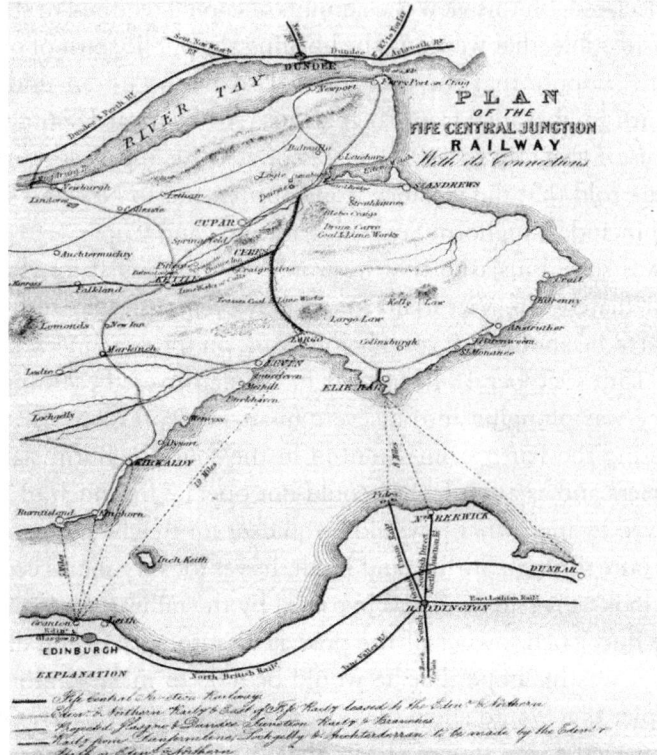

The *Fife Herald* of 6th November 1845 published the map above. Here we see not only the already proposed line from Burntisland to Newport but another that originates at Elie and stretches to the main line north of Cupar and includes a branch from Kettle past Cults lime works and joining the line north of Ceres. This was to take advantage of the Teases coal and lime works and that of Cults and Burnturk. The junction for Newburgh and Perth is clearly seen about a mile north of Kettle. This is, of course, exactly where Ladybank was to be established.

November 1845 finds a notice in the *Fife Herald* intimating the intention to take a branch line from Ladybank to Kinross. Clearly Ladybank junction was increasing in complexity, with branches to Cupar and the north, Perth and Kinross.[128]

---

127   *Fife Herald and Kinross, Strathearn and Clackmannan Advertiser* 31st October 1844
128   *Stirling Observer* 11th December 1845

On Monday 20th September 1847 the *Fife Herald* proudly announced the 'partial' opening of the Edinburgh and Northern Railway. The train left Burntisland at 12.20 p.m. (20 minutes after the arranged time) and set off for Cupar. The people of Fife lined the route with flags waving and bands playing. The reporter used his eloquence to describe how the train, with 20 carriages, gave passengers a magnificent view of the Firth and the Lothians as it headed first for Kinghorn. The crowds cheered as they passed through Kirkcaldy. It

Ladybank railway from Heatherinch

was then on to Thornton, Markinch and New Inn, which had its own station, and down into the Howe of Fife. With a decline of 1:100 it is northwards to Kettle and the great vista of the Howe is revealed to the traveller. Among the settlements described are Falkland, Auchtermuchty, Strathmiglo, Freuchie, Dunshelt, Springfield and Letham. Again Kettle is mentioned and so is Pitlessie.

Then, Ladybank is mentioned: 'At a place called Ladybank, about a mile beyond the Kettle station, the line divides.' We are not told at what time the train arrived at Cupar but apparently the 'whole population' was there to greet the first steam locomotive to arrive in the town. A pavilion had been constructed with banners and decorations by Messrs Sharp and Duncan of Cupar. There was an 'unlimited allowance of Champaign' for the pleasure of the 600–700 present (1 in 10 being ladies). Dignitaries from around the county and the cities of Edinburgh and Perth brought gravity to the proceedings and clearly everyone had a wonderful time.[129] All of the celebrating took place in centres away from the new railway junction of Ladybank, but it soon grew in size and importance and before long it became the foremost village in the Howe of Fife.

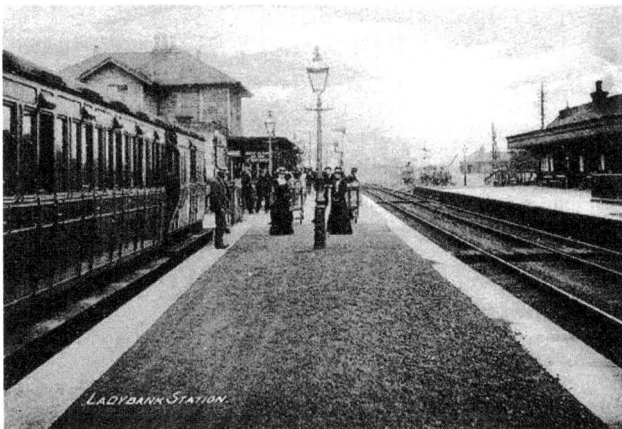

---

[129] *Caledonian Mercury* 20th September 1847

A Growing Community

At first the development of the new town was slow. In 1846, Samuel Lewis in *A Topographical Dictionary of Scotland* tells us that it consists of 102 inhabitants. On the six-inch OS map published in 1856 (survey done in 1854) we find a very scattered community. Monkstown was quite separate and the row of cottages faced the railway line to Kinross. This left the main line at Ladybank junction, which was situated opposite the farm of Heatherinch. The station stood in its present position and there were about seven properties on Kinloch Street and about 17 dotted around Hill Street and Victoria Road. The school appears to have been in its present position and was standing on its own and quite separate from the houses. This was the only property on Church Street.

Compared with Kettle, Ladybank was a very small community. Perhaps this is what upset a reader of the *Fife Herald* and caused him to complain that, 'while six passenger trains use the line daily, only two stop at Kettle. The first is at 7 minutes past 10 a.m. and the second 19 minutes past 6 p.m'. The letter was written in January 1848 and the author felt it was unreasonable to expect people to walk the mile between Ladybank and Kettle when the weather was bad.

The people of Ladybank did not get it all their own way either. In October 1849 there is a report in the *Dundee, Perth & Cupar Advertiser* of Ladybank people cheating the railway company of the proper fare when travelling from Dundee. It would appear that competition from the Tay ferries caused the company to reduce the fares of passengers travelling from Dundee to Newburgh or Collessie. The reporter tells us that 'Some of the sharp residents in the neighbourhood of Ladybank have in consequence attempted to defraud the Railway Company by taking tickets from Dundee to Newburgh or Collessie'. In fact, these passengers alighted the train at Ladybank and the company felt it was being robbed! One hapless passenger found himself before the Sheriff in Cupar for doing this. Although he expressed his regret an hour before the case was due to be heard, he had to agree to pay most of the expenses incurred.

A Description of Ladybank Past and Present Dated 1877

The following is part of a larger document under the heading 'Weavers & Weaving' and gives us a contemporary view of life in Ladybank and the Howe of Fife 140 years ago.[130]

> *Little difference has taken place in the number of hands employed within the last five years, and no alteration in prices paid for the past seven years. The employers are Messrs. Wilson & Hill, who supply a number of hands in a few of the small manufacturing villages in the county – webs being supplied to persons in Newburgh, Dunshalt, Falkland and Freuchie, &c. The goods manufactured by this firm are all linen, and some of them are of a fine fabric. The average wage earned by the broad linen weaver will amount to about 3s per day, while the extra good hands may earn a little more where fine 'stuff' has been put in. Few if any women are engaged at the handloom – the factories all being busy, all*

---

[130]   *Fife Herald* June **1877**

are employed in them. Although there seems no direct dullness, still the prices are low for the seller. Some thirty-eight years ago Ladybank was a place almost unknown. Only a few houses were then built in what was called the Moor. Monksmoss, however, was erected before that time, and this small village, which consisted only of some 24 houses, formed an important centre in the Howe of Fife. A great meeting of those who were favourable to the Chartist movement was held at Ladybank. No fewer than 7,000 politicians attended. The main body of the great assemblage consisted of weavers from almost all the villages within half-a-day's journey. The utmost enthusiasm prevailed on that day, and the speeches were delivered with much spirit and impression, as the whole audience were Chartists to the 'backbone'. Exactly on the spot where the 'hustings' were erected at that time stands the power loom factory of Messrs. Wilson and Hill. The weavers arrived from the villages with bands and music playing, and all the banners floating in the breeze. Auchtermuchty itself sent down about 1,000 of the good sort of hands, and Leslie and Markinch also contributed a good representation.

About twenty-two years ago Mr Lawson of Kettle, who succeeded his two uncles, Messrs. David and Alex. Adamson, in the handloom linen manufacturing trade, employed from 1,000 to 1,400 hands, and kept upwards of a dozen of warping mills in constant operation. In addition to his large business in Kettle he had extensive agencies in Kennoway, Lundimill, Pitlessie, Falkland, and Strathmiglo, &c. Ladybank has become now a small town, and many 'little lairds' can point to the shuttle as the means of their success. The railways and factories employ a great bulk of the working class. Wages are fair and steady, the average on the railway being about 18s per week. The female population have found employment in the powerloom factories, where the average wages range from 8s to 10s per week, while some extra good hands can realise with flue fabrics and good machinery 15s at times. The weavers at the present day are like their forefathers in principle and politics; and to use an expression of one of their own number, 'There is a strong sprig among us of the Chartist men still.' In earlier times the weavers all had their tidy gardens, fed their own pigs, and fed on the home produce; were exceedingly industrious, and for general knowledge could be compared with any equal number of artisans of a different class. 'Tick' was a thing which at one time was despised among weavers, who proudly maintained their independence.

The 19th century saw the steady demise of handloom weavers throughout the country as factories proved to be so much more efficient and cost-effective. In Paisley in 1841 a crisis occurred as unemployment and hardship became endemic in the town. The Chartist movement became popular among many at that time as it gave hope of a more equal society. The above article from the *Fife Herald* shows how popular it was, not only in the west but also in the east of Scotland. Having said that, it appears to me that a gathering of 7,000 people in the area that is now Ladybank may well be something of an exaggeration. Nevertheless, it does reflect the strength of feeling in the Howe of Fife at that time. The article also shows the importance of the linen industry to the growing Ladybank. No doubt the proximity of the railway helped in the growth of this industry.

The Ladybank Schools

As Ladybank began to grow it was clear the little school that was located in one of the cottages in Monkstown was too small. The future of the school, and the church, in this developing community was to be greatly influenced by Rev. Robert Williamson, minister of Collessie. Before entering the ministry he had been tutor in the families of Sir Robert Calder and William Johnston of Lathrisk. With this background it is not surprising that he should have an interest in the young of the parish and particularly in their education. This is why he was instrumental in founding a new school to serve the needs of the young in the area of Ladybank.[131]

The school in the home of Mr Bannerman in Monkstown, which he established in 1840, was a fee-paying school and served 25 scholars. When Mr Bannerman died in 1843, Mr James Myles of Hill Street opened another school and charged his pupils 1*d.* (penny) per week. Another in Golf Street was similar to Mr Bannerman's and Mr Myles' establishments but is more part of folk memory than included in any official records. Although these schools met the needs of the community in the early years, as Ladybank grew they became inadequate to cope with demand. Other schools in the parish included the Free Church School at Charlottetown and the Established Church school at Collessie, but these were some distance away and were limited in their capacity. Kettle, which was nearer, was also unable to take more pupils.

Towards the end of 1852 the people of Monkstown and Ladybank approached Mr Williamson, minister at Collessie, seeking his help in establishing the new school. The community comprised people of different religious persuasions and it was intended to have a school that was not connected to any particular church. There were at that time a sizeable number in the community who were members of the Free Church and the United Presbyterian Church as well as the Established Church of Scotland. Mr Williamson promised to promote their desire for the erection of the school.

In the spring of 1853, Mr Williamson found a site for the school and schoolmaster's house, but it soon became clear that subscriptions could not be found to establish an independent school. At a meeting with interested parties he explained that he would have to turn to the Established Church for the necessary funding. As a result, the school and the teacher had to be connected with the Church of Scotland. Mr Williamson then asked a friend, Dr Woodford, who was the Government Inspector of Schools, to draw up a draft constitution to guide its management. Because it needed to be a Church of Scotland school it was agreed that, in order to reflect the religious diversity of the community, membership of the Board should comprise one Heritor (the Heritors were involved in financing the project), one of the parents of the pupils and the minister,

---

[131] Scott, *Fasti Ecclesiae Scoticanae*, vol. 5

who was also to act as convener. It was to be an essential condition that the teacher be a member of the Church of Scotland. The new school was to be for both boys and girls and to include a department for sewing and knitting.

One might have supposed this to be welcomed by the community at large, but Mr John Boyd Kinnear of Kinloch, a supporter of the Free Church, was less easily pleased. He saw the activities of Mr Williamson in establishing a Church of Scotland school as trying to undermine the proposed intention of a government Bill which came before Parliament in 1854. While it would be easy to praise Mr Williamson and condemn Mr Kinnear, to fully understand the disagreement between the two men we must first understand the state of education in Scotland at that time.

After the Disruption of 1843 and the establishment of the Free Kirk, the recognised position of the Established Church in education was brought into question. From the beginning the Free Kirk set up its own schools, like the one in Collessie, and the United Presbyterians had also been running schools for some time. In addition, there was the immigration of Irish Catholics in the west of Scotland, who wanted their own schools, as well as a small number of Episcopalians who also provided education for their children. As a result, attendance at the Church of Scotland schools had, over the years, diminished and it could no longer run its own schools without government grants and inspection. Clearly the situation throughout the country was in disarray and the Lord Advocate, James Moncrieff, wanted to create non-sectarian, publicly funded schools controlled by a central authority. He brought several Bills before Parliament between 1854 and 1869. While all got the support of Scottish MPs, their English counterparts would not agree because they were afraid of a knock-on effect that would undermine the position of the Church of England. We now know that the Education Acts of 1870 in England and 1872 in Scotland brought the matter under control, but neither Mr Williamson nor Mr Kinnear had our advantage of knowing what was going to happen.[132]

Mr Kinnear was on the side of the Lord Advocate and he saw Mr Williamson as one trying to perpetrate a system that was no longer viable. The two men clashed publicly through the pages of the *Fife Herald*. Mr Boyd Kinnear's concern was that Ladybank School 'has connected itself, wholly and forever, with the Established Church of Scotland. It has made itself even worse than Parish schools; for the Government cannot touch this Ladybank School, which is to be coeval with the Establishment itself, and to be sectarian as long as that sect calling itself the Church of Scotland is established!' He then went on to make a personal attack by calling Mr Williamson a 'shrewd minister of the obscure parish of Collessie', and charged him with devising the constitution of the school in such a way that government reforms could not change its relationship with the Established Church of Scotland. A personal letter to Mr Williamson, as well as public communications, accused him of deception. This was seen as a libel and the matter came to court in Perth in September 1854.

---

132 Smout, *A Century of the Scottish People*

The people of the area were well pleased with the arrangements for the new school and supported Mr Williamson wholeheartedly. This is made evident by the fact that a number of residents of Monkstown and Ladybank attended the court in Perth in support of Mr Williamson. They consisted of four members of the United Presbyterian Church, two members of the Free Church and one member of the Established Church. They made it clear that at no point had they been deceived about the proposed constitution of the new school and that the community were fully supportive of it.[133]

Mr Kinnear dropped his allegations and Mr Williamson was cleared of all charges against him. There can be no doubt that the ties with Collessie were strong and that the Established Church still had an important role to play in the developing community of Ladybank. The project progressed unhindered throughout 1853. The school was erected on the same site as the present primary school, which over the years has been expanded to cope with the rising population and developing needs of education.[134]

The School, Ladybank

The school became known as Ladybank Madras School. This curious name was widespread throughout Fife with establishments at St Andrews, Cupar and Auchtermuchty as well as Ladybank. The name reflects the system of education that was devised by a St Andrews man, Rev. Dr Andrew Bell. Having become a clergyman in the Church of England, he was sent, as chaplain, to a regiment of the East India Company based in Madras. While there his duties included teaching the children of the soldiers. Teachers were in short supply and so he used older boys who had received instruction to pass on their knowledge to younger boys. He found this method to be so successful that when he returned to Fife he used his considerable wealth to found schools that adopted his ways. This was a popular method and became widely used across the county.[135]

---

[133] *Fife Herald, and Kinross, Strathearn, and Clackmanan Advertiser* 28th September 1854
[134] Calley, *Collessie: A Parish Alphabet*
[135] www.madras.fife.sch.uk/

In November 1857 we read in the *Fife Herald* the third annual report of the Ladybank Madras School. There were 166 pupils on the roll, but the greatest number present on any one day was only 138. Fees, which amounted to £45, were paid regularly by the parents. A third pupil teacher was appointed as a result of a rising roll and the head teacher, Mr Graham, received the unqualified support of the managers. One of the managers donated £50 for the purpose of creating 'a female industrial department'. This was to teach girls to sew and knit, important tasks for aspiring wives and mothers and stated as necessary by those who established the school. The report added that such education was important at Ladybank because most of the 1,500 people who lived there were employed as handloom weavers. The variety of religious denominations was celebrated. Ninety inhabitants of the district contributed to an annual payment of £5 as part payment of the salary of the schoolmistress. This amounted to a considerable financial commitment accepted by the community at large and reflects the widespread support for the school. The article concluded with a plea for greater financial support from the Heritors. It is pointed out that, while elsewhere parents meet only a quarter, one third, or even one fifth of the cost, the parents in Ladybank were meeting half of the cost of education in the community. It was to be another 15 years before the Education Act would remove this burden from the families.

An Act was passed by Parliament in 1872 which made school attendance compulsory between the ages of 5 and 13. It also removed parochial responsibility for education. This displeased the reverend gentlemen of Cupar Presbytery and they are recorded in the minute of 3rd December 1872 as lamenting the 'dissolving of the connection which from the time of the Reformation has subsisted betwix the Parish Schools and the Courts of this Church'. They remind the Church that the 'Godly upbringing of the Young has always been and still is one of the most important objects of the Church'. I am sure the majority of members today would concur that the Kirk has retained its responsibility for the young. On the other hand, few have regretted the passing of the responsibility for education to the state. It was not long before illiteracy rates began to drop across the country as a whole. It soon became clear that the majority of folk in the community could no longer be expected to follow the example of 28 stalwarts that travelled the three miles, twice each Sunday, to attend church in Collessie. Even the shorter distance to Charlottetown for Free Church members was becoming difficult to sustain. Kettle was nearer but it belonged to a different parish; nevertheless, 90 members of the Established Kirk travelled the mile across the River Eden. Any United Free Church members in Ladybank would also find their way to Kettle on Sunday mornings.[136]

Ladybank: A Growing Community

By 1866 Ladybank was the post town for the parish of Collessie – no doubt its proximity to the railway gave it that distinction – with Mr James Crombie the postmaster. Post

---

[136] Calley, *Collessie: A Parish Alphabet*

was delivered by 'a walking postman' who left the Post Office at 9 a.m. and made deliveries along a route through Edentown and Giffordtown to Collessie. On his return he left Collessie at 2.55 p.m. and arrived at Ladybank in time for the afternoon dispatch at 4.05 p.m. At the time Ladybank was boasting one shoemaker, three builders, a carter, two china merchants, two dressmakers, six grocers, three joiners, two sawmills, two vintners, including Mrs Elder of the railway refreshment rooms, a railway contractor, auctioneer, tailor and Wilson and Hill, Hand & Power Loom Linen Manufacturers. There can be little doubt that the community was growing rapidly. With three builders, there must have been a bit of a local building boom as Ladybank expanded.[137]

This first photograph shows the Royal Hotel standing on the corner of Commercial Road and Victoria Road, just opposite the station. This was built for a Newburgh man, Baillie Taylor, who became Provost of Ladybank in 1910. On the ground floor were shops with the hotel on the upper level. Built in 1877, it was a substantial building with ornate panels and mouldings. Although an important landmark in the town, it was destroyed by fire in 1968. The building was then completely redesigned as flats and it no longer bears any resemblance to the feature that once stood there.

Ladybank was well served with shops. Pictured below is William Law on Commercial Road. This was the sort of shop that could provide almost anything anyone could want. Groceries, ironmongery, boots and shoes, ladies under- and overgarments, not to mention the linoleum and baskets behind the lady at the door. William Law, Sandy Scott's (see Chapter 3 on Kettle) maternal great-grandfather is standing second from the right. The other people are not known to the author.

William Law's shop on Commercial Road

---

137   Trades & Professions Directory for Fifeshire 1866

According to the Ordnance Survey map, Ladybank lies at a height of only 41 metres (about 133 feet) above sea level. Those who live in the town know that drainage problems follow from being at such a low elevation. About 1879 it was decided to improve the storm drainage system and redirect water that flowed continuously from artesian wells. The plan was to dig a ditch from the station through Ramornie Estate to the River Eden. A large number of men were employed in this undertaking and the greatest difficulty they encountered was getting sufficient gradient to ensure a free flow to the river. Indeed, it was feared that if this was not done properly there was a danger of the Eden flowing up the drain in time of spate and causing flooding in Ladybank. In fact, their fears were unnecessary for this never happened. The ditch was lined with 20-inch glazed fireclay pipes, more than adequate for the task they had to undertake.

At about the same time it was realised that the railway bridge built in 1846 was too low and too narrow to allow the free flow of horse-drawn vehicles on the road to Pitlessie and Kettle. The decision was made to build a new bridge some 60 feet south of the existing one. The old stone bridge was only 8 feet 6 inches high and 11 feet wide. The new girder bridge would give a clearance of 14 feet with a width of 20 feet. In order to achieve the greater height it was necessary to excavate under the railway. The spoil from this was dumped nearby where the Coronation Park stands today. The old bridge became the pedestrian subway that connects the two platforms. The present reduced dimensions of the bridge were created when it was lined with bricks.

With the increased rail traffic passing through Ladybank the steam engines created a great demand for water. By the 1870s this demand reached about 54,000 gallons each day. Existing water supplies were inadequate and it was necessary to sink wells to reach untapped supplies. This was more than adequate for the job. Because of the geology they were all artesian wells requiring no pump to access the water.

There was a downside to the combination of artesian wells and industrial expansion and that was contamination. As artesian wells were supplying domestic as well as industrial water the local authority decided that a supply should be found that could be piped to all houses in Ladybank. Boring began in 1906 at the north end of Golf Street and soon a good supply of clean water was located. The following year the plans for a water tower were approved and the pumps for it were to be driven by a wind-operated mechanism situated on top of the tower. Two large tanks were housed in the upper part of the tower which gave a gravity supply to every house in the town. It was not until after World War II that an electric pump was installed.[138]

Ladybank water tower

In 1975 it became obsolete when a regional water supply took over.

---

[138] Calley, *Collessie: A Parish Alphabet*

A Free Kirk

As a popular rhyme from times past goes:

> *The Auld Kirk, the cauld Kirk*
> *The Kirk that has the steeple.*
> *The Free Kirk, the wee Kirk*
> *The kirk wi' a' the people*

As we saw in the section on Collessie, with the Disruption of 1843 Rev. John. McFarlane, minister of Collessie, led a very large part of the congregation there to form a breakaway Free Church in Giffordtown, which became known as 'the kirk in the wood'. A year later he became minister of Dalkeith and Rev. William Reid arrived. The work started by Mr McFarlane of building a church, manse, school and house for the schoolmaster became his to complete. Ten years later Mr Reid died suddenly in the manse at the age of 61. The sadness of the congregation at losing such a faithful friend and pastor is recorded in the Kirk Session minutes. The next minister was Rev. John Anderson, who remained for 11 years, being followed by Rev. James Cameron, who was transferred to Pathhead Church, Kirkcaldy. In November 1870 Rev. Hugh Ross was ordained as minister at Giffordtown.

Mr Ross found himself to be the last minister at Giffordtown and the first in the Free Kirk at Ladybank. As the new railway town grew in size and importance, so the Giffordtown Church found itself with an ever larger part of its congregation having to walk from Ladybank on Sunday morning. The church at Giffordtown was also in need of costly repairs and building a new church made sense. The plan was to erect a building that could provide seating for 600–700 people.[139]

Rev. Hugh Ross

It was in 1872 that the idea of moving was first raised. In May 1874 the *Fife Herald* reported that a subscription had been opened to fund the project and, in a few days, £1,000 was raised and soon a piece of ground found in Ladybank. It extended to about an acre in area with room for a church, manse, garden and glebe. On Saturday 13th March 1875, the foundation stone of the new church was laid by Francis Brown Douglas of Edinburgh. It was positioned just below the sill of the large window above the main entrance. A sealed glass bottle was placed in a cavity in the stone containing information about the origin of the congregation, a list of office bearers and workers as well as coins, local newspapers and a photograph of the minister, Hugh Ross. A glass tube containing documents placed in the foundation stone of the Giffordtown Kirk was also placed in the stone at Ladybank.

---

[139] *Fife Herald* Thursday 21st May 1874

Later that year, as the church was in process of being built, a grand bazaar was held in the Corn Exchange in Cupar to increase funds. It was hoped to raise sufficient to clear the debt before the new building was opened. The band of the *Mars* training ship in Dundee was present for the two days the event was running. The North British Railway Company sold tickets in all classes and from all stations in the country to Cupar at the full price plus 25 per cent. Presumably the 25 per cent went to the new church building.[140] Another bazaar in 1876 brought in £530 after expenses were paid. Although the church opened in 1876 it was not until 1879 that it could be reported that the total cost of £2,600 had been cleared. Generous donations by Mrs Haig and Miss Walker of Pitlair brought the finances into credit. So, in spite of the rhyme above, the Free Kirk had a steeple and, with hot water central heating from pipes under the aisles, it certainly was not the 'cauld Kirk'.

The historic connection of Ladybank with the Abbey of Lindores was maintained in the name, St Mary's Free Church. The following year work commenced on building a new manse next to the

St Mary's Free Church and manse some time after 1900

church. The estimated cost was £900. At this time the minister, Mr Ross, continued to live in the manse at Giffordtown until the new manse was ready for him.

The interior of St Mary's Church, Ladybank

---

140 *Dundee Courier* Friday 17th September 1875

In October 1883 the Free St Andrews Church, Kilmarnock, decided to call Rev. Hugh Ross to fill the vacancy in their charge. Mr Ross accepted the call and in December 1883 the folk of Ladybank said a sad farewell to their minister. Hugh Ross had been both friend and support as well as pastor to the folk during an exciting time in the life of the church. His 13-year ministry saw a new church and manse built in an expanding community and the Collessie Free Church (the name still linked it to Collessie) was looking very positively to the future. Mr Ross was presented with a marble clock and Mrs Ross received a silver salver.[141]

At a meeting of the Free Kirk Presbytery and members of the congregation on 2nd April 1884, it was decided to call Mr Peter Carmichael Stewart, a probationer in a Dundee church. Of the 212 members of the congregation 159 (including 15 adherents) were present and their decision was unanimous. In 1892 he married Mary Jane Crichton, daughter of Thomas Crichton, Roslea House. The church was packed for the wedding with standing room only in the gallery.[142]

It was during Mr Stewart's ministry that the church found itself in need of a new organist. Music had played an important part in the life of the Free Church in recent years and it was necessary to find a reliable and capable

Rev. Peter Carmichael Stewart

replacement. One person to come forward was Robert Carswell, who was known to Rev. James Bell, minister of the Free Church in Auchtermuchty. This letter was sent to Mr Stewart in support of the application:

> Mr Robt. Carswell, who is applying for the post of organist, has been known to me from his earliest years, and I have much pleasure in bearing testimony to his irreproachable moral character, and fitness from this side to occupy this responsible position. He is also well fitted by training in recent years for the technical work, and his diligence in study is ever improving his technique. He has for the past year taken turns with others in playing the organ in my congregation, and his services have been much appreciated. I wish him all success, & I am sure he will give satisfaction where he may be appointed. James Bell B.D.

This was to prove a long and fruitful relationship between Mr Carswell and the Free Kirk. In the fullness of time he became green convener of Ladybank Golf Club, a position which earned him the respect and affection of the members. In time the Carswell family home was built in Golf Street, where his daughter Margaret still lives.

Ladybank in 1888 was not free from crime. One young man was sentenced to five years' imprisonment for breaking into the Free Kirk in Ladybank and stealing £1 5s. from the 'missionary boxes'. Another was sentenced at the same court for stealing 15s. from a woman at Ladybank station and got 18 months' imprisonment as a result.

---

141   *Dundee Courier* Friday 21st December 1883
142   *Dundee Courier* 29th April 1892

Mr Stewart was to remain in the charge for 20 years until 1904. His resignation, reported in the *Courier* on 27th April, was a matter of great regret for many in the congregation. Only seven years earlier Mr and Mrs Stewart were presented with gifts by the members of the church because of the esteem in which Mr Stewart was held. In 1904 a petition was drawn up trying to persuade him to change his mind. His decision was made, however, and we are told it was for family reasons.[143]

Rev. David Affleck

This left the church in vacancy, but not for long. On the evening of 5th July a unanimous decision was made on the election of the new minister, Rev. David Affleck. This was to be the start of a very long relationship between Mr Affleck and the people of Ladybank and the Howe of Fife. According to the *Courier* of 29th August 1904 Mr Affleck not only had a striking personality but at six foot four inches had a commanding physical presence also. Mr Affleck married Sarah Currie in 1910 and two years later his daughter Margaret was born. The minister's daughter too was to become an important person in the congregation, becoming organist in January 1931. While this appointment might, at first sight, appear to be inspired by her father's position as minister of the church, to draw such a conclusion would be very unfair to Miss Affleck. There is no doubt she was a very capable musician, passing an important national exam on musical theory at the age of 16 in 1928 and being awarded LRAM in 1932.[144] As a result of this her contribution to the musical life of the church was considerable. In 1938 she became head of music at Madras College in St Andrews.

The Parish Kirk

By 1885 the status of Ladybank in the *Trades & Professions Directory for Fifeshire* had changed markedly. It was no longer listed under Collessie but alongside Kettle. Collessie is named along with Cults and Pitlessie as a sub-heading and we are told that these places, and Kettle, have the postal address 'near Ladybank'. As its importance grew, so did its size and the variety of trades and services available in the town. Now, in addition to a baker, two boot and shoemakers, 10 grocers (including William Wann, a beer retailer), there were the Royal Hotel and the Railway Hotel, the Union Bank of Scotland, various drapers, malsters, dressmaker, doctor Laidlaw, and James Bell the chemist. It even boasted a public hall, School Board, stationmaster and Free Church. There is, however, no mention of an Established Church in Ladybank.

This lack of a church was brought to the attention of Dr Williamson, the Collessie minister, in July 1878. A petition by 250 Ladybank folk was brought to their parish minister to ask for his help to build a church in the village. Dr Williamson tabled the petition at Presbytery, along with a sketch plan of the proposed church and written

---

[143] *Dundee Courier* 27th April 1904
[144] *Dundee Courier* Tuesday 20th September 1932

answers to queries sent down by the Home Mission Committee, following an application for a church building grant. After giving the matter due consideration Presbytery resolved to back the plan for the new church in Ladybank.

The Kerr Memorial Church from Well Road with the Spire of St Mary's Church just to the left

Interior of Ladybank Parish Church, later known as the Kerr Memorial Church

Building started in May 1881 and took 14 months to complete. The cost of £5,600 came from Church of Scotland Home Mission and various endowment schemes, the Baird Trust and donations by many well-wishers. Among the private donors was Dr Williamson himself, who is reputed to have contributed £2,000 to the scheme.[145]

On 24th January of the following year William Wallace from Newton of Collessie represented Dr Williamson at Presbytery when he presented a petition concerning the creation of an endowment of a new parish of Ladybank. He tabled a draft constitution, a plan of the proposed boundaries of the parish and a certificate of intimation of disjunction that would separate Ladybank and district from Collessie parish, which had been drawn up at Collessie Church. Presbytery approved the proposed disjunction and set in motion the procedure that would lead to an Act of Parliament that brought this into effect.

In June of that year a decree of the Court of Teinds was presented to Presbytery confirming the disjunction from Collessie: 'the Church of Ladybank and district attached thereto are hereby recognised as a Church and Parish *quoad sacra* within the bounds.' The term *quoad sacra* is often referred to as the model constitution. This is

---

[145]   Scott, *Fasti Ecclesiae Scoticanae*, vol. 5

the sort of church that until recently had become the 'normal' pattern, with the Kirk Session being responsible for spiritual matters in the congregation and a Congregational Board with responsibility for the temporal aspects of the life of the congregation. The Howe of Fife Parish Church was, until recently, a *quoad sacra* church.

In the past the Kirk Sessions had sole responsibility for all aspects of the church's life, spiritual and temporal. This was known as a *quoad omnia* church, which means 'responsible for all things' and has strong parallels to the more recent innovation, popular with many Church of Scotland congregations and recently adopted by the Howe of Fife, the unitary constitution. *Quoad sacra* churches were the exception in Cupar Presbytery in the 19th century but the preferred option when new churches were established. As a result, in addition to Ladybank, the churches at Springfield and Freuchie were the only others at that time. These churches were monitored carefully by Presbytery and annual reports given by a committee established to oversee them. The main concern was that the fabric of the buildings was maintained in good repair.

On 9th July 1882 the new church was opened and received its bell from Mr and Mrs Tullis of Rothes, Markinch. The guest minister, Rev. Dr James McGregor of St Cuthbert's, Edinburgh, 'preached a most picturesque and attention-riveting sermon of eighty minutes on the subject of Public Worship'. Well, at least the congregation got its money's worth! By all accounts it was a very warm day and one gentleman in the congregation had walked a considerable distance. When the long sermon had reached its conclusion and the congregation rose to sing, his back stuck to the varnish of the pew. His comment was, 'My Sunday coat was ruined, but I had the consolation of having been, for once, very closely connected with the Church of Scotland!'[146]

Dr Williamson was pronounced Moderator of the charge until such time as a minister could be found. This did not take long because on 13th September Dr Williamson tabled an appointment by the trustees of the parish of Ladybank in favour of **Robert Hagart Kerr**. Accompanying this was a call in favour of Mr Kerr which 134 parishioners had signed in support. There was also a letter accepting the call from Mr Kerr. Before ordination could take place all applicants for ordination had to undergo 'The Trials'. This was an examination of the candidate's knowledge and abilities and was undertaken by Presbytery. Mr Kerr passed with the unanimous agreement of Presbytery and ordination took place at Ladybank on 5th October 1882 at 12 noon.[147]

Rev. Robert Haggart Kerr

One month later a meeting took place between Mr Kerr and his assessors, who included Rev. Aeneas Gordon of Kettle. The new minister's first responsibility was to constitute a Kirk Session and to this end the congregation were asked to give the

---

[146] *The Presbytery of Cupar Magazine* July 1882
[147] Register of the Proceedings of the Presbytery of Cupar from 17th March 1863 – 24th January 1882 & 1882–1910

names of up to nine suitable people. The ordination of A. Henderson, A. Webster, T.M. McLaggan, Walter Williamson, William Williamson, J. Crombie and J. Simpson took place on 3rd December 1883. Kirk Session meetings seem to have been called as and when it was considered necessary. This was still the time when people were called before the elders and reprimanded for 'pre-nuptial fornication'. It appears that this, and increasing the roll, were the main occupations of the Kirk Session at that time. In May 1886 it is noted that the gallery was available for public worship, but it was not until 1889 that the matter of instrumental music was considered. This gained the approval of both the Session and the congregation, and so in February 1890 an organ, costing less than £35, was purchased and installed. One must assume that someone played the organ during the first three years but it was not until February 1893 that Alice Anderson was appointed organist.

The Golf Course

Ladybank Golf Club was formed in the Royal Hotel on 23rd July 1879. The original six-hole course was laid out by the legendary Tom Morris. It was subsequently extended to a nine-hole course in 1910 and then in May 1961 the 18-hole course was opened.

Over the years Ladybank Golf Club has been very much on the golfing map, especially since 1978 when it was first chosen as a final qualifying course for the Open Championship at St Andrews. Many well-known golfers have played there including Bernard Langer, Sam Torrance, Ian Woosnam, Jack Nicklaus and Seve Ballesteros. Jack and Seve played an exhibition match there in 1983. Both were made honorary members and their photograph hangs proudly in the clubhouse.

The Burgh O' Ladybank

As Ladybank continued to grow in the closing years of the 19th century, so its importance increased. In 1900 it received burgh status and had a Town Council with baillies, councillors and a Provost; Mr James Crichton was the first. It also had a Burgh Seal, which was approved by the Lord Lyon. Prior to the Town Councils (Scotland) Act of 1900 the town had operated as a police burgh when responsibility for running the town was in the hands of elected police commissioners.

It was also in 1900 when the recently formed Fifeshire Auction Company acquired a site close to the railway, on Golf Street. This was an extensive market where cattle, sheep, pigs and horses were sold. The site included a slaughter house, stables and byres.

The railway was responsible for the town becoming increasingly busy. A linen factory had been opened in 1853 where cheap coarse linen was produced for export to America. During World War I a type of canvas called 'tent duck' was produced for the forces. At its peak the factory employed 100 people, mostly women, and it remained an important source of employment until 1932 when it closed down. On a smaller scale, but still noteworthy, was the Ladybank Lemonade Works, which opened in 1909. The town was chosen for this venture because the recently opened water works, which centred on the water tower on the corner of Golf Street and The Beeches, provided a reliable source of good-quality water. The factory employed about seven women up to the end of World War II but production soon stopped in the mid 1940s and the building became a store for bottles of lemonade and similar products manufactured in Kirkcaldy and Dunfermline.

Life in Ladybank Quoad Sacra Church

In 1903 a Bible Class was established, supervised by the minister. A few years earlier the Sunday School 'lady teachers' were asked to collect subscriptions to meet the cost of the 'annual trip to Ramornie'. In June 1911 the General Assembly instructed all churches to hold a 'Coronation Service' on 22nd June to celebrate the coronation of King George V. All the local public bodies were invited to this mid-week service in the Parish Church. Mr Affleck of St Mary's was not best pleased about this arrangement and wrote to Mr Kerr claiming that a previous agreement had decided that St Mary's would be used for the next coronation. Presumably the Parish Church had performed a similar service when King Edward VII was crowned in 1902, but there is no mention of that in the minutes. The Session decided to continue with their arrangements and, presumably, they went ahead.

Communication and cooperation between the two Ladybank churches was normally healthy. In March 1913, for example, when the Town Council of Ladybank was considering adoption of the Shop Hours Act and its effect on Sunday opening hours, the two Kirk Sessions made joint representation. It was their hope that all places of business would be closed. In fact the Kirks were misinformed and a subsequent letter from the Council assured them that the Act was not under consideration. They had decided to recommend that places providing refreshment should close at 10 p.m. during the week and 9 p.m. on Sunday. Clearly this referred to bars and public houses and the Kirk Sessions agreed that this was a step in the right direction.

On another occasion, in 1915, St Mary's initiated a proposal that it, together with the Established Church and the churches at Collessie, Kettle parish and United Free, as well as Balmalcolm, would make strong representation to the North British Railway Company to curtail or cease work on the agreed Sunday in order to allow members to attend communion. They believed that by acting together they would promote a spirit of unity in the area that would have a positive moral effect in the district. This was agreed and they sent representatives to a meeting. The Sunday chosen for this communion was Easter Sunday, with the intention of holding a service of preparation on Good Friday. While the North British Railway Company did not cooperate with the request, the sense of goodwill and unity engendered throughout the parishes was very positive.

Apart from one or two entries, we read little about the war in the Kirk Session minutes. One record dated 1916 informs us that members of the Ayrshire Yeomanry, who were billeted at Annsmuir, came to worship on Sunday mornings; another that Mr Kerr had assisted in communion at the Annsmuir Camp when 44 men attended.

Later in the same year we learn of the change in timing of the evening service to 3 p.m. in order to comply with government lighting restrictions. In 1919 Provost Sime offered a clock, to be installed in the church, to commemorate the signing of the peace at Versailles. The Kirk Session accepted this gift gratefully and it was duly installed the following July. The clock bore the inscription: 'Presented by Provost and Mrs Sime to the Minister and Kirk Session of Ladybank Parish Church to commemorate the end of the Great War by the signing of peace at Versailles on June 28th 1919.'

A War Memorial for Ladybank

A significant year in the history of Ladybank was 1921, for it was on Sunday 13th November that the war memorial was unveiled. Provost Crichton chaired the War Memorial Committee and the site chosen, close to the station, is prominent.[148]

An Aberdeen granite cairn with a Celtic cross rises to a height of 16 feet 5 inches backed by a 6-foot high wall. In 1929 this was lowered because it was seen as obstructing the view of drivers. The memorial was designed by Mr C.G. Campbell of Methil and carved and built by Mr J.Y. Thomson of Leven. On that November afternoon a large crowd gathered with four clergymen: R.H. Kerr, John Henderson of Collessie, David Affleck of the United Free Church and Canon G.W. Paterson. Mrs Millbank Leslie Melville of Melville House unveiled the memorial; the Town Clerk read the names of the fallen; pipers played a lament and the last post was sounded.

When the provost accepted the memorial on behalf of the town Council, the Ladybank and District Choral Union sang the Hallelujah Chorus and many wreaths were placed at the memorial. This was an important day in the life of Ladybank; a small town that lost so many of its young men. Almost 100 years later, the ceremony is repeated annually.[149]

Also in 1921 problems with the manse emerged. Apart from the fact that the title deeds were lost, and remained lost for some time, repairs were needed. The windows required painting on the outside, while the kitchen range was in need of maintenance.

---

148   *Dundee Evening Telegraph* Friday 16th September 1921
149   *Dundee Courier* Monday 14th November 1921

There was broken plaster in the ceilings of the porch and washhouse and the boiler flue was in need of overhauling. There was also a large upper pane in the staircase window that was broken. It was necessary for the Clerk to draw attention of this to the trustees of Ladybank with the intention of having the repairs carried out.

In October 1924 Mr Kerr intimated that, owing to an infection of the throat and nervous debility, he intended retiring after 42 years. The Kirk Session agreed to disband evening services to lighten his load so that he could continue. While Mr Kerr continued for a time, he seemed unable to go on indefinitely and on 10th February 1925 he made an application to the Aged and Infirm Minister's Fund and sought Presbytery's support.

In April of the same year it was reported that Mr Kerr had been awarded £135 plus £22 for long service on condition that he retire not later than 15th June.

In May the Presbytery Clerk read a letter from Mr Kerr asking to be relieved of his charge as soon as possible and Presbytery agreed, so Mr Kerr retired on 18th May. He received a certificate allowing him to retain his full status as a minister of the Church of Scotland and a Presbyterial certificate confirming that his conduct was, in every respect, becoming of his profession. In July the Kirk Session received a letter from their minister gifting his late wife's piano to the church, especially for the use of the Women's Guild.

Mr Kerr left the folk of Ladybank and moved to Southampton where he died on 2nd December 1927. The following tribute was delivered to Presbytery by Mr Glennie, his successor:

> *The Presbytery regret to record the death of the Rev. Robert Haggart Kerr M.A. late minister of Ladybank, on the second current. Mr. Kerr was ordained as the first minister of Ladybank on 5th October 1882 and retired in 1925. The situation when he came was naturally a difficult one, but Mr. Kerr made his influence felt on the virgin soil. Soon after his induction the present Communion Service was gifted by the original elders: the manse was gifted by Mr Williamson, Collessie (our mother parish) in 1885; instrumental music and a heating system were inaugurated by Mr. Kerr. The Communion Roll rose to 500; and a vigorous Woman's Guild and successful Sunday School are results of his labours. His activities were not confined to the church for he was a member of the School Board of Collessie and the local school management committee, Chairman of the Parish Council, Chaplain to Masonic Lodge King Robert the Bruce (no. 304) and an original member of the local golf, curling and bowling clubs, where he learned a new side of human life. During the War he gave valuable service as Chairman of the Military Tribunal and Joint Chaplain to the Troops in Annsmuir Camp. Although he rests in a new grave in distant Southampton, his memory is enshrined in the hearts of those he loved, for despite many grievous personal sorrows he sought to show the joy of the Gospel and the Presbytery today mourn the loss of one who never hung his head. The Presbytery expresses their sympathy to his surviving son and daughter.[150]*

---

[150] Minute of the Presbytery of Cupar 13th December 1927

A memorial service was conducted in the Parish Church by Rev. Henry Porter of Cults. The congregation, which included the local company of Boys' Brigade, was well attended as Mr Kerr was a very popular minister.

A letter was presented to the Clerk of the Presbytery in favour of calling **Mr John Douglas Glennie** BA to the church and parish of Ladybank. When Presbytery met at Ladybank to examine the call, they found it contained the names of 290 out of the 530 on the electoral register. So the appointment was sustained and Mr Glennie was found to be entirely satisfactory following his trials. On 17th September 1925 Mr Glennie was ordained and inducted as the second minister of Ladybank Parish Church.

At his first Kirk Session meeting Mr Glennie made it known that he wanted to become chaplain to Fife and Forfar section of the Territorial Army. This is not surprising when we learn that he fought in World War I from 1915 to 1919 as a Territorial and that he was wounded twice[151] and awarded three medals.[152] He welcomed plans to build a church hall for use by the Boys' Brigade and Lads' Club. He raised the subject of monthly Kirk Session meetings but agreed to have it meet as and when it was necessary.

Rev. John Douglas Glennie

Young Mr Glennie came in as something of a new broom, full of enthusiasm and trying to get things right. All church organisations had to give annual reports to the minister. It would appear this did not meet with universal approval. The Women's Guild was slow in responding to this. But John Glennie was working very hard and in February 1926 reported to Session that he had completed his first visitation of members. Moves were afoot to initiate the use of freewill offering envelopes and he was keen to establish a Girls' Guild. In the following March he received his commission in the Territorial Army. By doing this he had put himself under pressure of time through his efforts within the church and this extra responsibility. Somehow he managed to work in a private life as he courted Margaret McWhirter, who lived in Pollokshields, where he served as an assistant before coming to Ladybank. They were married the following year in June 1927.[153]

Miss Margaret M. McWhirter, Pollokshields, who married Mr Glennie in Pollokshields Parish Church

The church seemed to continue to flourish under its new minister and arrangements for a church hall were going ahead. April 1926 saw an application to Presbytery for a grant for additional endowment, £237 having been raised locally. By June plans were

---

[151] *Aberdeen Journal* 3rd October 1940
[152] *Dundee, Perth, Forfar, and Fife's People's Journal* Saturday 1st March 1930
[153] *Dundee Courier* Saturday 2nd July 1927

laid before Presbytery and those promoting the scheme were authorised to approach the Baird Trust for funds. Life in the congregation was lively and one parishioner, Isabella Duncan, described a Sunday School Picnic at Ramornie in the verse on the next page.

In spite of this, it would appear that some things were not going so well. In June 1928 the communion roll was 'purged' of members who had failed to attend communion without good reason. The number on the roll on 31st December 1927 was 474, which, on the face of it, appears very healthy, but this was 56 fewer than in 1925. We can imagine there were many folk with hurt feelings at having their names removed. It also appears that there was disagreement about the new hall.

In 1928 the *Dundee Courier* carried the strange story of Mr Glennie's disappearance. He had decided to go for a walk after taking evening service and did not return home. It was thought that he might have had some memory loss. Some recalled that he had served in the First World War and was wounded in 1916. He had been unable to return to active duty before being demobbed in 1919. The inclusion of this information suggests that some may have thought there was a connection. Just after midnight on Wednesday following, he turned up at his sister's home in Laurencekirk. He said that he had walked to Perth, taken a bus to Johnshaven and then walked to Laurencekirk.

It was apparent that the minister was unwell and he wrote to Mr Taylor of Collessie Church asking him to act as Moderator during his absence. He also asked the elders to take steps to 'clear up the Hall matters and have a hall built according to the wishes of the Session, Hall Committee and Congregation'. Perhaps the disagreements surrounding the hall had caused him stress and he wanted to be rid of the matter. In December the minister returned to his duties but he remained in Ladybank for only a few months. In April Presbytery gave him responsibility for the temperance movement in Cupar Presbytery. Taking the role seriously, he sought Session's permission to open a branch in Ladybank and they agreed. There was little time to develop this, for in September 1929 Mr Glennie was translated to West Parish Stirling and Ladybank was again in vacancy.[154]

We should remember that Mr Glennie's departure was at almost exactly the same time as the union of the Free and Established Churches and the Presbyteries. This was clearly in the minds of the reverend gentlemen when they decided to try to get the two congregations in Ladybank to unite. But this was not in the minds of the congregations. Discussions took place with the Kirk Sessions regarding a union with St Mary's. In the end it was agreed that a vote of the congregation was the only way to establish the will of the people. A vote was taken and the idea overwhelmingly defeated.

On 10th December 1929 the minutes of Presbytery show that Mr Taylor of Collessie, convener of a committee to explore this possibility of union, reported back. He declared that they had explored every avenue to pursue the union without success. The committee was of the opinion that, in effect, Presbytery had to accept the will of the people and that the congregation of the Kerr Memorial Church should be allowed to elect a minister.

---

[154] Information from Kirk Session minutes, *Dundee Courier* 30th and 31st October 1928 and Scott, *Fasti Ecclesiae Scoticanae*

The Bairns Picnic from Ladybank to Ramornie, a Poem by Isabella Duncan

Fu' bricht shone the sun on a fair summer morning,
The lintie was singin' on ilka green tree;
In oor wee cottage gairden the roses were bloomin',
While the rowan an' the clover bespangled the lea.

Bit nae sun shone brichter, an' nae bird sang blither,
An' nae flo'er in the gairden bloomed bonnier I ween
Than oor dear little bairns that have met for their picnic,
An' stan' roon the kirk door sae tidy an' clean.

Their kindly young Minister sets them in order,
An' noo they are ready tae mairch thro' the toon;
Ah ! here comes piper Braid wi' his pipes and his chanter,
This is a' that is needed their pleasure tae croon.

Noo on the green gress they sit roon in a circle,
While Kininmonth comes in tae the field wi' supplies
Then each gets their fiz, an' a big paper baggie
Fu' up tae the tap o' buns, cookies, an' pies.

Then efter that's finished they're up an' awa',
The laddies tae fitba', the lassies tae swings;
While Jenny an' Nellie assist the wee totties
Wi' lucky magroats or the auld jinger ring.

Their mithers hae left a' their dull care behind them,
An' enjoy in the frolic their bairns tae please;
They romp an' they dance an' enjoy the daffin',
While their grannies sit watchin' frae under the trees.

An' noo comes the racin'; what excitement an' hurry;
Like dogs on the leash they would like to be free.
But no, they must wait, an' be ready tae start
When Ellis has gi'en them the one, two, an' three.

Oh' its graun tae be racin' for prizes an' pennies;
See hoo their wee tootsies thud, thud ower the grun';
While ilka ane tries tae get in 'fore his neebour;
Was there e're sic a picnic o' daffin' an' fun.

Oh be kind tae the bairns, it's the day o' their summer,
The day when their sky shud be cloudless an' clear;
Then love them an' guide them, an' never refuse them
The pleasure that tae their young herts is sae dear.

An' never forget when ye pass a wee bairn,
A smile or a kind word aye brings its reward;
For as much as ye dae tae the least an' the wee-est,
Ye hae rendered yer kind deed as unto the Lord.

116

In the end, after much debate, Presbytery agreed to this and it was confirmed in a minute of the Committee on Unions and Readjustment at the next meeting. Presbytery now lifted the ban on calling a new minister and the process could begin.

Now that the union of the Established Church and the United Free Church had taken place, Ladybank had two churches of the same denomination and they had to be distinguished. In October 1929 Mr Ellis, the Session Clerk, moved that the church should take the name Kerr Memorial Ladybank in memory of their first and very popular minister. This was enthusiastically approved by the Session.[155]

Rev. John Law Smith

In June 1930 Mr Taylor laid on the table a minute of election and appointment in favour of **Mr John Law Smith** to the Kerr Memorial Church. Presbytery resolved to meet in Ladybank to examine the call and, if it was acceptable, Mr Smith would undergo his trials for ordination. The call was sustained and, following successful trials, he was ordained and inducted on 20th July 1930.

Ladybank Boys' Brigade 2nd Company c.1930
Front row – Tom Calley, George Calley, Matthew Lindsay, Alex Thomson, Philip Clacher, W, Lawrie, P. Arnot
Second Row – Ian Graham, Staff-Sergeant Faill, Lieutenant Hutchison, Captain Adams, Lieutenant Howell, Pipe Instructor Anderson, Gra ?
Third Row – Corporal Adams, Corporal Graham, P. Prentice, James Easton, George Black, John Paton, Corporal Knox, Wm Ronaldson
Fourth Row – Alex Easton, Alex Smith, Kenneth Clark, Robert Grieve, T. Cunningham, Robert Cunningham, Corporal Walker

---

[155] *Dundee Courier* 23rd September 1929

How to Build a Hall, by Isabella Duncan

When nature in bright robes was dressed,
An' simmer time was at its best,
Oor dear parson needin' rest
Jist stapt aside.
A fine young lad cam frae the west
To be oor guide.
He stappit oot tae view the laund,

The kirk an' manse baith plased him graund,
Bit when the meetin' hoose he scanned
'Twas rather small,
His fiat went forth, a mild command,
Ye'll build a hall.

Noo, tho' we're puir, we hae some grit,
We didna in oor meetin's sit
An' say, 'No, no, we ar'na fit
Tae build a hall.
Ilk ane cam oot tae dae his bit,
Baith young an' aul.

Toffee an' tablet baith were made,
Soda scones an' curran' breid,
Jars o' jam an' marmalade,
We're a' intilt,
E'en bowls o' tasty potted heid
Were made an' selt.

Mony a cockerel an' hen
Were torn ruthless frae their pen,
An' slaughtered by the haunds o' men
Tae bring in money.
An' even frae its lonely den,
Puir, timid bunny.

Then at oor sales what awfu' stocks
O' little bairns' dainty frocks,
Young ladies hose, an' auld men's socks,
We're a' displayed.
An' even a few white linen pocks
A lady made.

Pyjama suits an' camisoles,
Pullovers bricht, an' cosy shawls,
An' lots o' ladies' overalls

A' sorts an' sizes.
Load o' sticks, an' tons o' coals
Sent in for prizes

The bairn frae its mither's side
Across the road would swiftly glide,
Noo; what is that ye're tryin' tae hide
Ye little caper?
It holds it oot, an' shows wi' pride
Some silver paper.

Ye ken I telt my granny, maw,
What e'er I fund I'd gier it a'.
Its disna matter tho' its sma'
Their need'nt all.
There's bags an' bags o't sent awa
Tae build a hall.

The things we've selt this twa three year,
Somethings cheap and somethings dear,
So langs they didna interfere
Wi' oor releegin.
I canna write them a' doon here,
Their name is legion.

Bit noo I think we've made a hit,
We've gaithered sillar bit by bit,
The last time that I heard o' it
Was six hunner fifty.
Noo we hae been, ye will admit,
Eident an' thrifty.

An' noo I think oor goal is seen,
Tho' weeks an' months shud intervene,
If we're as lucky as we've been,
Its plain to all
We'll maybe hold next Hallowe'en
In oor ain hall.

Noo friens, if you'll jist let me say it,
Tho' steeps the brae an far's the gaet,
An' tho' ye may hae lang tae wait,
Advice is here.
Ne'er sit an say I canna daet,
Just persevere.

A New Hall

Meantime plans for a church hall at the Kerr Memorial were approved and Presbytery attested an application for a grant from the Home Mission Committee. Three months later, on 8th May 1930, a grant of £52 was awarded against the total cost of £882. The hall was opened on 14th December 1930 with great ceremony by the Right Rev. Dr Bogle, Moderator of the General Assembly of the Church of Scotland.[156] Straight away it was decided to hold services in the hall while the church was redecorated. Two years later a special service was arranged to mark the Jubilee of the Kerr Memorial Church, it being 50 years since it was opened in 1882. Rev. Dr Patrick of Edinburgh agreed to take the service.

On the page opposite is another poem written to mark the occasion by Isabella Duncan. Surely her advice is just as relevant today as it was in the 1920s and 30s. Challenges never seem to go away, and it is up to us, God's people, to rise to them.

In 1931 both Ladybank churches sought grants for musical instruments. St Mary's wanted to refurbish its organ while the Kerr Memorial Church wanted to buy a new American organ. By September of that year the *Courier* reported that the new organ was dedicated by Rev. John Law Smith.

The opening of Ladybank memorial garden

The *Dundee Courier* of Monday 21st September 1931 recorded the opening of the memorial garden in Ladybank by Lady Haig, widow of Field Marshal Haig. The garden, designed by Ramornie's head gardener, Mr D. McKenzie, was laid out by ex-servicemen and is situated behind the war memorial. About 70 ex-servicemen attended and there was a good representation of the great and the good of north-east Fife. Both noble and military titles were in abundance as well as two sheriffs and the Dean of Guild from Cupar, provosts from around the area and some from further afield, whose presence remained unexplained. Colonel Hutchison was proud to speak for the local

---

156 *Dundee Evening Telegraph* **Monday 8th December 1930**

ex-servicemen who created the lasting tribute to Earl Haig and who 'was a Scotsman, one of themselves, a man of Fife'. He said the memorial was well suited 'near the doors of Ramornie which he knew so well'. Lady Haig named it the Douglas Haig Garden and asked the locals to care for it.[157]

In December 1933 Presbytery agreed to the appointment of women to the diaconate on the same basis as men and at the same time removed the barrier of their eligibility to the eldership on the grounds of sex. At the same meeting, however, they unanimously disapproved the admittance of women to the General Assembly as corresponding members. While the Kirk was beginning to tackle sexual inequality, it had a long way to go, for it was not until 1968 that women were ordained as ministers. Cults was the first of the Howe of Fife churches to agree to the ordination of women as elders in 1945, but Kettle and Ladybank did not achieve that degree of equality until the 1960s.

In February 1935 there was a visitation to the Kerr Memorial Church and it was discovered that the titles for the property could not be found. The following month the Secretary to the General Trustees wrote to Presbytery giving particulars as to the titles and so that concern was laid to rest.

Mr Smith, the minister, was having health problems. In July 1934 he wrote to Presbytery with his resignation 'for health reasons'. Presbytery reacted as it always does at such times and a small number approached Mr Smith to discuss the situation. As a result of this he withdrew his resignation in July and instead sought sick leave. This was granted but it was not until 15th December that he resumed his duties. It is important to note that Mr Smith's offer of resignation was viewed as a very unselfish act. His interests were with the congregation and he was placing himself in a difficult situation by resigning without any firm plans for his future. The congregation were sympathetic and supportive of their minister at this time. His return was short-lived and in March 1935 he finally resigned due to his ill health. Mr and Mrs Smith were both popular during the 5½ year ministry. The Women's Guild presented Mr Smith with a gold watch, which was accepted on his behalf by Mrs Smith, who was given a crystal vase.[158]

With the Kerr Memorial Church now in vacancy, and St Mary's so close by, readjustment was again considered. According to the *Dundee Courier*, it was Mr Affleck of St Mary's who declined offers to vacate his charge in order to make a union of the two churches possible. While one can imagine the difficulties that would have arisen in discussions about such a union, it appears to be Mr Affleck's decision that was held responsible.[159] So it was that on 8th September 1936 the schedule for the Kerr Memorial Church was laid before Presbytery and approved. In the following month, on 19th October, the congregation elected **Rev. Angus Duncan**, minister of Kilmeny, Islay. The call was considered at the following meeting and sustained. He was inducted to the charge of Kerr Memorial Church, Ladybank on 26th November 1936.

---

[157] *Dundee Courier* Monday 21st September 1931
[158] *Dundee Evening Telegraph* Wednesday 18th March 1936
[159] *Dundee Courier* Wednesday 17th June 1936

The War Years

Within a few years of Mr Duncan's arrival, Britain found itself once again in the midst of a terrible war. At this time the church continued to play an important part in the life of the community. Whist drives, parties and concerts provided entertainment and an opportunity for social gatherings. A special service was held for the Polish soldiers, who Marion Calley told me were billeted in the linen factory. In 1943 they presented a bronze plaque to the town, which was unveiled in the Burgh Chambers. The Women's Guild opened the Kerr Memorial Church hall every night running a canteen to provide tea for the soldiers, which included those billeted where Bonsford potato store once stood. The WRI met

Rev. Angus Duncan

regularly and film shows were run in the Masonic Hall for the troops. The films were up to date and sometimes the children were allowed in to see them and sometimes they were not.[160] Collections took place around the town to raise money for 'comforts for the soldiers'. Major events were held annually supporting the armed services. Each had a slogan and there was a parade with the Guides, Boys' Brigade and other voluntary organisations that raised money for the 'comfort fund'.

Presbytery instructed congregations to organise 'Fife Fighting Parties' and they were encouraged to form 'War Savings Groups'. A committee was created to advise Kirk Sessions on war damage insurance, and ministers were requested to avail themselves to the local authority to bring comfort to any made homeless due to bombing. The warden for the district had suggested that the Kirk should have a ladder for fire-fighting. It was agreed to arrange for a 21-foot ladder that would reach the roof of both the church and the manse.

Evacuees arrived at the station in Ladybank and they were given accommodation at Kinloch House and in more humble homes in the town. Marion Calley remembered that these children were taken to the church hall and local folk came and chose the ones they wanted to take home. Marion particularly remembered one black girl who was left until everyone else had been chosen. These children from the big cities attended the school in Ladybank and mixed well with the local children. Annsmuir was the site of a prisoner of war camp and so 'the enemy' could be observed by the locals.

In March 1940 Mr Duncan informed Presbytery that he had been offered and accepted the position of 'Hut Leader' in the north-west of Scotland, subject to Presbytery's approval. The Kirk Session was agreeable provided Presbytery arranged cover for the period of Mr Duncan's absence. The discussion that followed revealed concern that the congregation of the Kerr Memorial Church should be properly served during Mr Duncan's absence. Presbytery was, of course, very aware of the need many

---

160   Marion Calley, Giffordtown, personal communication

ministers had to contribute in some way to the war effort. As a result, a committee was formed to see how best the Ladybank folk could be cared for without their minister. At the April meeting six months' leave of absence was granted to Mr Duncan. Presbytery had consulted with the National Service Committee of the Church of Scotland and the terms of Mr Duncan's release were agreed. The purpose of the approval was to undertake 'hut and canteen duties' in service of the forces, for a period of six months. During that time Mr Flint of Kettle was to act as Moderator and a Mr Ewan McLean was appointed locum. Mr Duncan received a grant of £78 from the National Service Committee, which he used to pay the locum. The arrangement suited the congregation and in September 1940 we find in the *Courier* an account of a presentation made by the 'canteen workers of the Women's Guild' to Mr McLean. Mrs Wotherspoon presented him with a wristwatch and it was an opportunity for a social gathering.

It was also in 1940 that Presbytery asked the Kirk Session to consider a resolution regarding declining church attendances. The following conclusions were reached: 'A call should be made to faithful members to make public and private worship a matter of conscience'. Clear and positive preaching from the pulpit was required and in the Young Communicant Class, Bible Class and Sabbath School. Also parents were exhorted to fulfil their vows and teach their children by 'precept and example the truths of our religion'. It was also decided that a more frequent and faithful visitation of parishioners, especially the sick and aged, and cultivation of a spirit of Christian brotherhood within the congregation and community should draw people into the Christian fellowship.

When the war ended in 1945 the first Ladybank prisoner of war to come home was Jackie Hepburn. He arrived at the station on the 10.30 train and was given a hero's welcome by the whole community. Jack had served with the Royal Artillery and was taken prisoner at Tobruk in June 1942. Before the war he worked in the military store and lived with his aunt, Mrs Duff, in Melville Road.[161] Sadly, Mrs Duff died the following year but at least she had lived to see her nephew's return.

Resentment began to grow against the German prisoners of war who were kept in the local camp. Ladybank folk resented them filling the morning buses, making it difficult for the locals to find suitable transport. There was also a letter in the *Courier* in January 1947 expressing anger at a plan to provide hospitality to them in St Andrews. It took time for the folk in Fife, like those in the rest of Britain, to lose their dislike of Germans.

Strains were also occurring in the Kirk Session. In 1945 the Session Clerk and some other elders resigned without giving an explanation. The minister was unable to find a replacement and he acted as Clerk for the remainder of his time at Ladybank.

End of an Era

With the death of the Rev. David Affleck on 28th May 1946, change in Ladybank was inevitable. Mr Affleck's long ministry in St Mary's, which lasted 42 years, covered

---

[161]   *Dundee Evening Telegraph* 24th May 1945

such momentous events as two world wars and the union of the Free and Established Churches. With the two churches being close to one another, both aid-receiving, and Angus Duncan of the Established Church prepared to retire, a union was clearly in the interests of all concerned. While the Kerr Memorial had a congregation of 319, St Mary's had 209. Together they would have a congregation of 528, which Presbytery considered reasonable for one minister. At the end of September 1946 meetings were held in both churches to consider union. While the Kerr Memorial was in favour, St Mary's rejected it by a sizeable majority. This was not the first time the old Free Kirk had rejected the proposal so Presbytery decided to refer the matter to a Commission of the General Assembly.

At a special meeting held on 11th September with the congregation, proposals were drawn up jointly by the office bearers of the Kerr Memorial and St Mary's churches as well as the Presbytery Committee on Unions and Readjustment. It was agreed that the following should be recorded in the Kirk Session minutes:

> At Ladybank in the Kerr Memorial Church, the seventh day of September 1946, a duly convened meeting of the congregation was held. Present: fifty members of the congregation, with members of the Unions and Readjustments Committee of the Presbytery of Cupar. Mr Flint, Convener of the Presbytery's Committee, presided and constituted the meeting with prayer.
>
> Mr Flint gave a resume of the procedure followed by the Presbytery in consultation with the Unions and Readjustments Committee of the General Assembly since the death of Mr Affleck, minister of Ladybank St Mary's. Copies of a proposed Basis of Union for the congregations of Ladybank St Mary's and Ladybank Kerr Memorial drawn up by the office bearers of the two congregations and the Presbytery's Unions and Readjustments Committee and approved by Presbytery were submitted to the meeting. It was moved that the congregation approve the Basis of Union. The motion was seconded. There was no counter motion or amendment. On the motion being put to the vote it was carried unanimously. A draft minute of the meeting was read and approved, and the meeting closed with prayer.

In February 1947, Rev. T.J. Bunting, who was a member of the special commission appointed by the Assembly commission which had met in November 1946, reported its findings on the question of the union of the two congregations in Ladybank. In intimating the commission's decision to unite the congregations, under the name Ladybank Parish Church, Mr Bunting spoke at some length of the architect's report, and intimated that the church, hall and manse of St Mary's would be those retained for use of the united church. A revised Basis of Union was read. This was followed by another meeting when the Basis of Union was read out and the date of union was to be Tuesday 8th April 1947 at 7.30 p.m. So in the end a union did take place. This was marked by a special service. The Basis of Union stated:

- The congregation was to be named Ladybank Parish Church from 8th April 1947.
- All property and funds of each congregation would be shared equally.
- Worship was to take place in the building used by the former St Mary's congregation and the Kerr Memorial Church would be disposed of as the congregation saw fit. (This was decided by the special commission of the General Assembly, on advice from an architect.)
- The 'Bounds' were to include the united bounds of each congregation.
- The Kirk Sessions were to unite.
- The Board of Kerr Memorial Church and the Deacon's Court of St Mary's were to act as a united Congregational Board for three years, when the model deed of constitution was to be adopted.
- Rev. Angus Duncan, minister of Kerr Memorial Church, was to retire in the interests of union and the united congregation were to call a minister.
- The stipend was to be that set by the General Assembly Maintenance of Ministry Committee.
- The united congregation would readjust the arrangements under the authority of Presbytery.

The Kerr Memorial Church became a hall where youth organisations could meet. A Congregational Board was formed by the managers and deacons of both churches. After serving for three years it would be a *quoad sacra* church, adopting the model constitution. It was also agreed that the manse of St Mary's was to be used and that of Kerr Memorial sold, after Mr Duncan had been given a period of 18 months to find alternative accommodation. The proceeds of the sale were to go into a fabric fund for the maintenance of the manse. With the locum for St Mary's acting as locum for the united congregation after April 8th, it was time to seek a new minister.

The New Parish Kirk

As stated above, the union of the two churches took place on 8th April 1947. Rev. L.C. Phillips, Moderator of Cupar Presbytery conducted the service assisted by Rev. A. Duncan of Kerr Memorial and Rev. J. Henderson, Interim Moderator of St Mary's. The Presbytery Clerk read the decision of the Special Commission appointed by the General Assembly of the Church of Scotland and Mr Phillips then declared the congregations united in one church. After the service the Kirk Session met and it was agreed that the Interim Moderator of St Mary's should continue as Interim Moderator of the United Church. It was also agreed that the Kerr Memorial Church interests were not sufficiently represented on the Session and the Congregational Board would be consulted regarding appointing more Kerr Memorial elders.

Making such administrative decisions for a church and implementing them are two different things. There were those who disliked the idea of the union so much that they decided they would 'never darken the door o' the Kirk again', and many kept their word. Others did make the migration from Church Lane to the top end of Church Street, but felt their reception on arrival was less than welcoming. This was the time when, in order to maximise income, rents were charged for pews. As a result, the resident congregation did not take too kindly to these incomers occupying 'their seats'. The Kirk Session recognised the problem and sought to address it by setting aside two dates when people could come and pay their 4s. seat rent for one year. Somehow this did not resolve the matter. Feelings ran high and, as always, it took time for the 'dust to settle'. Such situations also take the exceptional qualities of a good leader.

The Ladybank folk did not appreciate how fortunate they were going to be when the *Courier* announced on Thursday 4th September 1947 the call of the **Rev. Sandy Philp**. Sandy was presented to the congregation as sole nominee with the unanimous support of the Vacancy Committee. He was duly elected by the congregation with 128 votes in favour and only 29 against the appointment. So it was that on 28th October 1947 Sandy Philp was inducted as first minister of Ladybank Parish Church.

Rev. Alexander Philp.

The time came when Mr Duncan was due to move, although he was a little delayed in order for work to be carried out on his new home. It was decided that the Kerr Memorial Church would become the Kerr Memorial Hall. To achieve this would take funds and so Presbytery was approached to have the Basis of Union changed so that money could be released from the sale of the old manse to renovate the old Kirk. This was agreed and wording was changed to read: 'The proceeds of the Manse are to be divided as follows: one third or £1,000, whichever is smaller, to be used to convert the Kerr Memorial Church into a Parish Hall and one tenth or £300 to be used to make necessary changes to St Mary's Church.'

In November 1959 the question of the records of St Mary's Church stretching back from its inception to the union of 1947 was raised. Mr Philp had searched for them including in the National Archives in Edinburgh and the special collections at St Andrews University library. Miss Affleck, daughter of the previous minister, was approached and she said her father had mislaid them one night on the way home from Presbytery where they had been taken for inspection. A search was made and the police informed but they were never found.

Soon the folk began to make the Parish Church a place where they all felt at home. In 1955 a gift to the church brought the old and the new together in the form of the lectern. The family of Margaret Fleming, a parishioner of St Mary's, had the baptismal font of St Mary's converted into a lectern for Ladybank Parish Church. This was dedicated on 18th December 1955. Mrs Brodie, widow of William, a past elder and Session Clerk from 1949 to 1958, wanted to gift a stained glass window in memory of her husband. The Kirk Session suggested, instead of one large window, three small windows in the vestibule. Mrs Brodie agreed to this and sketches by the artist William

Wilson RSA OBE were well received. The beautiful little windows in the vestibule were installed and enjoyed by those who entered the church Sunday by Sunday.

In memory of William Brodie, Elder and Session Clerk 1949 to 1958

Plans to Improve St Mary's Church

In 1959 discussions started regarding the improvement of the church. The organ had been refurbished and it was decided that it should be repositioned in the church. Lengthy discussion continued not only about the site of the organ but the position of the choir and the siting of the pulpit. There were also decisions to be made regarding the colour of the paintwork.

In spite of the many changes that took place in modernising the church, the beautiful windows in the apse remained (pictured opposite). All of this involved the Committee on Artistic Matters as well as the architect, T. Rodger of St Andrews, and a great deal of time. It was not until September 1962 that a special service of dedication took place. This was a big event with a visiting preacher and specially invited guests, including the architect and his wife, contractors and workmen.

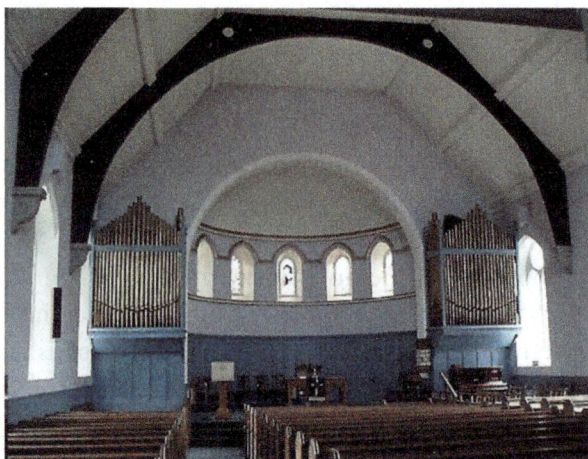

The interior of Ladybank Parish Church in about 2007

Sandy, as he was affectionately known by everyone, served Ladybank loyally for 25 years. He was ably supported by his wife, who seems to have been loved by the congregation as much as he was. When Mrs Philp died in 1976 Rev. Ian Wotherspoon, Sandy's successor, paid tribute to her in the parish magazine, *The News Review*. It is a wonderful tribute to a lady who supported her husband's ministry so well for many years: 'I have heard so much about her, her complete devotion to her duty to Church and parish, a duty which was so often made difficult by ill health, which in turn would have provided lesser souls with a valid excuse for withdrawing from all activities. Her warmth and kindness will be remembered with love and affection in Collessie and Ladybank and her memory will be honoured by all who knew her.'

Apse windows in St Mary's Church

Activities in the church blossomed with a badminton club in 1951 and a youth club, as well as an active choir under the direction of Miss Affleck, daughter of the last minister of St Mary's. Early in 1948 the vexed question of renting pews came up again at the Kirk Session. After considerable discussion it was decided to ask the congregation to choose between two possibilities, or propose something else if they preferred. The two suggestions put to congregation were (a) every family has a name on a pew but no allotted number of seats and everyone pays 4s. or (b) all names removed from pews and everyone pays 4s. At the next meeting when ballot papers were counted there was a clear preference to approved scheme (a). Somehow, in the printing of the voting papers, the pew rent increased to 5s. Sandy Philp accepted responsibility for this and it would appear there were no objections. In December the innovative Sandy suggested to the all-male Kirk Session that women be appointed to help elders in their duties. He must have been very persuasive because the proposal was passed without any dissention.

In 1952 there were plans to build a stage in the Kerr Memorial Hall and create a new doorway. These plans were approved by Presbytery and in September it was decided to hold a concert to celebrate the grand opening of the Parish Hall.

Coronation

The following year saw much excitement in the area with celebrations for the coronation on 4th June. In a competition Mr and Mrs T. Henderson were awarded the accolade of having the best-decorated house for the coronation at 14 Beechgrove. On 31st May there was a service of thanksgiving preceding the coronation in which local organisations were represented. A few days later, 7th June, Rev. Sandy Philp marked the culmination of a week of festivities in the village by dedicating the Coronation Gardens.

Graham Bell

Not everyone was completely happy with Queen Elizabeth II. Graham Bell, manager of the Royal Hotel in Ladybank, and his friend Simon Alston of Leslie, were each fined £5 for defacing a Royal Mail van at Auchtermuchty by painting out the II of the EɪɪR cipher on the side of the van and replacing it with EɪR. It was made clear at the trial that their action did not reflect negative attitudes towards the Queen. Indeed, Graham Bell had served on the Coronation Committee for Ladybank. His objection was the use of II rather than I in the cipher because she is the first Queen Elizabeth of the United Kingdom of Great Britain and Northern Ireland.[162]

In June the following year it was intimated that a Boys' Brigade company (BB) was to be formed. It was said that the Scouts were in a bad state through lack of leaders. New leaders had been appointed so it was decided not to pursue the BB idea. Life continued in the 1960s with Sandy Philp performing his duties, leading worship and conducting baptisms, funerals and weddings like the one pictured on the right of Jane and John Buchanan. The following year George Nicol was appointed superintendent of

The Buchanans at Ladybank Church on their wedding day

the Sunday School and by 1966 he was running the Bible Class.

It is in November 1968 that the proposed merger between Collessie and Ladybank is first mentioned. The Union and Readjustments Committee had approached the minister and asked if he would be willing for the union to take place. Mr Taylor was soon to retire, which would leave Collessie in a vacancy. The congregation was too small to remain independent and so union with Ladybank seemed to be the obvious way forward. Sandy Philp's answer to this request was that he had no objection so long as the office bearers and congregation of Ladybank had no objection. A subsequent

---

[162] *Dundee Courier* Friday 3rd April 1953

meeting took place with the office bearers of both congregations. The Basis of Union was read and approved. Another meeting followed which included the congregations of both churches. Again the Basis of Union was read and again there was no objection. This was an entirely happy union of Collessie, the mother Kirk, and Ladybank, the daughter Kirk. It was a happy day when on Sunday 7th January 1968 the Moderator of Presbytery proclaimed the Act of Union at morning worship in Ladybank and at the induction of Sandy Philp to Collessie Kirk in the afternoon. The name of the new congregation was Collessie and Ladybank Parish Church.

On 10th May, just four months after the union, Mr Taylor died and his wife died in October of the same year. So ended an era for the folk of Collessie. Following the union with Collessie in 1968 the new enlarged Kirk Session, complete with female members, were brought together for the photograph shown on the next page.

Sunday School teachers 1964.
Standing: George Nicol, Margaret Nicol, Bill Wanliss, Alex Easton, Doreen Clacher, Bill Harrison.
Seated: Joyce Blair, Margaret Watt, Margaret Robertson, Meg Pearson

Bible Class.
Back: Patrick Mangan, Rodney Maxwell, Alex Coull, David Norris, Keith Nicol, Forbes Catto, Graeme Halley.
Front: Lewis Hendry, ? Crawford, James Anderson, Bibby Hastings, (visitor?), Samson Hewlet, Mr George Nicol (Bible Class superintendent)

With the deaths of Mr and Mrs Taylor the Collessie manse became available to sell. Under the terms of union the funds raised from the sale of the manse were to be invested and the income from them deposited in the fabric fund. The Kirk Session applied to the trustees to change the terms of union to allow £2,000 of the £6,000 raised by the sale to be used to refurbish the Ladybank manse. This was agreed and the remaining funds were invested with the income being deposited in the fabric fund.

In 1971 the sister of the late Rev. Affleck died as well as Mrs Duncan, wife of the previous minister. Later in the year Rev. Angus Duncan also died. As old friends departed so memorials were presented to the church to ensure that they would be remembered by future generations. In 1974 two flower stands were gifted by Mrs Robertson of Cupar in memory of her mother Mrs M. Wilson. The following year the widow of John Miller, elder from 1951–1963, presented a pulpit Bible (NEV), markers, falls, a runner for the communion table and a pulpit hymnary.

Kirk Session following union with Collessie. John Watt, Hugh Munro, ???, A. Wilson, Hamish Mercer, George Skinner, George Baillie, ???, David Barclay, ???, ???, Mr Drury, Avril Corbett, John Stark, Mrs Aitken, Ian Leslie, Miss Philip(?), Bunty Watson, Mrs Komorowska, ???, Dorothy Fin(d)lay, David Maillie, Mr Patrick, George Nicol, John Adamson, WS Leslie, Mr Stark, Hugh Black, Bob Williamson, Mrs P?, Mr P?, Wull Pryde, Provost Allan, ???

A Time to Celebrate

The anniversary of Sandy Philp's induction to the parish of Ladybank was celebrated with a joint Collessie and Ladybank service and a gathering in the Lomond Hotel, Freuchie. Sandy was presented with a desk and chair and Mrs Philp (Vera) was given a cheque. Also in the picture is Miss Affleck, daughter of the former minister, organist for 42 years and head of music at Madras College in St Andrews. She received a gold watch in

recognition of her services. These were good years for the church and the parish.

Three years later Sandy retired and he and his wife moved to Upper Largo. Sadly, Mrs Philp's time there was short for she died in November 1976. Four years later Sandy too passed away in St Columba's Hospice in Edinburgh only a few days after the death of his daughter Diana, who was in the next ward. Diana left her husband 'Jock' and two boys aged 10 and 8. The whole family was loved by all who knew them and their passing was deeply mourned throughout the parish of Ladybank and Collessie. The obituary in *Life and Work* said that Mr Philp had 'the gift of making you feel you were ministering to him, rather than he to you, though in fact it was the other way round'. It concluded by saying that he represented the best in Scottish thought and character.

The retirement of Sandy in 1975 meant that the charge was once again vacant. In due course a young minister, **Rev. Ian Wotherspoon**, and his wife Rosemary started another very popular ministry in Ladybank. Mr Wotherspoon received 171 votes and a very warm welcome. His ministry was to be a time of great change in the parish.

The year after he arrived, Mr Wotherspoon proposed the sale of Kerr Memorial Church and grounds. He also proposed the sale of the Ladybank manse with the funds raised used to fund the building of a new hall and manse. While the old manse was a very fine Victorian building it was badly in need of renovation and modernisation. Heating the big old house

Rev. Ian Wotherspoon

had become a major problem and it was felt that a modern building would be more economic to run. The Kerr Memorial Hall had been allowed to reach a very poor state of repair and major work would have been required to make it suitable for purpose.

Demolition of Ladybank Church

Keystone of Kerr Memorial Church

The Session approved the plans and elder John Stark was a leading light of the project. He designed the new hall as a place where badminton and other sports that need a high ceiling could be played. The grand opening took place on 14th April 1978. A committee was appointed to oversee the event. Rev. James Cairnie of Dunlop was the guest speaker.

On 4th May 1982, much to the sadness of the Kirk Session, Mr Wotherspoon announced his intended departure at the beginning of July to allow a union with the linked charge of Cults and Kettle to take place. The Rev. Peter Wallace was to be Interim Moderator and Rev. James Turnbull, who had retired to Ladybank, was locum. At his last meeting with the Kirk Session Mr Wotherspoon warned them that the Union and Readjustments Committee would come to discuss the union with them. The sadness at losing this popular minister is clear in the tribute paid to him and recorded in the Kirk Session minutes. There we are told of 'his inspired leadership, his enthusiasm, his wit and humour, but above all that inner depth of care and concern, clothed in real feeling, which has so enriched us all in body, heart and mind'. Losing a popular minister is never a happy time. When that minister leaves in order to allow an unwanted union to take place we find it lays the foundation of unhappiness for a long time to come.

Just one month after the minister left the first of three meetings took place with the Union and Readjustments Committee under the convenorship of Rev. William Henny. The first was with the Congregational Board, the second with the united congregation of Collessie and Ladybank and the third with the congregations of Ladybank and Collessie and the linked charge of Cults and Kettle. On each occasion the draft Basis of Deferred Union was read out. The meetings with the congregations were poorly attended with only 62 at the Ladybank and Collessie meeting and 20 from Cults and Kettle. This reflected both a lack of enthusiasm for the plan and the belief that the inevitable would happen whether or not they attended.

At a meeting of 14th December 1982 the call to the Rev. Iain Forbes was intimated and that the relevant papers for members of the congregation to sign would be available in the churches on 19th December. The final entry in the Kirk Session minute book for Collessie and Ladybank was as follows:

> *The Congregations of Collessie and Ladybank were united with the neighbouring Parishes of Cults linked with Kettle to form the new charge of Howe of Fife Church. The minister called to the charge is Rev. I. M. Forbes, BSc., BD., who is to be inducted on 23rd February 1983.*

Other Churches in the Town

The Mission or Gospel Hall

The Railway Mission is a religious organisation which works in partnership with the London City Mission. It aims to provide a national chaplaincy service for the staff of the railways throughout the length and breadth of Britain. This organisation, which has been in existence for over 130 years, has chaplains in most major cities including Glasgow. From this centre the representative Christians who promoted a brand of the faith that was the same as that of the Plymouth Brethren came to Ladybank. Their aim was to set up a Mission for the many in the town who were employed on the railway.

While an exact date of the establishment of this organisation in Ladybank is not available to me, it was recorded in the *Courier* on Thursday 24th November 1904 that a meeting of the Heritors of Collessie Church took place in the Railway Mission Hall. This date is some six years earlier than that stated in the BBC Domesday project of 1986 and some 16 years earlier than other sources.

People came from different parts of Scotland and of different backgrounds to assist in the work. There was a family from Montrose and others with a Baptist background who felt the Mission could provide for their spiritual needs. The growing congregation drew upon not only those within the Ladybank community but also those from the neighbouring villages. This meant a walk of four or five miles for some and they attended worship in the wooden hut regularly and in all weathers. Cold and icy weather could give rise to frozen pipes with kitchen and toilets out of action.

Relations with other churches were always very good and the ministers of the Free and Established Churches frequently attended meetings there.

The Mission or Gospel Hall

One such meeting was the Scottish Girls Friendly Society, which met in February 1904 when both Mr Stewart of St Mary's Free Kirk and Mr Gordon of Kettle Kirk addressed the meeting. Miss Muckersie of Ladybank St Mary's began a Sunday School in the Mission Hall. This gave rise to a joint campaign of the churches in Ladybank with Commander Wolf-Murray of the Glasgow Mission playing a leading role. Even the Liberal Party held a meeting there in 1906. The work of the Sunday School has always been important for folk of all denominations in Ladybank, many being set on a road of dedicated Christian service.

While all this was taking place in Ladybank in the early years of the 20th century a Mission was also established in Kettle. Among the most active members was Miss Mary Scott, whose virtues have already been revealed in Chapter 2.

During the First World War the Railway Mission ceased to operate in Ladybank, but many who had been involved over the years continued the work in the area. After the end of the war missionary work in the area once again became active and many were attracted to the worship there. After the Second World War membership increased to about 40, mainly elderly people who had moved into the area. Believers from the small Mission in Ladybank have become active missionaries all over the world. India, New Zealand, Nigeria, South America and Canada are countries where local preachers have gone having felt called to serve the folk in these distant lands.

Today the Mission attracts a congregation from a wide area. Since the war, numbers have gone through times of increase and times of decrease. Many local folk belonging to the Parish Church find the Mission more convenient on Sundays and the weekly coffee mornings are popular. This is an opportunity for mid-week worship in addition to socialising and enjoying coffee. Whoever attends can be assured of a warm welcome.

St Mary's Episcopal Church

No history of the church in Ladybank would be complete without including what is the smallest church in Fife, St Mary's Episcopal Church, number 1 Monkstown. The Scottish Episcopal Church has had a presence in the Ladybank area since 1892. This was a time of great optimism in that church. St James the Great Church had replaced an 1818 building in Cupar in 1868.

Sister churches had developed Missions in neighbouring towns and villages leaving Kettle and Ladybank the only places available for St James to expand into. The first Mission held Sunday services in the Masonic Hall until 1897 when it moved to Kettle. Here services were conducted by the Church Army. This Anglican organisation was run rather like the Salvation Army with lay people holding positions which were given military-sounding ranks. It worked with people wherever need was identified and they were especially noted for providing for homeless men.

This continued until 1900 when the present building was acquired and converted into a church. The *Dundee Courier* of 10th December 1900 informs us that the new Mission Hall in connection with St James Episcopal Church, Cupar, had been opened at a service on the previous morning. Rev. C.E. Cook of St James conducted the service.

The building at number 1 Monkstown had originally been a dwellinghouse, one of the Monkstown cottages built by Andrew Thomson of Wester Kinloch in 1810. By 1896 the building had come into the hands of Andrew Young of Kinloch and he rented the premises to St James of Cupar. This situation continued until 1927 when the Heritors of Mr Young's estate sold it to St James' for £144.

Membership of the church has always been small but with a capacity of only 24 it was never designed for a large congregation. Records show that in 1929 with 25 on the roll it would have been very full if everyone attended. During World War II, with an influx of military personnel from all over the UK, its membership continued to grow. By the 1970s, however, the number had fallen to six or eight but increased to 12 by the beginning of the millennium.

At first services took place at 8.30 a.m. and 2.30 p.m. each Sunday. Eventually, frequency was reduced to fortnightly, though in 2000 evensong services were held when there was a fifth Sunday in the month.

It was not until 1951 that the little church in Ladybank was dedicated to St Mary at a special service, conducted by the Bishop of St Andrews, the Right Rev. Brian Burrowes OBE MA, on 10th June. A full congregation attended this important service, which was shared by the Rector of St James of Cupar, Rev. C.V. Lawson.

Worship in this tiny sanctuary brings the small congregation into a close fellowship and fulfilling experience.

The Masons

One of the most prominent buildings in Ladybank lies on the Kingskettle Road. It is the Masonic Hall. This body has been prominent in the town since early times and its contribution to the life of the community must not go un-noticed.

The history of freemasonry in Scotland is so very ancient that it is difficult to say when it started. With some certainty it is known that James I was a Mason, as was his son James II. It would appear that in these early times freemasonry in Scotland lacked cohesion and to put this right a Grand Lodge was established in Edinburgh in 1736.

Fife's early connection with Masons was through Dunfermline and St Andrews. There is also a connection with Falkland at the time of the building of the Palace there. With such a long history of freemasonry in Fife, it is not surprising that a lodge was established in the new town of Ladybank.

The lodge which is housed in the hall on the Kettle Road bears the name 'King Robert de Bruce' and the number 304. Its motto reads 'Tyde what May' (Come what May) and its charter dates back to 1823 in Auchtermuchty. Another lodge existed in Auchtermuchty at that time and the two operated until the 1860s when the King Robert de Bruce lodge became inactive.

As Ladybank continued to develop and the population increased, the charter was transferred to Ladybank by the Grand Lodge in 1887. Initially, the lodge met in accommodation in Church Street and among their membership was Rev. Robert H. Kerr of the Established Church in Ladybank. This accommodation, consecrated in 1888, was seen as temporary, for a year later plans were being made to build a new hall. The site chosen was on the Kettle Road beyond the railway bridge, which was made freely available to them by Mr Haig of Ramornie. Mr Haig also made available half the cost of the new building, which was estimated to be £600.

In April 1890 the members of the lodge met in Church Street and then processed to their new site, led by a band from Kettle and joined by about 300 people. Once gathered there a stone was officially laid above the main window. A recess cut into the stone holds a glass jar containing contemporary newspapers, coins and a history of the lodge. A social evening was then held in the Old Free Church Halls on Commercial Road (where Ladybank Tyres is today). In October 1890 the new hall was officially opened by Captain John Gilmore of Montrave. There was general celebration in the village and the local Liberal MP, John Boyd Kinnear of Kinloch, though not a Mason, presided. At the time the hall was opened the membership of the lodge was 80.

So, an important asset to Ladybank was opened and celebrated. It has been used by the community for many activities over the years. Still commemorated are the times when Liberal Prime Minister from 1908–1916 and MP for East Fife H.H. Asquith made many of his great speeches there. A plaque at the Masonic Hall commemorates the 50th anniversary of Asquith's entrance to Parliament in 1886.

A Door is Closed but a Window is Opened

Ladybank's history up to the formation of the Howe of Fife Parish Church was only 136 years, not long compared with the other communities in the newly formed parish. Nevertheless, it is the largest community. This makes it important, not only because of the size of population but also because it has become the business hub of the parish. It is here that we find the chemist, butcher and local supermarkets. It is here too that the doctor and library are located as well as the station that serves the whole community.

While this chapter has been split into two parts, it is telling one story. The beginning of Ladybank goes back to Collessie and the rededication of the church by Bishop David de Bernham in 1243. Ladybank Church has its roots firmly planted in the Abbey of Lindores and the monks who collected peats at Our Lady's Bog all these centuries ago, and it was the mother church of Collessie. It is for this reason that I have placed the story of these two communities into one chapter.

CHAPTER THREE: KETTLE

Churches in Kettle

~

The Origins of Kettle Kirk

The story of the parish of Kettle starts so very long ago that it is difficult to put a date on its origins. Of course, Kettle is not where our story begins, but at Lathrisk, which lies west of Kettle and quite near to Falkland. At the centre of the tale is Orabilis, a lady of high social status, who lived in the second half of the 12th century and had a propensity to change husbands.

Orabilis's father, Ness, was very wealthy and had estates at Leuchars, Lathrisk and Gask in Strathearn. Although he appears to have had two illegitimate sons, Patrick and Constantine, it was Orabilis he wanted to inherit his wealth. Inspection of a number of charters of the Priory of St Andrews reveals much about the life of this medieval woman. We know she married Robert de Quincy, an English knight with French roots and the first de Quincy to be recorded in Scotland. Before long she gave birth to an heir, Saher (Saer) de Quincy. Some time after, in 1172, she divorced her husband and married Adam Donnachad (Duncan), brother of Duncan II Earl of Fife. It would appear this marriage too faltered and by 1188 she had become Countess of Mar through her marriage to Earl Gillecrist (Gilchrist).[163]

Matthew Hammond tells us that Orabilis's father, Ness, gifted the church of Lathrisk to St Andrews Priory in about 1170.[164] When he did this he included 'Orabilis his daughter and heiress' so making it a joint gift. This is confirmed in the Chartulary of Lindores.[165] Furthermore, Hammond states that Robert de Quincy, her husband, and Stephen de Quincy, parson of Locres (Leuchars), witnessed this charter. Later, when she made another gift to the Priory of St Andrews, she did so as *Orabilis filia et heres Domini Nessii* (Orabilis, daughter and heiress of her master Ness). So it is that she identified herself as daughter of Ness and not as the wife of any man.

---

[163] M. Hammond, 'Charters of Ness son of William and his daughter Orabilis, lords of Leuchars, Fife', (n.d.) https://scottishmedievalcharters.files.wordpress.com/2014/02/ness-and-orabilis-for-web.pdf

[164] M. Hammond, 'Women and the adoption of charters in Scotland north of the Forth, c. 1150–1286, *Innes Review*, 62(1) 2011, pp. 5–46, doi: 10.3366/inr.2011.0003

[165] Dowden, Chartulary of Lindores, p. 232

The medieval records of the lands of Lathrisk and Kettle are complex. As stated above they appear to have belonged to Ness of Leuchars in the 1170s. His gift was confirmed by Bishop Richard of St Andrews and King William between 1173 and 1178. Uncertainty has arisen about whether or not this gift included the chapel of Kettle because Earl Duncan of Fife, second husband of Orabilis, made a separate gift of the chapel at Kettle in the mid 1170s. The church of Lathrisk was again granted to the Priory of St Andrews by Bishop William between 1202 and 1238. It was intended that the revenue from Lathrisk would be used for building the new church in St Andrews. In 1257 Roger de Quincy, who had succeeded Ness as feudal superior of Lathrisk, repeated the grant. This may reflect a dispute over the right of patronage as there was a disagreement between the Priory of St Andrews and the vicar of Lathrisk concerning the right to appoint a chaplain at Kettle in 1323. This is all telling a very complicated and somewhat confusing story. One thing that does emerge is that the totality of Earl Duncan's bequest makes the chapel at Kettle sound more like a church as it included a burial ground, which was unusual for medieval chapels.[166]

What is important is that the link between Lathrisk and Kettle has an ancient history and that link was maintained through gifts to the Priory of St Andrews. In 1340 a document also refers to the chapel as a Parish Church with its cemetery.[167] This chapel was significant both in its size and its function, which is not surprising, given the size of the parish of Lathrisk and the remoteness of the Parish Church from most of those it sought to serve. While the site of the chapel is known and remembered by the retention of the name 'Chapel', which was given to the farm at the south end of the village, no evidence of the building has survived.

Not only have chapels at Kettle and Forthar disappeared but there is also little to reveal the nature or extent of the church of Lathrisk. The land in the area is fertile and dry though

A view of the area where an ancient graveyard was excavated at Lathrisk

surrounded by bogs and marshland. Archaeological excavations in 1995 revealed numerous graves, suggesting an ancient graveyard, and the remnants of a wall that could have belonged to one of the ecclesiastical buildings. Old Lathrisk House contains evidence of an ancient tower which is erected over substantial vaulted cellars and it has been suggested that they may have provided the foundation for a small monastery. One-time minister of Kettle Rev. Aeneas Gordon states quite categorically that this building

---

166 S. Taylor and G. Markus, *The Place-names of Fife*, vol. 2 (Donnington, Shaun Tyas, 2008)
167 POMS Viewing Document Record: 3/16/11 (St A. Lib., 244)

with its arched ceiling was the vestry of the church at Lathrisk.[168] While it is tempting to draw such conclusions, the site of the old church and burial ground that belonged to it are marked on modern maps as lying close to, but not part of, the present house and there is no evidence of the church above ground level. Ample documentation exists to confirm that a church once stood in the locality. The building was consecrated (probably reconsecrated) by Bishop David de Bernham on 28th July 1243. It was dedicated to St Athernase and to St John the Evangelist. At the time of Bishop de Bernham's tenure as Bishop of St Andrews he granted permission for a chapel at Clatto to be built.[169] According to Scottish Church Heritage Research it was demolished about 1560, just as the Reformed Church was established throughout Scotland. With the main ecclesiastical centre at Lathrisk and chapels at Kettle, Kirkforthar and Clatto, the folk of this large parish were well served.

Old Lathrisk House

In a comprehensive charter dated 12th August 1471 King James III confirmed these gifts to the church of St Andrews and special mention is made of the 'church of Lotheresky' with the 'chapel of Cattull'. The latter seems to have been specially endowed as the lands of Chapel–Kettle and was granted to the Duke of Lennox in 1593. Less well known is the existence of a private chapel at Clatto and possibly also one at Devon.

St Athernase

While there is uncertainty about the origin of St Athernase, he is generally believed also to be named St Ethernascus, the Confessor, and is apparently so named because of his withdrawn life. This Irish saint's name Ethernascus means 'who spoke not' or 'The Silent'. He was one of the chief patrons of Clane, in county Kildare. It is difficult to determine what his precise connection with Scotland was, but his office occurs with a proper prayer in the Breviary of Aberdeen. His saint's day is 22nd December. (The Aberdeen Breviary is a prayer book which is 500 years old and believed to be Scotland's oldest large printed book.)

The Parish of Kettle

We hear of Kettle first in a charter by Malcolm IV in 1166 when he granted certain estates in Fife and Perthshire to Duncan, Earl of Fife, father-in-law of Orabilis, daughter of Ness, on his marriage to Ada, who was the King's niece. At some point after this the

[168]   Rev. G.W. Walker (ed.), *Church and Parish: Being Brief Historical Papers on the Parishes within the Presbytery of Cupar* (Cupar, J. & G. Innes, 1925)
[169]   J. Dowden, *The Medieval Church in Scotland: Its Constitution, Organisation and Law* (Glasgow, James Maclehose, 1910)

family of Duncan forfeited the lands and they were returned to the Crown. The lands of Kettle formed a portion of the 'Stewartry of Fife' and as such were in the King's gift. This may well be what gave rise to the name Kingskettle. The name 'Kingis Kettle' first appears in a charter dated 1541. Hoill Kettil, which lies south of Kingskettle, was the possession of the Beaton family of Balfour by the end of the 15th century and on 9th August 1507 King James IV confirmed the estate to John Beaton of Balfour. With the death of his descendant Robert Beaton this family name disappears from the area.[170]

As we can see, Kettle has a long history and, notwithstanding the above, its curious name is believed by some to be derived from the Gaelic word 'Cattul', which means 'battlefield'.[171] Not everyone is satisfied with this explanation. The land around the village was very marshy, which would make it an unsuitable site for a battle. It has been suggested that the name has emerged from a corruption of the word 'chapel', and as we know there is the site of a very ancient chapel in the land to the south of the A914 at Kettlebridge. An early document dated about 1180 records the granting of the chapel of Kettle to St Andrews Priory by Malcolm, son of Earl Duncan (II) of Fife.[172] All that can be said with certainty is that the origin of the name remains a mystery.

There is archaeological evidence of human activity in the area since Neolithic times. Aerial photography of a field west of Kettlebridge reveals the marks of two barrows or burial mounds, as can be seen in the RCAHMS photograph. The larger measures about 35 m in diameter while the smaller is about 15 m. At the present time there is little more that can be said about these ancient monuments because generations of agricultural activity has removed much of the original structures. The circular and square shapes that are so clear reveal ditches that had been dug around the burial tombs about 4,000 years ago.

Aerial view SW of back park revealing ancient burial site

In 1636 it was decided that with the closing of the chapels at Chapel and Clatto in 1560 the church at Lathrisk was too remote from the most populous parts of the parish. As a result, the building at Lathrisk was replaced by another that lay in what is now the old cemetery in Kettle. When the centre of the parish moved to Kettle the name moved with it. So it is that the ancient parish of Lathrisk is now the parish of Kettle.

---

[170] Millar, *Fife: Pictorial and Historical*
[171] Taylor and Markus, *Place-names of Fife*, vol. 2
[172] http://db.poms.ac.uk/record/source/2437/

Clatto

When a private chapel was to be erected the bishop's approval had to be sought. It was the bishop's concern that the Parish Church should not suffer any loss in either status or income as a result of the new establishment, and so when agreement was given it was always with conditions attached. It was felt necessary to maintain the superiority of the Parish Church and responsibility for the eucharist and the chaplain's oath of fealty was to the Parish Church.[173] This was the case when permission was granted by Bishop David de Bernham for the establishment of the chapel at Clatyn or, as we now say, Clatto.[174]

Clatto lies at the eastern extremity of the parish and was, until 1930, part of Balbirnie Estate and so within the parish of Kettle. There is a legend, widely reported, that many believe to be more than just a tale, about a family that lived there in the days of King James IV, between 1488 and 1513. The following was recorded in the Old Statistical Account by Rev. Barclay:

> The lands of Clatto, which constitute the east end of the parish of Kettle, and through which lay the old road from Cupar to Kinghorn, belonged to a family of Seton, who are celebrated in tradition for the most cruel robberies and murders. The grounds about Clatto Den are still desert. In the face of the brae, which forms one side of the den, is a cave that is said to communicate with the old castle or tower of Clatto, a long distance, the remains of which are still visible. The same cave is said to have had another opening to the road, at which the assailant rushed out on the heedless passengers and dragged them into the cavern, whence there was no return. All appearance of a cave is now obliterated, by the breaking down of the banks. A similar cavern was found, not many years ago, at Craighall in Ceres parish. Of these Setons many stories, replete with superstitions of preceding ages, are still current among the country people. One may suffice.

> One of the Scottish Kings, said to be James IV, was passing that way alone. As was common in those days, he was attacked by a son of Seton. The King, having a dagger concealed under his garment, drew it, and with a blow cut off the right hand that seized his horse's bridle. This hand he took up, and rode off. Next day, attended by a proper retinue, he visited the Castle of Clatto, wishing to see Seton and his sons, who were noted as hardy enterprising men, fitted to shine in more public station. The old man conducted his family into the King's presence. One son alone was absent: it was said he was hurt in an accident and confined to bed. The King insisted on seeing him, and desired to feel his pulse. The young man held out his left hand. The King would feel the other also. After many ineffectual excuses he was obliged to confess that he had lost his right hand. The King told him that he had a hand in his pocket, which was at his service if it would fit him. Upon this they were all seized and executed.[175]

---

[173] Dowden, *The Medieval Church in Scotland*
[174] http://db.poms.ac.uk/record/source/2248/
[175] Old Statistical Account, vol. 1, p. 369

I felt this intriguing tale deserved some attention and met Mr Harry Sangster who had owned Clatto Farm from 1954 until his retirement in 1984. Mr Sangster, who died in 2011, knew the tale of the Setons very well. He told me he had identified the cave both at the road end and at the site of the tower. He no longer told people how to find the cave as, when he did, some attempted to excavate in such a way as to endanger themselves. The castle was gone long before Mr Sangster arrived but he was aware that stones from the old building had been used in the construction of some farm buildings. A tread from a spiral staircase was built into the house Mr and Mrs Sangster retired to. Little is left of the old road except a bridge between Montrave den and Muirhead Farm as much of it has been reclaimed for agriculture.

Soon after his arrival Mr Sangster found it necessary to cut down a very large and very old ash tree. It was in a dangerous state and so hollow it was possible to walk into. This was known locally as the hanging tree and when it was cut down two sets of iron artefacts that he called 'hanging irons' were found. One set is now in an Edinburgh museum, but the other was in Mr Sangster's possession and I was able to see it.

Before Mr Sangster bought Clatto it was owned by Cupar Council. They purchased it in 1930 in order to acquire the land to extend Clatto reservoir. Mr Sangster said that the land was pretty wild and he worked hard to bring the 450 acres under control as an upland arable and stock-rearing farm.

Many people lived in the lands of Clatto both before and after the Setons. In 1435–36 Bishop Wardlaw gifted one sixth of the lands to one Willelmus de Forsyth de Nydy. In 1240 part of Clattow (Clatto) was granted by Prior John to Duncan de Ramsay on condition he maintained the chapel there. It continued in his hands until 1593. A member of this family, Andrew Ramsay, presented the accounts of St Andrews at Stirling castle in 1435. He was seen as an important man, for in 1443 he was sent on an embassy to Cologne. He also became provost of St Andrews in 1443 and again in 1450. The story of the ownership of Clatto is convoluted and there are many references to the pre-Reformation chapel there, but like the chapels at Kettle and Forthar no evidence of the structure survives.

The Parish Through its Ministers

It is hard to discover the names and identities of pre-Reformation clergymen who tended the parish of Lathrisk. One name does appear in 1517 in the *Register of the Ministers, Elders and Deacons of the Christian Congregation of St Andrews*.[176] This reveals that the Parish Church of Crail was on the petition and endowment of Sir William Myreton (vicar of Lathrisk, and a relative of the Cambo family). At least this gives us a name and an identity but we have no more information about him. The pre-Reformation ecclesiastical records that would give us a fuller account of the men (and they would all have been men) who faithfully served Lathrisk were destroyed around 1560.

---

[176] D.H. Fleming (trans. and ed.), *Register of the Minister Elders and Deacons of the Christian Congregation of St Andrews 1559–1600* (Edinburgh University Press for the Scottish History Society, 1889, p. 106)

The story of the ministers of Lathrisk and Kettle Kirk since the Reformation clearly reveals the part played by Kettle folk in the troubled times that Scotland endured over the centuries. The first entry in the *Fasti Ecclesiae Scoticanae*,[177] the record of ministers of the Church of Scotland since the Reformation, is as follows: '**David Cuke**: formerly Canon of St Andrews; reader 18th Jan. 1565–6.' This simple statement tells us that David Cuke had, before the Reformation, held a prestigious ecclesiastical position in St Andrews Cathedral. Now he was a reader, one who was trained but not considered ordained and so not appointed minister of the parish. At first sight it would appear this was a great humiliation for one who had held an important office in the most significant religious centre in pre-Reformation Scotland. In fact, in the preface of the *Register of the Ministers, Elders and Deacons of the Christian Congregation of St Andrews*,[178] we discover that by 1571–72, of 14 canons, 12 had become parish ministers of the Reformed Church.

Indeed, another 31 of the clergymen had already joined the Reformers by 1559–60. Clearly the Reformation in Scotland was not just about John Knox and a rabble he had raised against powerful and corrupt clergy. The reality was that the movement arose within the Church as well as outwith it and this presents a much more complex picture of events.

The second incumbent was **Mr John Balfour**, reader from 1574 to 1588 and called as vicar on 14th March 1580. This is not the only mention of Mr Balfour in the Howe of Fife. As we shall see in the chapter on Cults, John Balfour was 'vicar of Quiltis' in 1550 and, 'having embraced the faith', he remained in that parish until 1563. It is generally believed that the two John Balfours are in fact the same person. He was removed from Cults and placed in an obscure congregation by the General Assembly in 1563 because he 'usurped the place of a minister'. Clearly Mr Balfour had learned a lot between 1563 and 1574.

For about a year **John Pitcairn**, who had been removed from Strathmiglo, accepted the charge at Lathrisk. He also had the parish of Kilgour, which now lies in Falkland parish and is listed in *Fasti Ecclesiae Scoticanae* as 'Falkland, of Old Kilgour'. This resulted from a decision of the General Assembly in March 1574 that 'syndrie kirks be appointit to ane man' (one minister may be appointed to several churches at the same time). His residence would be at one church, where he would be called the principal minister, but assistance would be made available in the other churches. Such measures were necessary in the early years after the Reformation due to the shortage of qualified clergymen. Clearly this arrangement created an impossible load for Mr Pitcairn to carry and so in 1589 he was removed from Lathrisk to the sole charge of Kilgour. In *Fasti Ecclesiae Scoticanae* he is listed as James Pitcairn, though he is undoubtedly the same person because his translation to Lathrisk in 1588 is noted. He was the second son of Andrew Pitcairn of Innernethy and Janet Chalmers and was presented to Kilgour

---

[177] Scott, *Fasti Ecclesiae Scoticanae*
[178] Fleming, *Ministers Elders and Deacons of St Andrews*

by James VI. He fell out of favour, however, and was confined to his parish because the King was displeased with him for taking part in the admission of a minister to Strathmiglo without the archbishop's authority in 1611.

William Cranstoun arrived in 1589. He was born in 1556, the son of Robert Cranstoun and Margaret Myllis who belonged to St Andrews. At one time he was regent in St Salvator's College. Approved by the Presbytery on 27th November 1589, the year he came to Lathrisk, he served as a member of the Assembly in 1590. Mr Cranstoun was, however, a follower of Andrew Melville and disliked King James's insistence on appointing bishops. Nevertheless, he became a member of the General Assembly in 1597–98 and again in 1602 and served as Moderator of the Synod of Fife on 9th June 1607. It was, apparently, about this time that he had a major brush with authority.

The King, as patron to the parish of Lathrisk/Kettle, decided that Mr Cranstoun should be replaced as Moderator by Archbishop Gladstone. By the time the commissioners arrived Mr Cranstoun had gone up to the pulpit. As he sat there a messenger delivered a letter, which he put in his pocket without reading. A little later another letter was delivered in the Lord Commissioner's name instructing him to come down. His answer was that he came in the name of a greater Lord whose message he had not discharged. At that he named a psalm to be sung. Then one of the baillies whispered to him that he was commanded by the lords to come down. To this the minister replied, 'And I command you in the name of God to sit down in your own seat and hear what God will say to you by me!' The chastened baillie did as he was told. It was then that a councillor went to him and told him to stop as another had been appointed to preach. To this Cranstoun is reputed to have replied, 'But the Lord and his Kirk have appointed me, therefore, beware how you trouble his work.' At that he continued with his sermon. This resulted in the commissioners declaring him to be in contempt and 'an outlaw'![179]

Nevertheless, Mr Cranstoun opened the next meeting of the Synod on 18th August 1607 in the presence of the Royal Commissioner. This led to him being outlawed in September of that year. Clearly he was a persistent thorn in the flesh of the King and his Episcopal bishops because he was deprived of his charge by Archbishop John Spottiswood, who convened the Court of High Commission on 10th March 1620. The shortage of qualified ministers was such, however, that he was presented to the Kirk Session again by James VI on 10th December 1623, but he demitted the charge some time before his son was ordained to the same parish three years later. William Cranstoun died in January 1633 at the age of 77. He married three times, first to Agnes Rutherfurd, who died on 23rd November 1593. They had six children: Robert, who would succeed him as minister of the parish, Edward, Walter, Margaret, Elspet (married 1612 to John Brown, skipper burgess of Dysart) and Agnes (married David Ramsay, brother of John, who became minister of the parish in 1633). His second wife was Margaret Balcanquall, who died on 28th November 1595 and there was one child, Janet. His third wife was

---

[179]   D. Calderwood, *History of the Kirk of Scotland*, vol. 6 (Edinburgh, printed for the Wodrow Society, 1842, p. 674)

Janet Alexander, and they too had a daughter, Sarah. She later married John Ramsay, who, as we shall see, also became minister of the parish.

The ecclesiastical powers of the time must have thought the Cranstoun family had well and truly redeemed themselves, for in 1626 King Charles I presented **Robert Cranstoun**, son of William, to the charge of Lathrisk. He was ordained in April 1626 but his ministry in Lathrisk was short and he was translated to Scoonie in 1630. He had little time as his father's successor to make his mark on the parish but while at Scoonie he became a member of the 1638 Assembly that did away with bishops, and in 1641 his chambers were burned down while he was preaching. Scoonie's Session minutes perished in that fire. Mr Cranstoun died in 1643.

John Ramsay was also presented by Charles I. This followed Mr Ramsay's promotion to regent of St Salvator's College, St Andrews, and his ordination took place on 14th March 1633. As we have seen above, his first wife, Sarah, was the daughter of William Cranstoun and they had a son named James. His second wife was Anna but they had no children. Mr Ramsay died in December 1666. Very little seems to be recorded about John Ramsay, though it was he who brought the parish through the troubled years when the National Covenant was signed and then the trauma of the Civil War and persecution under Oliver Cromwell. He is also the one who was at the helm when the decision was made to move the Kirk from Lathrisk to Kettle in 1636. This meant building not only a new church but also a manse and a school. Mr Ramsay must have had an eventful ministry but sadly the record of this time seems to be missing and the Kirk Session minutes reveal nothing.[180]

The next incumbent arrived in 1667. He was **John Barclay**, the son of William, who was minister of the neighbouring parish of Falkland. Educated at Glasgow University he graduated with an MA in 1663 and was ordained to Dunino Church in 1664. When he was translated to Kettle in July 1667 he brought with him ecclesiastical beliefs that were more in tune with King Charles II than with some of his parishioners.

It was just over one year into the ministry that Archbishop James Sharp was assassinated. To understand this incident we must remember that the year 1679 was in the midst of the 'Killing Times' when anyone not willing to accept the Episcopal authority imposed upon them by the King was seen to be a traitor and treated accordingly. As we saw in Chapter 1, King Charles II ensured that bishops replaced the General Assembly, though Synods and Presbyteries were allowed to remain. While many ministers felt able to conform to this arrangement, 300 broke with the Church. Secret open-air services known as conventicles were held on the hillsides and were considered seditious both by the Crown and the official Episcopal Church in Scotland. Troops under the leadership of Sir Thomas Dalzell of the Binns and Sir James Turner took it upon themselves to disperse these conventicles by allowing their troops to ride down on them with swords drawn. There were those among the people who believed that James Sharp, Archbishop

---

180   Scott, *Fasti Ecclesiae Scoticanae*

of St Andrews, condoned and may even have encouraged this brutality and they hated him for it. They also hated him because he was seen to have curried favour with the restored monarchy and the King rewarded him by elevating this loyal Episcopalian to the position of Archbishop of St Andrews.

While the history of the Covenanters is one that is littered with perpetrators of foul deeds, James Sharp is probably the most reviled of all the perceived villains of the piece. It must be said, however, that this view of the man is not held universally, yet many consider his actions against the Covenanters displayed greater enthusiasm than was required. It is also noteworthy that the government's men were not alone in issuing summary justice and great cruelty. There were those among the Covenanters who were equally zealous in their dealings with anyone perceived to be a sympathiser with the Crown. At times those who attended the conventicles were so well armed for protection against the soldiers that they looked more like an army than a worshipping community.

Having been minister of Crail Parish Church, James Sharp was elevated to the position of Archbishop of St Andrews. It is said that he was more noted for his absence as minister of Crail than for his presence, for he spent a great deal of time in London where he found himself getting close to the court of Charles II. He played a part in making plans for the return of the monarchy in 1660 and it would appear his elevation to archbishop was a reward for his service to the Crown. There is no doubt that he was loyal to Charles and so he would have seen those who defied their King as little more than traitors. Soon he set about picking off those he saw as betraying their monarch and defying the law regarding the Church. Others gathered the evidence and Sharp sat in judgment, serving severe

Memorial to Archbishop Sharp on Magusmuir where he fell

penalties including death. The powers of the court were without limit and many hapless souls were hauled before it on the flimsiest of pretexts. Battles ensued and those who were behind the uprisings were executed without mercy and their heads fixed above the city gates. These were the circumstances that led nine men to make a fateful decision.

It was 3rd May 1679 when John Balfour of Kinloch and a band of Covenanters, which included James Russell, Andrew Henderson, George Fleman, Alexander Henderson, William Dalziel and Andrew Guillan, laid siege to the archbishop's coach on Magusmuir as he returned home to St Andrews with his daughter. The whole event was nasty and bloody and watched by his daughter. She was not physically harmed as it was James Sharp they were after, seeking retribution for his professed crimes against ordinary folk.[181]

---

[181] Goring, *Scotland: The Autobiography*

Two years after this brutal assassination, James Russell returned to Kettle and fixed his protest to the door of the Kirk. This document lists the crimes of the archbishop who, he says, 'has made murderers of honest God fearing men'. His anger is directed not only against Archbishop Sharp but also against the Episcopal John Barclay, minister of Kettle, whom he describes as 'both a thief and a robber'. He says it is a 'blasphemy to say' that John Barclay is a minister of Jesus Christ, and gives his reason for writing 'these two or three Lines, and cause put it on the Kirk-door of Kettle, being the most public place, as my testimony against all the wrongs and injuries done to my sweet Lord Jesus Christ'. He goes on to describe Chares II as a tyrant and to recommend his assassination.

Memorial at Magusmuir to those executed in retaliation for the assassination of Archbishop Sharp

He quotes liberally from both the New and Old Testaments and the whole sorry petition reads like the outburst of a desperate man. James Russell declared it written in his own hand at Kettle. It was signed and dated the third day of the fourth month 1681. James described himself as a 'Portioner', that is, one who had inherited part of an estate. In fact, he is described in *Historical Antiquities of Fife* as 'proprietor of Bankton and Kettle' and lived in the 'old house of Bankton' which stood near the house of Chapel.[182] James Russell escaped execution but the sad postscript to this is that five men who had nothing to do with the assassination of James Sharp were executed at Magusmuir in retribution. Their bodies were left on display as a warning to any who might wish to follow the example of James Russell and his compatriots until James VII and II fled to France and William and Mary ascended to the throne. It was a time of great brutality that encouraged many Scots to support the demise of the Stewart dynasty as monarchs of Great Britain.

In August 1683 it is recorded in the minutes of the Kirk Session that the King's proclamation had been received appointing an eight-day thanksgiving for the unsuccessful attempt on the lives of King Charles II and the Duke of York. This referred to what became known as the Rye House Plot when Charles II's illegitimate son, the Duke of Monmouth, hatched a plot to kill the King and the Duke of York (to become James VII and II) and have himself placed on the throne.

This was a difficult time in the history of Scotland and Great Britain. Those supporting James VII were considered to be Episcopalians if not Catholics, while those supporting William and Mary were viewed as supporters of the Presbyterian Church

---

[182] J. Russell, 'A True and Exact Copy of a Prodigious and Traiterous Libel, affixt upon the Church-door of Kettle, in Fife', (Edinburgh, **1681**) (see Appendix)

of Scotland and traitors to the Jacobite cause. At the time of the Settlement, that is the accession of William and Mary, Presbyterianism in Scotland was secured under the new monarchy. Many, mainly in the Highlands, wanted to retain the Stewart dynasty on the throne, blaming William for the Darien Disaster and adhering to the divine right of the Stewarts to reign.

This came to a head at the Battle of Killiecrankie in 1689 when the supporters of James VII defeated the government troops. Victory for the highlanders was short-lived as they were heavily defeated at the Battle of Dunkeld the following month. Three years later the Massacre of Glencoe took place, which was indicative of the feelings of unease of the supporters of the Crown in Scotland. As a result, anyone who failed to offer full support to the new order would be seen as a threat. Clearly John Barclay was providing just such a threat in Kettle and it was for that reason that he had to be put out of harm's way and deprived of the opportunity to spread his Episcopalian beliefs. In August 1689, the year after the 'Glorious Revolution', when James VII and II fled to France, John Barclay was deprived of his charge by the Privy Council for neither reading the Proclamation of the Estates nor praying for William and Mary but for King James. Finally, his Episcopal sympathies had caught up with him and he was removed from his post after serving the parish for 22 years. Two years after being deprived of his charge, in July 1691, John Barclay was found dead at the bottom of a well in Edinburgh aged about 62. While neither suicide nor murder is mentioned one does wonder why Mr Barclay's body was found down a well. The sadness of the situation is reinforced by the fact that after a 22- year ministry his expulsion from his charge is of such little importance to the Kirk Session that they did not record it.[183]

On 20th July 1690 the Moderator of the Session was Rev. Edward Jameson, minister of Monimail. Present at that meeting was William Pitcairn of Forthar, representing the Heritors of the parish. The Heritors were a body in the parish that normally comprised landowners. Their responsibilities included the upkeep of the church, manse and school. They also had to ensure that the minister received his stipend and the schoolmaster his salary. Provision for the poor and dispensing justice also lay within their responsibilities, as did the maintenance of roads. Clearly these were wealthy landowners, though not always living in the parish. Nevertheless, they were a very influential group of men, and sometimes also women. At this meeting, Mr William Pitcairn, one of the Heritors, expressed concern that the church had been in a vacancy and that the congregation had been without a sermon for some 'considerable time'. Mr Pitcairn felt there must be some way of calling a Presbyterian minister and that he and the rest of the Heritors had picked one, his son **John Pitcairn**, Minister of Burntisland, as a suitable candidate. So it was that on 15th April 1691 Mr John Pitcairn was admitted to the charge at the age of 43. One cannot help feeling that there had been some exercising of influence in this choice. Nevertheless, he remained Kettle's minister until his death in 1712 aged 64.

---

[183]   Scott, *Fasti Ecclesiae Scoticanae*

Mr Pitcairn's mother, Ann, was the daughter of Sir David Crichton of Lugton, an important family in both Church and State in the 17th century. John came not only with notable family connections but also with experience, for he had been ordained Presbyterian Minister at Ballymena in 1676 and called to Burntisland in 1688. His wife Elizabeth, daughter of Sir Francis Ruthven of Freeland, bore him a son, Alexander, and a daughter, Janet.

Kettle and Queen Anne

The death of Mr Pitcairn coincided with the decision of Queen Anne, on advice of the British Parliament, to pass the Act of Toleration which restored the right of the lay patron to choose the parish minister. In Kettle the patron was the Crown and so the new minister had to be approved by Queen Anne. In effect, the Crown acted on the recommendation of the Heritors and, as already stated, they did not all belong to the parish or worship at Kettle Kirk. The folk of Kettle clearly did not like this arrangement and were willing and able to voice their objections.

On 7th January 1713, Presbytery met and considered a representation made by the elders of Kettle. They were concerned that eight months had elapsed since the death of Mr Pitcairn and a successor had not been appointed. In addition, they suggested a minister they considered to be suitable. This representation had been drawn up in November 1712 but it had taken two months to come to the notice of Presbytery. To be fair, Presbytery had ensured at each meeting that the pulpit of Kettle was properly covered during the vacancy thus far, but there is no evidence that they had considered the need for ensuring that a permanent minister was in place.

The Heritors of Kettle pointed out that it was Presbytery's responsibility to ensure a minister was settled in the parish. They recommended that following the next Sunday service a meeting of the Heritors, elders and heads of families be called and that 'Representatives of Presbytery will attend to find out their thoughts on a new appointment'. The Moderator was also to write to those who had made representation to the Presbytery to make it clear that they (Presbytery) 'could not comply with their desire in regard to the young man they desired a hearing of'. Their reason was that he was 'not under their inspection, and testimonials had not been produced'. It was also pointed out that the Heritors did not agree with them. We can imagine the reaction of the good folk of Kettle to that reply to their request. Indeed, it drew up the battle lines between Kettle, the Heritors and Presbytery.

A meeting was called by Presbytery which comprised some of the Heritors and they announced their intention that Mr John Meldrum be appointed the new minister. The elders of Kettle, however, along with 'the whole body of the people' declared 'an utter aversion to Master Meldrum'. Some of the Heritors, trying to push things forward, presented Presbytery with a petition which included testimonials as to the suitability of Mr Meldrum from the Presbytery of Kilbaldie. The majority in Kettle was still against this minister and refused to pursue the matter. Presbytery was also pushing the issue when it decided to appoint Mr Meldrum to preach at Kettle on the next Sabbath. Another meeting was also called with the Heritors, elders and heads of families so that Presbytery could 'understand their minds'. At that meeting it became clear that, while some wanted this minister and others that minister, still others wanted the matter referred to Presbytery. Only four or five wanted Mr Meldrum!

At that a 'parchment' was produced which they called 'a presentation from the Queen'. That Queen was, of course, Anne and she was, we must remember, the legal patron of Kettle Kirk and so she had a legal right to declare the next minister. Cupar Presbytery then acted bravely and decisively. They met 'in camera' and rejected the principle of patronage. It was, they said, 'the right of Christian Congregations to have the free choice of their own pastors, which is the only foundation on which a pastoral relationship can be established between minister and people according to the word of God'. While these brave words probably reflected the will of the majority of people, and they certainly reflected the will of the people of Kettle, Presbytery still had the legal responsibility to ensure a minister was settled in Kettle. So, straight after that declaration the Heritors were called back and told it was decided that Presbytery would see to it that Mr Meldrum was settled in Kettle as soon as possible. Given the resolve behind closed doors, it is strange that the honourable men of Presbytery would have implied the opposite to the Heritors. The Heritors were then asked to leave and Presbytery decided that because of the feelings of the folk at Kettle against Mr Meldrum it would not pursue the matter until the next meeting.[184] Is this not so often the way of the courts of the Kirk when faced with a tricky problem? They delayed the decision until a later date.

On 3rd March David Boswell, Laird of Devon Farm and a leader among the Heritors, asked Presbytery what it had done to have Master Meldrum settled. Meldrum had not in fact preached at Kettle and so it was not known if the popular aversion to him would be sustained. Presbytery decided to put the matter forward to the next meeting. Mr Meldrum would be called and questioned. At that meeting Mr Meldrum was asked four questions. 'Do you know what way this presentation was procured?' He answered that the Laird of Balbarton had proposed him and the gentlemen seemed pleased with the proposal. When asked if he had any hand in procuring this proposal he said he had not. He was then asked if he had paid for the presentation and he said he had not. Finally, he was asked 'Do you think this is sufficient foundation for setting up a pastoral relationship with the people with most of the folk against you?' In reply Mr Meldrum said, 'If the folk think they have good reason against me they should bring it to Presbytery', then 'it is out in the open and Presbytery can be the judge.'

On 31st March the elders from Kettle were called before Presbytery where they declared that the body of the folk of Kettle was 'utterly averse to Mr Meldrum'. They then asked Presbytery to 'present a man in an orderly way'. Once again a decision was delayed, this time until after the General Assembly.

---

[184] Minutes of the Meetings of Cupar Presbytery, Special Collections, St Andrews University Library

This decision was not adhered to because on 10th May 1714 both the Kettle folk and Mr Meldrum were called to Presbytery and again the folk said they did not want him. In reply Mr Meldrum said that if the objectors would not state their objections in detail he should be given a chance to preach. Presbytery agreed and Mr Meldrum was to preach the following Sunday. A furious David Boswell expressed his frustration at further delay and threatened to bring the matter before the General Assembly.

The matter did indeed go to the General Assembly and it found in favour of Mr Meldrum, but no more appears in the Presbytery minutes until 8th August. At this meeting Mr Meldrum was present, as were the Heritors. Mr Boswell read a letter from the Heritors. In it he accused the folk of Kettle of opposing Mr Meldrum 'as a result of humour and pride'. He claimed that, when Mr Meldrum went to Kettle to preach, no one went to church to hear him and so he was rejected without reason. 'There is no hope of satisfying people that are so abandoned and unreasonable and to decline all possible means of being informed or satisfied.' The letter also blames Presbytery for procrastination.

The Crown sent a lengthy document entitled 'Memorial for the Presentation of settling Master John Meldrum preacher of the Gospel, Minister of Kettle' condemning Presbytery's action as the Queen had, it said, a monopoly as patron. Nevertheless, in conclusion it stated that 'it is hoped that a suitable minister can be found'.

So it is that Presbytery decided that Mr Meldrum should not be called because he was not wanted except by a few Heritors who did not live in the parish. According to the Kirk Session minutes the issue dragged on until 1715 when again the matter of Mr Meldrum was taken to the General Assembly. There Thomas Arnott of Chapel–Kettle and David Philp of Kettle represented the Kirk Session. Presbytery minutes record that it was not until 9th October 1716 that Mr Meldrum relinquished his hopes of becoming Kettle's minister. In the end it would appear the parishioners of Kettle won an important battle. They enforced the right of the membership to choose their pastor according to their conscience. This can be viewed both as a spiritual triumph, with the believing people of God having the right to decide on their minister according to the divine promptings of the spirit, and as a victory for democracy at a time when ordinary folk had few democratic rights.

It also reflected the feelings of the wider Church at the time with the developing unease at the perceived interference of Crown and state on the liberties of the individual. Certainly, it was an important step towards the Disruption of 1843. Throughout the 18th century the folk of Kettle were to reflect the unhappiness in the Church at patrons exercising their legal authority.

In this long and sorry tale there was a victim in the name of John Meldrum. We have not at any point had the reasons for the Kettle folk's objections clearly stated, and one does wonder if they were acting out of principle. I have been unable to find any further certain reference to the unfortunate man. There is, however, one John Meldrum who appeared in the *Fasti Ecclesiae Scoticanae* for 1718. The entry is for the parish of

Unst or Norwick Ballista and Lund and reads as follows: 'John Meldrum, M.A.; called May 1718, but became so melancholy and disturbed in mind that the Presbytery, 16th April 1719, refused to proceed with his settlement, and prohibited him from preaching in all time coming.' We will never know for certain if this is the John Meldrum who might have been minster of Kettle. But if it is, then one is left wondering whether his 'melancholy' was the cause or result of his rejection.

Matters may have been settled more readily regarding Mr Meldrum had it not been for the 1715 Jacobite Rebellion. The first entry in the Presbytery minute for 7th February 1716 explained that there had been no meeting after October the previous year because of the 'Unnatural Rebellion raised by the Jacobite party'. The rebels had threatened to arrest ministers who prayed for King George from the pulpit and imprison them in Perth. By the beginning of February the government forces had pushed the rebels north of Perth and so the reverend gentlemen of Cupar Presbytery felt safe to continue business. This is a glimpse into the effect of one of our country's most historic moments on the lives of the parishioners here in the Howe of Fife.

On 22nd February a meeting was called after the morning service. Heritors, elders and heads of families were asked to sign a call for Mr James Munro to be their next minister. This was agreed unanimously and the document was duly signed. Mr Munro preached at Kettle on 22nd March and was ordained as minister on April 25th. So it was that **James Munro** was welcomed into the parish after a turbulent five-year vacancy. James's father, John, was minister of Rothesay and his son became chaplain to Thomas, Earl of Haddington. He was ordained to Kettle on 25th April 1717. His ministry in the parish was to last 12 years and in 1729 he was called to Third Church (latterly St Paul's) in Dundee. One year after leaving Kettle, in 1730, he married Katherine, daughter of Sir Michael Balfour of Denmyln, and they had one daughter, Helen.

On 29th December 1729 Mr Munro preached his farewell sermon at Kettle. The Kirk Session minutes tell us 'he seriously exhorted the congregation to the diligent pursuit of Religion and exhorted the Elders to unity and prudence in the choice of another pastor. He then ended by commending the congregation to God in prayer'. This entry into the Kirk Session minutes was unusual at that time and it suggests that Mr Munro was popular and had had a successful ministry in the parish as his words were of sufficient importance to his folk that they recorded them for posterity.

By June 1730 there was still no sign of a successor. We find in the Presbytery minute for 9th June a petition from the elders of Kettle. In it they express their sadness at the loss of Mr Munro and ask Presbytery to help them to get the matter of a minister settled. Presbytery asked them if the Heritors were in agreement with their direct approach to Presbytery. They answered that they were not in agreement, except for Lady Lathrisk, who supported their move. Presbytery agreed to meet the folk at Kettle and find out their thoughts on the matter and report back at the next meeting. The representatives reported back that a meeting had taken place with the Heritors, elders and heads of families.

Two young preachers were regularly filling the pulpit during the vacancy. One was Mr Hugh Glass, from Kirkcaldy, and the other Mr Patrick Glass, also from Kirkcaldy. While it would appear reasonable to assume they were brothers, there is no indication of this in the records. Both were young, Hugh the elder by one year, and both were popular with the Kettle folk. In February 1730 the Kirk Session minutes tell us the Moderator, Mr Alexander Stoddart of Falkland, sought to acquaint Presbytery that the Session would like to hear the two probationers. April of the same year reveals that one member of the Session was to attend a meeting of the Synod and Presbytery in Cupar. On 27th May the Moderator, Rev. Mr Thomas Thomson of Auchtermuchty, 'exhorted the Elders in obedience to the Presbytery, to unanimity in their choice of minister'. Clearly once again there was trouble in the Kirk at Kettle!

Hugh Glass tended to be most popular with the Heritors while Patrick won favour with the ordinary members. The result of this was that there was deadlock with neither side being willing to give way to the other. Perhaps it was *because* Hugh was backed by the Heritors that the majority of ordinary folk supported Patrick. Whatever the truth of that, stalemate ensued for many months. In the end Presbytery made the decision and **Mr Hugh Glass** was duly ordained to Kettle Parish Church on 23rd September 1731. Mr Patrick Glass was called to Crail three years later so hopefully this was a happy ending for both men.

The seriousness of this affair prompted the publication of two documents: 'The case of the parish of Kettle, and the Reverend Synod of Fife respondents. Against the appeal of the callers of Mr Hugh Glass' and 'The callers of Mr Hugh Glass to the Parish of Kettle, appellants, against the callers of Mr Patrick Glass, and the Reverend Synod of Fife defendants'. At the General Assembly in 1732 the first schism of the 18th century took place and once again we find the feelings that gave rise to that dispute being played out in Kettle. From the account of events as revealed in the Kirk Session and Presbytery minutes it seems clear that the people of Kettle are reflecting the mood of many in the nation as a whole with regard to the role of patrons. Although the Heritors had responsibility for the financial welfare of the Church, they tended to be wealthy gentry and some were Episcopalians rather than Presbyterians. Should any elder have succeeded in joining their number, he would have been at a social disadvantage and would have felt obliged to do the bidding of his 'betters'.

The *Fasti Ecclessiae Scoticanae* 1731 relates the arrival of the 30-year-old Hugh Glass. Like many of his predecessors he had graduated with MA from St Andrews University. In 1720 he started his working life as a schoolmaster in Markinch. His licence to preach came in 1728 and ordination at Kettle on 23rd September 1731. In spite of the troubles prior to his arrival he must have been happy, for he remained in Kettle until his death 46 years later.

These were eventful years in Scottish history, which included the Jacobite Rebellion of 1745 with Bonnie Prince Charlie and the Battle of Culloden. In the Kirk, dissent about the use of patrons rumbled on. Very little appears in the Kirk Session minutes during Mr Glass's tenure apart from the dispersal of money to the poor, with £1 10*s*. to this one and £2 to that. The children of one John Good-Wilkies received £4 while the precentor was paid £1 4*s*. We learn a little about Hugh Glass the man of principle in the *Scots Magazine* of May 1751. An account of the General Assembly of that year is published in which we discover that there was a decision taken to censure the Presbytery of Linlithgow for failing to appoint Rev. James Watson, minister of Torphichen, as previously directed. This resulted in a petition signed by 21 ministers, including Mr Glass, and one elder, stating 'censures of the church are never to be inflicted, but upon open transgressors of the laws of Christ himself its only lawgiver: nor can we think that any man is to be constructed an open transgressor for the laws of Christ, merely for not obeying commands of any assembly of fallible men, when he declares it was a conscientious regard to the will of Christ himself … that led him to this disobedience'. Clearly Mr Hugh Glass was a rebel at heart. I think that suited the folk of Kettle very well indeed, for they had shown themselves to be independent-minded folk in the past and they were soon to do so again. Mr Glass must not be written off as being of little consequence, for he was highly thought of by parishioners and colleagues alike. The publication *The North British Intelligence* recorded his death in the following words: 'June 14. The Manse of Kettle, Fifeshire, the Rev. Mr Hugh Glass, in the 77th year of his age, and the 46th of his ministry. He was eminent in his station as a faithful and laborious gospel-minister, and had on the Thursday preceding preached before a very numerous congregation at the ordination of Elders in the Parish.'

It would appear from the little that is revealed that Mr Glass was a popular and effective minister and a man of principle.

The vacancy that occurred at the death of Mr Glass yet again revealed divisions within the parish of Kettle that reflected the differences of opinion to be found in the General Assembly. So it was that opposition in Kettle was inflamed at the new arrival when Peter Barclay was presented to the Session by the King George III on 5th July 1777. He came with excellent credentials, being a graduate of Marischal College, Aberdeen. Forty years later, in 1817, he was to receive a DD from St Andrews University.

Mr Barclay was presented by the Crown at Cupar Presbytery on 23rd September 1777 and it was agreed that he would, within the coming weeks, preach at Kettle. On 14th October a petition was presented to Presbytery asking it to 'Moderate Mr Barclay's call'. This meant that there was unrest in the parish at the prospect of Mr Barclay becoming their minister and they wanted Presbytery to look into it. On the 6th of November at Kettle a petition was again presented listing objections to Mr Barclay. The list of objections was long-winded, full of biblical references and vague. The underlying reason was that in Kettle it was generally believed that the real influence behind the appointment was a principal Heritor, in whose family he had been tutor. The name of that Heritor is not divulged. Once again the people of the congregation felt that their feelings and concerns had been ignored by those with influence. A report from the Synod of 28th April 1778 recommended that Mr Barclay be settled with all speed.

By the time of Mr Barclay's ordination, feelings in the parish were running so high that it was felt necessary to have the presence of a company of 'Dragoon Guards' in case of trouble. As it turned out the fears were unfounded, for all passed peacefully. Presbytery met in Kettle schoolhouse and, as is the custom, sent officers to the door of the church to ask if anyone had any 'Relevant Objections' to his life and doctrine. There were no objections. **Mr Barclay** was duly ordained on 14th May 1778.

Peter Barclay enjoyed a successful ministry, all be it with a reduced congregation. A considerable number had broken away from the Parish Church when he was ordained and when Mr Barclay wrote the Old Statistical Account in 1790 he revealed that 587 out of a total population of 1,643 were members of the 'Separatists', as he referred to the Relief Church.

During his long ministry Mr Barclay had the distinction of writing the Kettle contribution for not only the Old Statistical Account in 1791 but also for the New Statistical Account in 1836. In addition, he was responsible for building a new manse in 1792 and a new church in 1833.

On 28th December 1830 Dr Barclay, as he had become, with the agreement of the Heritors, invited Presbytery to hold a visitation to Kettle Church in order to examine its condition and decide whether it should be repaired or replaced. This took place and Presbytery invited two local and trusted tradesmen, George Buist and John Inglis, to carry out the inspection and deliver a report. This was done and the following report was presented on 25th February 1831:

> The roof of the body of the church is very much wasted and the roof of the aisle is completely wasted and at present unsafe. We also minutely examined the state of the galleries and find part of the joisting almost entirely gone and the rest of it done in so un-tradesman-like manner and put up in apparently temporary manner that we consider it unsafe. The seating which is for the most part without flooring is in a wasted and deranged state and may be said to be uninhabitable according to the modern ideas of church accommodation. With regard to walls we are of the opinion that they are in a bad state, some parts of them having given way. The stone stairs are quite in ruins. If an attempt was made to repair we are of opinion that it could not be done without almost a total renewal and therefore we have no hesitation in stating that it is our opinion that the church ought to be condemned and a new one built.[185]

Clearly the church was of a reasonable size with nave and aisle as well as galleries. On the other hand, it had been allowed to deteriorate so that it had become dangerous. So it was that Presbytery encouraged building a new church as quickly as possible. They wanted it occupied by Christmas 1832. The Heritors met and agreed to fund the new building. Plans were drawn up and approved, though Presbytery wanted two communion tables to be installed stretching from the pulpit up to the back of the church.

---

[185]   Minute of Meetings of Kettle Parish Church, Special Collections, St Andrews University Library

Evidently they still had the idea of holding old-style communions and the arrangement they wanted was the same as can be seen at Ceres Church. It was decided to build the new church on a new site. It was planned to seat 1,200 people and so would be bigger than the old building. Putting it on the old site would involve disturbing graves in the old graveyard and Presbytery was of the opinion that Kettle folk would not like that. As we saw, Collessie folk didn't like it either, but that is another story!

View of the 'new church'

An ideal piece of land belonging to Rev. David Symers was identified just across from the entrance to the graveyard. It was purchased at a cost of £280 and the tenants who lived there had to be rehoused because the buildings had to be demolished. The plans, specification and costs were presented to Presbytery and the £2,400 bill approved. It was not until 13th August 1833 that Presbytery met in the new church in order to inspect it. At that meeting the Heritors pointed out that there had been a considerable underestimation of the cost. Several things had been omitted like levelling the ground around the church, a new bell (which cost £100), a lightning conductor, painting the new church and a clock for the tower (also £100). In all there was a shortfall of £796 9s. 10d.

Clearly the money was sourced from somewhere as the church was approved by Presbytery, which said it was completed 'in a good, sufficient and substantial workmanlike manner'. The new building was now the legal church of Kettle and the old one had to be 'shut up as a place of public worship'.

But it was not demolished for some time and the Ordnance Survey map with a survey date of 1854 and published in 1856 shows the remains of the building in the old graveyard as a sort of T-shape.

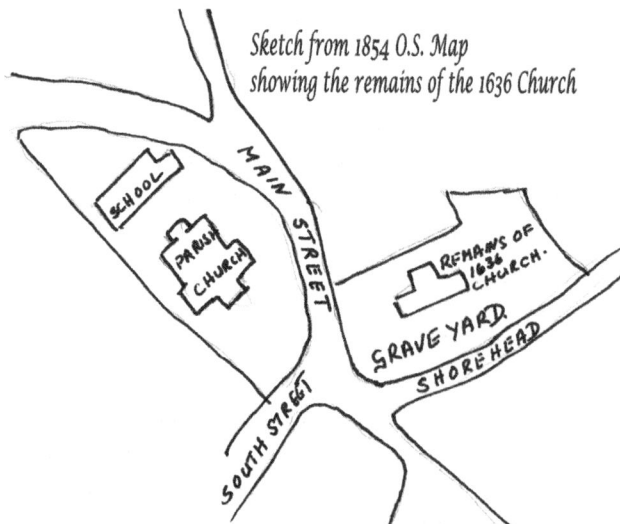

Sketch from 1854 O.S. Map showing the remains of the 1636 Church

The picture here is a view of the old Kettle Kirk (probably the only one) as it was seen through the dominie's window in Sir David Wilkie's painting of a village school. The school in question later became the smiddy and is now a private dwellinghouse standing next to the graveyard.

Much of the information above was gleaned from the Presbytery minutes. The Kirk Session minutes say nothing about the troubles when Mr Barclay arrived, the building of the new manse or the new church. What it does show is a very caring church that takes its responsibilities to the people of the parish very seriously. Perhaps it was Mr Barclay's influence that allowed this to be the case. We learn, for example, that the Session was responsible for providing a nurse to care for a foundling. She was given £11 Scots to pay for its needs but she asked the Kirk Session for more and got it.

In 1831 Dr Barclay ran into debt because he disbursed funds to the poor in the name of the Heritors but it was he and not they who provided it. When he sought reimbursement of the £350 from them they were not very pleased but he got his money. Also in 1831 we learn that Agnes Norman, who had been widowed, became ill when visiting her sister in Haddington. She was one of the needy poor of the parish so, when she became ill, the minister of Haddington contacted Dr Barclay to reach an agreement between the two Sessions about paying for her care. Later she died and the Kirk Session paid for her funeral and her care and gave something extra to her sister for her trouble.

There is the very sad but quite extended story of the Brown family. We first come across them in 1831 when David Brown tells the Kirk Session that he is unable to work and his wife is ill and they have four children to care for. By the time the Session met, Mrs Brown had died. Clearly financial support was required and the Session gave money to the family and paid for Mrs Brown's burial. When David died four years later the Session made provision for the children, ensuring the elder two had employment and the younger two were cared for by an uncle who received 1s. 6d. per week to help with expenses. In addition, each child received a new suit of clothes and, while the family home had to be disbanded, the furnishings were put in store for the children when they got a place of their own.

In 1837 the two eldest boys, John and James, are mentioned. The Session decided they needed to learn a trade. John was found a master, John Paterson, who was to teach him to be a shoemaker and provide full board, clothes and teach him his trade over a period of five years. James also learned to be a shoemaker but we know a little more about him. Contained in the minute book is the certificate of indenture dated December 1837 (see Appendix) that was signed by James.

In it we learn that James Brown of Kettle was to go to George Galloway, shoemaker in Markinch, to learn a trade. The agreement details James's responsibilities to attend to learning the trade and not to take time off without the express permission of Mr Galloway. In return, and in addition to teaching him his trade, Mr Galloway would provide accommodation, food and clothing and when James finished his apprenticeship he would get a new suit of clothes. If either party broke the agreement they would have to pay the other party £40 Scots. George Galloway and James Brown signed the document. James's beautiful handwriting was particularly noteworthy and reflects the pride with which he entered into this agreement.

A year later George Galloway contacted the minister because James had developed 'a large gathering upon his thigh'. Dr Barclay visited him and prescribed wine, which the Session agreed to pay for. Things must have deteriorated because a month later a surgeon, Dr Reid, was called and he prescribed a large quantity of wine, porter and beef steaks, which poor Mr Galloway could not afford to pay for. The Session agreed to meet the costs. Two months later the Heritors were asked to meet the cost of James's care.

Clearly the matter was causing much concern. A letter, included in the Kirk Session minutes, was sent to Robert Lynn, the Session Clerk, explaining that the 'boy Brown requires weekly a bottle of wine, 1 ½ of porter, 7 of beer and 3 ½ of beef for soup'. It also explains that Mr Galloway could not always give the boy the attention he needed and a woman should be employed to care for him. It appears James was weak and had to remain where he was until 'the part' was completely healed. It was being dressed with a 'great deal of barley and tacu'. The Kirk Session was, in effect, being asked to pay for a nurse. In the tone of the letter, signed 'M. Reid', it is clear that James is being cared for as well as he could be. We don't know what the outcome was as all mention of the Brown family suddenly stops. We can only hope that all the alcohol that he was prescribed made him feel a little happier, whether or not it addressed the infection that caused 'the gathering' on his leg.[186]

One interesting entry of 22nd December 1833 was when Dr Barclay asked the Kirk Session if anyone knew a James Watt. It was confirmed that indeed he was known and that he had been married by the minister of the Secession Church. At that Dr Barclay read a letter from someone in Aberdeen telling him not to marry James Watt for he already had a wife in Aberdeen whom he had married in the lifetime of his previous wife! The Kirk Session decided to pass the letter on to the father of Mr Watt's latest 'wife'. Once again we are left to imagine the end of the story.

It was about this time that a very remarkable man was taken by his parents to live, for a time, in the family home at Kettle. This man was Thomas Edward who was born in 1815.[187] Thomas grew to become one of the foremost Scottish biologists of the 19th century and spent most of his life in the north-east of Scotland. He earned his living as a shoemaker and never graduated above amateur status as a biologist. His contribution

---

186 Minutes of the Kirk Session of Kettle Church, Special Collections, St Andrews University Library
187 S. Smiles, *Life of a Scotch Naturalist: Thomas Edward, Associate of the Linnean Society* (London, John Murray, **1877**)

to understanding of the wildlife of his native land is, however, great and was recognised to be so in his lifetime. Edward's love of animals becomes clear in the earliest recollections of his young childhood in Kettle. Once able to walk he became friends with the cats and dogs about the house. When he was able to 'toddle out of doors' he discovered hens and ducks, of which, apparently, the village was full.

Eventually he discovered a much larger and more dangerous animal. Bet, a sow with a litter of pigs, was known to be ferocious, especially when she had piglets. Whenever he went missing he was found looking at the pigs as they fascinated him but, being unable to climb over the 'paling', he had to look through the slits. His mother tried to discourage Thomas in case he was bitten by Bet. One day the youngster disappeared. When she asked if anyone had seen 'Tam' the answer was always 'Oh! He's awa wi the pigs'. Every hen house and pigsty in the village was searched. At this point, according to his biographer, he was only a little over a year old so when he couldn't be found someone raised the cry that he had been stolen by the gypsies. It was remembered that 'tinkers' had been in the village selling brooms and pans and so it was concluded that they had stolen the child. Next morning Tom's uncle

Thomas Edward as an old man

and some volunteers went off to confront the gypsies in their camp, which was about three miles off. Understandably the gypsies were highly indignant at the charge being laid against them and the would-be rescuers were set upon by a number of women and girls. The men were 'unmercifully pummelled and scratched' before they escaped.

Just as another group of men were organised to go off in another direction to continue the search they were stopped by a scream. Into the house ran the 'pig-wife' and threw the child on his mother's lap. 'There woman, there's yer bairn! But keep him awa frae yon place, or he may fare war next time.' But where was he? 'Whar wud he be but below Bet and her pigs a' night.'

This story gives a lot of detail of life in Kettle in the early 19th century: the hens and ducks having free range around the streets; rearing pigs for food; and the tinkers and gypsies (both terms are used to describe the travelling folk) providing essentials to the villagers like brooms and pans. Perhaps most important was the concern each one in the community had for the welfare of the others and the reaction of the 'gypsies' to the insulting accusation made against them. It is also noteworthy that it was the women who sorted out the accusers, not the men!

Thomas returned to 'The Kettle', as he called it, later in the story. He was still a youngster and had run away from home in Aberdeen and walked to Kettle to see his uncle. Sadly, the uncle's Kettle relations were all dead and he was now lodging with a friend. The house in which he stayed was full of lodgers and there was no spare bed for

Thomas. A bed was provided, however, in the stick shed. In the evening after supper Thomas was asked to read two chapters from the Bible. Then he was asked if he could sing and when he said he could not he was sent to bed. As he lay there in the stick shed the young lad heard the folk of the house reading more from the Bible and singing a psalm. Here we get a glimpse of the kindness and the faith of our forefathers and how that was expressed in their daily lives.

In October 1835 a meeting of the Kirk Session was called on the insistence of the elders. They were concerned that Dr Barclay was no longer able to perform his duties as minister. In the minute we are told they expressed concern with regard to the spiritual wants of the parish 'considering the advanced years of our aged and venerable pastor who has laboured among us with zeal and efficiency for the long period of 57 years and who is now in his 87th year'. They wrote to the Crown, the patron of the parish, asking that a Mr Dickie, who had served in the parish for two years, be named assistant and successor to Dr Barclay. We can only assume this was not granted because when, on 28th December 1841, Dr Barclay passed away, there is no mention of Mr Dickie.

The death of Dr Barclay was recognised by Presbytery. Mr Murray, otherwise unidentified, spoke of his visit to his old friend only a few days before his death. He was, he said, 'in calm contemplation of death and entering no longer the hope of meeting again with the Brethren in the Presbytery'. He had asked Mr Murray to remember him 'most kindly' to them when they next met. Presbytery wanted this entered in their record and at the same time expressed their regret at the loss of such a respected member who had 'attained the 92nd year of his age, the 63rd in his ministry and who was the Father of the Church of Scotland'.

Once again there was a vacancy at a crucial time in church history with 1843, the year of the Disruption, only two years away. For over a hundred years Kettle had found that filling a vacancy could be a difficult process. The old story was to be played out again. In April 1842 Rev. Mr William Reid, minister of Inverteil, was presented by the Crown to Presbytery. The presentation was supported by 12 Heritors, 38 elders and heads of families and five communicants who were not heads of families. An objection was lodged by a small group who claimed he held beliefs inconsistent with the Church of Scotland. They further accused him of not believing in Christ as the head of the Church and that he had formed a close friendship with the patron in order to be presented as the new minister of Kettle. A grainy photograph of Mr Reid in an old newspaper shows the face of a strong character, so it is not surprising that he wrote to Presbytery and addressed the charges of his critics as follows: (1) he believed in the doctrine as found in the Confession of Faith, (2) he believed in Christ as the head of the Church and (3) there was no agreement or understanding with the patron. Eventually the objectors accepted that Mr Reid's faith was acceptable but they needed proof that there was no understanding with the patron. The patron was, of course, Queen Victoria. Mr Reid knew he could prove his innocence but this involved revealing the contents of correspondence he had entered into with Sir James Graham, the Queen's secretary.

Agreement for publication of these letters was gained from Sir James and the last of the objections disappeared. So it was that on 16th September 1842 Kettle had a new minister in the form of **William Reid**.

Mr Reid was the son of a schoolmaster and graduate of Glasgow University. He arrived at Kettle with his wife, Amelia Carstairs, whom he married the previous year, and soon they had four children. William Reid remained minister of the parish until his retirement. Kettle Primary School log tells us that he was chairman of the School Board, which he visited frequently. At times his wife and daughter accompanied him and in June 1878 his son, Robert, visited in his place. This suggests that Mr Reid was well supported in his ministry by his family.

A Young Canadian Comes to the Parish Church

Mr Reid died in Stirling in February 1884 and the next man to arrive in Kettle was 32-year-old **Aeneas Gunn Gordon**. He was the son of Gilbert Gordon and Mary Ann Gunn. Those who remember the Rev. Gordon do so with great affection.

Mr Gordon was born on 4th September 1846 and educated at Pictou Academy in Nova Scotia, one of the oldest institutions of secondary education in Canada, and the Universities of Dalhousie, Glasgow, Edinburgh and Bonn. He graduated with an MA in 1875. In that year he was licensed to preach by the Presbytery of Edinburgh and served as assistant minister at Caputh, Stornoway, Cupar and Kettle. He was ordained assistant and successor to Mr Reid on 12th December 1878. On 25th August 1905 he married Christina Moncur.

Rev. Aeneas Gunn Gordon

Unlike so many of his predecessors, when Aeneas Gordon presented himself to the people of Kettle he met with unanimous approval. This was not his first attempt at finding a charge in Cupar Presbytery. He had served as assistant to Rev. Dr James Cochrane at Cupar Old who died in 1877. Aeneas Gordon was interested in filling the vacancy but there was so much trouble about the appointment of the new minister that it became known as 'The Battle of the Charges'. In the end Mr Gordon gained 12 more votes than his rival but declined the charge because there had been so much strife. Mr Scoular became the minister of Cupar Old and Aeneas Gordon went off to Stornoway. Soon he returned to Kettle to assist an ailing Mr Reid and when the charge became vacant he was welcomed with open arms by the whole congregation.

Within a year of his arrival Mr Gordon found himself pastor to the people of the parish at the time of the Tay Bridge disaster. Many people from Fife were deeply affected by the terrible events on the night of 28th December 1879. One tale that has been recorded locally is of the foreman of Downfield Farm who took the farmer's son to Ladybank station. He had been home from Dundee for the weekend and wanted to get the train back to the city on the Sunday evening for work next day. It was a terrible night of wind with a gale blowing and the pony was unable to travel fast enough to catch the train.

They returned to Downfield and stopped at the Cotter Houses as the pony could not travel any further. There they visited 'Grandfather Robertson', who took the pony to the farm and made it comfortable. The foreman and the farmer's son were given warm food and rest by 'Gran'. When they eventually arrived back at the farm the farmer was very annoyed at the foreman for missing the train. Next day, however, when news of the Tay Bridge disaster broke, he gave his foreman £5 and thanked him for saving his son as the train he was to catch was the one that was lost. Grandfather Robertson was also thanked for his part and he too received £5.

Much has changed in the life and customs of the Kettle folk since the young Mr Gordon arrived in the parish. An article in the *Evening Telegraph* of 12th December 1928, which noted the forthcoming 50th Jubilee celebrations of the ordination of the minister, recalled some strange superstitious practices in the 19th century at the time of a wedding. Apparently it was a custom for pigs to be driven out to wander among the guests. The presiding clergyman would be stopped on his way to the church to have a blunderbuss fired over his shoulder and boots and shoes were thrown at the minister – whether or not that happened during the service is not clear! All of this was done in the name of 'good luck' for the young couple. I cannot imagine the minister feeling very happy about good luck wishes being passed on through him with such rituals!

Almost everyone who knew Mr Gordon had the greatest respect for him. Indeed, whenever he is mentioned it is always with a certain reverence. The *Evening Telegraph* said he was 'modest in demeanour' and did 'good by stealth'. In my research I spoke to the man who, at the time of writing, was probably the oldest resident in the Howe of Fife, Mr John Ronaldson. He remembers Mr Gordon quite clearly as a very strong man yet plain and humble. He was very fond of children, attending Kettle Primary School twice a week. Each Sunday he could be found at the door of the church welcoming folk – especially children. He was, however, no walkover and if members of the congregation were talking during the service he would bang his fists on the table and his beard would shake with emotion. Yet he was much loved by his flock, being just as at home in the farmworker's cottage as he was in the big house at Ramornie with Colonel Haig.

Among John Ronaldson's many memories is the annual Sunday School picnic. It usually meant a train journey to Burntisland, Kinghorn or some such place. Food was purchased from the Co-op bakery and John and his friend Robbie Skinner were earmarked to collect the food and take it up to the station and load it onto the train. Mr and Mrs Gordon would be organising the pupils onto the special train that had been hired for the occasion. Once at their destination John and Robbie would have to carry all the food to the beach where the picnic was being held. Only then were they told they could go off and have time to themselves. They had to return in time to take all the leftovers to the station, onto the train and back to the Co-op in Kettle. It was quite a day, but clearly the young lads were up to it and did it willingly.

Throughout his ministry Aeneas Gordon clerked the Kirk Session meetings as well as acting as Moderator. The downside of this from my point of view, as a researcher, is that the readability of his writing varied. It was always neat, but not always legible. The minutes also tend to be brief and lack information. No mention is made of youth organisations, though I believe there were Scouts and Girls Guildry.

According to the *Evening Telegraph* of 12th December 1928, Kingskettle Parish Church was the first in the Presbytery to introduce instrumental music and the second to have Sunday School trips. It was also during Mr Gordon's tenure that gas for lighting was installed, as were hot water pipes for heating and a new bell in the tower. The church had also been redecorated three times in the 50 years of Aeneas Gordon's ministry.

Mr Gordon retired from the charge of Kettle in 1930, 52 years after his induction. His last Kirk Session meeting took place on 7th November. It recorded a communion service which was attended by 304 people and Mr Gordon was assisted by Rev. Henry Porter of Cults. Prior to this on 26th October Mr Gordon read the Basis of Union to the congregation and, at a well-attended meeting after the service, the union with the United Free Kirks in Kettle and Balmalcolm was unanimously approved. This was a local manifestation of the union of the Free Kirk and the Church of Scotland in 1930.

A service was held when Aeneas Gordon said farewell to the people of Kettle. He did not attend personally but his friend Rev. D. Affleck from Ladybank presided and dedicated the brass lectern that adorns the church to this day. He also read Mr Gordon's farewell message, which shows the bond between minister and people. It was incorporated in the minute of the Kirk Session and reads as follows:

> My dear friends, The time has come when, as minister and people, we must part. My official connection with the parish terminates today. The Presbytery accepted my resignation on Tuesday last. You will forgive me, I hope, for not saying farewell to you myself; I have entrusted my message to my good friend, Mr Affleck. In taking leave of you I would like to say, as I think you must know, if any minister loved his people, I loved mine; and if any people have been good and kind, gracious and courteous to a minister, you have been so to me. For all your goodness and kindness, the grace and courtesy you have shown me during all these years, I thank you as much as I am able to do. Kettle shall always be my home. I shall think of you every Sunday. My chief delight in the future shall be to hear of your welfare and prosperity and the success of your children, whom I loved so dearly. As minister and people we part, but friends we remain; friends ever. Good bye. God bless you all.

In November 1931, exactly one year after he retired, Aeneas Gordon died at his home in Leuchars. The minutes of the Kirk Session record the following: 'We do here record our deep sense of loss at his passing, and with reverence and with love did we carry out his last request that he should be laid to rest by the Elders of his old Session.' His long ministry, sound Christian teaching and the high intelligence that were a mark of his sermons were recalled. As was his loving kindness to all and 'particularly to the children'.

His generosity to the church was also remembered in his gifts of the harmonium, communion table and chairs, and the lectern, which was a parting gift. The money that had been raised to mark his long ministry he had invested in a new 'public clock' in the church tower. Few who knew Rev. Aeneas Gordon had an unkind word to say about

him. He was known to enjoy a whisky and some among his congregation who were teetotal would keep a bottle in the house so that they could give him a dram when he called. He was loved, not because he had no faults, but in spite of his faults. That is also how he loved his flock. Aeneas Gunn Gordon truly was the shepherd and friend to God's people in Kettle and a faithful servant of God.

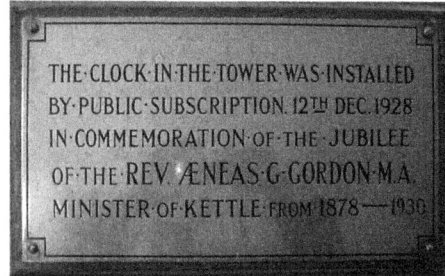

THE·CLOCK·IN·THE·TOWER·WAS·INSTALLED BY·PUBLIC·SUBSCRIPTION. 12TH DEC. 1928 IN·COMMEMORATION·OF·THE·JUBILEE OF·THE·REV·ÆNEAS·G·GORDON·M.A. MINISTER·OF·KETTLE·FROM 1878——1930

The End of an Era

A.G. Gordon in later years

With the retiral of Aeneas Gunn Gordon came an end to the old ways. Mr Gordon had cared for the parish through many hard times, not least World War 1. He saw how the local men were called into service and the resulting shortage of labour on the farms in the parish. There can be little doubt too that he knew the 36 local men who died and supported their families in their grief.

When the war was over, he played a leading role as parish minister in the ceremonial occasions when memorials to the fallen were unveiled.

A War Memorial for Kettle

It was reported in the *Dundee Courier* of 21st April 1919 that a public meeting had been called by Major Lawson to consider the form the war memorial for Kettle should take. After discussion it was agreed to extend the public hall to allow provision of a public library and reading room. In addition, a tablet was to be erected bearing the names of those who died and those who served in the war. A committee was elected to supervise the execution of the task. The *Dundee Courier* of 5th April 1920 tells us that Major Alexander Lawson of Annfield House unveiled the memorial to the 36 men who died.

On Sunday 19th October 1919 the local MP, Colonel Sir Alex Sprot, with his wife and daughter, unveiled a memorial in Kettle Church. It takes the form of an illuminated scroll containing 198 names presented in 40 regiments.[188] The service, which was conducted by the ministers of Kettle, Strathmiglo, Dunbog and Cults, was well attended by dignitaries from around the Presbytery.

D·BENNIE	D·GRAHAM	C·M·MUNRO
J·H·BISHOP	T·B·HAWKINS	A·NAIRN
J·S·BOYLE	D·N·JACKSON	G·R·NICOLL
A·CARGILL	R·JOHNSTON	J·G·NICOLL
J·CRERAR·JUN	W·KERR	J·OGILVIE
W·DALGLEISH	T·C·LAMB	J·ROBERTSON
J·K·DRUMMOND	J·LATTO	G·ROSS
C·DUFF	J·LAWRIE	W·TURNER
H·DUFF	A·MAYNE	R·TURNER
W·DUNCAN	J·MILLAR	R·WHITE
D·GIBSON	J·MILNE	R·WILKIE·JUN
W·GIBSON	F·MORRISON	G·SOMERS

In total 181 men from Kettle parish volunteered to 'do their bit' between 1914 and 1918. The Kettle folk were very proud of those who fought and died and stained glass windows were placed in the UF Church in memory of those who did not return. All of this was completed before the war memorial was unveiled on 3rd April 1920.

Rev. William Flint

It was not many months after being inducted into the new charge that Rev. **William Flint** had the sad duty of officiating at his esteemed predecessor's funeral at Kettle Church on 26th November, three days after his death. Mr Flint shared the service with the Moderator of Presbytery, Mr Craig, the retired minister of Balmalcolm, and Rev. Henry Porter of Cults, who officiated at the graveside. Rev. David Affleck of Ladybank conducted a special service at the Kerr Memorial Church. The whole Howe of Fife was in mourning and the world seemed to be a sadder place without Mr Gordon.

As Aeneas Gordon's successor, William Flint was the first minister of the combined churches of Kettle East, Kettle West and Balmalcolm. He was translated from Glasgow Tron and inducted on 14th May 1931. With the union in 1930, the retirement of Aeneas Gordon and the translation of Rev. Alexander Mitchell of the Free Kirk, the way was clear for him to become minister of the newly united charge. Aeneas Gordon was, however, a hard act to follow. This is so often the case. When a minister is as loved by his people as Aeneas Gordon was there seems to be some resistance to his successor, and this can be hard to break down.

---

188 *Dundee Courier* Monday 29th October 1919

Nevertheless, Mr Flint had a successful ministry and remained in Kettle until 1962. The early years of his ministry were a time of adjustment, rationalising buildings and uniting congregations. He was also minister during the war, which itself was a difficult time for the folk of Kettle as well as the country and, indeed, the world.

The Relief Church

The UF Church and Sunday School circa 1900

The Relief Church was formed by a group of ministers who broke with the Church of Scotland in 1761. Their objection to that Church was the role of patrons in the selection of ministers, the very reason for objections to Mr Barclay only seven years later.

As stated above, when Mr Barclay was ordained the local people made their unhappiness known at the appointment of the new parish minister and feelings ran high. While the fear of open revolt at his ordination proved groundless, a large number of parishioners decided to leave the Church of Scotland. It was because of this that a church was built to sit 500 people at a cost of £500. The first minister of the new Kirk in Kettle was John King and, while we do not have a date for his induction, we know he resigned as a probationer in Kilmarnock in 1779 and that he was a member of the Relief Church Synod in 1781. A manse was built in 1793 at a cost of £220, the funds for this and for the church being met by the people of the congregation. In 1803 Mr King died at the age of 66.

The second minister of the Relief Kirk was William Familton and he was inducted in January 1804. His previous charge was in Newcastle but there was little interest in Relief Churches in that town, so Mr Familton was ready for the move when he was called to Kettle. The stipend was to be paid in two parts. The main element was £85 but an additional £15 was to be paid annually. By 1819 it appears there was a decline

167

in numbers and the congregation decided to withhold the £15. Mr Familton raised an objection and the matter was brought before the Relief Kirk Presbytery.

No agreement was reached and the congregation made a strong petition that the connection with Mr Familton be dissolved because he had lost the affection of the people. The matter was taken to the Synod, which decided that Mr Familton should receive £200 in compensation for his trouble and on 11th May 1820 he was relieved of his charge. In 1822 he was recorded as doing pulpit supply in Edinburgh, but it is said that he finally made his way to America where he was drowned in a lake in 1825.[189]

The Relief Kirk was once again in vacancy, but not for long. The next year 1821 saw the ordination of Daniel Gorrie into the charge. He came from Glenalmond and was licensed to preach by the Presbytery of Edinburgh. The promised stipend was £100, which his predecessor received before the difficulty that ended his ministry there. Mr Gorrie served his flock for 30 years and of his congregation he said 'there had not been one discordant voice among them', which showed he had a happier experience than his predecessor. He preached his last sermon in the old church but died in March 1852 aged only 53. One who knew him described him as a stately man with white hair 'and a good amount of the figurative in his pulpit style'.

The United Presbyterian Church built in 1852 and manse built in 1879

A new United Presbyterian Church in Kettle was built in 1852 and provided seating for 700 souls at a cost of just under £1,850. The UP Church was formed by the union of the Relief Church and the United Secession Church in 1847. The church was opened on Sunday 9th January 1853 and is said to have kept the people together through troubled times. The troubles centred on the calling of a new minister. First one minister was called, but he preferred a charge in Auchtermuchty, and then another, but he preferred to go to Musselburgh. The congregation had already made it known that they did not want to be 'supplied with very aged men, almost incapable for duty, or by one who, from other engagements [the Synod probably], cannot *commit* his sermons, but

---

[189]   D. Small, *History of the Congregations of the United Presbyterian Church from 1733 to 1900*, vol. 1 (Edinburgh, David M. Small, 1904)

only reads a paper whether of his own or another's production'. In conclusion they said that 'if any such be *pawned* on us, we should shut the door against them, and instruct the treasurer to allow no payment for services'. Clearly the Free Kirk Presbytery had to tread very carefully when seeking to supply the pulpit of Kettle during the vacancy and in the selection of a minister. The good people of this congregation were to be handled with care!

Interior of the United Presbyterian Church

The Reverend Hugh Barr from Kilbrachan was ordained on 27th September 1854. Mr Barr had a successful ministry that lasted 20 years but in November 1873 he caught an infection and died at the age of 49. On his death Mr Barr was remembered fondly by his colleagues on the School Board. In the minute of 27th December 1873 his popularity as a preacher and pastor was recorded. It is also noted that Mr Barr had a deep interest in education and was an advocate of the 'National Scheme of Education'. They say he spoke his views frankly but was always prepared to 'listen and to fairly weigh the arguments of any who might differ from him'. The minute records that the members of the Board felt they had lost 'not only a faithful and pleasant counsellor but a very great friend and brother'. Clearly Mr Barr made an impression on the folk of Kettle.

A special year for the folk of the UP Kirk in Kettle was 1878, as it was the anniversary of its formation. Before the Relief Church had its first building the congregation met out of doors, even in bad weather. There is a tale of a dove that accompanied the worshippers both outside and in. This was seen as such a great omen that the original building built about 1778 had a dove carved on its ceiling and

The communion tokens struck for the centenary communion

painted on a pillar. When it was decided to commemorate their centenary with a communion service a special token was struck for the occasion and the dove, regarded as their emblem, was included in the design.

The next minister, William Tees from Glasgow, was ordained on 9th July 1874. Five years later the old manse, which by then had served for 85 years, was demolished and a new one built on the same site for £1,440. In 1884 Mr Tees was called to Rochdale, serving there for five years before moving to South Africa, where he became the minister of a Presbyterian church in Durban. After Mr Tees left, James B. Nicholson from Leven was ordained in February 1885. He stayed only a short time, accepting a call to Hutchestown, Glasgow, in 1889. Membership was dropping and short ministries did not help to build numbers. When Arthur Simmons arrived from Dalry, Ayrshire, in 1889 the membership stood at 325 and the stipend was £225, with manse and garden. The UP Church in Kettle was beginning to wonder if the establishment of the St Mary's Free Church in Ladybank, which had moved from Giffordtown and now had 300 members, was having an effect on its growth.

UF Church Choir 23rd August 1890, Minister Mr Arthur Simmons

Kettle was, however, holding its own and Mr Simmons remained for 20 years, being translated to Gateshead in July 1909. During his tenure the UF Church and the Free Church united to form the United Free Church. On 31st December Rev. John Gilmour was ordained and he remained until 1920 when he was translated to Edinburgh Holyrood Abbey. The next minister, Rev. George Mitchell, was the last UF minister in Kettle. He had first been ordained into the Congregational Church at Broughty Ferry in 1907 but was admitted into the UF Church by the General Assembly in 1920. He was inducted into the church at Kettle in 1921. With the union of the Established Church and the United Free Church in 1929, Mr Mitchell was expected to seek another charge to make way for adjustment. Aeneas Gordon of the Parish Church had already retired. Mr Mitchell moved to Shotts Erskine in May 1930, but sadly died in March 1931.

The Free Church of Kettle and Cults at Balmalcolm

U. F. Church and Manse, Kettle and Cults.

Another Free Church was opened at Balmalcolm following the Disruption of 1843. Initially it was thought that the planned Free Church at Giffordtown would also serve Kettle. Within a few weeks of leaving his charge at Collessie, John MacFarlane was also preaching at Pitlessie and in Annfield Den, finding support from Kettle as well as Pitlessie. It was quickly realised that this was not a viable option for the long term. The distance between Kettle and Giffordtown was too great for folk to walk on Sunday morning and the area too large for a minister to serve.

Interior of the Free Church of Kettle and Cults in Balmalcolm

By December 1843 the church at Balmalcolm was opened for public worship, though it was not quite complete. Rev. Mr McGregor was ordained its first minister. Mr Manson, an Edinburgh minister, preached in the afternoon and Mr McGregor preached in the evening. The offering on the first day was £21 13s. 7d. This new church was to serve the needs of people in both Kettle and Cults. The earliest known record of Balmalcolm (Malcolm's Town) is 1166 in a charter of Malcolm IV to Duncan, Earl of Fife, on his marriage to the King's niece Ada. This was a wedding gift to the Earl. By the 18th century it was well known as a weaving village producing coarse linen cloth or 'dowlas' and material for window blinds. Today it serves as a dormitory village in the midst of the fertile Howe of Fife. The largest business in the area is Kettle Produce, which is a major supplier of fresh fruit and vegetables to supermarkets throughout the country.

A very popular early minister of the church at Balmalcolm was Rev. William Stewart. He was inducted to the charge on 6th September 1854. When he was called to Dudhope Church, Dundee, in 1860, the Presbytery of Cupar refused to lose him. The Synod, however, overruled them and Mr Stewart moved to Dundee. There he served for seven years before succumbing to pleurisy. He was highly respected as a preacher having a clear, strong voice presenting sermons that were easy to follow.

Rev. William Stewart

Rev. William Craig

In 1879 Rev. William Low Craig was ordained and inducted into the charge and he served the folk of Kettle and Cults loyally until the church was closed. The union was to include Balmalcolm, the UF and the Parish Church. Both the Parish, or East Church, and the UF, or West Church, were used every Sunday with morning services taking place in the East Church and evening services taking place in the West Church. Balmalcolm Church was closed and Colonel Haig of Ramornie arranged for the transference of the two stained glass windows in the photograph on the next page to the East Church. The two windows showing St Peter on the left and St Andrew on the right, which once adorned Balmalcolm Church on either side of the pulpit, can now be seen to advantage only from the gallery. This is unfortunate because they are very fine windows. Mr Haig of Ramornie House, Ladybank, donated the windows to the UP Church in Balmalcolm in 1898 in memory of his wife Anne. He was a member of the well-known whisky family of Haig in Markinch.

On 12th December 1934 the death of Mr Craig was intimated to a meeting of the Board. In tribute to the Free Kirk minister the Moderator, Mr Flint, expressed the deep sense of loss felt by the congregation and the parish. He had been in post for more than 50 years. Mrs Craig was permitted to continue to live in the Balmalcolm manse until

May 1935 but she was given the option to leave earlier if she so wished! When the minister died, the manse had to become available quickly for the convenience of the church and perhaps a new minister. In this case, the house was sold with the £640 raised going to Kettle Church fabric fund. The church itself was sold for £30. It was in 1936 that Mrs Craig, widow of Rev. William Craig, unveiled a memorial to her husband in Kettle Church following the morning service on 11th October. Originally in the vestibule it was moved to its present position in the sanctuary in 1970.

Windows transferred from Balmalcolm UF Church to Kettle Parish Church

The United Parish Church of Kettle

With the union of the Free Kirk and the Parish Kirk in 1930, a new minute book was opened on 23rd November of that year. The opening paragraph reads: 'The Kirk Session of Kettle (consisting of the Sessions of Kettle East, Kettle West, and Balmalcolm Churches now united in terms of the Basis of Union affixed on the page opposite to this minute) met this evening and was constituted.' The document containing the terms of the Basis of Union can be found in the Appendix.

The Kirk was in vacancy and the Interim Moderator was Rev. Anson Wood, minister of Cupar First Church, now called Cupar Old. The opening business concerned the appointment of office bearers and a Board to ensure the new united Kirk was properly managed. This seemed to occupy the Session until the end of the year. On 9th March of the following year the Session met for the purpose of counting the ballot which had been held for the appointment of the new minister. The result was 159 in favour and 19 against, and so it was that Rev. William Flint was elected minister of Kettle Parish Church. As we saw above, his induction would take place on 14th May 1931.

It was decided to hold communion on Sunday 19th April, the first for the united congregation. Mr Craig officiated at the afternoon service in the West Church, where individual cups were used and 329 attended. The morning service had 221 attendees, which used the common cup and was led by the Rev. John Gilmour.

At the Kirk Session meeting of 25th November the death of Rev. Aeneas Gordon, two days earlier, was announced and funeral arrangements made. At a special meeting the following Sunday a tribute to Mr Gordon was read. At the April 1932 meeting of the Kirk Session the terms of Aeneas Gunn Gordon's will was read out. It stated that £600 was to be set aside and invested in the name of the Kirk Session. The interest accrued was to pay for: (1) the upkeep of the graveyard, (2) the insurance of the church and manse and (3) the upkeep of the church clock and tower. This was to continue for 14 years and on the 15th year the money was to pay for maintenance of church and manse; on the 16th year the whole process was to start again. It was embodied in the will that any change to this distribution of the money could only take place with the approval of Presbytery. It was also Mr Gordon's will that this be embodied in the Kirk Session minute. In conclusion, however, there was some doubt about the availability of the whole sum. As it turned out, the final figure was £540. This was a considerable amount of money in 1934, and would have been the cost of a very nice modern bungalow.

In January 1936 the death of George V was minuted along with loyalty to Edward VIII. The minister had decided to mark this with a memorial service on the following Sunday and a funeral service on the 28th. On 10th March it was recorded that the Kirk Session was very concerned at the 'phenomenal growth of Football Pool Betting', being convinced that serious social and moral consequences were involved, and so they welcomed a Bill that was being introduced to Parliament for the 'suppression of this phase of the gambling evil'.

In June 1936 the post of organist became vacant and was advertised with an annual salary of £30. A list of four candidates was drawn up and the successful applicant chosen by a ballot of the congregation. In November of the following year the Moderator of the Church of Scotland was visiting Cupar Presbytery. On the Sunday he was to preach at the Kerr Memorial Church in Ladybank and it was agreed that Kettle should cancel its evening service and encourage its members to attend the service there.

On 21st April 1938 John E. Brown MA BD, a member of Kettle Church, was licensed by the Presbytery of Cupar to preach the Gospel. The Session recorded its gratification that a member of the congregation had entered the ministry of the Church of Scotland. Little did the good folk of Kettle know that the 24-year-old John Ebenezer Brown was to father a son who would one day be Chancellor of the Exchequer and Prime Minister, so bringing international recognition to their village.

John Brown was born just one month after the outbreak of the First World War. He attended primary school at Cults and at Kettle, going on to Bell Baxter Secondary School in Cupar. After graduating with an MA from St Andrews University and a BD three years later, he served at Newburgh in Fife, Govan and Dunoon, where he was ordained in 1939. Mr Brown then returned to Govan as minister before going to St Brycedale in Kirkcaldy. His marriage to Elizabeth Souter brought three sons into the world and each has made his mark. John became head of public relations for Glasgow City Council, Gordon became Prime Minister and Andrew a Channel Four television producer. The *Herald* of 8th December 1998 carried an obituary in which it said he was greatly loved both as an able preacher and 'superb pastor' and that he was 'distinguished by his selfless concern for those committed to his care'. Mr Brown is remembered with affection by local folk, some experiencing his kindness long after he left the area.

World War II

The 3rd September 1939 saw the outbreak of World War II and at the Kirk Session meeting of the 11th we find this already touching the lives of the folk of Kettle. They were concerned about the lighting restrictions affecting the work of the church. It was decided not to provide blackout for either church but to change the time of the second Sunday service from 6 p.m. to 3 p.m. and to hold the second service in the East Hall instead of the West Church. It was also decided to provide blackout for the East Hall so that it could be used for church functions in the evening. One year later a Presbytery resolution was read 'deploring the spiritual apathy in our Church and Nation and calling for renewed efforts on the part of the Church to influence members and others in the way of Godliness and righteousness'.

An important entry was made in the Session minute for 26th August 1942. We are told that Mr Flint, the minster, read 'an intimation he had received through the Church Offices that Private John Low, Prisoner of War, Germany, had taken his first communion after instruction from Rev. John McIntyre, C.F., also a Prisoner of War'. It was agreed to add the name of John Low to Kettle's communion roll.

On 10th November 1942 the minister had received a letter from the officer commanding the local Polish forces requesting that the Session accept and place in the East Church a plaque commemorating the stay of the Polish troops for over two years in the community of Kettle. We know the request was granted as that plaque remains

Plaque in memory of the Polish forces in Kingskettle 1942

in a prominent place in the middle window on the east wall of the church. Sandy Scott, a young lad in the congregation on the Sunday when the plaque was dedicated, remembered being in the balcony when all of the Polish soldiers filled the pews below. The singing that Sunday was, he said, wonderful.

It was not until 12th June 1947 that the Congregational Board of Kettle Church got around to considering the erection of a fitting memorial to those of the parish who had fallen during the Second World War. A member of the Board was instructed to look into the matter and report back in September, but there is no more mention of it until 26th August 1948 when it was decided that the memorial windows located in the West Church should be removed and installed in the East Church. An estimate of £90 had been received from Alexander Kerr of Edinburgh to carry out the work and this was accepted.

The building was derequisitioned in April 1947 and the church given the opportunity to make a claim for compensation. A sum of £500 was received and the money placed in the Church of Scotland Fund as a local fabric fund. By the end of the war it was in such a bad state that it was decided it was unsuitable as a place of worship and the Board investigated letting the church to Fife Poultry Products. As a result of this decision the removal of the windows became a matter of urgency.

World War II memorial window

It was also decided that there should be a memorial in the church containing the names of the fallen in both wars. Presumably this refers to members of the Parish Church who died during World War I because those of the UF Church are remembered on the windows moved to the East Church. A member of the Board was instructed to look into the matter and report back.

On 20th November 1949 it was intimated to the Board that a letter had been received from the Welcome Home Committee (Kettle) informing them that £85 had been set aside for the erection of a stained glass memorial window in the Parish Church. It was agreed that McKee, Stained Glass Artists, Edinburgh, be asked to offer a quotation for the window and in the meantime the money would be lodged with the Co-operative Society.

The windows were installed in the church as planned. The window referring to World War II remembers G. Balsillie, R.I. Booth, R.S. Clazy, G.R. Dawson, T.E. Jamieson, P. McL. Prentice and J.M. Turner. Each one was known to the people of Kettle, loved and missed.

These names are also found on a plaque which was added to the war memorial.

Post-war Period

On 13th October 1945 there was a special meeting of the Roll of Communicant Members, called to consider an overture (presumably from the General Assembly) to remove the barrier to the appointment of women as elders. A vote took place and of the 15 who attended only two voted in favour. The Kirk Session of Kettle was not ready for women to be allowed to hold their proper place in the fellowship of the church.

The First World War memorial window was removed from the UF Church and installed in the Parish Church. It accompanied the other window, which is in memory of David Beveridge, the founder of the factory. On 13th April 1950 Kettle's minister, Rev. William Flint, put Kettle on the world map by leading a radio broadcast service from Cupar St John's Church celebrating the tercentenary of the Scottish Psalter.

Left: window in Established Church in memory of David Beveridge
Right: 1914–18 war memorial window from United Free Church

The building was now 125 years old and showing signs of wear and tear. It was considered necessary in 1958 to replace the roof. Funding was, as ever, a problem and the work was not carried out until 1962. Repairs were also needed to the ceiling and in 1961 services had to take place in the hall to allow work to proceed.

Mr Flint had seen the parish through troubled times but now his time as minister of Kettle was coming to an end. In July 1962 he celebrated 50 years in the ministry and it is recorded in the Kirk Session minutes that a special congregational function was held in the Kettle Memorial Hall – principal guest Rev. W.J. Baxter DD from Glasgow. Mr Flint was presented with a wallet containing Treasury notes to mark his Jubilee and his retiral. In November of that year he conducted his last service and demitted the charge in December. Rev. Peter R.G. Wallace of Falkland became Interim Moderator to see the Kirk through another vacancy.

The first mention of a linkage with Cults Kirk is in the May 1963 Kirk Session minutes and in the June meeting of the Board. It appears the Kirk Sessions and Boards held joint as opposed to separate meetings while the churches were in a vacancy. In December 1962 Kettle Kirk appeared to be in a strong position with 373 on the roll, 285 having 'communicated' at least once in the previous year. The Woman's Guild had a membership of 49 and the Sunday School catered for 90 youngsters.

The joint meeting of the Kirk Sessions in February 1964 recorded that **Rev. Angus Macaskill** was chosen to fill the vacancy with 228 votes in favour and only 9 against. Mr Macaskill was a popular choice and his ministry was to be a short but happy one. His induction took place on 23rd April 1964. A quinquennial report by Presbytery in December 1965 was full of praise for the way he had endeared himself to the whole congregation as a result of 'his strong and vigorous preaching of the Word, and his efficient pastoral care of his people'. They also predicted that under his leadership the linkage with Cults would 'progress smoothly and favourably'.

Three years later, following the death of Rev. William Flint, the Kirk Session approved a memorial service to their late minister and sought subscriptions to finance a suitable lasting memorial to his ministry at Kettle between 1931 and 1962. It was decided this would take the form of a pair of vase stands and flower vases. On the morning of 11th May 1969 the Kirk Session met with Angus Macaskill as the Moderator, although it was clear that he was preparing the church for vacancy because he was retiring. The Kirk Session met again at 4.15 p.m. and the Interim Moderator, Rev. Johnstone Titterington, had been appointed, though Rev. A.G. MacKenzie of Newburgh led the meeting because Mr Titterington was ill.

On 19th June the Kirk Session met with Angus Macaskill acting as Moderator for the last time. He expressed gratitude to the elders for their devotion and recalled his happy relationship with the congregation. In reply John Balmain, the Session Clerk, expressed the congregation's gratitude for Mr Macaskill's devotion to duty. It was also remarked that he provided the inspiration for the renovation work which was now well advanced.

A New Face to an Old Kirk

In December 1966 the Board decided to install a Hammond electronic organ at a cost of £559. The next entry in the Board's minute book is July 1968 and this meeting considered the possibility of a refurbishment programme. The intention was to install a roof to seal off the balcony, replace the pews with some purchased from Victoria Street Church in Dundee and redecorate the vestibule, sanctuary and vestry. The total cost of the whole project was estimated to be £1,851 15s.

The December 1968 meeting recorded the approval of the General Trustees and the Advisory Committee on Artistic Matters to the proposal. Mr Tom Rodger had accepted an invitation to act as architect and a plan was being prepared to put before the Board.

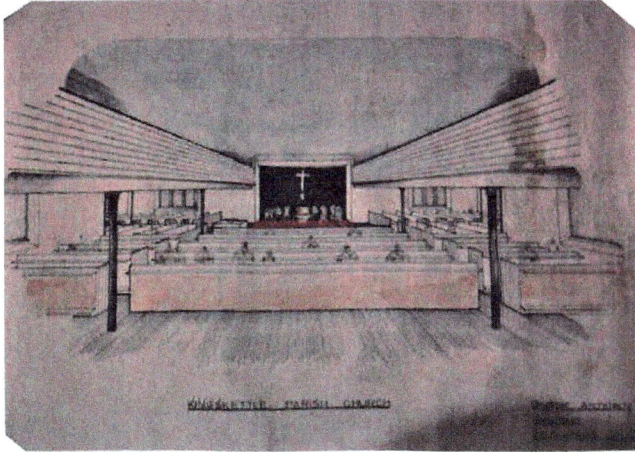

The plan presented to the Board for their approval

At the May meeting it was reported that the General Trustees and Advisory Committee had approved the plan produced by the architect. There had also been a meeting with the Session Clerk, Property Convener and Clerk to the Board (the Treasurer was unable to attend) and it was decided to seek competitive offers to carry out the work. This was to include work on the central heating system and the re-siting of four memorial stained glass windows. The final bill as revealed to the Board on March 24th 1970 was £3,442 3s. 1d.

Interior of Kettle Church early in the 20th century

The 11th January 1970 was a red letter day for Kettle Kirk. It was on this day that there was a service of rededication of the church following the extensive renovation that had taken place. It was a communion service and the guest preacher was Rev. Hugh. O. Douglas, Moderator designate of Dundee Presbytery. At the same service a Bible marker and a pulpit fall, gifted by the Woman's Guild, were dedicated as were the pair of vase stands and flower vases in memory of Mr Flint. It was at the time of the renovation that the Hammond electric organ was purchased. This was a great improvement on its predecessor and it served the congregation well for about 12 years.

The interior of Kettle Church in 2016

The Last Minister of Kettle and Cults

The vacancy, following the departure of Mr Macaskill, was a short one as on 8th October 1969 the joint Sessions of Kettle and Cults met in the reading room at the Wilkie Hall, Pitlessie. There it was revealed that **Rev. George Henderson** had been overwhelmingly approved by the congregation. George preached as sole nominee at the time of the renovations of the church. Because of this the church was closed and he had to preach in the Memorial Hall, the church hall being too small to accommodate the congregation. George told the Vacancy Committee that although he was a bachelor at that time, if he was accepted by the congregation he would return a married man. So it was that when he came to Kettle as the parish minister he brought Hilda, his wife, with him. Rev. George McLean Henderson was inducted by Cupar Presbytery on 15th January 1970.

Rev. George Henderson

Mr Henderson arrived at a difficult time in the history of the church, not only in Kettle but nationally. It is said that *The Forsyte Saga* on BBC television on Sunday nights killed the evening services in churches throughout the land. Well, that may or may not be the reason, but the fact is that not only did the evening services stop over the country as a whole, but attendances at morning worship and at Sunday Schools also began to drop off. This pattern of diminishing membership was followed in Kettle, just as it was elsewhere, and it caused a great deal of soul-searching at that time, just as it continues to occupy hearts and minds today. Nevertheless, several important measures were taken in the life of the Kirk.

It is recorded in the Kirk Session minutes of 10th December 1971 that, subject to the approval of the Social Work Department, the Kirk Session agreed to the formation of a playgroup 'to be known as Kettle Parish Church Play Group'. This was an opportunity for the church to provide an important service to the community and in the care and education of the young, which is a traditional concern of the Kirk. By 21st October 1973 there was a request to the Kirk Session to approve the establishment of a mothers and toddlers group, which was to be under the management of the Playgroup Committee. This organisation was popular and doing well in Kettle but on 6th July a letter was read to the Session to the effect that the playgroup was no longer an organisation of Kettle Parish Church. There is no lead up to this and no explanation regarding the decision. It may well be that the provision of the service was taken over by the local authority. It certainly continued to function because in May 1982 the Kirk Session received a request from the committee of the playgroup to hold an event in the church hall to celebrate their anniversary. This was to include serving punch and the Kirk Session felt that serving alcohol was inappropriate on church premises and so refused permission.

In the minute of the AGM of 30th March 1980 the minister expressed thanks to Mr Richard Galloway and friends for 'the building of the organ acquired from Uddingston Congregational Church'. Mr Galloway was one-time Assistant Advisor of Music to Fife Education Authority before becoming Advisor in Music to Central Region. His wife Margot, who became church organist at Kettle in 1968, noticed an article regarding the demolition of Uddingston Church and that the organ was freely available to anyone who would give it a good home. Richard and his friends worked very hard at weekends and sometimes until late into the night to install the organ. Once finished, it looked as though it had been made for the church, fitting perfectly into the chosen location.

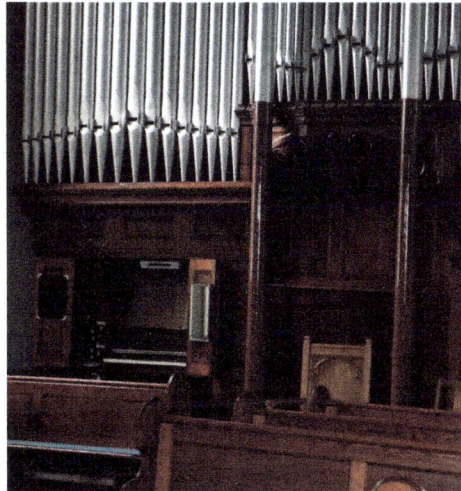

Later that year, on 16th November, the Kirk Session nominated Mrs Ann Page to be the first female elder at Kettle. It may have taken 35 years since the matter of women as elders was first raised in 1945, but in the end equality in the Kirk Session was achieved. After all, the Kirk had been appointing women as ministers since 1968 so it could be argued that it was high time the role of women in the government of the church was recognised in Kettle. Mrs Page was ordained by Rev. George Henderson on Sunday 30th November 1980. The first Kirk Session she attended was on 4th December 1980 and the minister gave her a warm welcome.

It was during Mr Henderson's time as minister that the wife of John Balmain died. John had been a prominent figure in the parish ever since his arrival. He had acted as Session Clerk, Clerk to the Board, Sunday School superintendent and organist at various times over the years. When his wife Mary died in 1972 the white and gold pulpit fall that is used at Christmas, Easter and on communions was presented to the Kirk in memory of her. The Bible marker which matches the pulpit fall was also a gift, in memory of another of the Kettle ladies, Mrs Grace McNeil.

On 2nd May 1982 the minister informed the Kirk Session that he had written to Presbytery intimating his intention to demit the charge on 16th January 1983 in the interests of readjustment: so started a difficult time in the history of Kettle Kirk. On 12th August the Rev. Walter Learmonth attended the meeting of the Session to explain a draft Basis of Deferred Union between the united parish of Collessie and Ladybank and the linked charge of Kettle and Cults. After a detailed explanation when each clause was covered the draft was accepted by all 39 elders present.

On 31st October 1982 the final entry in the Kirk Session book records the celebration of communion led by Rev. George McLean Henderson. A total of 101 members participated that day, which was the last when this ancient congregation acted as the Parish Church for Kettle. From January 1983 it would be part of the larger Parish of the Howe of Fife.

Life in Kettle: The School

Education has long been considered important in Scotland. The first Education Act goes back to 1496. James IV was behind this as he wanted the eldest sons of the ruling classes, barons and freeholders, to be proficient in Latin, arts and the law. This was to ensure that local government was in the hands of those knowledgeable in the necessary skills. Universities were a natural offshoot of these early schools.

The first evidence of a school in Kettle is recorded in the Kirk Session minutes during Mr James Barclay's ministry, in about 1688, when a schoolmaster, Mr Thomas, was appointed. The appointment of the schoolmaster was seen locally as an important step forward and Mr Thomas received £2 13s. 4d. for teaching two boys for two quarters. By 1689 his annual salary had increased to £5 11s. 8d.

Throughout the history of Kettle Kirk, the provision of education in the parish was taken seriously and the schoolmaster normally acted also as Session Clerk. On 14th

February 1697, during the ministry of John Pitcairn, Mr Robert Grieg was presented by the Heritors to become the new schoolmaster, precentor and Session Clerk. This was all in line with the efforts of the Kirk and Scottish Parliament to make provision for schools in every parish. While the intention to have such schools had been laid down at the very beginning of the Reformed Kirk, lack of money, civil war and difficulties caused by the monarchy made it hard to put into effect until the accession of the Protestant monarchy of William and Mary.

In the Old Statistical Account, Rev. Peter Barclay tells us that while the schoolmaster's house was in good repair, the master himself was 'rather too old for much activity'. This disadvantage was offset by his assistant who was 'of considerable abilities'. The master had a salary of £22 per annum plus school fees as follows: English 1s. 3d.; writing 1s. 8d.; arithmetic 2s.; Latin 2s. 6d. While this education was available to all, it was really accessible only to those who could afford the fees.

By 1836 Mr Barclay's entry in the New Statistical Account tells us that a new school had been built which was 'capacious and airy'. The schoolmaster was paid the maximum salary which, with school fees that 'are very low', provided him with an annual income of £60–£70. 'Everyone', we are told, 'without exception learns to read.'

Following the Education Act of 1872 when education became compulsory for all children aged between 5 and 13, a School Board was established in Kettle. It first met on 29th March 1873 and lost no time setting about its business. It consisted of eight members, including local manufacturer David Beveridge and the UP minister Rev. Hugh Barr. Mr Keddie, the headmaster of Kettle School, was appointed treasurer and he also took the minutes.

Boys at drill, Kettle Public School

The first priority was to establish the property that was available to the Board and the number of actual and potential pupils requiring places. Mr Beveridge led a committee to investigate. They reported to the next meeting that their main concern was the Parish School which stood on the land adjacent to the church, which had 161 pupils on the roll comprising 111 boys and 50 girls. The remit of the Board covered not only Kettle but the surrounding area and so a census of the young people throughout the parish between the ages of 5 and 13 was conducted. This established that there were 432 eligible youngsters including 81 not on the roll of any school.

The following information about the Parish School in Kettle and the other schools in the parish was minuted:

The Parish School is taught by Mr Keddie and the area is sufficient for 118 scholars allowing 8sq feet per scholar. The Free Church Infant and Industrial School taught by Miss Thom in a hired room is very unsuitable as to site, size and ventilation and without any playground. The area space is barely sufficient for 38 scholars while there are 59 on the roll and an ordinary attendance of 52. Distance from the Parish School is 200 yards. The Subscription School at Kettlebridge is taught by Mr Archibald: The walls are damp, the building in want of repair and the office almost in ruins while the playground is only 283 square yards in extent. The area space is sufficient for 76 scholars. There are 70 on the roll and an ordinary attendance of 59. Distance from the Parish school about 1,200 yards. The Adventure School at Coaltown of Burnturk is taught by Mr Turpie in a hired room with area space for 27 scholars. There are 29 on the roll and an ordinary attendance of 16. The house is very much out of repair and damp. The floor is under the level of the road. No playground is attached. Distance from the Parish School is about 1 ¼ miles.

On consideration of these findings the Board concluded that only the Parish School and Kettlebridge School 'were worthy of the name of school'. The sites of both schools were too small for development so it was decided that Kettlebridge, the Infant School and Coaltown School should be closed and the scholars placed at the disposal of the Board. Furthermore, it was agreed that a new site be found on which to build a new school suitable for containing 400 scholars. It was also recognised that because of the lack of suitable accommodation the Board would be unable to enforce attendance until the new school had been built. The Parish School would have to be sold and the Heritors were consulted regarding the whereabouts of the title deeds. It transpired that there were no title deeds but the following explanation was included in the minute:

With reference to this it may be necessary to explain that the ground in which the Parish School and Schoolhouse are built forms part of that which was purchased originally for the erection of the Parish church, and that the building of the Parish School and Schoolhouse in a portion of the same ground being apparently an afterthought in the part of the Heritors, it may have been considered unnecessary to have other special Titles prepared than the Instrument of the Sasine and disposition with the purchase of the ground for the church which are both in the hands of the Heritors Clerk.

In June 1873 two pieces of land were identified as suitable for the new school. One on the junction of the Kettle Road and the Kirkcaldy–Cupar turnpike (now A914) was rejected in favour of the other site on Rumdewan. By 5th July plans for the new school were submitted. The Board was in communication with the Education Department regarding receiving a loan which would be used to pay for the new building. By October Mr Keddie was told to consider the enrolment of additional staff members. The Board was in a hurry but involvement with the Education Department slowed progress considerably.

There was a great deal of discussion about the plans and letters were sent back and forth between the Board and the Department. Eventually in 1874 a loan of £2,800 over a 40-year period was secured. The building progressed with the use of local tradesmen from Kettle, Freuchie and Markinch. The opening date finally came on 20th September 1875 and the members of the Board were in attendance. Once the classrooms had been furnished, parents, pupils and members of the public were invited to see the new school.

Kettle Primary School Log Book

The first entry in the log book was 15th October 1875. The roll stood at 200 and the staff consisted of Mr Keddie, headmaster, Miss May Russell, infant teacher, and pupil teachers David Duff, William Seath and Andrew Birrell. The minister was Mr Maxwell of the Free Church at Balmalcolm.

The opening sentence states: 'Many children appear to have forgotten all they had learned before vacation.' Mr Keddie felt the solution was to 'Drill Standard II in Multiplication and Addition Table. Standard I requires great practice in Arithmetic. Writing also requires improving'. It appears that much teaching involved drilling the pupils in tables, dates in history and addition. By 5th November it is noted that 'Children learning to sit in better position for which new desk seems to be well adapted'. In history James VI and Robert the Bruce were studied. On 20th December a temporary timetable had to be used because attendance was below average due to a storm.

Sadly, Mr Keddie, who had been so involved in establishing the new school, became unwell and died. The children were dismissed on the afternoon that his death was announced and they had the day off to mark his funeral. This was followed by another day off to mark the Queen's birthday, which was an annual public holiday.

The new school won high praise from the school inspectors when they made their annual visit in June, although they recommended improvement to the lighting and ventilation of the principal room.

Attendance was a constant concern and seems to have dropped when the youngsters were needed to help out on the farms, especially in October when the potato harvest was being gathered. Outbreaks of infectious diseases like measles, scarlet fever, chicken pox and whooping cough also caused attendance to drop dramatically. This was a time when the idea of compulsory education was being introduced and many families resented its effect on their incomes as youngsters were needed on the farms.

There was also concern among the families in outlying areas about the distance the children had to travel to school. In October 1879 a letter was received from Mr Morton, who was the farmer at Clatto, requesting that the Board consider a 'side school' at Coaltown for the village and surrounding farms. After consideration, however, the Board declined the request because, they said, the accommodation of the school had been provided for all the pupils in the parish and the pupils at Coaltown were within the statutory walking distance. Those measuring the distance from the village of Coaltown to the new school did not, of course, take into account the additional distance children from outlying farms like Clatto and Devon would have to travel.

There was a new headmaster in the school, in the form of Mr Alex Murray, but he had a very unhappy relationship with the Board. In October 1879 he communicated with them regarding the provision of needlework and knitting for the girls in accordance with the wishes of the government inspectors. He requested money be made available to Mrs Rollo for cloth. The Board rejected this saying the parents should make such provision. He then made further requests regarding the alteration of staffing (details not available) and alterations to the school and schoolhouse. These were inevitably 'left to lie on the table' and so no decision was taken. A request from Mrs Rollo, however, for an increase in salary because of increased work resulted in a rise in salary from £67 per annum to £70. Mr Murray's thoughts on this are not recorded.

In April 1881 the Board resolved that there should be a supply of books and paper to the scholars at a reduced rate. Mr Murray was to make up a list of books required and give it to the Clerk to order. He was then to superintend the sale of the books to the scholars and to account to the Clerk. On 2nd May the headmaster wrote in the school log that the Board had 'laid upon me the extra duty of selling books to pupils but they said nothing as to increased salary on that account'. By 4th June 1887 Mr Murray was still unhappy and wrote to the Board intimating his intention to comply with their request regarding the sale of books. He referred to a deputation from the Board, who had visited him when he voiced several concerns. These he listed in his letter as follows: (1) what salary increase was he to receive for the extra work involved in selling the books; (2) what credit was he to gain, and (3) what was to happen to pupils whose parents did not supply the books? The Board responded by saying that his services during the school day were at the disposal of the School Board and that they considered his salary sufficient. The Board also accused Mr Murray of holding certain pupils back 'notwithstanding their equipment for the work'. In reply Mr Murray pled 'not guilty'. Other charges in the Board's reply are contested and it is clear that the relationship between the Board and the headmaster were reaching a very low point.

Matters escalated as parents came before the Board holding Mr Murray responsible for the requirement to purchase books. They seemed to be unaware that it was at the insistence of the Board, not Mr Murray, that this measure had been instigated. The Board was coming to the conclusion that Mr Murray was refusing to comply with their wishes and that they should 'decline to continue' his services. Mr Murray maintained that he did comply with the wishes of the Board except that he reserved the 'classification of my pupils which I must keep in my own hands if I am to be any use at all in the management of Kettle Public School and in doing so I have the gratification of showing that I am acting in accordance with a resolution of the Board still barely a year old'.

The School Board decided to reduce the salary of the headteacher, which Mr Murray did not accept. Apparently, they were trying to take into account the possible rent of the schoolhouse and reduce his salary by that amount. The Education Department made it clear this was not possible. In September 1881 the Board decided to dispense with the services of Mr Murray and to publish all correspondence and relevant papers between the School Board and the headmaster (in the *People's Journal* 12th November 1881) 'to the Ratepayers enlightenment'! The advert for the new headmaster stated the salary was £150, plus a tied house.

On 2nd December we find the following announcement in the school log: 'My connection with the school terminates on Wednesday 7th December.' This terse announcement does, I believe, say it all! The new headmaster, James Calder who hailed from Aberdeen, arrived the next day.

Time to Move On

The Board members came to the end of their tenure shortly after Mr Murray's departure but questions remained about the treatment of the former headmaster. On 18th April 1882 at the meeting of the newly elected Board, which followed an annual inspection of the school, it emerged that the inspectors were seeking clarity on the events surrounding his departure. It also became clear that the new Board members were at odds with their predecessors regarding this issue. We hear no more of Mr Murray and we can only hope he found a position where his gifts were appreciated and he enjoyed a positive relationship with the Board.

During the 1890s the annual school inspection regularly reports that discipline is of a high standard. But perhaps it was a little too inhibiting even for the standards of the 19th century. On 29th April 1891 the Inspector writes: 'The Discipline is highly satisfactory in most respects, but a more confident and frank manner of answering should be cultivated.' It would appear his words were taken seriously as subsequent reports were positively glowing regarding the discipline and demeanour of the pupils.

Holidays were frequent. There was a week at New Year and several weeks during August and September. One-day holidays marked market days at Freuchie, Ladybank and Kettle. On 15th July 1880 the pupils were allowed a half-day holiday in order to gather wildflowers for the flower show which was part of Kettle market. The school was also used as a polling station and so closed to scholars on these days. Pupils were also given days off to mark the death of prominent people in the community like Rev. Hugh Barr, School Board member and minister of the UF Church, and Mr G. Beveridge, who had also been an active member of the Board as well as being the owner of an important source of employment in the town.

Mr Calder's beautiful cursive writing used in his entries in the school log is a pleasure to read. As ever, the main concern seems to be attendance. In October the potato harvest continued to create an unofficial 'tattie holiday', with large numbers of pupils finding themselves engaged in the fields of the parish. Also of concern were the frequent outbreaks of scarlet fever, measles, mumps and, occasionally, diphtheria. As the number of absences increased so the concern increased. The Medical Officer of Health for the county often became involved. At times the school was closed for a day to allow disinfection of the building to take place. When an outbreak of infection was persistent and widespread the school would be closed for up to a month until there was evidence that the infection in the community had begun to abate.

In 1903 the Scottish Education Department introduced the qualifying exam. The point of the exam was to establish which pupils had completed their primary education to a satisfactory standard and to categorise them into small groups capable of completing either a five-year education course or a two- or three-year course. The former was classified as a 'secondary' course while the shorter courses were classified first as the supplementary course and later 'post-primary' or 'non-secondary'. In Fife it was decided to centralise supplementary pupils and Kettle was recognised as the official centre, although those at Ladybank and Collessie could choose between Ladybank and Kettle. This would have suited the facilities that were available at Kettle, where laundry and cooking were part of the curriculum, as was woodwork, all subjects that would have appeared suitable for the non-academic 'supplementary pupils'. This was an expansion of the remit of the school and took up much of the time of the headmaster and staff.

In 1906 this purpose-built school was beginning to struggle to cope with the numbers of pupils. The Inspector's report of 18th May 1906 contains the following: 'The staff in the Infant room is technically sufficient, but the strain thrown upon the Infant Mistress, who, with the aid of a pupil Teacher, is responsible for the instruction of 80 pupils, is severe, and adequate individual supervision, so essential at this stage, is almost impossible.' The roll at the time of this inspection was 210 and the staff consisted of two certificated and four pupil teachers. A year later one of the certificated teachers was absent due to illness and a pupil teacher, Mary Wilkie, 'who has been making good progress in her studies', was put in charge of senior class III *and* junior class I.

Pupil teacher studies followed a correspondence course through Skerry's College in Glasgow. In addition they were tutored by the qualified staff in Latin or some other subject in which the teacher had a special skill. Examination of their subjects was frequent and good marks were expected. It must have been very hard work for these young people to be studying at night and working so hard during the day as they learned the skill controlling and teaching such large classes.

There was another Inspector's report on 30th April 1910. In this the state of the school is noted: 'The school is being repainted. Heating inadequate for the large classrooms – The closets should have doors'! On 20th May 1910 the school had a day off to mark the funeral of King Edward VII. The first day after the summer holiday, 16th August, saw the new headmaster, Mr Forsyth, take up the post. Mr Calder's illness is recorded, for he had to have his duties taken over by someone else, but soon his incapacity made it necessary for him to retire. On 12th October 1917 it is recorded that Mr Calder, who had been headmaster of Kettle School for almost 20 years, passed away.

Mr Forsyth, a 30-year-old hailed from Macduff in Banffshire. He lived in the 10-roomed schoolhouse with his wife Grace, whom he married at Collace in 1910, and Isabella Hogg, an 18-year-old servant. The new headmaster was critical of the standards achieved by the classes and was determined to improve matters. He was also concerned about truancy and was ready to punish severely those who absented themselves from school. On 15th September 1910 he records: 'The attendance is very unsatisfactory this week. Many children whose parents are railway servants are being kept at home for a holiday as these people are obtaining cheap fares.'

In June 1911 he complains to the Board that Mr George Duncan of Arthurfield had taken his two daughters, both in the infant department, away from school because of a family holiday. He also complained that Mr Craig, UF minister of Balmalcolm, had done the same thing the previous year. The Board made no decision about this non-attendance and in response the headmaster said, 'I cannot be responsible for keeping the attendance at all in the circumstance.' There were times, however, when the Board felt it necessary to grant permission for a child to be excused attendance. One girl was exempt because she was needed at home due to her mother's illness.

The April 1911 Inspector's report is very critical of the school building:

> Accommodation for the infants and juniors is not suitable; the lighting is not good; wash hand basins, though of a substantial structure, are rusty and are without paint or enamel; drinking water is said sometimes to be warm, owing to the nearness of the different sets of supply pipes; desks are not of a modern type, and there are no physical maps. The staff is necessarily sufficient, but the variation in size of rooms makes it extremely difficult to distribute the numbers properly, and the organisation of the school suffers in consequence. The necessity for re-modelling the premises must now be pressed upon the attention of the Managers.

Mr Forsyth was also unhappy with the accommodation as in May 1911 he records: 'The school rooms have been exceedingly close during the week. Today none of the rooms are below 650 and both the Infant Room and the Supplementary classroom stood at 700 although the windows are kept steadily open.'

On 28th June 1911 there was another holiday to mark the coronation of King George V and in January the following year the architect visited the school. It was not until 1914 that work began and pupils had to be moved out of the building. The infants found themselves in the Public Hall and the Junior II and III classes were located in the Parish Church hall. On 25th April the contractors began their work. It would appear that this was the big event in 1914 Kettle!

Kettle School and the First World War

On 1st September when the school returned, Britain had been at war since 4th August. We now know that this war was to continue for four long and devastating years. No mention of this is made in the school log because on 1st September the significance of the war that was to embrace virtually the whole world was not apparent.

In any case, the headmaster, Mr Forsyth, was still concerned about the school being disrupted as the reconstruction work continued. It had been a hot summer and the Parish Hall lacked adequate ventilation for the four classes that were housed there. Teachers were concerned that pupils were drowsy because of the heat and many complained of headaches. On one occasion a temperature of 80 degrees was recorded and the headmaster felt that work was suffering. He was very disappointed that the reconstruction was not finished after the summer vacation and he believed that the disruption would continue until November. In fact, the pupils did not return to the school until 15th January 1915. Even then classes had to be conducted around tradesmen who were completing the work.

Absence due to the potato harvest continued to cause problems. Those over 12 years of age could get an exemption from school for the harvest by completing a form. In fact, many under the age of 12 also absented themselves. The work of the qualifying class was severely disrupted and this caused the headteacher a great deal of concern. The following year it was decided that children should be allowed off for the potato harvest because of 'the great shortage of field labour'. This is the first recorded sign of the impact of the war on the life of the school and the shortage of labour due to the demands of the war was having its effect on all the farms around Kettle.

A year after it began, the war was still not mentioned in the school log, though clearly it was not far from the thoughts of Mr Forsyth. On 31st January 1916 he records that he had attended the Scottish Board of Selection and on return requested permission of the School Board to enlist in the armed services immediately, but the permission was refused. A member of Mr Forsyth's staff, Mr Couston, was called up on 29th February and perhaps the headmaster felt that he too should be pulling his weight in the war effort. William Couston at 28 was a younger man than the 36-year-old headmaster and he lived in two rented rooms in Kettlebridge. As a qualified assistant teacher, his absence caused some disruption in arranging adequate cover for the classes. The shortage of staff was to be a recurring problem throughout the period of the war.

On 7th June Mr Forsyth visited Cupar in order to make enquiries regarding his position under the Military Service Act. On the 20th he received a letter from the School Board intimating that no Appeal for Exemption would be lodged by them on his behalf. We do not know what was in Mr Forsyth's mind at this time but he must have felt very strongly that he had to go, for on 30th October he sent his resignation to the School Board. This was accepted and they were willing to relieve him of his duties within a month. So it is that he took his wife and four-year-old son and left Kettle. His last entry in the school log book was on 15th October 1916.

The new headmaster, Mr Patrick Murray, soon took up his post but the lack of qualified staff was increasingly affecting the work and discipline of the pupils and the morale of the staff. Pupils too were being affected by the war and in October 1918 the School Board decided to provide free books 'to all soldiers' orphans attending Kettle School'. It was also decided to start presenting prizes to the pupils at the end of the year and the Board and members of the community subscribed to this. Mr Couston, who was still in the forces, sent £1. The following year he contributed 30s. In March 1918 £8 10s. had been collected for the troops and was sent along with packs of cards, sets of draughts, dominoes and Ludo. There was also 24 ¾ dozen eggs sent to the Red Cross Hospital and a flag day was held which raised £5 16s. 5d. for Springfield Hospital. Red Cross Week 1918 raised £8 8s. The school was playing its part in the community in its support of those serving in this enduring war. Lighting restrictions were imposed on the school in 1917 and on 25th September blinds were being installed in some classrooms and the windows of others being covered with dark paper.

On 11th November 1918 there is a single entry in the school log: 'Armistice signed at 5 a.m. and hostilities ceased this morning at 11 a.m.'

It was not until 3rd April 1919 that Mr Couston returned to his duties in Kettle School. For him, and the whole community, 11th November 1919 was a very serious day carrying much sadness and thankfulness. So it is recorded: 'Today from 11am to 11.02am the scholars assembled in the Hall and gave tribute to the dead by lowering heads and closing eyes, after which the Dead March in Saul was played by Mr Couston.'

In 1922 Mr Murray moved to Lochgelly South School and he was replaced by Mr John Ross. Entries in the school log were now more brief than previously and lacked the detail we have become accustomed to. We learn that the 'control' (or qualifying) exam was held in Ladybank; that there were occasional problems of pupils with 'verminous heads' and that the evening classes in dressmaking, cookery, English and arithmetic attracted 50 students. Most classes in the day school were large by today's standards with 34 to 40 pupils. By 1924 rural courses were introduced, comprising woodwork, gardening and agriculture, and science, all well suited to the youngsters of the area. The railway strike of 1926 prevented Miss Kinnear from travelling to Strathmiglo and she took needlework classes at Kettle instead. On a sad note, in May the headmaster and Mr Watt, one of the teachers, attended the funeral of a pupil, John Grieg.

On 7th May 1935 there was a holiday to mark the King's Silver Jubilee and sports and a picnic were held in the public park. Each child received a Jubilee shilling from the County Council to mark the occasion. Again in May 1937 the children received a shilling from the Council to mark the coronation of King George VI and Queen Elizabeth.

In 1939 the country found itself once more at war but entries in the school log continue to be sparse and there is little mention of the effect the war was having on the pupils or the school. In November of that year classes were rearranged to accommodate the new lighting restrictions, and in the spring of 1940 boys were recruited to make a piece of spare ground in the schoolhouse garden suitable for growing vegetables. VE day was marked by a holiday, and two years later Mr Ross retired from office as headmaster having served in that post for 26 ½ years. He was clearly highly thought of and the Inspector's report included a word of praise for his endeavours over the years.

Kettle Folk

Throughout the history recounted so far it is clear that the folk are at the heart of the parish. They have shown great generosity, great stubbornness, great principle and great wisdom. Up to this point they have been seen through the ministers and teachers who came to serve them. It is time we began to see the ordinary folk of Kettle through their own eyes.

A major source of information in this regard has been Sandy Scott. Sandy was principal of music at Moray House in Edinburgh, but his family roots are deeply planted here in Kettle. Indeed, his roots go back to James Moyes, who was born in 1813, and his wife Isabella Stevenson. Their daughter, Jean, married Robert Scott in Falkland in 1856 but they lived in Kettlebridge at the time of Robert's death in 1913. They were Sandy's great-grandparents.

There were 10 children including Alexander, Sandy's grandfather, who was born in 1869. At the

Alexander Scott looking over a wall with a friend in dress uniform of the Scottish Rifles

time of Robert senior's death he was a retired railway linesman, though when Alexander was born he was a handloom weaver. Weaving was an important industry not only in

Kettle but throughout the Howe of Fife. Alexander went on to have an extremely interesting life. Having completed his apprenticeship as a tailor, in December 1888 the 19-year-old joined the Scottish Rifles. He saw action in South Africa in 1899/1900 (relief of Ladysmith and Tugela Heights also in 1900) before being discharged in 1901, his conduct and character being described as 'exemplary'.

Sandy's grandfather, Alexander, as an apprentice tailor working for William Seath; it is interesting to note how young the apprentices are

Sandy's great-grandmother's father, William Law, started up a general merchant's business in Kettle. In the 1871 census William Law, born 1837, was an employee of the Co-operative Provision Society. By 1881 he was a master grocer. The business came to the Scotts through Alexander's marriage to Janet Law in 1896.

In the photograph above taken about 1910 lined up are, from the left, Sandy's father, William Scott, a young lad whose name is not known, Jean Scott, his aunt, whose surname became Mackie after she married, Janet Scott, his grandmother, and Alexander Scott, his grandfather, of South Africa. William Law opened a general merchant's shop in Ladybank as well and this too was run by Alexander Scott.

Today, the shop in the pictures belongs to the Singing Kettle. The second photograph shows the same shop with Sandy's aunt Jean on the left and his grandfather Alexander and grandmother Janet. Clearly the business was still doing well in the 1920s.

One person well worth remembering is Mary Scott, Sandy's great-aunt. By all accounts she was a lovely lady with a very deep Christian faith which was combined with a love of children. Her Bible, 'The Christian Worker's Bible', was presented to her in 1908 and inscribed 'With love from the members of her Bible Class'. This Bible was clearly well used and heavily annotated by her. She was involved with the Gospel Mission which met in Kettlebridge Hall. On her untimely death in 1929 a stone was erected to mark her final resting place and is probably the best tribute to a very special lady.

Born in 1932, Sandy spent his childhood in Kettle in the 1930s and 40s. In 1950 and 1952 when he was a student he spent his summer vacation working as a postman, with a round that stretched from Ladybank to Kettlebridge. He has many memories of the people and the places where he delivered the post and he writes in a style that brings it all to life.

Mary Scott

As he approached Kettle from the north, laden with a heavy bag of mail, the first house Sandy came to was known as 'Puddenha', and at that time it appeared to him as a 'poor, rather bleak place'. More recently it has been substantially upgraded.

The next property was occupied by the Lawsons, who later lived in Annfield House. They had been involved in the linen trade in handloom weaving days and, owning property in the area around Ullapool, tended to recruit servants from there. The family also owned much of the property in Kettle and, as a result, Mr Lawson became known as 'the Laird'. William Lawson, an Edinburgh stockbroker, died in the 1940s and Alexander Lawson acted as the district councillor in the 1950s. The family was well known to Sandy as his mother had worked as cook for the Lawsons in the 1920s.

Up a very narrow lane was Parliament Square, so called, we are told, because it was a meeting place for the men of the village to buy newspapers and discuss current affairs. It is here that a breakaway 'Free Church' was established after

Annfield House

the union of the Parish Church with the Free Church in 1930. Sandy tells us that 'Tam Allan, a local tailor who had been Beadle at the Parish Church, set up a breakaway Free Church in a two-room cottage in Parliament Square'. Sandy was often called upon to play at services there while still at school. He also recalls the Ancells, neighbours of his great-grandparents in the early 1900s, who had a black mongrel dog that was a nuisance to cyclists, including him, as it snapped at them as they pedalled hard to escape.

Hazel Cottage and Jim Seath was the next stop. He was, apparently, of 'somewhat military demeanour and took a great pride in turning his annual berry crop into jam'. A relative of his, William Seath, was known as the local bard and had published a book of poetry in 1905. One poem in particular is relevant here and refers to the old church clock, which is the one before the present illuminated clock:

Kettle Kirk's old black clock face

> Ye wise an' douce Kingskettle folk,
> O, pity me, yer auld toon clock;
> Consider weel my waefu' case,
> An' renovate my bruckit face.
> I've faces four (folk whiles hae twa).
> But ane o' mine's nae face ava;.
> The three look north, south and east,
> Are half respectable at least,
> But that whilk glowers oot tae the west
> Has thold sae mony a bitter blast
> That deil ane frae that airt can see
> That time o' day it is by me.

A solution to the problem is put forward later in the poem below. This explains why the new clock installed in 1928 was such a good idea.

> Send Martin Annan up my vent
> To gie my face a slaik o' pent,
> An I will wad a groat that he
> Would mak' it like the ither three.

Next to Hazel Cottage was the old Police Station where the Scotts lived in the 1940s before moving to 'Speed's Corner', so called because Andrew Speed, the local watchmaker, stayed there, while 'upstairs from him lived Miss Christina Yuill – otherwise Teen Yale'.

Sandy recalls that his family had run the Post Office since the time of the 1914–18 war and it remained with the family up to the 1950s. In the 1980s it moved to its present location next to the church hall. At one time Kettle also had its own telephone exchange but that was closed before the Second World War.

Continuing on his postal round, Sandy encountered Jim Muirie's horse-drawn milk delivery cart. Donald, the horse, was supplied with slices of bread and was known to leave Jim behind and move on to the next place where food would be supplied. Sandy tells us that Jim swore profusely, and he was totally unaware of any impropriety in doing so. When the Minister Bill Flint passed, he would say something like, 'Not a very good morning, Jim!' The reply would be totally relevant but quite inappropriate when addressing a gentleman of the cloth in the 1950s!

Along Rumdewan is a house called Rylea where 1930s film star Diana Napier is said to have stayed for a brief spell when serving as a member of the Field and Nursing Yeomanry. Her husband, tenor Richard Tauber, sought accommodation at the Post Office for easy access to phones, which were rare in those days, so that he and his wife could easily talk to one another, but the request was turned down.

With the Samons taking over Kettle Farm in the 1950s, improvements in management were rewarded with expansion of the business until it reached the importance it has today as a supplier of fruit and vegetables to supermarkets across the UK. Local tailor Jim Seath's wooden shack at Shorehead was where Sandy's grandfather learned his trade.

Also found on Shorehead was 'Bell Smith's Chip cairt', which served the locals with their fish and chips. There had been a 'chip cairt' in Kettle for a long time, started by the parents of Bob, Bell's husband. This was located at the Crown Hotel. Sandy has an early memory of 'Chippie Hain' from Ladybank, who pre-dated the Smiths and served the locals from a brightly painted, pony-driven cart that was lit by paraffin lamps.

Then it was on to South Street and Maggie and Bell Peebles, the newsagents, where a certain amount of betting was known to take place 'unofficially'. Betting shops at this time were illegal but a mysterious system seemed to work very well and it included the milkman, Jim Murie, and the Co-op barber, known as Sweeney Todd, collecting betting slips. The connection between the two in this matter is not entirely clear.

Next it was up to the Co-operative Society, which was always very popular in Kettle. John Ronaldson told me how he could get anything he, and his parents, wanted there. It dates from 1843 and provided a valuable service to the community, and in Sandy's memory the honorary treasurer was Willie Birrell.

During World War II a tank trap extended across Fife and an associated pillbox remains above the site once occupied by Annfield House, though now heavily overgrown. Nevertheless, it is a reminder of times when Kettle, like the rest of the UK, felt under threat. As the war was drawing to a close, Italian prisoners of war based at Annsmuir Camp near Ladybank were put to work filling in the ditch which formed the trap.

Then it was 'up the Wynd', which was dominated by the UF building and where 'Russian Jimmie' (Mr Fraser, chairman of the local Communist Party) lived, and then there was mail for the egg-packing station which occupied the UF Kirk. While the Kirk was closed after the war, Sandy has childhood memories of magical gaslit evening services there. With the closure of the UF Church the beadle, William Smart (or Wull Smairt as he was known), took over the Parish Church. He and his wife Queenie held the church keys and Sandy had to collect them when he went to practise on the 'derelict old American organ that had survived from Balmalcolm Kirk'. He says, 'It was not so much the wish to practise as the need to discover how many more keys had stopped functioning on the instrument since the last time I had played it.'

Sandy then had to pass under the station as he progressed along Station Road. He remembers one character in particular:

Jim Marshall, the Station Clerk, who used to have a daredevil act he performed before an 'up platform' of waiting passengers. He would rush across the track at the last possible moment as the engine was driving hard uphill from Ladybank into the station. His leap onto the platform was always greeted with a sigh of relief. Collecting wartime deliveries meant that I visited the goods shed regularly. There was a chute and a crane. After raising each other up to the rafters in the crane's large scoop, the ploy was to let it plunge down and apply the brake at the last possible moment. How we were able to avoid injuring ourselves seems, in retrospect, impossible. We borrowed the railway company's two large handcarts regularly to collect scrap iron, rubber and waste paper round the village during the war years.

Under the bridge and Sandy was through to Bankton Park and it consisted then, as it does today, of handloom weavers' cottages. There was Maggie Turner, whose husband Harry was the village pharmacist. Their house looked over towards the railway line. Maggie, Sandy says, 'was a merry old chatterbox. Throughout the years of rationing, she used to appear in our Main Street shop every morning to entertain fellow customers with a barrage of gossip and stale jokes'. Then there was 'An old couple, Rachel and Ebenezer Brown, who lived near the southwest corner of Bankton Park. They were the grandparents of Prime Minister Gordon Brown. My very first visit to a morning service at the Parish Church was the occasion when their son John preached there for the first time. Gordon and Sarah Brown have buried Jennifer, the first child they so sadly lost, beside her great-grandparents in the village cemetery.'

After Bankton Park there was the rough road to Orkie Mill where two cottages lay, now gone. Here too was sited the gas works, now long since dismantled. The manager of the gas works always gave the regular postman a cup of tea but Sandy was not so fortunate. Once a week he would have to go out to Glenorkie Old manse with a postcard confirming that there would be a market in Cupar the following Tuesday. Sandy felt this was a waste of time because everyone knew when the Cupar market was held.

The mail for Kettlebridge was usually light. He would proceed up the main road and then take a detour off to Boghall. Chapel was also included but Sandy cannot remember the exact order in which he delivered the mail. Mrs Catherine Black was the resident of Chapel in Sandy's days as a postman. It had belonged to the Arnott family in the 19th century and James Moncrieff Arnott FRS (1794–1885) had twice been president of the London College of Surgeons. Then it was down North Street and half way up Mid Street and along Hall Street to where Sandy's grandparents had lived. 'Fiddly Adamson, the local dancing master, lived opposite their house. He could play Reels and Strathspeys on his violin whilst demonstrating the steps simultaneously.'

A friend of Sandy's grandfather, Davie Wishart, lived at the west end of Needle Street and, his father, Sandy tells us, 'had been responsible for track maintenance on the first

Tay Bridge. On the morning of 29th December, 1879, after its central girders collapsed, father, Wishart and a group of officials had walked out to where the structural break had occurred. Despite having been repeatedly told to go back, ten-year-old Davie followed them all the way out. He told me that story when I was a schoolboy, and I believed it. With so many railway men in the village, he would not have risked ridicule by peddling a tall tale.'

So ended Sandy's round as a postman and our look at the people and personalities that were Kettle folk in the 1930s, 40s and into the 50s. There is, however, another whose memory is longer that Sandy's and so we turn now to Mr John Ronaldson.

A Farmer's Memories

John Ronaldson was the oldest member of the congregation at the time of writing this book. He was 101 years of age and, as a retired farmer and son of the manager of the farm at Ramornie Estate, remembers the people and events of the parish over a very long time.

Going back to his childhood days at Kettle Church, Mr Ronaldson had one memory of Aeneas Gordon that he shared. At the end of the road on which the manse was situated there was the old gas works. On this particular occasion some Travelling folk were camped there and the minister went up to see them. They were in the midst of a party and Mr Gordon joined in and everyone had a wonderful time. When the time came to leave, the minister told some of the Travellers to come to the manse next day for some milk. The Gordons kept a family of goats for their milk. The next day the Travellers duly arrived and received the milk. A little later the minister discovered that his pony had been exchanged for the Travellers' pony.

John Ronaldson

This was something of a tragedy because he used to tour the parish and the replacement did not like pulling the carriage, and indeed did some damage to it. The local policeman was called but he was none too interested in the 'exchange' and wanted to pass it off. Mr Gordon did not like that idea and went off to sort it out himself. Exactly what happened is a mystery but the minister returned with his own pony!

Mr Ronaldson had been born in the vicinity of Largo but the family moved to Ramornie when he was very young. He and his mother took the train from Windygates to Markinch and then to Ladybank. She was told that when they left the station they were to take the road to the right of the war memorial and follow it down under the railway bridge, then straight ahead was a wooden gate which was the entrance to Ramornie Estate. There was a house on the estate for the Ronaldson family and there John, his two brothers and sister were raised. John loved being in the country and he always wanted to be with the men working on the land. It was not possible for a

young lad to spend all of his time in the outdoors as school beckoned. He was sent to Pitlessie Primary School but did not like it one bit. He frequently ran away at the first opportunity and punishments had no effect. Eventually John's mother decided she would teach him at home. This worked quite well for a time as Mrs Ronaldson was an able woman and John a bright pupil.

One day the butcher from Kettle arrived in his van. Mrs Ronaldson had told him about her son who didn't like school. The butcher suggested that she try sending him to Kettle School and this she did. This was a good move and John happily walked across the estate, along avenues of poplar trees, to Kettle and on to the school.

Ramornie House

John aged about 7 on his way to school

The headmaster was Mr J. Ross and he had the knack of encouraging John and his friend Robbie Skinner. Eventually they had to sit the qualifying exam to gain entry to Bell Baxter. John and Robbie sat the exam and to their surprise Mr Ross told them they had achieved a higher grade than anyone else in the school. There was only one problem: they didn't want to go to Bell Baxter. Realising that the move would not benefit the boys in any way, the headteacher agreed to keep them at Kettle and teach them there what they would learn at the high school. This worked out very well. The boys worked hard, but dared not copy from one another. When they had completed their work Mr Ross would send them out into the garden to see what his wife had for them to do. The arrangement suited John and Robbie very well, for they were both more interested in the outdoors than school.

It was because John got to know Mr Gordon, who attended school assemblies twice each week, that he started to attend Kettle Church. As we have seen, Aeneas Gordon always welcomed the Sunday School pupils as they arrived. They were divided into 'classes', each sitting in a different corner of the church. The minister would ask if they had learned a tract from the book that was provided, and he always asked some poor soul to recite it, and too often nerves made the hapless youngster lose his memory.

Ramornie was a beautiful house situated in a lovely, leafy estate. It was filled with trees of all sorts and there were many beautiful walks. It was World War II that saw the removal of the trees, which were required for the war effort. When John's father arrived on the estate World War I was still in progress and Colonel Haig was injured and in hospital in France. Mr Ronaldson Sr worked on the land and when a trainee factor was sent from Edinburgh to learn his job, Mr Ronaldson took him under his wing. He learned a lot from John's father and so, when he left Ramornie for a job in Aberdeenshire, he knew the estate was in safe hands.

When Colonel Haig returned from France, the first person he wanted to see was old Mr Ronaldson as he was grateful to him for his dedication to the work of the estate. He did not do it alone, however, for Mrs Ronaldson was an able book-keeper and saw that the finances were in order. So when the tenancy of a farm became vacant at Lathrisk and Mr Ronaldson was interested in it, Colonel Haig saw to it that he did indeed become the new farmer there. When it came to buying the equipment that was being sold off by the previous tenant, Mrs Ronaldson had seen to it that there were sufficient funds to pay for everything in cash and on the spot!

John's younger brother, William, went off to the war in 1939. He was at Dunkirk and fought in Germany, Italy and Sicily. He had two friends who were killed beside him just before Armistice and this made its mark on him. He returned to Ladybank and worked for Updahl the baker before going to Edinburgh, returning to Ladybank to retire, where he spent the rest of his days.

John Ronaldson oh his 100th birthday

The Linen Factory

A panorama of Kettle showing Beveridge's factory on the left, the UF Church and the Established Church

For generations of Kettle folk the main source of employment in the area was weaving. For most it was handloom weaving in the cottages that characterise the village to this day. By the middle of the 19th century the industrial revolution had arrived in Kettle in the form of a factory. It was established in 1869 by David Beveridge. This man's great-great-grandson, also David Beveridge, has been able to furnish the following information and the sketch plan of this once dominant feature on the Kettle skyline.

The Kettle factory was established in 1869 by David Beveridge. After his death it was run by his sons and then it was passed on to their sons. One of the sons died young and this, together with the great recession of the 1920s, meant it went into general decline and closed around 1929 to 1930.

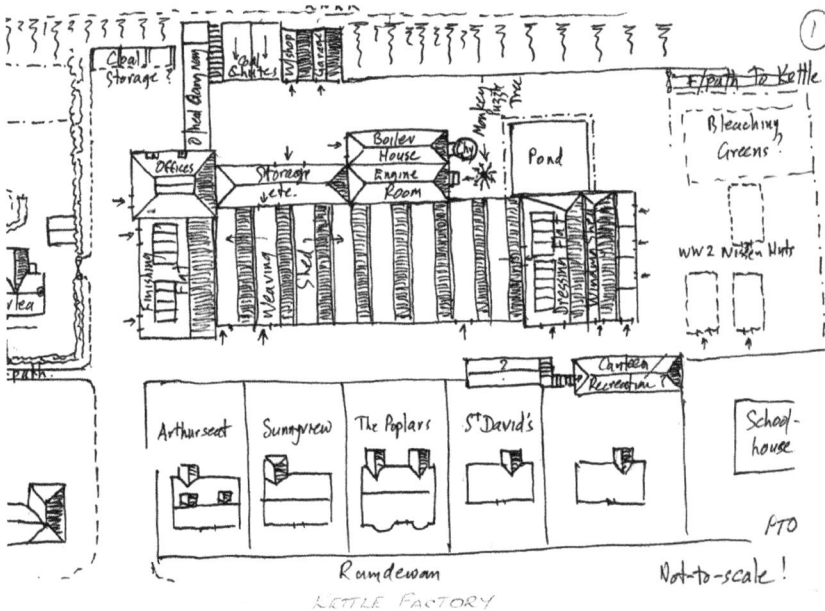

Sketch of Kettle factory by David Beveridge

This was a powerloom factory, unlike another on South Street which was a handloom works. There was a steam engine next to the boiler house and it drove the works machinery in all departments by means of underfloor shafts carrying belts and pulleys to each machine. Water for the boiler came from a natural pond. Coal was delivered by rail. The coal was offloaded at the station and stockpiled in the yard (there was no siding) and delivered to the boiler by means of two chutes and stored ready for the steam engine. The workforce was large, being a major source of employment in the area. High-quality damasks as well as other cotton and linen goods were produced. The company also traded in coal with the villagers. Lighting in the works was by electricity, which came from a generator powered by the steam engine.

The factory comprised a series of weaving sheds running parallel to Rumdewan. At the east end was a winding shed and dressing flat while on the west end was the finishing flat. Behind that and attached to these buildings were, from west to east, the offices, a storage shed, boiler house and engine room, and a monkey puzzle tree beside the pond. Some distance further east were the bleaching greens where Nissen huts stood during World War II.

During the war the weaving shed was used by the Poles for storage and as a workshop. The offices were used once again as the administrative centre. After the war a haulage firm, Thomson's of Ladybank, used the main building for lorries and latterly Charlie Samson of Kettle Farm installed a grass or hay drying plant in part of the building.

The Canal at Burnturk

Industry, other than farming, has a long history in the parish. Apart from whinstone quarries at Downfield and Kettlehill there was a coalmine at Burnturk. It lay due south of Smithfield and, according to the Ordnance Survey map of 1856, there was another a short distance to the west, the Downfield Pit. It is the one at Burnturk that is better known as its existence is embodied in the name of the settlement, Coaltown of Burnturk.

At one time this was a considerable enterprise. According to John Thomson, the owner was a local man, Mr Low. He considered it necessary to transport limestone from the nearby works to kilns he had built at the pit. To this end, it is recorded that two canals were cut, one between the lime works and the top of the kilns and another from the bottom of the kilns to Kettle.[190]

Canmore, the online archaeological catalogue, tells us they were constructed about 1800. The first, between lime works and coalmine, was two miles long and the other, from the kilns to Kettle, was half a mile. Thomson tells us they were about 9 to 10 feet wide and 3 feet deep. The water came from a flooded mine. The longer canal carried boats with a capacity of 4 to 10 tons, while the shorter canal carried boats with a capacity of only 2 tons. It was manpower that propelled the boats, with two men on the larger barges and one man on the smaller ones. Thomson tells us there were no locks on

---

[190]   J. Thomson, *General View of the Agriculture of the County of Fife, with Observations on the Means of its Improvement* (London, J. Moir, 1800)

either canal because there was no variation in levels. This is hard to imagine knowing the topography. The shorter canal must have stopped somewhere at the top of Annfield Brae as Thomson says the contents of the barges were loaded onto carriages with very broad wheels that acted as rollers rather than wheels, which would cut into the road surface. These were drawn by horses down to sheds in Kettle where the burnt lime and coal was stored before sale.

It is hard to identify the route this canal had taken because, although Canmore tells us there is some evidence of it, I have been unable to locate its exact route. What we do know is that these waterways were abandoned in 1830 and were not marked on the first Ordnance Survey map of the area which was surveyed in 1854.[191]

Living in Kettle

Ann Page, the first woman to become an elder, was born in 1923. Her mother and father were neighbours in Kinross before they got married and came to live in Kettlebridge. Strictly speaking Ann was born at her grandparent's home in Kinross, but she has lived all her life in Kettle. She had two younger sisters but sadly they died of meningitis when Ann was only 5 years of age. Ann was baptised by Rev. Aeneas Gordon, and she remembers him well as a lovely man who was very kind. Being raised in a church family she always attended Sunday School at 10 a.m. every Sunday morning and in the afternoon she went to the Mission in Kettlebridge in what is now the Scout Hall. She was also in the junior choir and we can identify her in the picture here of the choir taken in 1936. Ann is fourth from the left in the front row.

Junior choir 1936

---

[191]   https://canmore.org.uk/site/217653/burnturk-canals

Like John Ronaldson, Ann has fond memories of the Sunday School trips to seaside destinations like Buckhaven, Kinghorn, Crail and St Andrews. By the time she was herself a Sunday School teacher, after the war, they travelled by bus. The children had to carry their tin mug with them for tea and they were given a bag of food, purchased from Kettle Store (the Co-operative) once they were seated on the ground. A hall was always available in case it rained. Ann was also a member of the Girls Guildry until it was disbanded due to lack of numbers after the war.

Ann too remembers the Polish soldiers who were based at Beveridge's and in the Memorial Hall between 1939 and 1945. The church hall was used as a 'Church of Scotland Hut', which means it was a canteen for the soldiers. The WRI and Woman's Guild met in the week of a full moon, for there was no street lighting because of the blackout. This way they could see their way to the school where their meetings were held. Ann's father, a member of the Home Guard and the ARP, was based at the hall in Kettlebridge. During these years the Sunday School would be transported by the farmers' carts up to a field, just by the nasty bend, on the road between Coaltown of Burnturk and Limehills.

Sunday School picnic at Crail

Ann remembers 'Willie Flint' the minister, who was also a kind man, though he had one great vice: he was a heavy smoker. At the close of the service he would be found not at the door shaking hands with the congregation as they left but in the Session House having a smoke. His first wife, Ann, was also a lovely person and they had two daughters, though sadly one died and the other went to live in Canada. Mrs Flint died and the minister married for a second time. After Willie Flint died, his second wife, Mary, went on to marry the Session Clerk, John Balmain, who had also been widowed.

Mr Flint was cremated in Edinburgh and a stone erected in his memory in the old churchyard in Kettle.

Ann spent much of the war in the Army as a first-class clerk at Chilwell in Nottingham. She was demobbed and returned home in the winter of 1947. The train was unable to stop at Kettle so she had to go on to Ladybank. It had been her intention to walk to Kettle from the station but she was told the snow was so deep it was not advisable. After spending the night at Ladybank station she got the early morning train to Kettle, left her luggage at the station there and walked home to Kettlebridge.

Ann, centre back, with her Sunday School class on a picnic at Ravenscraig Park, Kirkcaldy

After the war Ann became involved in the Sunday School and she returned to serve in the Girls Guildry. When they folded due to lack of support, Ann was invited to form a pack of Brownies and a company of Guides. This she did in 1955 and these organisations are still functioning and providing a valuable service to the young folk in the community. The WRI and Eastern Star were also important organisations in the area and Ann was a curler, though she found it very cold on the ice.

Up to this point Ann's surname was Campbell, but that was to change in 1964 when she and Bill Page were married in Cults Kirk by Rev. Angus Macaskill. Bill had been married before and his son was Clerk to the Board. He introduced Ann to bowling and she became very much involved in that organisation, becoming president of the Women's Bowling Association and match secretary of the East of Scotland Bowling Association. When Bill died in 1973, Ann found the friendships formed through the bowling club were of tremendous importance to her.

Bill Page had known Angus Macaskill when he lived in Arbroath and so it was a reunion of old friends when he came to Kettle. As we have seen, Angus retired and went to live in Bridge of Earn. His successor was George Henderson. George was the minister who ordained Ann as an elder in 1980. She was amazed when he approached her and delighted to accept the honour and she has served the congregation in that capacity loyally ever since.

The End of a Chapter

Over the centuries Kettle always reflected the mood of the Kirk nationally. When Kings James and Charles I tried to impose Episcopacy on the people a Kettle minister, William Cranston, refused to comply and finished up being removed from the pulpit. When there was anger at the behaviour of Archbishop Sharp in the days of Charles II, a Kettle man was involved in his murder. When William and Mary came to the throne it was John Barclay who rebelled and paid the price. Just after Queen Anne passed an Act reintroducing patrons there was a vacancy and the Kettle folk refused to accept John Meldrum and held out against the Crown until they got their way.

Between 1729 and 1732 there was the vacancy when the parish again refused to accept the man the Crown wished to impose upon them. In 1768 the Dragoons had to be called because the folk of Kettle reflected the unhappiness of many in the Kirk at the involvement of patrons and so the Relief Kirk came to Kettle.

Over and over again Kettle found itself caught up in the great events of the history of the Kirk. So it is that in January1983 Kettle was reflecting what was happening across the country. More and more churches were finding it hard to remain independent. A new arrangement had to be made to ensure the work of the church in Kettle continued. It is at such a time that we must remember why the church exists. It is not for buildings or services, liturgy or pride but to do whatever it takes to be God's people striving to make God's kingdom of love, peace and justice a reality.

There were times in the past when it was achieving that, especially in the care of the poor, the sick and the orphans. There are times it failed through too narrow an interpretation of the faith, and sometimes showing a surprising ignorance of the Gospel. In the end both its successes and its failures reflect the humanity of the people that make it a church. Now these people must move on, learning from the past and working to create a better tomorrow. As part of the Howe of Fife, the folk are stronger and more able to achieve their great aim.

CHAPTER FOUR: CULTS

The Parish of Cults

∿

Cults Kirk and its People: A Special Place

Few come to Cults Kirk without commenting on its charm. It is simple in design and decoration. This is a place for Presbyterian worship and Presbyterians have gathered here for generations to give praise and devotion to God. But it is not only the building that makes Cults a special place. The fields, farms, cottages and nearby hills that surround the old Kirk create an ambiance that many find peaceful, quiet and healing. All of this glorifies the God worshipped in this place.

Cults Kirk

It's not that the architecture of this B-listed building is grand or even different from many other 18th-century churches in Scotland. The interior design with the pulpit on the long south wall, surrounded by pews and box pews, as seen in the 1947 wedding photograph of Bert and Jean Bradbury below, is not uncommon. It is, however, less common today as many other congregations are now removing the pews to create a more flexible space. There is no doubt that Cults has old-world charm but visitors frequently find that it also provides a sense of the spiritual presence that has arisen from generations of ordinary folk worshipping on this site for more than a thousand years. Rev. Henry Porter, when providing a definition for the name Cults, said it is 'a place where things are put to be in safety or out of sight; laid past till needed'.[192] This is true, for whoever enters Cults Kirk knows they are in a sanctuary, a safe place, where the evils and troubles of the world cannot touch them.

Marriage of Bert and Jean Bradbury 1947

The spelling of the name Cults varies according to which ancient document is consulted. Quilt, Quilte, Quiltis, Quhylt, Quilque and Quilques are frequent in pre-Reformation documents, while the more familiar forms of Cultis, Coults, Cowlts and Cult are more common after 1560. Most authorities agree that the name means 'a back-lying place', a niche or an inlet and probably refers to the fact that the ground on which it stands is surrounded by hills. The early history of the parish is sketchy. There is evidence of Iron Age settlements with a fort in Lady Mary's Wood on Walton Hill but that awaits further archaeological investigation. There are also Neolithic remains at Ramornie, and with so much evidence to be found in nearby Kettle parish it is clear that the whole area was well populated from the earliest times. There are few reliable records

---

[192]   W. Porter, *Cults and its Ministers 1560–1843* (Cupar, J. & G. Innes, 1906)

of a pre-Reformation church, although what we have are indications of its presence and a parish with the name of Cults. According to A.H. Millar, the estate of Quylts gave its name to the parish.[193] Of course, parishes came into being in the 12th and 13th centuries and it is believed that a place of worship probably existed on this site well before that time. This is supported by Simon Taylor in *The Place-names of Fife* where he refers to Dennyhogles Field, which appeared on a map of Lower Bunzion dated about 1900.[194]

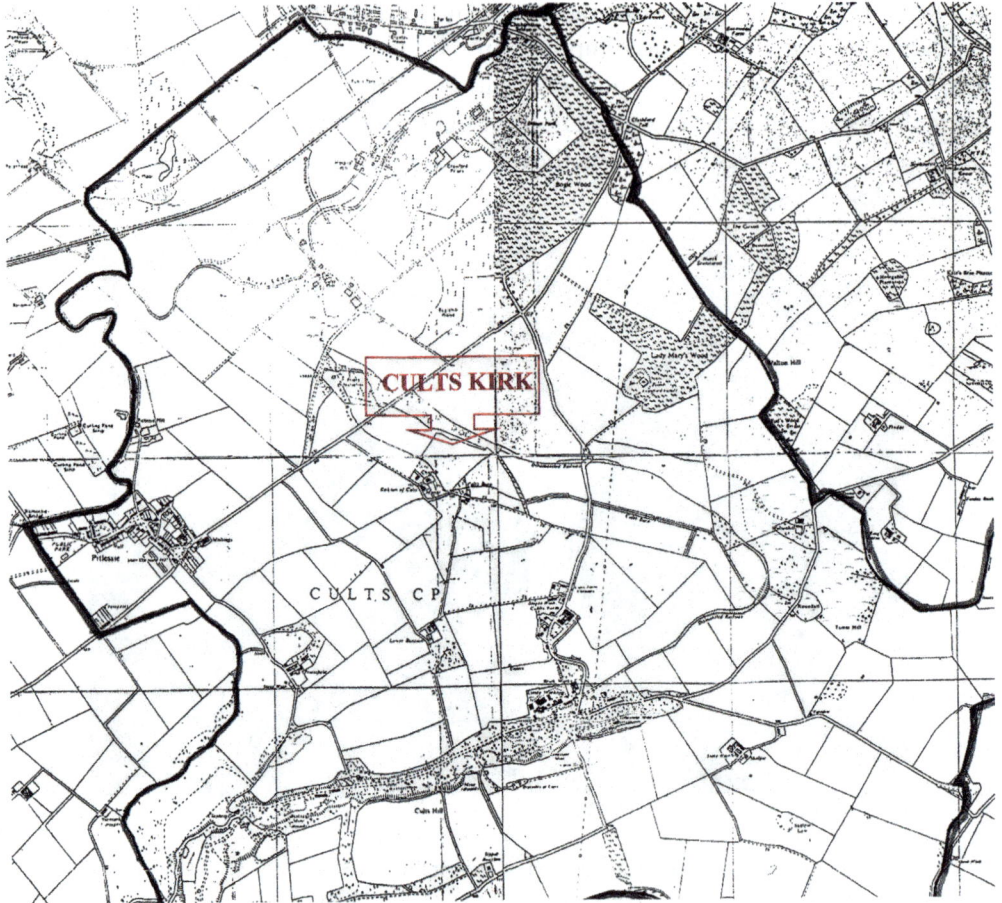

Map c. 1900 showing the extent of the parish of Cults with the church in the centre

He traces the origin of this name to the Gaelic language word *dun-na-h-eaglais*, which means 'hill-fort of the church'. Such a connection indicated that a church existed here long before the Romanisation of Christianity in Celtic Scotland. The earliest documented evidence for the church is the rededication of Cults Kirk on 8th August 1243. No saint is named in the rededication records and this is surprising because most churches were dedicated to at least one saint, and frequently, as in the case of Lathrisk, to a Celtic as well as a Roman saint.

---

193   Millar, *Fife: Pictorial and Historical*
194   Taylor and Markus, *Place-names of Fife*, vol. 2

The next time we hear of Cults we learn it is bestowed by David II on Robert Erskine and in 1369 granted by him to Patrick de Blair of the Blairs of Balthayock. The Blairs were settled in Fife at the time of William the Lion and Sir William de Blair was knighted and appointed hereditary steward of Fifeshire by Alexander II. The estate remained with his family until the mid 16th century. By a charter dated 19th August 1538, Thomas Blair of Balthayock sold the 'Kirkton of Cultis' to Magister Hendry White, dean of Brechin. This is the first time the name of Cults appears in a form recognisable to us, apart from the pontifical confirming the rededication of the 'church of Cuilte' by Bishop de Bernham. In 1550 Thomas Blair sold the remainder of the Cults property to John Balfour and his wife Jonet Smith. By 29th September 1664 the title for the property had passed to James Arnot of Fernie.[195]

In the year 1412 the 'Rector of Qwilt' was David Brown and he also held canonries in the Chapel Royal of Stirling and Dunbar. In 1426 records show that his association with Cults had continued. The year 1450 was, however, a very significant one for Cults as this is when Bishop James Kennedy founded St Salvator's College in St Andrews. There were to be three theologians on the staff of this new college and each was expected to act as rector in a local church. So it was stipulated that while the licentiate would take Kemback and the Bachelor Dunino, it was the provost who would take Cults. They were not expected to work in the parish themselves but to appoint vicars to fulfil the function of pastor.[196] The last named vicar of Cults before the Reformation is Martin Balfour. This name is connected to the vicar dating from before the Reformation and up to 1563. The name is also found in a charter dated 15th June 1503 'granting a tenement in St Andrews to Martin Balfour'.[197] While it is clear they are unlikely to be the same man, for age would prevent him from being active 60 years after this reference, they may well be related.

The relevance of all this detail is to show that, while records are thin, there was much activity going on regarding ownership of the land in the parish, and the church continued to exercise influence over the people in that place. The two most significant events recorded are the rededication by Bishop de Bernham and the acquisition of Cults by St Salvator's. The former legitimised Cults Kirk in the eyes of the Roman Catholic Church and the Cathedral of St Andrews, which was responsible for each church in the diocese; the latter established St Salvator's College as patron for Cults, appointing the clergymen who stood in the pulpit each Sunday. With only short interruptions due to historical events, this arrangement survived the Reformation and continued until 1930.

In the earlier part of the 15th century Pitlessie, the main centre of population in the parish and lying about a mile south of the church, was in the possession of Alexander de Ramorgany. He is believed to be the son of Sir John de Ramorgany of that Ilk. A special charter of James V on 2nd January 1541 granted the status of burgh of barony

---

195 Millar, *Fife: Pictorial and Historical*
196 Taylor and Markus, *Place-names of Fife*, vol. 2
197 St Andrews University Archive Catalogue UYSS110/W/6

on the village. This gave its inhabitants the power to buy and sell, to become burgesses with the right to choose baillies and to hold a weekly market at the market cross every Wednesday.

There were also four annual fairs on the feasts of the saints James and Philip, Maelrubh and Katherine; each of which was to last eight days. The marking of these feast days, remembering particular saints, raises the question again of the dedication of the church to saints. If there is no connection between these saints and the local church then why choose these feast days for the village fairs? It seems likely that they had a long association with Cults but that the records are lost.[198]

After The Reformation

It would appear that during the first few years after the Reformation little changed at Cults. It is recorded in the Great Seal of Scotland that 'Mr John Balfour, vicar of Quiltis, Fifeshire' witnessed a charter on 8th December 1550. That was 10 years before the establishment of the Reformed Presbyterian Church, yet he remained in post until 1563. While he was the first Protestant minister of the parish it is clear that he served the cure under the pre-Reformation Catholic Church. No doubt he proclaimed his support for the Reformed Church before retaining his position after 1560. Yet records show that this was without the approval of the General Assembly. Certainly, his name is not included among those deemed qualified by the first General Assembly to preach the ministry of word and sacrament.

In the *Fasti Ecclesiae Scoticanae* it is reported that on 25th June 1563 he was removed by the Assembly, having 'usurped the place of minister here' and was 'placed in an obscure congregation, according to the measure of his gifts'. It is hard to imagine which congregation was deemed sufficiently obscure to accept one considered to have so few gifts that he was unfit not only to preach the word and dispense the sacraments but even to read the prayers. While he disappears from the church and the community of Cults without leaving any trace as to his gifts or his reputation among the folk he had served there, it would appear he re-emerged as reader in the parish of Kettle. Be that as it may, one must feel more than a little pity for this man who was apparently so cruelly dispatched and whose tattered reputation has been inscribed forever in the official records of the new church.

These were exciting times. The new Presbyterian Church was sweeping across the land removing all traces of its Roman Catholic predecessor. It had to ensure that the preaching of the word and the serving of the sacraments were in accord with the new theology. All that smacked of 'Popery' had to be swept away. Clearly Mr Balfour was one of the symbols of the past that had to be removed.

On 26th June 1563 Mr Balfour was succeeded by Mr Johne Rutherford, principal of St Salvator's College. It was he who had complained to the General Assembly that

---

198   Taylor and Markus, *Place-names of Fife*, vol. 2

Mr Balfour was not qualified and so had him removed. Now Mr Rutherford, whom the General Assembly had considered 'maist qualified for ministering and teaching', offered himself to be minister of Cults 'according to the talent given him by God'. This is not altogether surprising for, as we have seen, Cults was the responsibility of the principal of St Salvator's, so no doubt Mr Rutherford felt obliged to ensure the parish was being properly served by a minister of the Reformed Church.

Mr Rutherford, or Rutherfuirde as it is recorded in some documents, was a learned gentleman. He hailed from Jedburgh but was educated at universities in Bordeaux, Coimbra in Portugal and Paris. When he was invited to St Mary's College in St Andrews in 1552 at the age of about 32 he had a considerable reputation as a scholar. It was in 1560 that he was translated to St Salvator's. Then he joined the Reformers and used his considerable intellectual powers to promote that cause.

Despite his abilities and standing, especially in philosophy, Mr Rutherford had a reputation for being hot-tempered and quick with his tongue. In 1563 a visitation to St Salvator's declared him to be 'too hasty and impatient'. As a result he was 'admonished not to let the sun go down upon his wrath, and to study to bridle his tongue, and conduct himself with greater humanity and mildness'.

It was not long before Mr Rutherford found himself on committees of the Kirk and working alongside John Knox, George Buchanan and David Ferguson. I suppose today we might say that he did not suffer fools gladly and he seemed never to be happy unless he was involved in a good argument. It soon became clear that his work as a professor, as well as serving on committees and disputing with his peers, took much of his time. The General Assembly of 1570 found him guilty of failing to do 'diligence in serving the said cure [Cults] at leist certain tymes in the year, admonishing him to the said fault in tymes coming, utherwayes the Kirk will proceed against him as ane neglector of dewtie'. We can only imagine how the fiery Mr Rutherford reacted to this!

There is no evidence that he stopped finding causes to fight and people to offend – including Knox himself – yet he continued to publish works in philosophy that were highly respected. On 26th September 1577 he resigned the 'half of the teind of Quilts' to Mr James Martin, second master under him at St Salvator's.

A few weeks later, on 18th December of the same year, there is reference to 'Christiane Forsyth, his relict and executrix'. It would appear then that between these dates Mr Rutherford died and a powerful character of great intellect and personal charisma departed this life.

As principal of St Salvator's Mr James Martin was *ex officio* minister of Dunino; then in 1570 he was translated to Kemback. In 1578 he became principal of St Salvator's and minister of Cults. Mr Martin was a much quieter man than his predecessor. He worked very hard for the church and served on the Assemblies of 1586 and 1610, and in the High Court, also in 1610. There he was involved in trying some who were thought not to conform to the new church. The Synod of Fife twice sent him to try to persuade Mr Adamson, Archbishop of St Andrews, to embrace the Kirk; and with others he interviewed the King, James VI, as to the jurisdiction of Presbyteries and Synods over bishops. In 1691, four years before he died, Mr Martin had the distinction of being one of the first in Scotland to have the degree of Doctor of Divinity conferred upon him.

In 1595 Patrick Peat was admitted as assistant and in 1608 Mr Andrew Morton came to Cults, but sadly failed to make his mark in any way as the next mention of him is in 1635 when he died.

Mr Morton was succeeded by Mr Edmond Cranston, the first of the Cults ministers to hold the degree of AM, which was conferred upon him at St Andrews in 1625. All was not well for Mr Cranston and on 7th October 1635 he was ordered to stop preaching by the Synod of Fife 'because the provost of the Old College has the title and charge of plantation'. Perhaps there had been a disagreement between Mr Cranston and Mr Morton; it is difficult to say. We must remember that in 1625 Charles I came to the throne and he was given an Anglican coronation in Edinburgh in1633. Five years later the National Covenant was signed with the consequent revolt against the Crown. With such events surrounding Mr Cranston's ministry at Cults, it is possible to speculate that the prohibition against his preaching was a reaction to the political sensibilities surrounding these times of high emotion. If Mr Cranston found himself at odds with the Synod of Fife because he viewed the role of the monarch differently from that body, this would surely have been considered sufficient reason to justify their action against him. This, however, can only be speculation because there is no available evidence to support such conclusions other than the strong feelings in the Synod only 48 years previously when it excommunicated the Archbishop of St Andrews for supporting James VI's 'Black Acts'. This was a time when imprudence in one's beliefs and a readiness to express them could have dire consequences.[199]

Following the departure of Mr Cranston, another Mr Martin, James, arrived at Cults in 1636. The few years he was in the parish appear to have been uneventful. After being translated to Auchtermuchty in 1641 his life met sadness and difficulty. His wife died in 1644 and this may have been the cause of his troubles. Having failed to give communion for two years and for 'somethings insert in the Session Book wronglie, and afterward blotted out' he was suspended in 1649. There is no record of how long the suspension lasted but he was translated to Ballingry in 1669.[200]

When William Glasfurd arrived in Cults in 1641 the country was still at war with itself. But Mr Glasfurd lasted only two years and was followed by Mr John Alexander in 1643. In 1654 he was translated to Creich and replaced by Mr George Dishington (or Diston) in 1655. Following the Restoration of the monarchy in 1660 Mr Alexander gave in and conformed to the re-established Episcopacy. At Cults Mr Dishington did not conform and so was 'deprived by Act of Parliament 11th June 1662; suspended October 1665; deprived 1st April 1668'. He finally departed from Cults in 1668, only five years before he died in 1773 at the age of 53.

---

[199]   Burleigh , *A Church History of Scotland*
[200]   Scott, *Fasti Ecclesiae Scoticanae*, vol. 5, p. 126

These were the days of Charles II, who reneged on his promises to uphold the Covenant that saw him crowned at Scone in 1650. He also forgot the consequent suffering of the Scots at the hands of Cromwell that resulted from their loyalty to him. It was that instrument of Charles in St Andrews, the infamous Archbishop Sharp, who had Mr Dishington removed. But, as we see from the various suspensions and deprivations, it appears the archbishop tried to give Mr Dishington every opportunity to conform. For several years there were discussions at the half-yearly diocesan Synod of Fife, which was moderated by the archbishop. Attempts were made to resolve the conflict. In the end the archbishop felt he had no alternative and we learn that Mr Dishington was deposed as minister of 'the Cowlts'. This did not herald his ruin and it would appear that he was a man of independent means as he went on to purchase the lands of Lochmalony, north of Cupar.[201]

It took five years after the removal of Mr Dishington for Mr John Mathers, his successor, to be called. He was an Episcopalian but little is known about him while in the parish. In 1685, the year of Charles II's death, Mr Mathers was translated to Ceres. While there, and being a confirmed Episcopalian, he refused to read the proclamation 'forbidding any to acknowledge the Catholic James [VII] as King' and to pray for the new Protestant sovereigns, William and Mary. It was as a result of this refusal that Mr Mathers was 'deprived of his charge' at Ceres on 16th May 1689.

These were hard times for all concerned. The ministers of nine congregations in the Presbytery were affected, with eight 'deprived' and one confined to his parish. Only one minister, William Tullidaff of Dunbog, survived until the abdication of James VII; the others conformed to the demands of the Crown. Mr Tullidaff certainly suffered for his beliefs. He was 'deprived' at Dunbog in 1662 and did not get another charge until 1670 at Kilbirnie in Ayrshire but was replaced in 1672. In 1673 he was fined a half year's stipend for not observing the anniversary of the Restoration. In 1684, 11 years later, he was imprisoned for refusing to promise not to exercise his ministry anywhere in Scotland. The Glorious Revolution restored this man's reputation in 1688 when he became minister of Wemyss, and three years later he was translated to St Leonard's in St Andrews. *Fasti Ecclesiae Scoticanae* was unsure how to spell this man's unusual name. At Dunbog he was Tullideff, at Kilbirnie Tullidaff, at Wemyss Tullielff and at St Leonard's Tullidelph. However his name is spelled, his story makes it clear that those who stood up to the Crown had to pay the price. It is little wonder so many succumbed to the King's demand.

Fines were also imposed on the congregations of dissenting ministers. Cults suffered fines and losses totalling £4,500, causing much hardship in the parish. This was greater per head of population than larger parishes and is surprising because there is no evidence of any of its parishioners having been punished for involvement in any Jacobite activity and there are no Cults names on the Martyr Roll of the Covenant.

---

[201] Porter, *Cults and its Ministers*

In addition, Porter tells us that there was not a single case of witchcraft recorded in the Session records.[202]

Mr Mathers was succeeded in 1685 by Mr Alexander Skene DD, principal of St Salvator's College. It would appear that Mr Skene saw his position at Cults to be temporary because in 1686 he was replaced by Mr John Keir AM. Mr Keir, who was a graduate of St Andrews, remained in Cults for only three years as in 1689 he was 'deprived' of the charge for 'not reading the Proclamation of the Estates, not praying for their Majesties William and Mary, and not observing the thanksgiving or the collection'. Clearly he, like Mr Mathers, was a confirmed Episcopalian and so suffered the same fate. The Presbyterians, like the Episcopalians before them, were uncompromising in their demand for conformity

After a vacancy of four years the next minister, Mr Alexander Wilson, came with a bit of a past. The *Fasti Ecclesiae Scoticanae* tells us that in 1676 he was living in Cupar with his wife and six children and that he was 'exposed to much persecution and hardship'. He had been minister of Cameron from 1650 but, like Mr Tullidaff of Dunbog and many other ministers, was expelled in 1662. In 1674 he was 'put to the horn', that is declared an outsider by three blasts of the horn, for not appearing before the Council when summoned, for holding conventicles (open-air services that were in accord with the Covenant of 1638) and 'intruding into pulpits contrary to law'. In 1678 he fled to Holland where he met up with other refugees from persecution.

The whole sorry saga is told in Woodrow's History and I shall allow him to relate the details which give some idea of the lengths to which the authorities would go in order to pursue their victims:

> About this time, Mr Alexander Wilson, minister of the Gospel at Cameron in the presbytery of St Andrews, a singularly pious and peaceable person, was brought to no small trouble; I shall give a hint of it in this place, altogether from an attested account of it before me. He was turned out, with others, for his nonconformity to prelacy, by the influence of the archbishop, in the year 1662, after he had diligently served his Master in that charge twelve years, being ordained minister of Cameron in 1650. This good man went and lived in Cupar of Fife about sixteen years, during which time, notwithstanding his sermons were mostly in his own house, he was frequently searched for, and many times narrowly escaped. We have heard he was intercommuned [ostracised by the church] some years ago, and towards the beginning of November this year, an order was sent, procured by the primate from the council, requiring the magistrates of Cupar, under the penalty of 500 merks, to banish Mr Wilson and his family from the town, in forty-eight hours after their receiving the orders. The orders came to their hands upon Saturday, when at the preparation-sermon, before the sacrament of the supper to be dispensed by the Episcopal minister next day; and they thought good to delay the execution of them till Monday. When sermon was over that day, the Magistrates, immediately after they

---

came out of the church, before they went home to their own houses, came straight with their attendants and the town-officers, to Mr Wilson's house, and searched for him. He had got some hint of the orders, and had withdrawn himself: however, they intimated the council's pleasure to Mrs Wilson, commanding her and her family to remove out of the town in twenty-four hours. Mrs Wilson signified to them that it was not possible for her to remove her family in so short a time, having six children, and one of them under sickness at present, and hoped they would not be so rigorous, considering the circumstances of her small family. However, to obtemperate as far as possible, that very night Mrs Wilson privately removed with her sick child, and the other five, and her servants, to lurk in a neighbour's house, till she should see what would become of the sick child, and till she might take some measures how to dispose of her family, and that the magistrates might be in no hazard of the penalty, for not executing their severe orders, which they alleged was the only reason of their harshness to her. Yet the very next day, the magistrates came to see whether their orders had been obeyed, and finding nothing but locked doors, they caused a smith, whom they had with them for this very end, fix iron plates upon all the doors of Mr Wilson's house, while the whole plenishing was remaining in the house. Mrs Wilson looking for no such treatment, when she had, as far as possible, complied with the orders she received : yea, as oft as Mrs Wilson privately went into the house, to get out such necessaries as she wanted, as often new plates were put on by the magistrates. Under these difficulties Mr Wilson's family continued for some time, till the lady Preston-hall, knowing their strait, made an offer of an empty house near the town, but not within its jurisdiction, in which her gardeners used to live, which was very thankfully embraced, though there was scarce so much room in it as to place the beds necessary for the family. Even there the persecuting temper followed them : Mr Wilson was frequently searched for in that little house, but never catched; and the magistrates, in conjunction with the Sheriff-depute, endeavoured to eject his family from that little shelter; but the foresaid lady protected them and, as soon as the season of the year would permit, the family removed to Kirkcaldy, where no house could be found to be set for money to Mr Wilson, save one that belonged to a person who was himself intercommuned for nonconformity. There and at Burntisland Mr Wilson and his family suffered very much till the revolution, when, in the year 1689, this excellent person, after twenty-seven years' persecution, returned to his old flock at Cameron.[203]

By the time Mr Wilson arrived in Cults the 'Revolution' had taken place and Presbyterianism was restored as the form of the national Church. This man who had been a villain under the Episcopal Church was a hero when, at the age of 73, he took up the charge at Cults. His period of tenure lasted only four years but, in spite of his age, he worked hard, enthusiastically engaging in the task of reorganising the parish, which Porter tells us 'since the deprivation of Mr Keir, had fallen into a state of neglect'.

---

[203]   R. Wodrow, *The History of the Sufferings of the Church of Scotland from the Restoration to the Revolution*, vol. 2 (Glasgow, Blackie, Fullarton & Co., 1828, p. 483)

We are told there was no Session book, no money in the Kirk box; there was no schoolmaster, both church and manse were in a state of disrepair. There was, however, a full Session of nine elders and, with their assistance, Mr Wilson restored the parish to full working condition. According to Porter it was recorded in the Kirk Session minutes that 'He began by asking if there was any scandal in the parish, and on being, fortunately, told there was none, exhorted the Elders to their deuty'.

Then, one Andrew Smith should 'continue precenture in taking up the psalm until the parioche be provided with a schoolmaster for which he is considred'. He then saw to the 'reparations of the roofe of the Kirke, and what also was needful to the doores and windowes of the Kirke'. Oversight of the work was entrusted to Thomas Morton, one of the nine elders. Mr Wilson then divided the parish into districts and allocated elders as follows: 'Tho: Morton for Waltoun and Fetters, Geo: Durie for Easter Cults, Jo: Hendersone for Rocklays and Bunzione grounde, Jo Nesse: for Wester Cults and the Kirktoune, Jo: Fairnie and Ja: Morton for Pitlessie and Pitlessie milne, Jo: Smith for Walke milne, Tho: Colzier for Hospital and Cult milnes'. William Dall, who was a senior elder, was not given a district, probably due to his age.

Then there were money matters to be attended to: 'ther was tuo little silver dishes belonging to the Kirke put into the Kirke box, which were delivered to Tho: Morton to be sold and the pryce therof to returne to the Sessione'. Next a scale of fees was drawn up and 'the Sessione appointed that every master (who is a Tennant) should pay fourteen shilling at the baptisme of his child and at his contract twentie shilling to be given to the precenture for proclaniatione. And that a Servant at Baptisme ten shillings and at contract and proclamation a fourteen. A stranger (having to pay his proclamation in the parish wher he resides) coming to be maried in this parish is to give twelve shillings to the box. And for a stranger that is a servt sex shillings.' The charge for the mortcloth was £1 10s. 0d. In addition, income was derived from 'rent of the Cult Park on the lands of Forthar, and ordinary collections'.

Soon the Session funds began to grow and be put to good use. Several pensioners were maintained, contributions were paid to the Presbytery bursar and in addition occasional amounts were paid to 'a poor woman', 'a young scholar' and 'a distressed man'. There were also records of money being lent or given to a pensioner to buy a loom and another received money to buy a cow. In addition, the congregation cared for orphans or destitute children. The local joiner, Patrick Groundiston, was often paid for making coffins for the poor, or repairing the church or the manse. At times money was lent for interest but sometimes it was difficult to get either the interest or the principal repaid. Special collections were made for building bridges and other projects in the neighbourhood and beyond.

Life at Cults was far from idyllic. Not everyone behaved themselves and we discover that there were drunken men and quarrelling women. One woman is specially mentioned as being a 'servant lass' who apparently slandered her neighbours and the minister's wife. She had started such rumours that the minister and his wife went before the Session to face charges, which were found to be groundless. As a result the following was recorded in the Session book:

> The sd Margt was sharply rebuked yt if ever she vented any such thing hereafter she should be brought in publicke. And because the sd Margt was removed out of this parioche to Ceres where her parents resides the minister there and oyrs [others] are to be advised yt notice should be taken of the sd Margt as of a notorious liar and ane incendiary in the place where she lives.[204]

In those days Kirk Sessions dealt with much that in modern times would be considered none of their business. But times have changed, and so have attitudes to behaviour, so it is difficult for us to judge an age that is like a foreign land to us. Certainly the Session took very seriously its responsibility to maintain order. Porter found evidence that using charms, even for good ends, was punishable, as was consulting with witches, blasphemy, failing to report blasphemy, 'flyting', drunkenness and profaning the Sabbath. Two publicans in the parish were 'engaged' to let no 'personne be drunken in their house' and to sell no 'yeall after eight houres' to any without business or strangers. Parents had to ensure their children did not play in the streets of Pitlessie on the Sabbath day.

I have given much space to this detail and have quoted much from Rev. Henry Porter's book as it contains a great deal of information from the Kirk Session books that were lost in a fire at the manse in 1926. As a result, I consider them gems that must be preserved as they throw light on the past of Cults and Pitlessie that otherwise is gone forever.

Before we leave Mr Wilson it is worth noting that Wodrow describes him as 'a singularly pious and peaceable person'. Clearly he had many fine qualities, being a man of principle and considerable ability, yet retaining those personal qualities that endeared him to his fellows. After three years of his ministry Mr Wilson was clearly beginning to struggle. Entries were found in the Kirk Session minutes telling us there was 'No sermone the minister being unweel'. At times Presbytery provided pulpit supply. Occasionally it was recorded that 'The minister's son Walter did preach'. Walter Wilson had been ordained in 1689 and in 1701 was admitted to the parish of Kilconquhar. In April 1697 Rev. Alexander Wilson died.[205]

On 12th May 1699, a successor to Mr Wilson was appointed in the form of Thomas Burrell, AM. The *Fasti Ecclesiae Scoticanae* tells us that he graduated from St Andrews in 1683 and passed as a probationer 'Under Episcopacy'. According to the Presbytery of Kirkcaldy of 1692, while he had presented himself well on the trials, they were not satisfied that he would be faithful to the government of the church.

Once again the purse was almost empty and on 14th June we find the following:

> It was moved in ye session that it was reasonable some consideration ought to be given to the Kirk box by these that ware allowed to place grave stones over the bodies of

204 Porter, *Cults and its Ministers*
205 Porter, *Cults and its Ministers*

yr deceased friends, and it was voted and enacted by ye Session that each to whom that priveledge is granted shall pay for each through stone the soume of five Merkes Scotts, and for each head stone the Half yr-of, and also that these who have had that benefit alreadie are lyable to pay the said soume asweel as these that are to have it in time comming and also that the money so gotten, with what shall be gotten for the mortcloath shall be putt togither & keep for such purposes as the Session shall think fitt.

It was during Mr Burrell's ministry that the bell in the belfry was acquired. It bears the inscription: 'john meikle, edinburgh, fecit [made] for the kirk of cults, 1699'. Also acquired at this time was the Cults Kirk box, which Porter tells us was 'in the custody of the present minister'. He describes it as 'a curious old oaken box about 18 inches long, 8 inches high, and 6 inches broad. The box is liberally supplied with iron clasps, and two locks, and has carved on its front, in incised letters, the cult kirk box, 1712'.

The drawing above of the Cults Kirk box is taken from the *Evening Telegraph* of Tuesday 3rd March 1908. The box, like the Session papers, was destroyed in the fire of 1926. Mr Burrell died in March 1726 at the age of 63.

Mr Burrell's successor was Andrew Melvill. A graduate of St Andrews, he was ordained to Cults in 1726. Although Mr Melvill was in post at Cults for 36 years, the only memorial to his ministry are two communion cups, each with the inscription 'this cup belongs to the k. session of cults mr. and. melvill, minr. an. mdccl'. There were also two salvers, which are no longer in the possession of the church and may have perished in the fire of 1926.

It is unfortunate too that Porter recorded that during this ministry there seems to have been a gap in the Session minutes. This, together with the lack of any alternative information, means that Mr Melvill's

ministry remains a mystery to us. This is a pity, for the years he spent in Cults covered dramatic times in both the country and the Kirk. His successor, Mr Andrew Hutton, was translated to Cults from Glenisla in October 1762, a few months after Mr Melvill's death at the age of about 71.

Eleven years later, in May 1773, Mr Hutton was translated to Kilmany. This left a vacancy which was not filled until the following year. On 14th April 1774 the Rev. David Wilkie, the most famous minister of Cults, arrived to take charge of the parish. This man, who apparently had 'a rapid delivery, and spoke thick', was not only considered 'a sensible preacher' but was held in very high esteem by those who knew him for his 'genuine piety and rectitude of conduct'.

Mr Wilkie was raised in the family farm of Ratho Byres in Midlothian. The land had, according to his son, been in the hands of the Wilkie family for 400 years but, through what he calls 'the imprudence of his ancestor', the farm of John Wilkie, father of Rev. David, was rented from a distant member of the family. David was born in 1738 and the family lived a frugal life. He won a bursary of £40 Scots (£31 6s. 8d. sterling) per annum, which allowed him to study Greek, Hebrew, philosophy and maths. He earned additional income from giving private tuition. Professor William Wilkie, professor of Divinity at St Andrews, was related to David and invited him to study in his department.

Rev. and Mrs Wilkie painted by their son; note the communion cups on the table, which are familiar to worshippers in Cults today

By the year 1768, and at the age of 30, David preached to the Presbytery of St Andrews and became assistant minister at Glamis. After moving for a brief spell to be assistant at Rescobie, he wrote in his diary: '1773, November 24. Received a presentation from the United College of St Andrews to the vacant church of Cults, which was sustained by them.' On 14th April of the following year he was ordained as minister of Cults.

Rev. David Wilkie was a man who knew great sorrow in his life, as the following extract from his diary shows:

1776 October 18. Was this day married to one of the most beautiful women in Fife, Mary Campbell, sister to George Campbell, one of the ministers of Cupar.

1777 February 8. This day my beloved wife departed this life, having been taken ill of a fever, attended by consumption—an event the most afflicting I ever met with.

Mary Campbell's beauty was well known in the area and remembered over 60 years after her death.[206] On 3rd November 1778 Mr Wilkie married his cousin Miss Peggy Wilkie, but on 28th March 1780 another sad entry reads 'this day my most indulgent wife departed this life after being delivered of a still-born male child'. So, the minister of Cults was, once again, deprived of the companionship and support of a wife.[207]

Cunningham provides a description of the life of the manse family at the end of the 18th century.[208] The stipend at Cults was £130 per annum. This was considered a meagre sum even at that time and the glebe attached to the manse was an indispensable part of the minister's income. At Cults the land forming the glebe extended to only three of four acres. This provided pasturage for the horse, which was essential for transporting the minister around the parish as well as to Presbytery meetings in Cupar. It may also have accommodated a couple of cows for milk, cheese and butter, which was normally produced in the manse kitchen. The herbs for adding season to the food were grown in the garden and the dove cot provided a meal for an unexpected visitor. Some also grew flax and Cunningham suggests this was the case at Cults. There was also poultry providing fresh eggs and, once past laying, a meal for the family. Clearly maintaining the glebe and dealing with the produce was a labour-intensive business taking much time from the vocational duties of the minister. In other words, a minister without a wife was, in effect, short not only of a companion but of labour.

So it was that on 4th October 1781 Mr Wilkie married Miss Isabel Lister, a Pitlessie girl, daughter of James Lister, farmer of Pitlessie Mill. This, the third Mrs Wilkie, was, at the age of only 18, 25 years younger than her husband, which caused some of the wagging local tongues to note that she was young enough to be his daughter. Nevertheless, the new Mrs Wilkie rose to the challenges of her position. She bore him four sons, John, James, David and Thomas, and one daughter, Helen. Mrs Wilkie's father was, of course, well known in the parish and had been a member of the Kirk Session of Kettle before coming to Cults parish in 1778. It was said of him that he was a man of 'singular worth and sagacity'. It appears his virtues were inherited by his daughter Isabel as it is said she 'discharged the duties of her station so as to win and retain the respect and affection of the parishioners'. This involved living the simple

---

[206] A. Cunningham, *The Life of Sir David Wilkie: With his Journals, Tours, and Critical Remarks on Works of Art and a Selection from his Correspondence*, vol. 1 (London, John Murray, 1843)
[207] Cunningham, *The Life of Sir David Wilkie*
[208] Cunningham, *The Life of Sir David Wilkie*

life of a Scottish Presbyterian clergyman's wife. Cunningham used the word 'frugal' to describe the standard of living they had to endure. She made her own clothes, spun wool and flax, and was prepared to make do and mend in order to ensure her family were well provided for. It was not unknown for the clergyman to find himself having to make his own furniture and it was seen as a virtue for the manse to 'be an example of thrift to my parish', as one young minister in Nithsdale said.[209]

It was into such an austere lifestyle that the minister's third son, David, was born. While it is tempting to indulge in some detail about the life of Sir David Wilkie RA, that biography is more properly dealt with by others better qualified to comment.

On the other hand, it must be recorded that the people of the parish were, and have remained, very proud of the Wilkie connection. But while the father did not win the accolades of the son, nevertheless he was a man respected both by his parishioners and his colleagues. In 1794 he published his *Theory of Interest, Simple and Compound, derived from first principles, and applied to Annuities of all Descriptions*. It was, he says, the result of four and a half years of study. Lord Napier, to whom it was dedicated, received the compliment courteously, and 'Mr Pitt, it is said, consulted it in all his calculations'. Mr Wilkie also published *Tables of Mortality in the parish of Torthorwald* and he was responsible for writing the Cults entry in the Old Statistical Account. According to Porter, the Kirk Session minutes were written by him with great care and there was a manuscript bound up in the Session of Kettle's copy of the Old Statistical Account. Clearly Mr Wilkie was a busy man.

Sir David Wilkie's biographer tells us that in 1793 'the minister of Cults was cured of a complaint by Dr Bell, which, brought on by study and anxiety, threatened his life', but we are not told what the complaint was. It is clear the Cults minister was working very hard and his anxiety may have been exacerbated by the poor condition of the manse and church and the need to replace both buildings.

The present church was built in 1793 and, Porter points out, the date is still to be seen on the belfry, which is composed of the supports of old table tombstones. Mr Wilkie, in the Old Statistical Account, tells us that, in 1791, the church and manse were about 150 years old and described as having an 'old and tottering fabric'. This would place the time of erection at about 1640.

Self-portrait of the young Sir David Wilkie

---

209   Cunningham, *The Life of Sir David Wilkie*

While there are no pictures of this building and we cannot estimate its size, it might be fair to assume the new building was built on the foundations of the old. There are also those who claim that the pews that are still to be found in the church came from its predecessor, though I could find nothing to substantiate that.

We have already learned that during Mr Burrell's ministry the church received its bell, which is dated 1699. This leads us to conclude that a bell tower of some sort either pre-existed the bell or was specially constructed to house it. Porter also provides a very detailed estimate of the work that was to be carried out in about 1762 when Mr Hutton was minister. Material required included 700 slates, lath, hair for plaster lime, glass windows and harling on the outside walls (see Appendix). An east door is also mentioned leading us to conclude there was a west door also. We can assume too that the interior walls and ceiling were plastered. Had these repairs been carried out in 1762 the total cost would have been £12 12s. 2d. The work actually carried out was, according to Porter, on a much more modest scale. While Porter refers to this, unfortunately the record of what was actually done has not survived.

Country churches have always had their own character but it may not be too far out of the way to imagine Cults to have been similar to many simple 17th-century rural churches now standing in ruins. In 1791 Cults had a population of 534 and so the building must have been a reasonable size to accommodate such a large congregation. This can only be a rough guide but I am sure that the building erected in about 1640 would have been simple both inside and out, providing only what was necessary to house the faithful when they gathered for worship on Sunday morning.

In 1796 the manse, being of a similar age to the church, was also rebuilt. One cannot but conclude that the Heritors of the parish were generous in providing such a sanctuary as Cults and a manse. With nine rooms and a kitchen the house was large, providing accommodation for entertaining guests and housing the manse family in comfort.

David Wilkie was 11 years old when he and his family moved into the new house. It is here that he is said to have decorated the walls of his room with 'humorous drawings', perhaps cartoons of visitors to the manse and members of the Kirk. Apparently these drawings were of chalk, charcoal, pencil, ink and ochre but were painted over with whitewash when the manse was prepared for the arrival of Mr Wilkie's successor. Porter tells us they remained visible for 40 or 50 years but, by the time he arrived in 1900, they had been completely obliterated.

When Rev. David Wilkie arrived in 1774, we are told that once again there was 'no money in the box'. In order to preserve a record from the now lost documents of Cults, I include the following from Porter's book:

> There were, however, eleven bills or bonds for small sums lent out by the Session. Four of these bonds were at once written off as 'desperate Debts'; of the other six it is written these are 'little better than desperate Debts.' 'A Disposition' (dated 7th July 1735) 'of David Pitcairn of Kirk-Forthar, to the minister and Kirk-Session of Cults, to a Pendicle of land and houses thereon, called the Beggars' Butts, but now called the Cult Park lying in

224

the parish of Kettle, together with an Instrument of Saisine' (dated 5th January 1737) 'of the said Inclosure and Houses thereon in Favours of the minister and Kirk Session of Cults, for the use and Benefit of the poor thereof' might promise more interesting reading. It turned out, unfortunately, that the rent of £2 5s. for this pendicle was not considered worth the trouble the property involved, and the Heritors and Session decided to sell 'the Cult Park'. It was accordingly exposed to public roup in Cupar, on the 19th of April 1810, and was bought by Mr Thomson of Nottingham Farm, the only bidder, for £340.

One thing that caused Mr Wilkie a great deal of unhappiness was the appearance of Mr Curror, who opened a chapel, part of the Haldane movement, in Pitlessie. This movement was started by two brothers, James and Robert Haldane, in the mid 1790s. It was their custom to attend the Parish Church on Sunday morning and then hold a meeting in the afternoon to criticise the theology of the minister according to their own Evangelical principles. A fair degree of success was achieved with Sunday Schools being established throughout Scotland. There was also a lot of resentment within the Kirk towards them. Many see this movement as being influential in the spread of both the Baptist and Congregational Churches in the early years of the 19th century.[210] While records show that he remained in Pitlessie for 10 years, I have been unable to discover the dates he came and left.

With the advancement of years, Mr Wilkie became very frail and in 1812 it was considered necessary to find an assistant minister, but he died before arrangements were completed. When he preached his last service on the last Sunday of October 1812 his parishioners thought his health was improving. The biographer Cunningham said: 'Though he continued calm and even cheerful, he only smiled when hopes of his being heard again in the pulpit were indulged in by his friends, and said, looking out of the window, "I will never see the leaves grow green on these trees again." He died 1st day of December 1812 aged 74 and in the 39th year of his ministry.'[211]

While no stone marks Mr Wilkie's grave, the memorial marble tablet to the right of the pulpit was commissioned by his son Sir David in memory of his parents after his mother died in 1824. It was placed on the north wall of the church in 1833 but removed to its present position in 1835 when it was decided to extend the gallery.

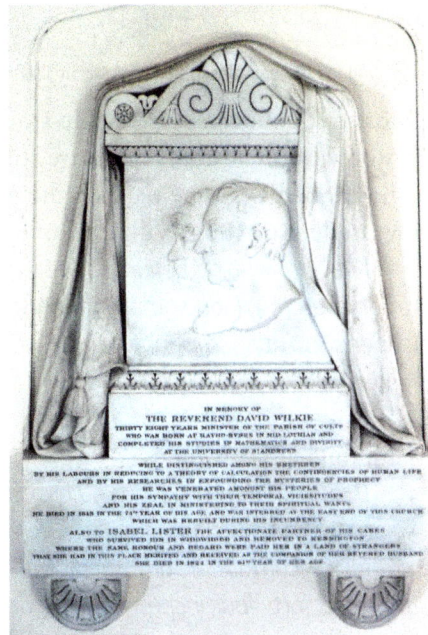

---

210   Burleigh, *A Church History of Scotland*
211   Scott, *Fasti Ecclesiae Scoticanae*, vol. 5

The monument on the other side of the pulpit commemorating Sir David was put there by his sister following his death in 1841. She also had the clock installed in 1843.

Apart from providing the world with wonderful works of art, Sir David Wilkie provided us with a window into a Pitlessie that is gone forever. While the famous painting *Pitlessie Fair* shows us an arrangement of the streets and houses that is quite different from the village of today, his preparatory sketch, pictured below, shows this even more clearly.

Background for the painting *Pitlessie Fair* by Sir David Wilkie RA

Most of the houses were single-storey weavers' cottages, many long since gone. The two-storey house just left of centre still stands and gives us an idea of where Sir David was positioned when he painted the picture. Cunningham tells us that in a letter to a fellow student in 1804 Wilkie said:[212]

I have now fairly begun to The Country Fair [the original name]. I have the advantage of our herd-boy and some children who live about the place as 'standers'; and I see how superior painting from nature is to anything that our imagination, assisted by our memory, can conceive.

Cunningham continues:

[He] made a working sketch of Pitlessie – house and street and stream – and drew in masses the various groups whom business or pleasure had called to market; then stretching canvass on a frame, the largest he had yet used, measuring twenty-five inches high and forty-four inches wide, he desired to begin, but was in want of an easel.

---

[212] Cunningham, *The Life of Sir David Wilkie*

In fact, Wilkie turned to a chest of drawers and, pulling out the centre drawer, leaned the canvas there with the top leaning against the top of the chest. Regarding the characters Wilkie chose in the village on market day, Cunningham continues:

> [H]e found the street, a long and somewhat winding one, occupied with shoemakers selling shoes, weavers selling webs, rustics selling hens and ducks, lasses selling fresh butter and eggs, and old women with stall or basket selling sugar-candy and sugar-plums: overall was heard the voice of a travelling auctioneer who sold coloured beads and striped ribbons for the gayer part of the audience, while the voice of a ballad singer vending provincial verse mingled its dolorous tones with the 'any one bids more' of the other. We may add to these sights and sounds the recruiting sergeant with his ribbons streaming in the air, the drum summoning the martial lads of Cults to the path of glory; and the lowing of cattle in the distance, from whose goaded steps the wandering dealer in tea dishes and jugs can scarce protect her brittle ware; while watching all, without seeming to do so, walk the grave dignitaries of the district – the ministers and elders – not insensible, as they go, to the charms of the lasses who enter now in bevies into the joys of the fair.

Cunningham tells us of the problem Wilkie had in finding his subjects, as 'the magnates of Strath-Eden opposed many obstacles, some on the score of vanity, some on that of religion, to have their faces recorded in the scenes of a fair'. In the end he decided to draw well-known faces when they were unaware. Cunningham explains:

> Wilkie one day, during sermon, saw one of the characters marked out for his picture nodding in his seat in the kirk; he glanced his quiet eye on him, and applying his pencil – it was one of red chalk – to the blank leaf of his Bible, fairly sketched him off without any one being aware. After the slumbering he ventured on those awake, with equal success, but not with like secrecy. All the notables of Pitlessie, with his douce grandfather included, found their way to book or to paper, and from thence to the canvass; nor were they quite aware of the extent of his limnings till the picture itself was finished...

According to Cunningham, of the 140 figures Wilkie painted, most were portraits. The Bible is now held by the National Library of Scotland and there we can see all 21 sketches Wilkie made of the folk in Cults Kirk in 1804. Some of the sketches are pictured on the following pages. These images, some strong and some faint, show us his father, grandfather and several of the farmers and folk of the village. It wasn't until the painting was finished that Wilkie's 'sitters' realised what he had done. Some took a righteous stance that something so frivolous as drawing could take place in the church – and by the minister's son! In reply to the criticism Wilkie is reported to have said that 'anyone who practised portrait painting knew that the ear was not engaged in the work, for, being a business of the eye and hand alone, he could draw as well as listen'. Wilkie did not spare the members of his family, including his grandfather on the Lister side, and his sister and cousin. Sir David's father was upset that he had been painted talking to the publican until his son pointed out that he admonished him for his trade.

Preparatory sketches for *Pitlessie Fair* **painting from David Wilkie's Bible**

The painting had been commissioned by Kinnear of Kinloch, who lived in the neighbouring parish of Collessie. Wilkie received £25 for it. Eight years later Wilkie said the picture was very badly painted yet confessed 'it has more subject, and more entertainment in it than any other pictures I have produced since'. Nevertheless, it was this picture, portraying ordinary folk enjoying a break from the hard work of daily life, that launched Wilkie onto the national and international stage as a painter of outstanding ability.

Pitlessie Fair by Sir David Wilkie

One of the local vagrants of Fife that Wilkie introduced us to in another picture is the blind fiddler. According to Wilkie's mother he was well known in the county. As a result of the work of Sir David Wilkie, who produced so many pictures reflecting the lives of the folk of Pitlessie and Cults, we have a picture of life in the parish at the beginning of the 19th century. The faces we see in these famous pictures are the faces of the folk who trod the streets of the village, who worked in the fields and sat in the seats in the kirk; seats now filled by other folk like you and me. How fortunate we are to see the ordinary people from whom we inherit our Kirk and village as they flirted with the girls, played and squabbled as children and tended their animals. We also see the minister scolding the publican for pursuing his trade. That publican is now recognisable to us, as is the whole life of the village over 200 years ago. Who knows, the once frequently quoted beadle of Cults Kirk, Tammas Young, may even be included. He gave rise to a local proverb: 'Seek a hole for yoursel', like Tammas Young's bairns.' The origin of this saying is apparently that Tammas was father of a large family. It is said that once his wife had undressed the 'bairns' he would pitch them into the box bed with the instruction 'Seek a hole for yoursel'. This, it is said, prepared the youngsters for the struggles of life in a world which, though larger than a box bed, also had its limits.

The folk and the picture of life in the village of Pitlessie would have changed little from Wilkie's famous painting when Rev. David Wilkie's successor, Rev. Prof. Thomas Gillespie was inducted to the charge in 1813 at the age of 35. Thomas Gillespie was born in 1778 at Dunns Yett, Gilchristland and Closeburn. He was educated at Wallacehall Academy, Dumfries Academy and the University of Edinburgh and became tutor to the family of Sir James Hay on Dunragit. In 1810 the Presbytery of Stranraer licensed him to preach and he was presented by University College, St Andrews, to the good folk of Cults. There he was ordained on 23rd March 1813. He demitted the post on 30th September 1828 to become assistant and successor to the Professor of Humanity at the University of St Andrews.

Thomas Gillespie was a larger-than-life character being a wit, journalist, author, poet, divine and professor. The loss of Wilkie's childhood drawings was a matter of regret for him and so he made it his task to collect all the information he could gather about the painter. This made him an important source for Cunningham when he wrote the biography of Wilkie shortly after his death in 1841.

Being 35 years of age when he was ordained at Cults, it seems he served a long probationary period of three years and his ordination may have come as a relief. Perhaps it is for this reason he inscribed the following on the lintel above the side gate into the manse garden: '*Inveni portum, spes et fortuna valete. Sett me lusistis, ludite nunc alias*', which has been translated as 'I have found a harbour, hope and fortune farewell, Me you have mocked enough, mock others now'.

Gillespie seems to have been a man who was full of fun and Porter includes many anecdotes about him both in the parish and at St Andrews University. He published a book of sermons in 1822 which was well received and he was also seen as a very eloquent speaker. With the death of his daughter Helen, known as Elly, in 1839, he wrote a very moving poem in memory of her and another on his return to Cults, which was clearly a place filled with happy memories. During the Disruption of 1843 and the controversy that led up to it, Dr Gillespie was Moderator of the General Assembly of the Church of Scotland. He expressed his viewpoint by writing satirical verse challenging Mr Maitland Makgill Crichton of Rankeilour, who was an Evangelical, the movement that sought to remove the privilege of the landed gentry to impose a minister on a congregation.

When Dr Gillespie demitted the charge in 1828 he made way for Rev. Dr George Crawford, who was presented to Cults in December of that year. Sadly, Mr Crawford's ministry was to be a short one as in November 1831 he died at the age of 29. According to the entry in the old parish records the cause of Dr Crawford's death was 'Decline', an old term for consumption or TB. A tablet in the church was erected in memory of him.

Dr Crawford's successor, Rev. John Cook, was ordained on 1st June 1832. His ministry in Cults was also to be a short one but it was during his tenure that Lady Mary Lindsay Crawford died. This resulted in the abandonment of a plan for poor relief that had been agreed by the Kirk Session and Heritors. Mr Cook was the son of Dr Cook, professor of philosophy at St Andrews, Moderator of the General Assembly in 1825 and chaplain to King George IV. Within 14 months of his arrival John Cook AM was admitted to the second charge of Haddington on 19th December 1833.

Thomas Jackson Crawford

Once again Cults found itself in a vacancy, but the brother of Rev. Dr George Crawford, Thomas Jackson Crawford, came to the rescue and was ordained on 13th June 1834. Mr Crawford remained four years and it was during his ministry that the middle gallery was built. The congregation had been complaining about the church being cold in winter and so two stoves were installed. There also seems to have been some disagreement about the right of the schoolmaster to a pew, but this was settled amicably. While at Cults Mr Crawford was responsible for the Cults entry in the New Statistical Account and during his long life he wrote many books, some considered to be of note in their day. Mr Crawford was a popular minister and he stemmed the tide of rebellion.

A Free Kirk for Pitlessie

Pitlessie UF Church

Like Kettle, a Secession Church was established in Pitlessie. Unlike Kettle, which had a Relief Church, Pitlessie found itself with the United Secession Church. It came about as a result of the translation of Rev. John Cook from Cults to Haddington in 1833. Without waiting to find out who the new incumbent of the parish might be, a petition was drawn up by those who objected to the role of the patron in choosing a new minister asking the Secession Presbytery of Cupar for a sermon. With 102 signatories the request was granted on 21st January 1834. Soon it was made known that the people were planning to build a place of worship. By August 1835 the first communion was observed and six elders ordained.

In September of that year an application was made for a minister with a stipend of £70 per annum and the rent of a house. In February 1836 John Lawson was ordained to the Pitlessie charge. The call was signed by 51 members and 33 adherents. The Secession Presbytery kept a close eye on the communion roll, and applicants, mostly from the Established Church, were subjected to an examination. While this may have affected the number of members, there was another problem in the form of the new minister of Cults, Rev. Mr Thomas Jackson Crawford, for on this occasion the patron, St Salvator's in St Andrews, had done its job well and selected a most popular minister. Such was his popularity that he stopped the flow of members leaving Cults for the new church in the village. Indeed, seating at Cults had to be extended by the erection of a new part to the balcony.

Five years later Mr Crawford was translated to another charge and Mr James Anderson was installed in the Parish Church. This did nothing to improve Mr Lawson's success and in the summer of 1841 we are told that he was in need of 'sympathy and assistance'. When he spoke of resigning in 1846, 141 people petitioned him to remain. His health continued to be poor and after struggling on a little longer he finally resigned in March 1847. On 1st June 1852 Mr Lawson died in Selkirk. Clearly he had been an ill man and perhaps he was lacking in the vigour that a new charge needed. Yet 141 people signing the petition for him to stay is a significant number so his ministry was not a failure.

The second minister was Andrew W. Smith. Ordained at Cambuslang, he was inducted at Pitlessie in September 1847, the year in which the United Secession Church joined with the Relief Church to form the United Presbyterian (UP) Church. The call was signed by 91 members and he too was to receive a stipend of £70 and it was decided that this should be increased at regular intervals. By 1849 membership was over 100 but, as the population of the village started to fall, the size of the congregation contracted also. Nevertheless, by 1869 the stipend reached £140. Half of this was raised by the congregation and half by a central fund.

In spite of falling numbers and the need for aid to pay the stipend, in 1865 it was decided that the old building was cheerless and required extensive and costly repairs. After much discussion it was decided to replace it with another on a more attractive site. The Earl of Glasgow kindly provided land on the east side of the village and on the south side of the turnpike from Cupar to Kirkcaldy. Building started in June 1885 and the foundation stone was laid with much ceremony. In attendance were Mr Maxwell, Free Church of Kettle and Cults, Rev. Barr, UP Church of Kettle and Mr Chrystal, minister of Cults Parish Church, reflecting the good relationship between the local clergymen. The new church, designed to offer seating for 400 people, was opened in May 1866 by Dr George Jeffry of Glasgow at a cost of £800 and it was opened free of debt.

With the retirement of Mr Smith in 1888, Pitlessie became known as a 'teaching station' where students and probationers gained experience. The congregation found this unacceptable and petitioned the Synod in 1899 to be restored to a fully functioning church. By this time membership had fallen to only 60 and they could afford to pay only £50 as a stipend and so Presbytery was hesitant at granting the request. Nevertheless, they relented and in August 1899 Rev. John Carmichael was inducted. He received a stipend of £130, but clearly assistance was required in meeting this sum.[213] This was to be a short ministry and he left in 1901 when Pitlessie UP Church (the UF Church since the union of the UP and the Free Church in 1900) was united with Kettle and Cults UF Church on 16th April 1901,[214] and Balmalcolm Church became the main place of worship for members of the UF Church in Pitlessie.

Cults Loses its Minister

At the time when the balcony was extended the membership of Cults was 678 people (150 families) but Mr Crawford confessed only 348 communicants.[215] This was remarked upon at the dinner held in his honour on the evening before he left the parish in September 1838. There were between 40 and 50 present and Mr Maitland Makgill proposed the toast and spoke of Mr Crawford's considerable intellectual qualities, clear simple preaching style and care and compassion for the sick and dying in the parish. He was highly respected not only by the people of the Parish Kirk but also by those tempted to join the Secession Church. In reply Mr Crawford told of his anxiety when he first came to Cults because he lacked experience as a minister. Yet he found he was met with such warmth and kindness by the parishioners that all his fears were allayed. He was sad to leave the people and hoped to return to see them again. So it was that with a heavy heart Mr Crawford left Cults to become minister of the parish of Glamis.

As Mr Crawford moved on there was again a vacancy and a new minister had to be found. So it was that in December 1838 the University of St Andrews presented Mr James Anderson to Cults and he was ordained in February the following year.

Mr Anderson was the son of James Anderson, a tenant farmer at Mill of Ardoch and nether Braco in the parish of Muthill, Perthshire. He was born on 26th May 1804 into a family that had been active in the church for several generations. His paternal and maternal grandfathers and grand-uncle (William Anderson) were responsible for the erection of a chapel of ease and graveyard at Ardoch in 1780. Indeed, his grandfather, James Anderson, had the honour of being the first occupant of the graveyard in 1782.

Mr Anderson's father inherited responsibility for the chapel and was involved in the selection of ministers and acted as a manager of the church. It is not surprising, therefore, that to James Anderson the Christian faith was at the very centre of daily life throughout his childhood and he was well acquainted with the catechisms at an early age.

---

213 Small, *Congregations of the United Presbyterian Church*
214 *Dundee Courier* Wednesday 17th April 1901
215 *New Statistical Account*

Mr Anderson had served as 'missionary' at Largoward before being ordained at Cults in February 1839. About the time he left Largoward there was a great deal of unhappiness in that place. Accusations had been levelled against the minister of Kilconquhar, which caused splits in the Presbytery of St Andrews, and Mr Anderson became involved in the heated debate in support of Dr William Ferrie, father of his wife Maria.

Rev. James Anderson

On one occasion when St Andrews Presbytery met at the Kirk of Kilconquhar and tempers became somewhat frayed, Rev. James Anderson was reported as having said to one speaker, 'You have no right to be heard here, Sir!' 'Just you be quiet, Mr Anderson,' came the reply, 'you are not a parishioner here!', which was true as Mr Anderson was a member of the Presbytery of Cupar, not St Andrews. Such a charge would not trump Mr Anderson's sense of outrage and he retorted, 'I have as much right to be heard as you – I will not be put down by any lawyer from St Andrews!' Despite the appearance of a mild-mannered man in the photograph, there was clearly plenty of spirit about the young James Anderson, and he was prepared to speak plainly when it suited.[216]

In contrast, we see the warmth of the new minister of Cults in the letter he wrote to Thomas Wilkie offering the condolences of the people of the parish at the death of his brother, Sir David Wilkie. Here he recounts the memories of those old enough to remember the Wilkie family in the manse and how they recalled 'the image of that social and happy fireside, around which you and the immortal deceased were accustomed to gather, under the venerable and watchful eye of a pastor father'.

The Death of Sir David Wilkie

The death of Sir David Wilkie in 1841, at the age of 54, affected the people of the parish deeply. They had been so very proud of their famous son and that pride would last for generations, down to the present day. In an article in the *Fife Herald* of 24th June 1841 a moving tribute is paid to the great national figure that Sir David was. It also records with great affection the memories of local folk of their minister's son.

Davie Wilkie was remembered as a clever boy whose father gave him a chisel and apron to 'help' in the building of the new church. As a boy he was a frequent visitor of William Graham, the local blacksmith, and was allowed to hammer on the anvil. It was recalled how he had a passion for drawing noses, eyes, trees and cottages using the burnt end of a stick as his tool.

---

[216] *Fife Herald* 14th April 1842

The following incident is recorded in the article. Lady B, whose nose happened to be somewhat prominent, had visited the manse at Cults and noticed the little boy (then only 5 years old) who was playing by her side. As soon as this noble lady had taken her departure 'wee Davie' went missing. When found he was in the act of drawing, with a piece of charred stick, the outline of a figure. When asked what he had drawn he replied, 'Gonie nose! Gonie nose!' Davie got little encouragement from his family in the pursuit of his artistic talents. His grandfather James Lister was often heard to say, 'Indeed, my man, it will be a long time ere daubing wi' a stick' will do onything for you.' It was his father who relented and allowed his son to pursue his artistic talents in Edinburgh. In conclusion, the author of the article asks the rhetorical question 'When shall we see his like again?' Indeed, this is the case, for his prominence brought fame to the parish in which he was born. To this day visitors travel from around the world to visit the birthplace of this great man.

The Wilkie Memorial

Discussion took place in the press about erecting a suitable monument to Wilkie and some based their ideas on the Hopetoun monument. Sites at Skelpie and Upper Bunzion were mentioned and even near to the proposed railway line where anyone passing through Fife would see it. In the end it was Wilkie's sister who had the tablet in the Kirk installed in 1844.[217] The marble for this memorial to Wilkie was, according to Lewis, cut from the same block of marble as a statue now in the Tate Gallery in London and also carved by Samuel Joseph.[218]

Memorial commissioned by Wilkie's sister in 1841

David Wilkie's sister kept in touch with Cults. She came to the parish to visit her aunt in 1842 and also visited the church to see the tablet that bore the images of her mother and father that Sir David commissioned Chantrey to create. She made a gift of £2 to be spent on the poor and promised to give the church an hour glass to replace the one her brother had given but which was broken.[219] A year later Miss Wilkie presented the Kirk with the gallery clock, made by Adam Thomson, who was, according to the *Fife Herald*, 'one of the most distinguished clock-makers in London'. That clock is still in the gallery opposite the pulpit to remind the preacher if sermons are too long! After a recent refurbishment it keeps perfect time.

[217] *Fife Herald* 17th February 1842
[218] Lewis, *A Topographical Dictionary of Scotland*
[219] *Fife Herald* 25th August 1842

Clerk to the Presbytery

In 1842 the Clerk to Presbytery died and so it was necessary to look for another. The discussion soon centred on two candidates, Mr Brodie of Monimail and Mr Anderson. It was pointed out that Mr Anderson was 'of good temper' and had a 'great desire to oblige'. Mr Brodie too was an amiable gentleman so how were they to decide? After much deliberation it was decided that Mr Brodie's church was very wealthy and so his stipend was generous. He also had further income from a school he ran and so he was financially better placed than Mr Anderson who, with his wife and children, depended on the meagre stipend that came from Cults, a poor congregation. As a result, it was agreed that the £15 per annum paid to the Presbytery Clerk would be better placed with Mr Anderson. With the benefit of hindsight this decision saved Presbytery from having to find another Clerk. In the following year Mr Brodie joined the Free Church and went on to establish the church at Bow of Fife. Mr Anderson's appointment was popular and he became a recognised expert in ecclesiastical law. He remained in the parish for 25 years and during that time turned his skills to editing and publishing several volumes.[220]

With the coming of the Disruption at the General Assembly in May 1843 we learn that Cults was not immune from the unhappiness that surrounded these times. On 30th March the *Fife Herald* makes charges against Mr Anderson, claiming that he had become a signatory of the 'Convocationalist Resolution'. This would put him clearly in support of the Dissenters who wanted to leave the Established Church. It was at this time that the one-time minister of Kilrenny and leading Dissenter Thomas Chalmers was preparing the ground for the new Free Kirk. One particular group, which included Dr Candlish, minister of St George's in Edinburgh, was the Convocationalists, which invited ministers to join them at a meeting in Edinburgh. Resolutions were adopted deploring the encroachment of the civil courts in spiritual matters. This was inspired by patrons who went to law feeling their position was being challenged when, as the law required, they sought a minister for the parish in their charge.

The Convocationalists became very active in spreading propaganda and public meetings were held in the large towns. Rural ministers were approached personally, with some protagonists being rather more zealous than they should when they threatened reluctant ministers that they would attempt to lead their congregations away from the Established Church or at least split them if the minister did not sign. We don't know whether such pressure was placed on Mr Anderson. One month after the charges appeared in the *Fife Herald*, it is reported that the Cults minister requested that his name be removed from the Convocationalist Resolution.[221] He was not alone in this and it may be that such men did sympathise with the aims of the Free Kirk but, for whatever reason, could not bring themselves to join it. This said much about the unhappiness of the times.[222]

---

[220] *Fife Herald* **17th February 1842**
[221] *Fife Herald* **17th April 1843**
[222] *Fife Herald* **30th March 1843**

By 11th May things were coming to a head in Presbytery and feelings were running high. Mr Anderson, as Presbytery Clerk, was publicly criticised for manipulating the election of commissioners to the General Assembly. This was repudiated and in his defence Mr Anderson pointed out that some members of Presbytery left that court to form their own Presbytery and so were not fully aware of the procedure being followed.[223] For many the very existence of the Church of Scotland was at stake. As Presbytery Clerk, the minister of Cults found himself in the midst of all the rancour of these times of high emotion.

The Glasgow Silver

During his ministry at Cults Mr Porter found the following entries in the Kirk Session minutes:

> *Schoolhouse, Pitlessie, 14th February 1856: On the 27th day of August 1855 the Earl of Glasgow presented to the Kirk and Parish of Cults, through the Revd. James Anderson, minister thereof, a Communion service, consisting of four cups, two flagons, and two plates – all of them of the most massive and elegant description. A representation having been made to his Lordship that the Parish of Cults was very inadequately supplied with Communion plate, his Lordship at once not only agreed to supply the defect, but now has most amply carried his good intentions into effect by the magnificent gift of Communion plate that has now been presented to the Parish of Cults. The several articles of Communion plate were forwarded by Messrs Mackay, Cunningham & Co., Edinburgh, goldsmiths to the Queen, and have been executed in their best style.*

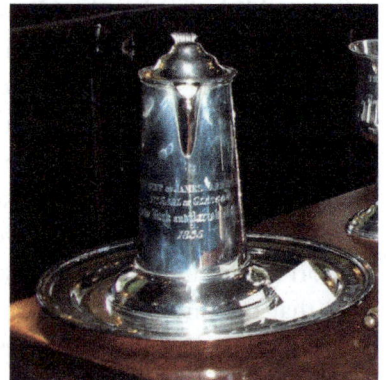

Communion jug and plate donated by the Earl of Glasgow

> *Session House of Cults, October 16th 1856: Thereafter, it was stated by the Moderator that John Neill M'Leod, Esqr., Crawfurd Priory, had on the 5th instant, given the valuable gift of a Bible and Psalm book to the Kirk Session and Parish of Cults for the use of the Minister for the time being, and which was presented on the occasion of his brother, Mr Donald McLeod preaching his first sermon. [Now 1907 Dr*

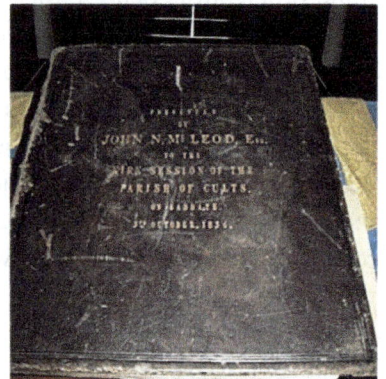

The Bible gifted to Cults Kirk in 1856

---

223 *Fife Herald* 11th May 1843

Donald Macleod of Park Church, Glasgow, was editor of Good Works.] As Mr McLeod in his letter which accompanied the gift very appropriately termed it a 'very sincere thank offering' on what we must all pray may be the opening of a career of much usefulness; we view it in that light and receive it accordingly, and we are thoroughly convinced that should health be granted to Mr M'Leod, he will become a 'burning and a shining light.' The Kirk Session therefore feel it to be their duty to record their deep sense of gratitude to Mr J. McLeod for the valuable gift received, and for the uniform kindness experienced by them from Mr McLeod as well as the many favours conferred upon them since he became Factor to the Earl of Glasgow.

That Bible is still in use and carried to the pulpit at Cults at the beginning of worship.

Lady Mary

The title Earl of Crawford is one of the most ancient titles in Britain, having been created in 1398 for Sir David Lindsay. Struthers, a castle with an interesting history said to date back to 1124, and the lands of Cults came into the hands of Sir William Lindsay in 1382 when he married into the Keith family and inherited the castle and lands. The Crawford family, and their ancestors, retained Struthers until the end of the 19th century. The castle is now a ruin but in its time it entertained Charles II and housed a detachment of Cromwell's army for three months in 1653.

Struthers Castle

Lady Mary, the daughter of the 21st Earl of Crawford, gained ownership of Crawford Lodge and the Struthers Estate on the death of her brother George, 22nd Earl of Crawford, in 1808. The title, Earl of Crawford, found no successor until 1848 when it was passed to her cousin, the Earl of Balcarres – now Earl of Crawford and Balcarres.

Not long after inheriting the land Lady Mary began work on extending and renovating Crawford Lodge, which had been built in 1758 as a hunting lodge. She employed the architects David Hamilton and James Gillespie Graham to build a Gothic fantasy. While there was no ecclesiastical connection until the Earl of Glasgow built a tower and Episcopal chapel some time later in the century, it was dubbed Crawford Priory from the beginning. The supervision of the work while running a large estate was no mean feat for a single lady, even one of noble birth, in the early part of the 19th century.

Crawford Priory, Cupar

On the ground floor were the main public rooms including the drawing room, the small and evening drawing rooms as well as the superb Gothic hall that was crowned with a magnificent fan-vaulted ceiling from which pendants hung. In niches suits of armour stood to attention, while lighting came through a stained glass that was in the medieval style. A beautiful staircase adorned with gilded panels ascended to the first floor where one would find the library, main bedrooms and chapel. The state bedroom was above the Gothic hall and nearby one would find the Psyche bedroom, so called due to it being decorated with wallpaper depicting the life of Psyche, a character in a classical tale by Apuleius. The photographs here, taken about 1873, give us a distant view of the great opulence that once graced the parish of Cults. Many changes took place over the years including removal of the stained glass and installation of an additional window to improve lighting in the Gothic hall and the installation of electricity in 1933 at a cost of £1,000.

The grand staircase

Top: the drawing room. *Bottom*: the small drawing room

Top: the evening drawing room. *Bottom*: the library

Top: the state bedroom. Bottom: the Psyche bedroom

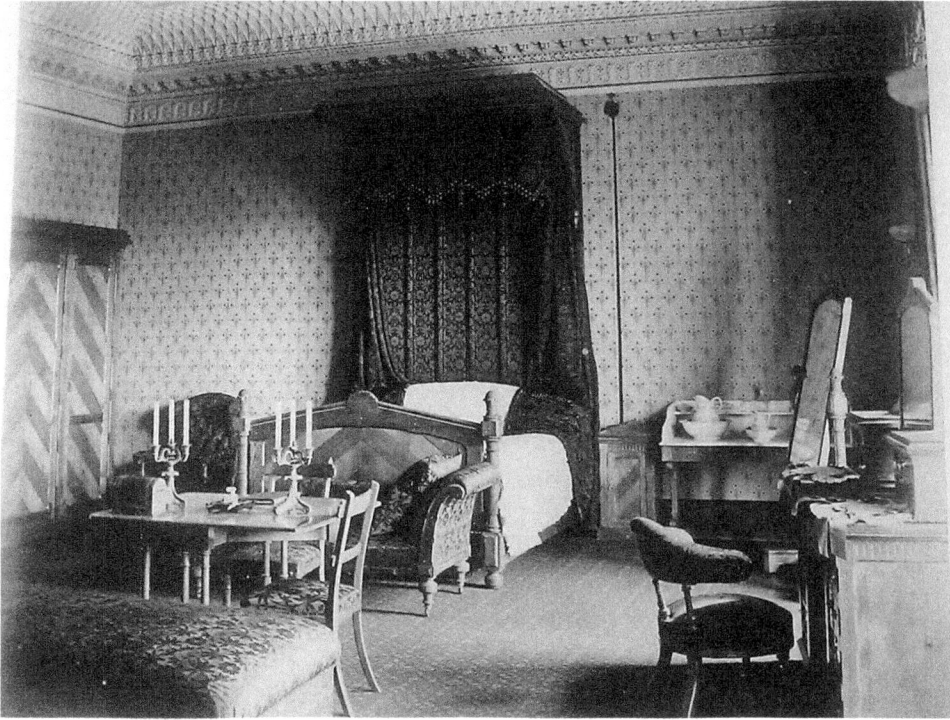

According to Millar in his *Fife: Pictorial and Historical*, Lady Mary was very beautiful in her youth, but she was also, in current language, feisty, having a clear understanding of her own principles and priorities and was not afraid to pursue them. We are told that this beautiful woman became the subject of numerous scandals but the Earl of Balcarres suppressed many of these. He said of her that 'her mind was of a masculine order' and she had a reputation for being of 'high spirit, independent and unscrupulous'. In later years Lady Mary wrote a letter to the Earl showing her appreciation for his support during those difficult days. She said he had been like a brother to her.

Correspondence relating to the construction of the Priory indicates that Lady Mary personally dealt with the builders in addition to running an estate which included lime kilns, coal mines and farms. Women in the early 19th century would not have been considered capable of such management and so the rumours may well have been ill-founded, malicious gossip, spread by prejudice and envy.

Nevertheless, Lady Mary was 'kind and considerate to her dependants that were devotedly attached to her'. Evidence of this can be found in the *Fife Herald* of 1st March 1832. Here it is recorded that she gave 'her usual 100 loads of coals' to the poor of Cults parish. In addition, there was 'a large quantity of flannels, stockings and shoes'. It was also recorded that she donated £25 to county funds for the prevention of cholera. The Earl of Balcarres was clearly very fond of Lady Mary, whose correspondence, discovered after her death, revealed a very kind and generous lady.

It is said that Lady Mary seldom left Crawford Priory and was extremely fond of animals. There are tales of her having a pet deer that accompanied her when she was out walking and she was even said to have kept a tame fox. In 1811 a party was held that brought the attention of the *Evening Post* of 24th June. It took place in the Argyle rooms and catered for over 500 guests. Supper was served during a break in the dancing, which continued until six in the morning!

Lady Mary's Episcopalian funeral service took place in the Gothic hall on 2nd December 1833. Once the service was over a procession carried the coffin from Crawford Priory along a specially cut road towards Walton Hill. When it arrived at the mausoleum in the woods, now known as Lady Mary's Wood, she was silently laid to rest next to her brother. A large number of people attended, including tenants of the estate and people from Cupar and Ceres. It was, according to the Earl of Balcarres, an impressive spectacle.

Mausoleum of George, 22nd Earl of Crawford and his sister Lady Mary Lindsay Crawford

Life in the Parish of Cults in the Mid 19th Century

Pitlessie was a different place in the 1800s from the one we are accustomed to in the 21st century. In 1846 889 people lived in the parish. In addition to the village of Pitlessie, the hamlets of Crossgates, Cults Mill, Hospital Mill and Walton were considered worthy of mention by Lewis in his *Topographical Dictionary of Scotland*. Indeed, Cults Mill with a population of 46 seems to have been the largest community outside Pitlessie, which in 1836 had 516 inhabitants. With agriculture and weaving being prominent industries in the area there was plenty of work for a blacksmith.

William Doig, blacksmith

Blacksmiths have always been important people in communities everywhere and Pitlessie is no exception. In the days when the Wilkies were in the manse there were two smiths in the parish, one in the village and the other at the Kirkton. Wee Davie Wilkie was known to visit the smith frequently. Later in the 19th century a family of smiths by the name of Doig served the Cults area for several generations.

First mention of the family in Pitlessie is in the 1851 census, which tells us that the blacksmith was Peter Doig, aged 37, and he had an 8-year-old son, William. The family continued living in Pitlessie at 8 Cupar Road until the 1901 census. On an early OS map of Pitlessie we see the smithy situated next to the inn (at the junction of the High Street and Cupar Road). An advertisement in the *Courier* of 22nd September 1853 tells us that there was malting, baking and brewing taking place in the inn. Mr Doig had the responsibility of showing people round the property, which was up for sale. We also know that he attended the funeral of Rev. Mr Forbes in 1900.

In 1888, for several consecutive years, Mr William Doig served on the School Board and the Curling Club, which seemed to consider him their 'Poet Laureate'. In 1903 he recited a poem he had written himself which extolled the virtues of the club's office bearers.

Mr Doig's death is recorded in the *Courier* on 13th January 1904 when intimation was made that debtors and creditors should contact his solicitor in Dundee who was winding up the estate. Nevertheless, Mr Doig left a legacy of many friends and good will. He also left a plough he had made, pictured below. Perhaps it was the one shown at Walton Farm when he received a prize for the plough costing less than £5.

This was not all, however, for the village, surrounded by 12 very productive farms, was thriving and contained: four boot and shoemakers, six carters, two china merchants, two churches (the Parish and the UF Churches), six grocers, three joiners and wrights, two libraries, two lime burners and merchants, five masons, two millers, two tailors, two teachers, three vintners, a dressmaker, a weaver's agent, one plash miller (operator of a water-driven fulling mill) and one basketmaker.[224]

In addition, there was the limestone in seams up to 14 feet thick in the quarries on Cults Hill. In 1846 it produced 25,000 bolls annually. (A boll is an old measure which varied according to the locality and material. As a guide, one boll of meal weighed 140 lbs or 63.5 kg.)[225] Most of the limestone, valued as a building material and for agriculture, was transported to Dundee and Perth. This was a very important contributor to the economy. Crawford in the New Statistical Account tells us that in the summer season over a hundred carters were employed from Cults, Ceres, Collessie, Largo, Kennoway, Cupar, Kettle and Cameron. By this time coal was no longer being worked here, and had to be imported from Teases for burning the lime. There were also several freestone quarries within the parish.

About 150 people were employed as linen weavers and they produced about 1,700 webs a year, each 140 yards long and 30 inches wide. These were sent to manufacturers in Kettle, Leslie and Newburgh and there were also agents in the parish. There were 85 men and 65 women employed in weaving, with nearly half of them under the age of 20. Payment was 14s. 6d. per web and looms were rented at 9s. annually. The average weekly wages were 5s. for a man and 3s. for a boy or girl.[226]

At Hospital Mill an old corn and flax mill was converted at a cost of £4,000 for spinning tow (hemp). The mill was driven by a waterwheel and the 160–180 tons produced annually were sent mainly to Dundee. Of the 50 people employed, many were women and children. There were six mills in total in 1836 including, in addition to the above, mills for flour, barley, malt and oatmeal as well as two sawmills, one water-powered and the other steam-driven.[227]

Pitlessie Fair still featured annually on the second Tuesday of May. It was well attended for the sale of farm animals and agricultural implements. It is also revealed that Mr Anderson's stipend was just £162 plus the glebe, which was valued at £11 per annum. This was widely considered a lowly income for the minister.[228]

There was a Parish School which served about 100 pupils and the teacher received an annual salary of £34, with an addition of £30 in fees as well as a house and garden. In the New Statistical Account we are told that he also received £6 for acting as Session Clerk and registrar. There was also a private school in 1836 with 45 pupils charging fees

[224] Parochial Directory for Fife and Kinross 1861, www.fifefhs.org/resources/records/parochial-directory-for-fife-and-kinross-1861
[225] M. Robinson (ed.), *The Concise Scots Dictionary* (Aberdeen University Press, 1985)
[226] New Statistical Account, vol. 9
[227] New Statistical Account, vol. 9
[228] Lewis, *A Topographical Dictionary of Scotland*

of 2*s*. (10p) for reading and 2*s*. 6*d*. (12.5p) for arithmetic. A further 'remote' school existed where the teacher was 'female' and it had about 20 young pupils who paid from 1*d*. to 2*d*. per week (1*d*. was 1/240th part of a pound). The Sabbath School had between 30 and 40 pupils 'according to the season of the year'.[229]

When we compare the annual incomes of the minister and schoolteacher with others we find that a ploughman in 1836 received £16 to £26 per annum and a female domestic servant £4 10*s*. to £6 10*s*. A male day-labourer received 8*s*. to 10*s*. per week and a female day-labourer from 4*s*. to 5*s*. per week. Perhaps in comparison with others the learned gentlemen were indeed well off.[230]

There were about 12 people in the parish who were identified as paupers. They received rent for their house, coal in the winter and from 4*s*. (20p) to 5*s*. (25p) per month. There were others who received occasional assistance. The average cost of caring for the poor in the parish was £50 each year. This came from Kirk Session funds, which relied upon collections at the church door and other voluntary contributions.

While the majority of the people attended the Established Church, a considerable minority chose dissenting churches. These include 136 members of the United Associate Synod, 57 members of the Relief Synod, 8 members of the Original Burgher Synod and 8 Independents. These were Crawford's figures and they indicate the degree of unhappiness there was in the parish with the Established Church at that time.

The statistics give a picture of a busy, thriving community which was quite independent in many ways. Employment was plentiful and the education of the young well catered for. We know from elsewhere in the history that the Kirk Session took its responsibility for the poor of the parish seriously and it would lend money, and not always to people who could pay back the loan. Altogether it looks like a happy community in the mid 19th century. One point that is worthy of note is that while the number of places of worship has decreased since the 1800s, so has the number of licensed premises.

Like so many of his predecessors, sadness became part of Mr Anderson's life. The loss of two daughters was said to be responsible for him suffering heart disease. One night he was driving to Presbytery in a carriage with a friend when there was a collision with a passing cart and he fell and suffered some injury. He continued to Cupar but after the business at Presbytery was completed he visited the house of a friend where he became ill. Having been taken home his condition deteriorated and he died on 30th September 1863 when he was 59 years of age. This was a great blow not only to the parish but to Presbytery, where the following tribute was recorded:

> *Cupar Presbytery 20th October 1863. It having pleased Almighty God, since last ordinary meeting of Presbytery, to remove by death their Brother, the Revd. J Anderson, minister of Cults, and Clerk of this Court, the Presbytery deem it incumbent upon them to record an expression of deep feeling of solemnity with which their minds have been affected by his sudden demise, so soon after he had been in the midst of them discharging*

---

[229] New Statistical Account, vol. 9
[230] New Statistical Account, vol. 9

his official duties; of the respect which they entertain of his memory; and of their sympathy with the congregation thereby deprived of a Pastor, and the widow and family of a Husband and Father. Having for a period of twenty-four years officiated as a minister within their bounds, during twenty-one of which, and upwards, he held the office of their Clerk, the Presbytery feel called upon to bear testimony to the attention, regularity, and faithfulness with which he uniformly discharged his duties, as well as the urbanity and kindness of disposition which he never failed to show in all his transactions with his brethren. They desire to improve in their own experience the lesson so solemnly set before them in his death, and they pray that the Spirit of Consolation may be granted to the bereaved Widow and family.

Clearly Mr Anderson was much loved. This became evident again a few months later when the Session Clerk of Cults, Charles Robertson, approached Presbytery seeking their help in finding another minister. He presented a petition to Presbytery seeking their support in drawing up a leet of prospective candidates to replace their 'late lamented minister'. This petition was for Mr James Chrystal.

Rev. James Robert Chrystal came to Cults in 1864 at the age of 25. He was the son of Rev. James Chrystal of Auchinleck and married to Margaret Riddell, born in 1841. Margaret's mother, also Margaret, was the daughter of John Wilkie, brother of Sir David Wilkie and son of Rev. David Wilkie of Cults. So it is that the new minister's wife was granddaughter of Rev. David Wilkie.

Rev. James Robert Chrystal   An elderly Mr Chrystal

On 28th January 1879 at the meeting of Presbytery a letter from Mr Chrystal expressing his intention to demit the charge at Cults in order to accept the charge of Newmains in the parish of Cambusnethan was tabled. The letter was dated 20th December and on 21st January he was admitted to the church at Coltness. Mr Chrystal was greatly loved by the people of Cults and when he left the children of the Sunday School presented him with a writing desk and from the parishioners he received 'a gold keyless lever watch, with Albert chain and seal'. It was inscribed with the words 'To the Rev. J. Chrystal, from his congregation and friends, on his leaving the parish of Cults, where he faithfully discharged the duties of the ministry for 15 years – Jan. 1879'. Mrs Chrystal received a brooch.[231] Rev. James Chrystal was also a popular man among his peers and when he made one of several return visits to the area he visited Presbytery and was warmly welcomed.

Mr and Mrs Chrystal had four children while at Cults: Alice in 1872, James in 1875, Walter in 1876 and Robert in 1878. John Playfair Chrystal was born in Newmains in 1880 and William in 1882. Alice died in 1948, while Robert became a soldier and died in action in Rhodesia in 1899. After moving to Coltness James Chrystal became a Baptist in 1886 and first minister of Hamilton Baptist Church and president of the Baptist Union of Scotland in 1910. He died on 27th January 1930 in Melrose.[232]

A view of Cults Kirk dated about 1876

The chair in the photograph was presented to Cults Kirk by Alice in memory of her father's ministry there. It was on 23rd September 1928 that the congregation gathered for the service led by their minister, Mr Porter. Mr Chrystal, who was then aged 89, delivered the sermon. The *Courier* tells us that his voice was 'still fresh and clear, and he carried his years wonderfully well'. Porter explained that Mr Chrystal and his wife had visited the manse three years previously and that he had returned with his daughter on two previous occasions. The people's fondness for this man did not diminish with the passage of time. Lady Glasgow wrote the following letter to him.

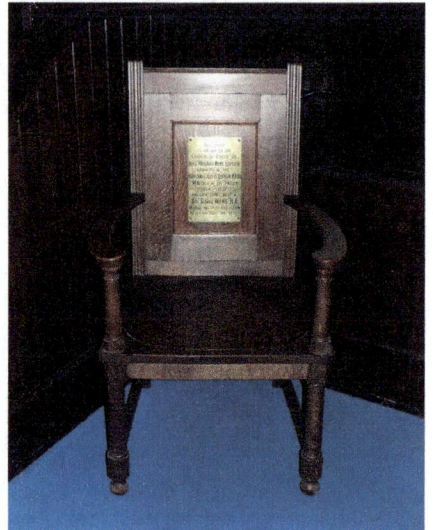

There must be some who remember you there, and who will be glad to be reminded of old times. I remember how good and sympathetic you were about the young women's Bible Class. I am quite invalid now, almost always in bed. I am sorry I shall not see you, but I feel you are a long ago friend.

---

[231] *Fife Herald* Thursday 9th January 1879
[232] Scott, *Fasti Ecclesiae Scoticanae*, vols 3, 8 and 9

This is a great tribute to the ministry of this man. Miss Chrystal also installed a plaque at the back of the church in memory of her happy childhood in the manse.

In May of 1879 documentation was laid before a Presbytery meeting held at Cults Kirk seeking permission to call Rev. James Forbes, minister of Cranshaw in the Presbytery of Dunse, to be minister of Cults. On the 4th of July Mr Forbes was inducted into the charge. This was an occasion of great celebration. Following the service of induction a dinner was held in the afternoon. Members of the Parish Kirk and friends attended giving Mr Forbes a very warm welcome. In the evening a congregational gathering took place in the church, which was filled. Members of Presbytery gave speeches and music was sung by the choir under the leadership of Mr Arthur Garland.

Rev. James Forbes was a popular minister. Only two years after his induction he was presented with a watch by Arthur Garland on behalf of the congregation 'as a mark of the esteem in which Mr Forbes had been appreciated'.[233] The Forbes family was very much involved in the life of the community. Agnes, the daughter of the manse, was a good musician and frequently played at local social and fundraising events. On one occasion when participating in a 'grand entertainment' under the auspices of Pitlessie Horticultural Society, she shared the stage with Harry Campbell, 'the famous skirt dancer and female "personator"'. On another occasion she performed 'a couple of tastefully executed violin solos'. Agnes was a pupil of Bell Baxter School in Cupar and she passed the preliminary exam (junior grade) with the Associated Board of the Royal Academy of Music and the Royal College of Music. Perhaps she got her musical talents from her mother, who was known to be accompanist at benefit concerts in the village.

Agnes's talents were not all musical, for she contributed a doll she had dressed for a sale and auction that Lord and Lady Glasgow held in the hall of Crawford Priory to raise money for the Zenana Missions (a charity that sent missionaries to approach Indian women in their own homes, with the aim of converting them to Christianity). This was a very grand occasion, which the *Courier* of 5th July 1889 tells us had stalls run by what must have been the members of a 'Who's Who' of Fife aristocracy. We are also told that it was visited by 'a large number of the resident gentry in the north of Fife'. Agnes Forbes was clearly a lady of many talents.

Welcome to the Earl of Glasgow

With the passing of Lady Mary the lands that had once belonged to the Lindsay Crawford family were passed to the Boyle family and John Boyle, the 3rd Earl of Glasgow. This was the result of a marriage that took place between a daughter on the Lindsay side and a member of the Boyle family. On his death in 1843 the title and Crawford Priory passed to his son, the 5th Earl, James. This gentleman seems to have found interest in the 'sport of Kings' and invested in horses. We are told that he was poorly rewarded for his interest and he refused to name a horse until it had proved itself

---

[233] *Dundee Courier* Monday 22nd August 1881

in the race. This practice had the disadvantage of causing great confusion in the stables. According to one yarn he had been persuaded that he really should name each of his three horses running in the same race. As a result they ran under the names 'Give-Him-a-Name', 'He-Hasn't-Got-a-Name' and 'He-Isn't-Worth-a-Name'. He was also known to have the horses that did not live up to expectations shot. On one morning he is said to have had six horses shot! This Earl's eccentricity was not confined to animals. Being always ready to join a hunt, he became frustrated if he failed to flush out any foxes and would choose one of his own huntsmen to take the place of the unfortunate quarry, who would be pursued for miles over the countryside.

George Boyle, 6th Earl of Glasgow

When the 5th Earl died in 1869 the title passed to his half-brother, George Frederick Boyle. In 1872 the 6th Earl and Countess of Glasgow decided to take up residence for part of the year at Crawford Priory. A welcome fit for royalty was prepared. During the previous three years the Earl had invested a considerable sum in extending and improving the building of Crawford Priory. This showed a commitment to the estate that had been lacking for some 30 years after the death of Lady Mary.

Schoolchildren from Ladybank and Kettle were allowed a holiday to gather at the station, and women from nearby factories used their lunch hour to attend. Mr John McLeod, factor to Crawford Priory, welcomed the family, and the tenants of the estate and their sons provided a mounted escort. Large numbers lined the procession in Kettle and Pitlessie and the bell of the church in Balmalcolm rang out. Three arches were built, each bedecked with flowers, surmounted by a crown and bearing the words 'Welcome Home'. Flags and banners were also displayed with words of welcome. Several had been prepared by the workers of the lime works with such mottos as 'Behold our Chieftain Comes', 'Long live our Noble Earl' and 'Long live the Countess'. The procession, which moved from Kettle to Crawford Priory, consisted of mounted escort, police, Kirkcaldy Artillery volunteer band and tenants on foot, farm servants, and carriages with Lord and Lady Glasgow and family. Other carriages carried contractors, masons and employees with the general public taking up the rear.

Words of welcome and a specially prepared joint statement from the tenants were given by Mr Hutton of Cults Farm. Lord Glasgow replied and invited the tenants and visitors into the Gothic hall. There he extended a further invitation to them to attend his birthday celebration on 9th October. Mr Smith of Walton Hill proposed a toast to His Lordship and his family and concluded the day by leading three cheers.[234]

[234] *Fife Herald* Thursday 9th May 1872

How strange this sounds to us in this more egalitarian age. It reflects the attitudes of a time when the local 'gentry' held a vital social as well as financial position in the parish. The relationship tended to be paternalistic, with those who lived and worked on the estate looking to the 'noble family' for both social and financial security. At the same time, the landowner depended on the income from his land and saw it as his responsibility to create employment for those who lived on the estate. In the parish of Cults and surrounding area the Earl and his family were at the apex of a social triangle that extended downwards to the large number of farm workers and labourers at the bottom. Each depended on the other for their position in life, which was fixed, and for their income.

The 6th Earl of Glasgow was a deeply religious man with a strong commitment to the Episcopalian Church in Scotland. He worked hard to improve the fortunes of this body and, in 1851, founded a theological college on the island of Cumbrae where the family owned land. This establishment became the seat of the Bishop of the Isles, the smallest cathedral in the whole of the United Kingdom.

There were other costly projects including the extension to Crawford Priory with its Episcopalian chapel, as well as financial support for church building in Perth and elsewhere. In addition, he owned several large houses. All of this led to severe financial difficulties. In 1886 we find notice in the *Courier* that the estate of Crawford Priory was up for sale. In the same edition there is also notice that the Estate of Moonzie is to be sold. This land

Painting showing interior of the chapel funded by Boyle

also belonged to the Earl and Countess of Glasgow, with an upset price of £41,000 – a fortune in 1886.[235] There were other lands in Fife, including Struthers, that belonged to his daughter as well as property in Ayrshire. The sale of much of this land not only saved Crawford Priory for the family, but cleared the Earl's considerable debts. One wonders if he was truly aware of the seriousness of the developing situation when only the previous year Lord Glasgow agreed to reduce the estate rents for the following five years.[236]

The year 1879 saw a grand occasion at Crawford Priory with the 'coming out' of Lady Gertrude. The Gothic mansion was filled with the nobility of Fife and beyond as

---

[235] *Dundee Advertiser* 30th October 1886
[236] *Dundee Courier* 16th February 1885

well as the tenant farmers and friends of the Cochrane family, for Lady Gertrude was to marry Hon. Thomas H.A.E. Cochrane, the younger son of the Earl of Dundonald the following year. The young couple were to take up residence at the Priory when they married in 1880.[237] Crawford Priory was very much at the heart of the community at the end of the 19th century.[238]

The *Fife Herald* of Thursday 7th October 1880 described a double event. In the first place there was the traditional celebration of harvest thanksgiving, which was held in the 'pretty little chapel' at the Priory. There was also that forthcoming marriage of Lady Gertrude to the Hon. Thomas Cochrane. Once again it was a grand occasion with the great and the good of the county along with the tenants of the estate present. Rev. Mr Forbes proposed thanks to the host and hostess for their generosity. Three years later, Rev. and Mrs Forbes, along with 150 guests including friends and tenants of Lord and Lady Glasgow, were invited back to the Priory to celebrate the baptism of their grandson, Thomas Cochrane, son of Lady Gertrude and the Hon. Thomas Cochrane MP. In addition to Mr and Mrs Forbes, we find familiar names and farms mentioned, though the farms and the names may no longer match as they did in 1883. So it is that we find the name Smith attached to Walton Hill and Cults Mill, while Martin is the name associated with Priestfield. It was the Graham family that farmed at Skelpie, with Mr Wilson at Muirhead.[239] On this occasion Mr Smith of Cults Mill thanked Lord and Lady Glasgow for their hospitality on behalf of the tenants, after the cake and wine had been served in the Gothic hall.

A Little Local Trouble

Although newspaper reports show Mr Forbes to be a busy and popular minister, we hear little of him in the Presbytery minutes until 3rd February 1885 when, it would appear, he was guilty of upsetting the reverend gentlemen.

The matter arose on 3rd February 1885 through some correspondence in the local press regarding the annexing of part of the glebe at Cults into the graveyard. Mr Forbes was required to confirm or deny the allegations. In his response Mr Forbes was clearly upset at this turn of events and he wrote the following letter to explain the situation:

> *24th February 1885 – letter Mr Forbes: The facts of the case are simply these. The Churchyard needed enlarging and an addition could only be made conveniently on one side. Lord Glasgow, who has always shown great kindness to the ministers of Cults, asked me if I would have any objection to a piece being taken off the little paddock, and I said I had not. I confess I see now that before saying either yes or no to Lord Glasgow I should have consulted the Presbytery, and I sincerely regret this, especially if it puts Presbytery or Lord Glasgow to any trouble. Honestly, I thought the matter of no importance; the piece of ground, less than a quarter of an acre, was of little value, and the compensation offered by*

237 *Dundee Courier* Wednesday 27th September 1899
238 *Evening Telegraph* Tuesday 24th April 1883
239 *Evening Telegraph* Tuesday 24th April 1883

Lord Glasgow – viz. £1 a year, seemed ample. As for it being near the manse, it is scarcely any nearer than the old ground is, and the ground about the manse is not curtailed in any way saving that the private door leading to the church yard is a little further in. As the ground was to be used for church and parish purposes, I thought there could be nothing wrong in the arrangement. I had no idea of a letter on the subject being in the public papers till I got your note, otherwise I would have come to the meeting of Presbytery and given this explanation.

There is no doubt that Mr Forbes was in a peck of trouble and he knew it. The fact is that responsibility for the land was in the hands of Presbytery and Mr Forbes usurped the authority of that court of the Kirk. Presbytery does not like its authority being challenged and it was about to ensure that Mr Forbes got the message and that he would not forget it. His contrite letter did not have the desired effect!

A letter from Lord Glasgow, dated 14th January, supporting Mr Forbes was produced and Presbytery decided to form a committee to visit Cults to view the situation. That committee reported that it could see no reason why the land should not be annexed. On receiving the report the whole of Presbytery decided all of its members should see the land and so a further meeting was arranged at Cults. Two local farmers were also to be present to act as arbiters. It was concluded at this meeting that time would have to be given to the arbiters to write their report and submit it to Presbytery. This was done by the next meeting. In the end it was concluded that the boundary of the disputed land should be marked by March stones and that Lord Glasgow should compensate the loss of 0.231 acres by adding 4.508 acres of the adjoining land to the glebe. While this exchange was clearly not in Lord Glasgow's favour, agreement was reached. The matter was settled and the extended graveyard is still used by the parishioners. While I have no doubt Mr Forbes learned to regret his hasty decision, succeeding generations have had cause to be grateful to him and to Lord Glasgow.

One gets the impression that there was a bond of friendship between Lord Glasgow and Mr Forbes, so it must have been painful for the minister to announce on Sunday 17th April 1890 the death of the local Laird. Next day the *Dundee Courier* recorded the following:

At the close of his sermon yesterday afternoon, the Rev. J. Forbes, parish minister, made a fitting allusion to the death of the Earl of Glasgow, and the loss the parish had sustained. For about 21 years he had been closely connected with it and up till recently had been sole heritor. His kindness to the poor and aged, his anxiety that all on the estate should be comfortably provided for, was dwelt on, as was also his consideration for those who had been long in his service.

Mr Forbes may have been popular and very active in the social life of the parish. This does not mean he was easy-going and lacked principle. On 5th January 1888 the *Courier* reports that he provided 'A Gospel Temperance address to Cupar Temperance Society'.

We are told he expressed concern at the indifference of the church regarding intemperance and pointed out that although attitudes had changed 'intemperance was still rampant, and many schemes which had been tried for the amelioration of the masses failed, and the public houses still afforded their attractions'. Clearly there was a serious side to Mr Forbes. In his concern for those 'who could not take care of themselves in regard to strong drink' he called upon the state to 'take charge of them'. In this case, the answer to the age-old question 'Does the minister take a dram' would have been a resounding no!

Again showing his rather conservative tendencies, we find him encouraging the establishment of the Church Defence Association at a meeting in Pitlessie School. This was an international body formed in 1881. It saw the courts as infringing the authority of the Church, which resulted, they claimed, in its making serious departures from 'the truth in matters of doctrine'. In particular, this body opposed the introduction of instrumental music in worship; the use of hymns 'of human composition'; the practice of sitting during the offering; and unscriptural means of raising money for the church. It added, 'Congregational choirs are an unwise innovation tending to destroy congregational singing.'[240] It seems strange that Mr Forbes would promote this stern body in the parish. His wife and daughter were very musical and there was every sign that music in the church was encouraged.

When the question of disestablishment of the Church arose in 1885, Rev. James Forbes addressed the matter from the pulpit. He said that the agitation for disestablishment was a serious religious question – not a political one. The question had been thrust upon the members and the future of the Church of Scotland rested upon them. If they were careless with their privileges and thought them not worth preserving then they would lose them. If they did value them then they must be resolute in their efforts. The Church, he said, does not exist for the clergy but for the people. He believed that all things worked for the good.[241] It is clear that he was, once again, holding conservative rather than progressive views regarding the Church and its future.

Agnes, wife of Rev. James Forbes, also had a wide variety of interests, serving on the School Board and attending, as well as contributing to, prize-giving events there. The school had a certain social importance and the Countess of Glasgow took a keen interest in its work and the welfare of the pupils. Mrs Forbes also wrote a book. While the title is not given, the *Berwickshire News* of 19th April 1892 tells us, 'For the most part [it contained] studies from real life, the stories are now published in book form at 1/-.'

We have no photograph of Mr Forbes except that in the composite opposite presented to the man at its centre, the Rev. John Duncan, in 1896 as he celebrated 60 years as minister of Abdie. We know that all 24 ministers of the Presbytery of Cupar are there and that Mr Gordon of Kettle can be identified. Of the others, it is hard to identify the reverend gentlemen who served the people of Cults so well for so many years.[242]

Life in Pitlessie in the closing years of the 19th century was lively. We read in the *Courier* of 1st February 1898 of a 'Magic Lantern Entertainment' in Cults Public School:

> Mr Forbes, Cults Manse, presided and lectured in the views thrown on the screen. The views illustrated 'The May Queen', 'Dan Dabberton's Dream', 'The Signal Box'. Mrs Forbes read an amusing Scottish Story. Mr Leitch, M.A., manipulated the lantern, and the slides were provided by Mr Peter Feathers, Dundee. During the evening the children sang several Sankey's hymns.

---

240 Testimony and Declaration of Principles of the Presbyterian Church Defence Association (Toronto, 3rd May 1881), https://archive.org/details/cihm_60227
241 *Fife Herald* Wednesday 11th November 1885
242 *Dundee Courier* Monday 8th November 1896

The church choir was invited to the manse for supper and the Sabbath School had an outing to a field for which local farmers provided transport. There were also prizes for good attendance and in that year the winners were Arthur Garland, Andrew Crawford, Alex. Garland, Mary Deas and Annie Stevenson.

Annual Excursion of Cults Parish Council and Cults School Board at Glenfarg, circa **1896**. *Back*: William Maxwell, lime works. *Middle*: John Lawson, Pitlessie Mill; W.B. Henderson, Pitlessie; John Graham, Skelpie; William Doig, Pitlessie; Alex Alison, Cults Mill; David Garland, Pitlessie. *Front*: David Speed, Pitlessie; Andrew Smith, Walton Hill; John Thoms, Bunzion

The turn of the century brought improvements in public amenities in the parish when, on 2nd December 1898, Mr Haig of Ramornie opened the public hall in Pitlessie as a memorial to Sir David Wilkie. According to the press there was a large number of people attending the event. This had been known as the Forsyth Hall after the UP Church had decided to move to its new location in May 1866.[243]

---

[243]   *Dundee Courier* 3rd December 1898

A Plan for the Parish Church

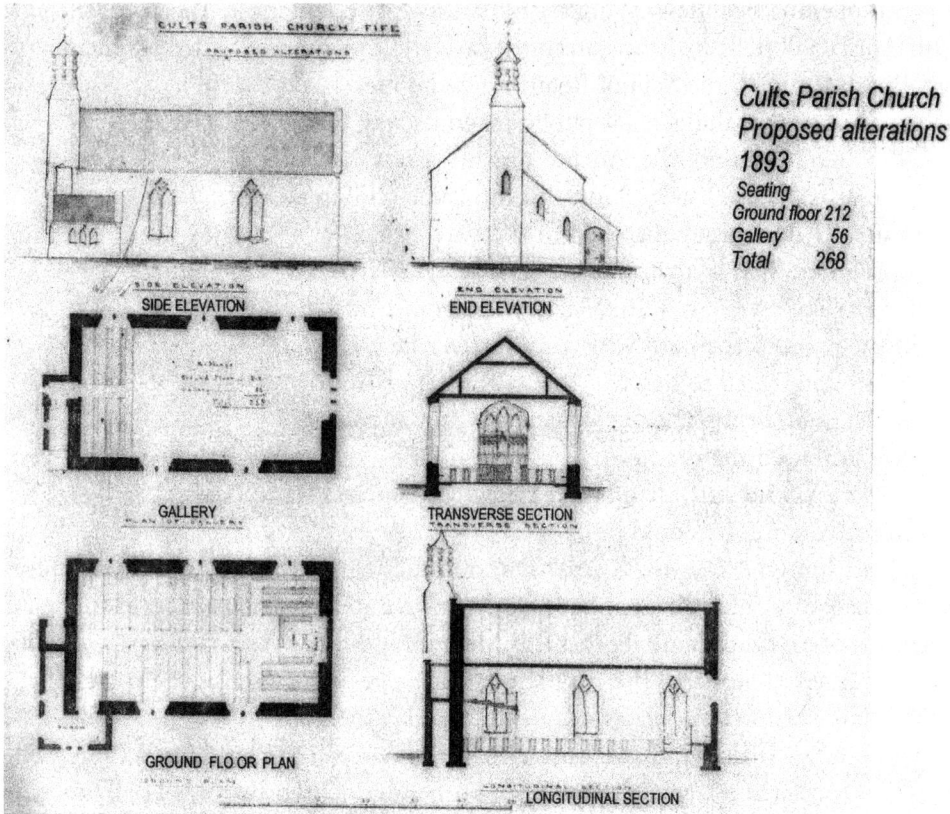

Cults Parish Church
Proposed alterations
1893
Seating
Ground floor 212
Gallery 56
Total 268

In 1893 a plan was drawn up which would have changed the church completely. The old gallery was to be removed and replaced with a new one at the west end of the church. Access to it was to be by a covered stairway up to the tower from a new porch. The box pews were to disappear and conventional pews installed facing east where the pulpit and communion table would be situated. In addition, it was intended to replace the quaint Georgian windows with large ones in the Gothic style. Had these plans been implemented we would have inherited a familiar Victorian mock Gothic building instead of an 18th-century gem.

We don't have a record of the discussions that took place so we don't know the reasons for dropping the plan. Perhaps the financial difficulties of the Earl of Glasgow at that time made it impossible. We can imagine that, while there would have been those who felt inspired at the prospect of 'modernising' the old place, there would have been other voices calling the plan a waste of money. An educated guess would suggest that, whoever won the debate, it all fell through because of lack of money. Only 10 years later when Mr Porter was in place he had to apply for financial assistance to make necessary repairs to the church and manse. I would suggest, then, that on this occasion it was a lack of money that preserved our architectural treasure.

In Pitlessie, public amenities were once again enhanced when in April 1900 there was the grand opening of Pitlessie Public Park amid great celebration. The *Dundee Courier* of 9th April 1900 tells us it was an impressive affair. A procession led by members of Cults Parish Council, the School Board, the schoolteachers and pupils as well as the general public made its way from the UP Church behind the Auchtermuchty brass band. Large Reform banners were unfurled and the children carried smaller ones. They marched to the park, which was to be opened by Miss Martin (daughter of James Martin of Priestfield), who was accompanied by her mother. She opened the gates to the park with a solid silver key, which was formally presented to her. Mr Andrew Smith of Walton Hill, as chairman of the Parish Council, gave an address in which he expressed the gratitude of the community to the late Mr Martin, who sadly died before the gift so generously given to the community could be opened.

DEATH OF A WELL-KNOWN FIFE FARMER.

James Martin

On 11th June the *Dundee Courier* reported that Mr Forbes suffered an 'apoplectic shock' (what we would call a stroke) and died two and a half hours later at the manse. At the time of his death James Forbes was Moderator of Presbytery and was held in high esteem by his parishioners. The people of Cults were very upset at the death of their minister. No worship took place at Cults on Sunday the 10th.

It was a large funeral and the *Courier* lists the names of many local folk as well as those from further afield who attended. Mr Forbes' son, Dr Forbes, was a pall bearer and among the general mourners, as the *Evening Telegraph* of 14th June dubbed them, were Mr John Garland, Mr John Elder, Mr A. Garland and more. The funeral arrangements were carried out by Mr David Garland.

A New Era

With the death of both the Earl of Glasgow and the minister, two prominent people in the community had gone, no doubt leaving many with a great sense of loss. At Crawford Priory the daughter of the Earl of Glasgow and her husband and family took over where her father had left off.

The Cochrane Family

Mr Thomas Horatio Arthur Ernest Cochrane MP was the third son of the 11th Earl of Dundonald. He distinguished himself with both his military and parliamentary career. Decorated in the Boer War he served as a Major with the Argyll and Southern

Thomas Horatio Arthur Ernest, First Baron Cochrane of Cults

Highlanders. His civilian career was no less successful as he served as MP for North Ayrshire between 1892 and 1910 and acted as Parliamentary Private Secretary for the Colonies between 1895 and 1901 and Undersecretary for the Home Department from 1902–1905. In 1919 he was created the First Baron Cochrane of Cults.

They had three sons, Thomas George Frederick, baptised in 1883 in Crawford Priory, Archibald Douglas and Ralph Alexander. Each went on to distinguish himself in the 20th century.

A New Minister

On the day of Mr Forbes' funeral Presbytery met to organise the vacancy at Cults. This resulted in several candidates coming to the parish to meet with the Session and Mrs Forbes kindly accommodated them in the manse. In appreciation for all that Mrs Forbes had done for the parish over the years, not only in support of her husband but also in her own right, she received a gift from the congregation. This took the form of a silver inkwell and pen and £26 in cash. In the days when the average weekly wage would have been £1–£2, this was a lot of money and reflected the affection this family had earned among the people.

It was not long before a candidate was elected in the form of Mr William Henry Porter, a probationer minister. He had been licensed by the Presbytery of Glasgow in June 1894 and he held a Presbyterial certificate in his favour by the Presbytery of Edinburgh dated September 1900. The call was supported by the Heritor, three elders and 67 members and parishioners. Mr Porter accepted the call and it was arranged for him to undergo the trials by Presbytery. He was to be examined on: 'Hebrew, the 19th Psalm; Greek New Testament and *apperturam* [openings]; Christian Doctrine – the Passion of Christ; Elements of Church law, and Pastoral Theology, all as prescribed by the regulation of the General Assembly'. Mr Porter met

Rev. William Henry Porter

the requirements of Presbytery and was ordained and inducted on 1st November 1900.

Henry Porter, born in 1865, was 35 years of age when he arrived at Cults. His father was William and his mother Euphemia Galloway. Educated at Falkland School before going on to Glasgow University, Henry Porter had acted as assistant at Hillside and St Paul's, Leith. Three years after his arrival at Cults he married Margaret, the younger daughter of Andrew and Grace Dickson of Haddington. Between 1904 and 1916 he had seven sons; one died in 1913 at the age of only 3. I know this information to be true because it was Mr Porter who had responsibility for updating the Cupar Presbytery contribution to volume 5 of the *Fasti Ecclesiae Scoticanae*, which was my source for this information.

Mr Porter had an interest in church history, which is reflected in his two publications *Cambuslang and its Ministers* (1897) and *Cults and its Ministers* (1906). I have been fortunate in having a copy of the latter available to me and I am indebted to Mr Porter for the information it contains.

When Henry Porter arrived he found the condition of the church and manse to be poor and in need of considerable attention. In a letter dated 16th November 1903 he informed Mr Thoms, the Heritor's Clerk, that the gallery was unsafe and the churchyard wall was badly in need of repair. The walls of the manse garden too were in need of attention, as were the drains, not least the positioning of the cess pool only three yards from the kitchen window! The windows upstairs could not be opened and smoke from the chimney invaded the upper rooms. Clearly the manse, which was over 100 years old, was feeling its age.

Cults Kirk choir about 1905; Mr Porter is centre and David Garland 2nd from right, front row

World War 1

It was during Mr Porter's ministry at Cults that our country, and the world, faced the great tragedy of World War 1. The folk of Cults did not escape this epoch-making event that affected so many around the globe between 1914 and 1918. With the loss of Kirk Session records it has been necessary to turn again to Presbytery minutes to uncover something of what was happening to this community at that time. While Cults seldom gets a specific mention, the following gives us a clue to how the church in this area was reacting to these events.

It is noteworthy that Presbytery says nothing about the war during the first two years. It is April 1916 when we find recorded a request made to the General Assembly to set aside a National Day of Prayer. They saw it as a way of expressing belief in 'the righteousness of the Country's cause' and of 'sharing the Christian faith, confidence and courage of the nation'. The matter was raised in several churches and different dates were suggested throughout the year. The idea was not universally popular. The following October a communication from the Commission of the General Assembly on the 'Spiritual and Moral issues of the war' resulted in Presbytery forming a committee to consider the communication and then report back to Presbytery. The outcome of their deliberations was that a devotional conference was to be held in January 1917.

Things were happening in the parishes that were affecting the work of Presbytery. It is reported that, 'While every parish contributed to the seven main schemes – foreign mission, home mission, Jews, Colonial, Endowment, small living and aged and infirm ministers' fund; only sixteen contributed to the remaining four schemes and Collessie & Ladybank contributed to none'. The reasons given for this were: Collessie – 'other collections were very numerous, and in addition, there were special collections for the War Fund'; and Ladybank – 'Seven Collections are enough for one parish with its collections for Congregational Purposes'. Money was getting tight and the war fund was having its impact on the ability of some to give.

In February 1917 Mr Porter proposed the following motion: 'The Presbytery instructs the Committee on Spiritual and Moral Issues of the war to consider the advisability of frequent devotional meetings of the Presbytery and occasional celebrations of the Lord's Supper.' No response to this motion is recorded. It was at the following meeting in March that Mr Porter, having raised the matter again, was rewarded with the formation of a committee to consider the matter and report back at the next meeting.

In April 1917 a report from the Committee on War Service was presented. This had been a joint committee with the United Free Church Presbytery. It is interesting to note that in these difficult times the Established Church and the United Free Church were able to find sufficient common ground to form a joint committee. Unfortunately, they were unable to agree on the final report and so the UF Presbytery War Committee and the Established Church War Committee delivered separate reports.

The joint committee had been presented with two questions: first, whether individual ministers would volunteer for national service; and second, if so, what form of service – in the Army, in munitions, whole-time or part-time. Almost every member of Presbytery had responded to the query, only two having failed to reply. The committee said it was sure these ministers were as ready as the others to do what they could for the work. Of those who replied, three were exempt from active service because of their age; two were 71 and the other 66. Mr Kerr of Ladybank (aged 62) was willing to do whatever he was considered fit for. Three were willing to do whatever was asked; Mr Porter (52) volunteered to undertake munitions making; three were prepared to cover for ministers who were involved in active service; seven felt able to offer part-time service in the local area; one decided that whatever he did he could be called to resume his work as a chaplain at any time; and another was free to work locally from Tuesday to Friday so that he could have the weekend for his duties in the parish.

All of these fine intentions were dependent upon there being sufficient cover for the work of the parish to continue. To this end it was decided to group the churches of the Presbytery according to what normally happens with the exchange of pulpits. As a result, Ladybank was with Collessie and Monimail, while Cults was put with Kettle, Falkland and Freuchie. Mr Forbes of Freuchie unsuccessfully applied to be relieved of his parish duties as he had been accepted as chaplain to the Armed Forces in October 1917, while Mr Alexander of Cupar was granted leave to accept a post as Army chaplain in February 1918 because he had arranged for an ordained minister from South Africa to cover the parish for him. In October 1917 Mr Porter was granted leave to go to France to work with the Scottish Churches Huts. This was established by the Church of Scotland's Guild and it set up 25 centres, staffed by 350 workers, in France and Flanders during the First World War. Its purpose was to provide physical and spiritual rest and the opportunity for recuperation. Although smaller than organisations like the YMCA it was fulfilling a similar purpose. This was the work that Mr Porter of Cults volunteered his services for in 1918.

THE SCOTTISH CHURCHES HUT MONTREUIL

Scottish churches' hut, Montreuil

In December 1917 there was a report from the Committee on War, which moved that communications should take place between their convener and his opposite number in the UF Presbytery. The purpose was to arrange a public meeting in Cupar in connection with the moral and spiritual issues of the war. The outcome of this was a public meeting in St John's UF Church in Cupar in the morning and a conference in the Parish Church in the afternoon. Once again this was a joint venture by the two Presbyteries in Cupar, displaying their ability to work together. It was reported in March that this had been a very successful event which was well attended. In this way both Presbyteries were fulfilling a need in the wider community.

In 1914 the ordinary folk of Cults could not escape the war, as the memorial outside the Wilkie Hall testifies. Not all who fought were lost and three members of the Garland family experienced the horrors of the Great War and returned home to Pitlessie. Pitlessie's local joiner, Andrew Garland, together with his older brother David and younger brother John, joined up to serve their country in the Great War. We are fortunate in that Andrew kept a diary covering his service in the Royal Engineers from 1st January 1917 until 31st December 1918. This gives us the following unique insight into the daily life of a local lad during these terrible times.

Andrew K. Garland, Royal Engineers; David Garland, aged 23, RAF; John Garland, aged 21, Royal Engineers

Monday 1st January 1917 was cold and showery in Rouen and Andrew was fully employed in his trade as a joiner, making doors. Being in the Royal Engineers he had to be adaptable and ready to do whatever was required, and often this did not involve being a journeyman joiner. So it was that on the following day he was at the Petit Quevilly Prison Camp, while Wednesday saw him back to joiner's duties shafting picks. On Thursday he returned to the Prison Camp marking foundations. Sunday was a working day although he did have time to attend a religious service in SCA.

On Tuesday 2nd he received the Cults Parish Christmas Gift, a reminder of home in a foreign land. One piece of excitement on the first Sunday of 1917 was searching for escaped Austrian POWs, but once they were found it was back to the daily routine, sometimes using his skills as a joiner and sometimes doing more mundane work like cleaning hangars. He said this was very hard work with small rations. Being in the engineers seems to have meant that he could be used for any work, including loading timber onto railway wagons or constructing a road in the Prison Camp. Occasionally he was chosen to guard wounded German prisoners.

Conditions could be harsh in that cold winter of 1917, with water pipes freezing and the men unable to wash. On more than one occasion he records washing on the main road 'in a biscuit tin'. On the lighter side, the YMCA hut provided meals and entertainment and there were football matches and cinema.

On Wednesday 28th February he was warned that he was going up to the front and he left the base for Rive Gauche Station at midnight. He journeyed in an old wooden carriage where he made tea and slept on the floor, travelling all day and night before joining his company. On arrival at the front line, and wearing a steel helmet as protection against the heavy shelling, Andrew had the mundane task of digging a two-foot-deep trench for the latrines.

It is difficult to imagine but in the midst of all this, recreation did take place. There were always football matches, which the engineers seemed invariably to win, and a concert given by The Balmorals of the 51st Division.

On the 26th of March Andrew saw the German lines 2 km away and they were told the 'big push' was coming. Next day he was shelled as he entered a shelter. It was raining and the trench was knee-deep in mud. He described it as 'an awful mess'. In the morning the damaged trenches had to be repaired while the shelling continued. On the last day of March he witnessed a terrible fire and saw an explosion on the German front line following a raid by the 66th Royal Highlanders. He recorded 16 casualties. Then the British ammunition dump exploded.

So the saga continued, with shelling being received daily and this followed by necessary repairs to the trenches, often involving the heavy work of shovelling mud. The weather was cold, sometimes with rain, often with snow. At times food was scarce and they were frequently bombarded by gas shells. Monday 9th March:

> Barrage fire all night, boys go over at 4.30 a.m. We watch artillery duels all day. Germans over the ridge by midday. Artillery move to advanced position during the afternoon and night. Reported heavy losses in our Division. Saw captured German Staff. One of our balloons breaks loose but the men on board escape by parachute.

Hydrogen-filled observation balloons were commonly used by both sides for gaining intelligence on the activities of the enemy. The flammable gas that filled the envelope made them vulnerable when attacked and the observers frequently had to use parachutes to escape. Inevitably young Andrew saw dead Germans lying in the snow, and he was often under machine-gun fire. Then it was back to filling sand bags, washing wagons and guarding prisoners.

On 22nd April he was hit by a piece of shrapnel. Although able to walk to the dressing station, it was necessary for him to receive treatment in hospital. While there he was expected to help clean the ward and its windows. On 1st May Andrew was discharged and declared fit for duty.

By now the weather was warm and he was able to have some relaxation, though once more there were various tasks that had to be done, including painting wagon wheels and making a table for the officers' mess. The death of comrades was frequent and always recorded. By summer filling in shell holes seemed to be the main activity for a while, until he found he had arrived at an 'Old German Dump' in 'No-man's-land' and was once again under fire.

In June the weather was hot and tiring. Andrew was billeted only one mile from Ypres. Allemande (it's interesting that he reverts to the French word for German) shelling of Ypres continued the whole day and for the next few days the only escape from the dugout was to search for drinking water. The battle raged with the 'screams' of artillery fire filling the air all day. A nearby railway and dump was shelled and a British plane hit by shrapnel and forced to land (safely behind British lines). In the midst of all this Andrew was busy making notice boards and a butcher's bench. The irony of performing these everyday tasks surrounded by such death and devastation is hard to escape. He tells us that German bombing raids got 'a hot reception' but usually got clear away. Air raids and shelling were, by then, a daily occurrence. Young Andrew found the dead lying everywhere, in shell holes and in trenches. Repairing trenches remained an important task. Clearly this young man was not being spared any of the horrors of the war.

Throughout this difficult time there were few pleasures but those noted seem to include the occasional and much-needed bath. Life in the trenches was such that there was little opportunity to maintain any sort of standard of personal hygiene and so disease was widespread. Another pleasure was receiving parcels sent by Miss Nairn of Rankeilour and, of course, pay day, which occurred on Fridays.

Andrew tells us that several men were gassed during heavy shelling on Saturday 14th June. The next day he reported sick and was sent to the hospital by motor ambulance having been diagnosed with 'Trench Fever'. This disease, which affected about one third of British troops who reported sick, was transmitted by lice, reflecting the unhygienic conditions under which the troops had to live. Andrew remained in bed in hospital all day. When he left the hospital he was transported on a train dedicated for the use of 'gas cases' and he added, 'of which there were not a few'. After a long journey he arrived at Le Havre and boarded a ship named the *Aberdonian* which took him to Southampton. There he transferred to a train for Edinburgh arriving there at midnight. Andrew was admitted to the Edinburgh Royal Infirmary where he remained until 20th August. Then it was off to Kelso for convalescence before he finally returned to Pitlessie on Friday 31st August.

Andrew had survived the Third Battle of Ypres, which continued until the fall of the village of Passchendaele on 6th November.

While in Pitlessie Andrew went to the pictures in Ladybank, and to Dundee where he visited the family of a friend he left in France. His uncle Harry took him rabbit shooting and he had tea with the Porters at the manse. Church attendance was important to Andrew and he seems to have taken every opportunity to worship God throughout the two years of his diary. It is not surprising then to discover that he took the opportunity to attend church at Cults while at home.

He was required to return to duty on 10th September when he was sent to Kilwinning and given light tasks including sawing firewood. While there he had the opportunity to go to Glasgow for a Rangers–Celtic match, where Rangers won 2–1, and also a Cup Final, where Rangers beat Partick Thistle 4–1.

Then it was on to Staines Castle to practise 'barbed wire entanglements'. Andrew and his comrades became expert in this skill and travelled around Scotland demonstrating to troops in Cromarty and Aberdeen.

Being considered fit for duty, he left for France on 1st April 1918, arriving at Le Havre on Wednesday 3rd, then back to Rouen. Soon he found himself digging trenches and 'wiring' in Forceville on the Somme. It wasn't long before Forceville came under enemy fire and one member of the wiring party was killed and seven injured on the first day. At this time food was in short supply, the canteen at times being unable to supply anything. On Thursday 2nd May Andrew and nine others were gassed. Two days later Forceville was again shelled and an escort of Borderers near his billet were all killed.

Andrew worked in several sites on the Somme at this time. He was transported in trestle wagons to such places as Acheux, Mailly-Maillet and Louvencourt. There he was required to dig out old trenches and lay barbed wire entanglements. At this time he said rations were decent with only four men to a loaf. A few days later, after laying wires while under enemy fire, there was nothing to eat when they got back to the canteen.

May 1918 was difficult for Andrew and his comrades as they were constantly under fire as they continued with their tasks of repairing trenches and laying wire entanglements. Gas forced them to retreat from their billet and one of their number was killed while laying the wire. Incendiary devices known as 'Golden Rain' were dropped from planes at night. Casualties continued as their work progressed while under attack by 'Fritz'. Day after day he was kept busy laying wires, digging out trenches, repairing damaged shelters, laying tapes marking an extension to the minefield and building a shelter for the 'Yanks' who had arrived, all while finding themselves under fire and seeing comrades killed and injured. Conditions were terrible with mud everywhere in the showery weather. On one occasion he was considered too untidy for guard duty, and on another he had to get a tooth extracted. Illness struck several times and he had to report to the MO. Searching for wood for the canteen was a constant job and, with food in short supply, they went scrounging for apples.

As the summer advanced so the number of casualties increased and, at times, Andrew was forced to stop work laying wire because they were under fire. Then on 16th August he fell ill, having been gassed, and attending the MO was necessary. This resulted in a return to Rouen and hospital. He was allowed only 11 days for treatment before he was back digging trenches. This did not last and he was soon put on to lighter duties, so clearly he was not yet fit for heavy work.

The men were finding this a difficult time. Andrew recalls a significant incident on the evening of 6th September though the details are unclear. He tells us that a Staff Commander spoke to Canadians in 'D.H.'. Then, 'The place gets rushed. We are lectured to by S.O. on parade.' He says 700 men from the base marched on Trouville and 'smashed the guard' on their return.

Andrew's condition seems to have been deteriorating because when the MO tried to mark him fit he was marked 'B' instead. He also found he was not 'officially employed' and so he seems to have kept himself busy by attending a French class at the YMCA, lying on the grass enjoying the sun and reading. A few days later he was declared officially employed again. By the beginning of October he was declared fit, though he seems to have continued do light duties for a time, being posted to Rive Gauche on the 11th. Soon he was back in the thick of the battlefield at Monchaux. There he was engaged in building and repairing bridges. At one point, he once again landed in no-man's land running out tape to a bridge.

As November arrived so did the rain, soaking everyone and, on one occasion, coming through the roof of their billet. On the 11th Andrew began to hear rumours of an armistice being signed at 11 a.m., otherwise life continued as before until he had to report to the MO with boils and was consequently given light duties. This seems to have involved working in the billet and stables. The church service the following Sunday was one of thanksgiving because the war had ended, but this made little difference to the life of this Sapper. Tending the horses and digging latrines continued to be the daily chore. At times food continued to be in short supply and hunger was noted in the diary. On the other hand, the opportunity to go to the cinema and theatre with his friends became a more frequent occurrence and on one occasion he said the dinner was good!

Sapper Andrew K. Garland's final entry on Tuesday 31st December 1918 reads: 'All quiet (On The Western Front).'

As 1918 progressed it was clear that there was more activity in support of the war. It is almost as if in August 1914 the war had little impact on the awareness of Presbytery. By October 1918 they were thinking of little else. It is noteworthy that in November 1918 there was not a Presbytery meeting.

On 10th December an expression of thanksgiving at the close of the Great War was placed on the records of Presbytery. When we read it today we find the language archaic as it refers to the 'Dominions of Canada, Australia, New Zealand and South Africa, and our Indian Empire' and of their gratitude for the 'unsolicited help of the Mother Country'. Its opening words, 'The Presbytery desire to put on record their deep thankfulness to Almighty God, the Sovereign Disposer, whose prerogative it is to "restrain the wrath of man" and to turn evil into good, that, through the achievements of the allied armies, an armistice was signed on the eleventh of November', express the heartfelt view of every citizen in every generation. There is no doubt of the sincerity of the sentiment and, while we would express ourselves very differently today, the heartfelt thankfulness that the horror had stopped was universal. This is a generation that had suffered untold misery and for so many of the injured, physically, spiritually and emotionally, as well as the bereaved, the agony did not stop on 11th November 1918.

A War Memorial for Pitlessie

The parish of Cults decided in March 1919 to have a monument erected as a war memorial, so Andrew Smith, Clerk to Cults Parish Council, called a public meeting in the Wilkie Hall for Monday 9th February 1920 to consider its site and form. It was not until 11th August that the *Dundee Courier* announced: 'The parish of Cults war memorial which is to take the form of an obelisk 20 feet high, with bronze panels for the names of the twenty men who made the supreme sacrifice, is to be erected in the grounds of the Sir David Wilkie Memorial Hall at Pitlessie facing the public road.'

With £115 having been collected in May 1919[244] and a further £230 gathered by February of the following year,[245] funds were available for the project. While on the face of it agreement had been reached, in fact there was a group who were highly dissatisfied at the proposed position of the memorial. A petition was drawn up which received sufficient support for it to be handed to the chairman of the Parish Council. The main objection was that the memorial would be placed in front of 'a place of amusement'.[246] This was considered to be unseemly and strong words appeared among the letters in the *Courier* on this subject.

The objections were overruled and on 14th May 1922 Lord Cochrane of Cults unveiled the memorial that is familiar to us today. It was reported that in his address Lord Cochrane said that, for a small country parish, Cults had done remarkably well. From a male population of 295, 70 to 80 had volunteered for the war. What struck Lord Cochrane most was the character of the men he had had the honour of training. It was not only the courage which brought them from their country villages and quiet homes to face the enemy but the grit and determination with which they

Pitlessie war memorial

244 *Dundee Courier* Wednesday 14th May 1919
245 *Evening Telegraph* Tuesday 10th February 1920
246 *Dundee Courier* Saturday 7th May 1921

endured the cruel hardships of the enemy's fire, the deadly bombs and the fumes of the poison gas. 'Surely', he said, 'these men were heroes, and their memory should be enshrined in every heart.'

This solemn occasion was attended by Revs W.H. Porter and W.R. Craig of Kettle and Cults UP Church, each taking part in the ceremony. A lament was played by a piper and the last post sounded.[247] This was a day for the parish of Cults to cherish, to mourn its dead and show pride in their contribution to the Great War.

Peace Time

In February 1919 the Committee on War reported that the church authorities in Edinburgh were considering a national rededication and that to this end they should cooperate with 'their brethren of the United Free Church'.[248] This national event marked the end of the Great War and the beginning of a new normality. As we now know, society changed after the war. The wealthy became less so and the majority of the population, both men and women, began to see the prospect of a better future while enduring hardship in the present. The war had a financial as well as a human cost and once again it was the people who had to pay.

In 1926 we are informed that Mr Porter is appointed to the committee of management of the Cupar Bell Baxter School at the request of Fife Education Authority. Clearly his interests in the younger members of the community were well known in educational circles. In April of that year we also find an interesting article in the *Courier* under the heading 'Greek Font in Cults Church – Relic of Crimean War'. Mr Porter had intimated to Cupar Presbytery that the gift of a Greek font was made to Cults Kirk by Miss Moon of Edenfield. The Moon family ran a spinning mill at Hospital Mill on the River Eden.[249] The gift was in memory of Miss Moon's father, mother, brothers and sisters. The font came into the possession of the Moon family during the Crimean War. A ship which had been of interest to Miss Moon's father was commandeered during the Crimean War. The captain, who was visiting Balaclava, found the font and retrieved it from among the ruins of a burned church.

---

[247] *Dundee Courier* Saturday 15th May 1922
[248] Presbytery of Cupar Minutes 1910–1938, University of St Andrews Special Collections Ref: CH 2/82/28
[249] Leighton, *History of the County of Fife*

Disaster Strikes Cults Manse

In December 1926 disaster struck Cults Kirk. The Clerk to Presbytery was instructed to note in the minutes that 'The Presbytery record their sympathy with Mr and Mrs Porter in the destructive fire which took place at Cults manse on the 13th November involving the loss of so many of their personal effects, and also the Parish records and other property of the Church. They deplore the loss and recommend the Kirk Sessions throughout the bounds to take steps for the safe custody of all records and their property of value.' It is clear that the loss Cults had suffered of its historical documents was so serious that others were to use it as a warning and ensure the safety of their own records. Henceforth the minutes of the courts of the Kirk were lodged in the Special Collections Department of St Andrews University or in the National Archive in Edinburgh. In addition to the documents, an old pewter baptismal font, said to have been used at the baptism of David Wilkie, and some pieces of communion plate were severely damaged. Damage to the manse was extensive and the following was reported in the press:

> During a brief absence from his study Rev. W.H. Porter, parish minister of Cults, said an oil stove which was in use for heating purposes burst, and set the building on fire. The manse was gutted, and the minister and his family were rendered homeless … A garret in the manse burned down was the nursery of young Wilkie, and on the Whitewashed walls he produced portraits in chalk, charcoal, pencil, keel, and ink of visitors to the manse and frequenters of the Kirk. Unfortunately all trace of these youthful efforts, which would have been priceless, have long since disappeared.

Cults manse after the fire in 1926; the left-hand side of the photograph has been sketched in

Dog Raises Alarm

Mrs Porter and her mother, Mrs Dickson, aged 86 years, and one of the young sons of the manse, who were in the drawing room downstairs, had their first intimation that something was amiss by the loud barking of Mr Porter's little spaniel. Going to ascertain what the cause of the dog's distress was, the boy found his father's study in flames.

The alarm was at once raised, and the inmates of the manse speedily made their way to safety, while in a comparatively short time a company of willing workers from Cults Farm and Pitlessie were lending assistance. When once the fire got hold of the roof it was evident that with the gale that was blowing the old home was doomed. Cupar Fire Brigade arrived to find the roof had fallen in but, with water pumped from a burn about 200 yards distant, they succeeded in subduing the flames. According to the *Dundee Courier* of 15th November 1926, only a comparatively small quantity of the furniture was saved.

Minister's Books Gone

In giving an account of the fire, Rev. Porter said:

Owing to the shortage of coal I was using an oil stove to heat my study. It had been working very well and in the evening when I left the manse to pay a sick visit to a house some distance from the manse I left the stove burning, as I did not intend to be gone for more than an hour, and wished to have the study warm and comfortable when I returned. The first indication I had of anything amiss was when one of my younger boys came running to the house I was visiting, and told me that the manse was on fire. When I arrived on the scene the fire had got a good hold and there was little chance of saving the building. Practically all my books have gone, and among other things that were destroyed are an old kirk box dating back to 1712, the Session records from 1693 onwards, all the Session books, such as the Communion roll and the baptismal register. The baptismal font which was used at the baptism of the late Sir David Wilkie has also perished, along with two full sets of Communion services. Several rare books have also been destroyed and all the bedding and personal apparel have gone.

Tribute to the Porters by the Parishioners of Cults

Mr and Mrs Porter were respected and loved by the people of Cults. There was a great deal of sympathy for the manse family who had lost everything. About a month after the fire a fund was set up and £100 raised and handed over to them by Mr John Garland, senior elder, at a gathering of the congregation in the Wilkie Hall.

Many people from the district attended including Lady Cochrane of Crawford Priory,

Rev. and Mrs Porter

Mrs Martin Smith of Priestfield, Rev. and Mrs Craig of Balmalcolm and Rev. and Mrs Laird of Springfield. Rev. Aeneas Gordon sent his apologies. Mr Porter, having spent 25 years in the parish, was described as 'a faithful friend, faithful in and out of the pulpit'. He was praised for 'his Christian charity, kindness, and sympathy in time of trouble and bereavement', and for the example he had shown them in his daily life, walk and conversation.

These were not idle words of praise. I have known people who remembered Mr Porter well and they had nothing but praise for this loyal servant. In reply Mr Porter said the support and sympathy that he and his family had received had done much to compensate their losses. A house had been made available and clothes, furniture, money and books given to them. The tragedy of the fire revealed the character of the people, minister and parishioners alike and was an opportunity for the love of God to manifest itself in the Howe of Fife.

There was nothing else to do but rebuild the manse as the minister and his family had no home. The Building Committee reported to Presbytery that estimates had been received and considered for rebuilding and they had accepted the lowest offer of £1,303 14s. 9d., leaving £296 to cover the paintwork, architect's fees, outlays and contingencies.

Cults manse from a postcard dated about 1912; the lady in the garden may be Mrs Porter

It would have been reasonable to expect that to be the end of the matter of the manse for many years to come. It was, after all, a new building. However, in March 1931 Mr Porter went to Presbytery seeking their approval for a grant to offset £116 8s. 11d. to repair dry rot at the manse. Presbytery minutes of the time are brief and to the point. Perhaps it is just as well that we hear none of the expressions of outrage at this problem arising so soon after the new manse was built. In March it is intimated that a grant of £21 11s. 6d. was given. The source of the balance is not recorded.

A United Presbytery

It was on 8th October 1929 that the first meeting of the new United Presbytery of Cupar first met. As arranged, it opened with a service of communion in Cupar Old Church with Rev. Aeneas Gordon of Kettle and Rev. Dr James Bell of Auchtermuchty conducting the service together. It was then to the hall of the Bonnygate Church. Mr Gordon was then elected Moderator after Mr Bell, the senior of the two, declined the privilege.

Rev. Dr James Bell

The UF Church in Pitlessie

Following the union of Pitlessie UF Church with that of Kettle and Cults in 1901 the building remained the responsibility of the Kettle Church until the union of 1929. Following this, the Presbytery of Cupar tried to get the Kirk Session of Cults to accept responsibility for it. This offer, which gained some local support, was declined by the Kirk Session on more than one occasion. Presbytery paid for essential repairs to maintain the building but in 1937 it had no alternative but to support an application from Kettle Kirk to the General Trustees for the property to be sold. The proceeds of this were granted to Kettle Church. The building was used for many years by Harry Beg, engineers, as a workshop before being demolished to make way for a modern bungalow.

Retiral

Like most people who are respected by their peers, Mr Porter had a clear idea of what he believed to be right and what was wrong, and he was not afraid to state his opinion. So it is that in 1925, when the proposed new hymnbook was being heavily criticised in Presbytery, Mr Porter is recorded in the *Courier* on 9th September as saying that he could not understand for the life of him why they put so much trash into the new hymnary and in the old too. Why hadn't they introduced Burns' verse to the 1st Psalm? (See Appendix). It was a disgrace to the committee that they hadn't put it in.

Nor was anyone in any doubt about Mr Porter's thoughts in 1929 during a debate on the unwillingness of churches to contribute financially to the work of the wider Church. He was again recorded in the *Courier* (on 25th March) as saying he was often asked in his own Kirk Session what the Presbytery did for them, and he knew that in the coming year he would have some difficulty in getting payment of the Presbytery's dues. He thought Presbytery should be more in evidence and not allow churches to drift into congregationalism. Once again his point was made and once again it was not to everyone's taste. Nevertheless, he was also one of a committee set up by Presbytery to consider the lack of church attendance in the rural areas and he was very critical of people who appeared only on communion Sundays. His concern was that improved transport had given people reason to neglect church services.[250]

---

[250] *Dundee Courier* 13th March 1929

Such criticisms did not prevent his opinions from being sought. Henry Porter was regularly present on committees of Presbytery and in education, where he served on the Board of Bell Baxter High School and Cupar Education Trust. When he retired in 1935 he and his wife moved to Monifeith where they named their house 'Cults' after the place that had been home for so many years. When Mr Porter died, quite suddenly, on 14th November 1953 at the age of 88, a service was held in Cults Church where all friends were invited.[251] There is no doubt he was a faithful pastor and friend to the people of Cults.

A Vacancy

Rev. John Goudie

With the retiral of Mr Porter the Kirk at Cults found itself once more in a vacancy. With a decision that no adjustment was needed the vacancy did not last long and Mr John Goudie was ordained and inducted on 2nd July 1936. The 'social' in the evening was held in the Wilkie Hall. Ministers from the area, including Mr Affleck of Ladybank, attended along with locals Miss Cunningham and Miss Syme, who provided music and recitations. Mrs Lawton and Mr Wright welcomed the new minister and presented him with new robes. These people, along with Mr Hoggan, Mr Ainslie Smith and Mrs Thoms were, in 1936, the 'pillars o' the Kirk' but their names have slipped from the memory of many today, particularly those of us who have come to the parish in recent years. Yet their presence, and that of current incumbents, is reassuring as they confirm the continuity of the Kirk in this place.

Life Boys pictured at the manse with Mr Goudie in 1941

---

[251] *Dundee Courier* 17th November 1953

While Mr Goudie no doubt appreciated the welcome, he was in need of more than this, for necessary repairs had to be carried out at the manse, and a grant was sought from the Church and Manse Buildings Committee. This shows that Cults continued to be a church that found it hard to maintain itself financially.

It was in 1940, during John Goudie's tenure at Cults, that the BB was formed. This was wartime and the Session Clerk, John Marr, was called to serve his country in 1942. Mr George Bryson agreed to take over the role in Mr Marr's place for the period of the war. It was also in 1942 that Mr Goudie intimated to the Kirk Session that he intended to accept a call to Regent Place and Cathedral Square Church in Glasgow.

This left Cults in a vacancy at a time when ministers were in short supply due to their involvement in World War II. So it was that the parish of Springfield agreed to share their minister, Mr Laird ,with Cults. This provided continuity as he was already acting as Interim Moderator since Mr Goudie left. The agreement was based on the understanding that this was to last only for the period of the war and that neither parish would lose its independent status. The costs of the ministry were shared and the agreement was reviewed at six-monthly intervals. Consequently, the manse was vacant. At first it was made available through the Ministry of Agriculture for itinerant farm workers. This lasted for only a season and when the Ministry indicated it no longer required the house it was let to Lord Cochrane at an annual rent of £32, which was set aside for the manse fabric fund.[252] Lord Cochrane wanted to install the manager of the lime works there, who, as it happened, was Mr Bryson, the acting Session Clerk.

During the war period attendance at the church fell considerably. On one communion the congregation numbered only 50. Before the war it would have numbered over 100. A meeting was held when it was agreed to write to every member in the parish and ask two questions: (1) do you want a full-time minister? and (2) will you support a full-time minister? It was pointed out that one cannot expect support from a minister if the congregation will not support him. The result was that 158 were in favour of a full-time minister and only 4 were against. This led to the decision to take measures to fill the vacancy, but with a candidate over the age of 50! This was a way of ensuring that this would be a ministry that would be reviewed within 15 years.

The new incumbent was Rev. Peter Lockhart, who came from Edinburgh where he had been chaplain at the Royal Infirmary. He remained at Cults until 1952 when poor health forced him to retire. His successor, Rev. Archibald Bell, arrived in November 1952. Once again the call had specified a man over the age of 50. It was during his ministry that a great deal of work had to be carried out on the property. In 1953 estimates were sought for a new roof for the church, though it appears the work was never carried out. Instead there were repairs at various times over the next few years. It was also agreed to install electric light in the church and the manse, as well as electric heating in the church. In 1961 the pulpit Bible, the one gifted by John Neil McLeod,

---

252   *Dundee Courier* Wednesday 10th January 1945

was rebound and the graveyard was extended. In the same year Andrew Garland, who was the Property Convener, reported that there had been an infestation of woodworm in flooring both on the ground floor and the balcony. It was felt to be urgently in need of repair, though to complete the job would be costly, at least £230. Mr Garland suggested that they should start by concreting the SW and he was given the job to do.

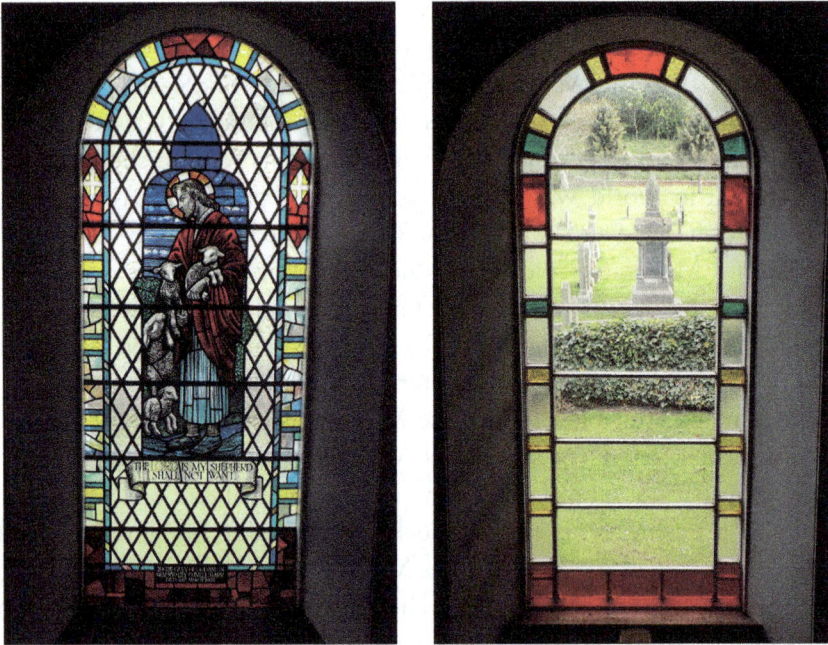

In 1958 the beautiful stained glass window above was installed on the left of the pulpit in memory of Lily Marr. Lily and her husband John were married in Cults in 1935. He was the same John Marr who resigned as Session Clerk in 1942 because he was called up to serve in the war. John was a local postman and a member of the Marr family of Crossgates. He was 11 years Lily's junior and they had no family. This made it so much harder on John when Lily died of cancer on 26th March 1957.

The window is a beautiful reminder of a lady who was greatly loved and carries a message of faith, hope and comfort: 'The Lord is my Shepherd'. This reminds all who worship in this place of the one on whom they can rely. The artist who created the window was Douglas Hamilton of Glasgow, who also created the windows at Collessie. It was unveiled on 22nd June 1958.

With the new memorial window on the left of the pulpit it was felt necessary to change the other window so that the two would complement one another. Andrew Garland set to work and drew up plans for the new window (pictured on the right above). While the two are quite different they accompany one another and enhance the appearance of the building.

There is, however, another stained glass window that is seldom seen. It is in the wall of the tower at the head of the outside staircase. A striking window with wonderful colours it depicts the burning bush. Cara McNeil, daughter of an elder of Cults Kirk and an art college graduate, made and gifted the window. There was nowhere suitable for it in the sanctuary and this little window beside the rope for the bell was the only place considered appropriate. Surely it could not have found a better location. Just as we find God in the most unexpected parts of our lives so we find this burning bush in a dark corner where it brings light, wonder and joy.

The church was not solely concerned with buildings during Mr Bell's time for it was in 1953 that the Women's Guild was formed. A year later the Kirk Session authorised the Cults Church Girls Club, which met in Pitlessie School under the leadership of Mr McNeil, Cara's father. While the BB seemed to be in decline, there was now a troupe of Boy Scouts and some of the young men of the parish were 'under the guidance of Hon. Vere Cochrane District Commissioner', now Baron Cochrane of Cults.

Cults Kirk before the windows were altered in 1958

Mr Bell was to be the last of the ministers of an independent Cults Kirk, for when he intimated his decision to retire, the Presbytery resolved to encourage a linkage with Kettle. Mr Bell's last service took place on 31st March 1963 and the following Sunday there was a special service officially linking Cults and Kettle. While by and large there were few problems with the linkage, one did emerge in the form of the manse. Presbytery recommended that Kettle manse be sold and that Cults manse become the official home of the new minister. There were those in Kettle who opposed this and tried to have that

279

decision reversed. Presbytery decided that Cults manse should be decorated and have its kitchen modernised so that the new minister could take up residence. If, after one year, it proved unsatisfactory then it could be sold and another found in its place.

When Rev. Angus Macaskill arrived in 1964 he was extremely appreciative of the work that had been carried out on the manse and seemed to be happy to stay there. Mr Macaskill, who was very popular, retired in 1969 leaving the linked charge vacant for the arrival of Rev. George McLean Henderson.

A Church Hall for Cults Kirk

The lack of a hall caused the congregation at Cults some concern and it was not until 1964 when Andrew Garland requested permission to convert the manse washing house into a place fit for the Sunday School that the matter was remedied. This was possible because Cults manse was the manse for the linked charge of Cults and Kettle. A toilet had to be installed and the walls lined. The area was only 15 feet square and so, when the Sunday School reached a roll of 50, there was the problem of space. This was settled by keeping those children under 7 at Cults and

Sunday School 1966

using the Wilkie Hall for the older pupils under the leadership of Jean Bradbury. This arrangement served Cults well until 1983 when the General Trustees decided to sell this building along with the manse. In consequence, Cults Kirk was denied not only a hall but also a toilet.[253]

In 1970 Rev. George Henderson was inducted into the linked charge of Cults and Kettle. It was just before his induction into the parish that George married Hilda Jervis. Soon they moved into the manse at Cults, which became their home until George retired in 1983. Then they moved to Cupar hoping to enjoy their later years together. Sadly, George's retirement was to be short, for in 1989 he died of cancer leaving Hilda a widow for many years. While his ministry in Cults and Kettle was stormy at times, he had many good colleagues in the ministry who gave him friendship and support. Hilda died after a long illness in August 2015.

Rev. George and Mrs Hilda Henderson

---

[253] *People's Journal* 29th October 1966

The problem of the remoteness of the manse was raised time and again. George wanted to sell it and buy The Poplars on Rumdewan in Kingskettle. While this almost went ahead, in the end it was considered financially unwise and so the Hendersons remained at Cults. When Andrew Garland died in 1977 he was mentioned in the Kirk Session minutes. His friendship, long service to Cults Kirk as an elder and as Property Convener had been highly valued and he was sorely missed. Three years later in 1980 Cults bought the Hammond organ from Kettle when it had its pipe organ installed. By now time was running out for the linked charge of Kettle and Cults as Presbytery was now seeking a union with Ladybank and Collessie. The last entry in the Session book was by the Session Clerk, Karen Garland, and dated 10th March 1983.

By the time of the union to form the Parish of the Howe of Fife, Cults found itself in financial difficulty. Its stipend contribution was £564.91 short, the Mission and Service was not paid and there were no investments with the Church of Scotland Trust. Clearly the finances of Cults were not in a good state. As we have seen, however, this was not new, for Cults had found itself with financial difficulties on many occasions before.

The Folk and Life in the Parish of Cults

Some family names seem to crop up time and again as we delve back into the history of the parish. Two such names are Smith and Garland. It is because they have clearly been pivotal in our history that we must make room to mention both.

The Smith family trace their Howe of Fife ancestry back many generations. The obituary to Mr Andrew Smith of Walton Hill, written in 1928, claimed that he traced his family connection to that farm back 200 years. It appears that the Smith family have for generations found themselves taking a leading role in the life of the community. Andrew founded the Hills and Howes o' Fife Ploughing Association, hosting many ploughing competitions at Walton Hill. He also founded the Cabbage Judging Association to promote the cultivation of that crop. In addition, he was a JP, a member of the County Council and chaired several committees including Weights and Measures and the Cults School Board. The list goes on and so when he died in 1928 he was mourned by many people.

Five years later and another county councillor by the name of Smith died, James Martin Smith of Priestfield. Having spent much of his farming life at Cults Farm he moved to Priestfield just a few years before he died.

Top: Andrew Smith of Walton Hill
Bottom: John Garland with his family outside Lister House, Pitlessie circa 1900

He too had been an important member of the farming and wider community for many years. The *Courier* described him as a 'kinsman' of Mr Andrew Smith. It would appear that service to the community ran in the veins of this family, for once again his life represented great service to the community. He was also heavily involved in the lime works and Martin, Henderson & Co., Maltsers. Since then the family has remained at Priestfield, where the current Mr Smith continues to work the land.

Anyone casually strolling around the graveyard at Cults could not fail to come across several stones dedicated to the Garland family. This family has provided Pitlessie's joiners since 1844 when David Garland founded the business. The Garlands, like most village joiners, also acted as the local undertakers. The smell of tar-coated coffins in the workshop, drifting up to the family above, would have been familiar to generations of Garlands in years gone by. It was in the 1960s, when Elder Garland, who inherited the family business, and his wife Karen took over, that the house and the workshop was moved to a separate building. They and their family lived in two caravans in the garden for several months while renovations took place to create a modern house large enough for their family, what is now known as Lister House. The workshop was on the ground floor and the family lived in a flat upstairs.

Another of the many families that contributed substantially to the community was the Marrs who lived at Crossgates. They owned much of the property there and were well known in the community. Mr Marr was an active elder in the Kirk. In years to come his daughter Jean would follow his example. The photograph on the left shows Mr and Mrs Marr with their granddaughter Kay. On the right is Jean Marr in 1938. Most of us knew her as Jean Bradbury following her marriage to Bert nine years later.

There were lots of activities in the parish during the interwar years. Below is a photograph of the Drama Group on their annual outing in 1938.

The whole community got together whenever possible and pictured below we have groups of older folk enjoying the Sunday School picnic. Age seems to have been no barrier to participation.

There are many others who should be mentioned, including the Scott family, with daughters Lena and Jean. Their father was one-time chairman of the Community Council and was sometimes referred to locally as 'The Provost of Pitlessie'. He not only chaired the Council but was also the man to see if it was necessary to arrange a visit from the doctor.

Skelpie

It is well known that a life in farming can be hard. Today it is EU and government regulations, cash flow and the loneliness of driving a tractor all day that make it hard. In years gone by it was the early mornings, long working days, few holidays and low wages that made many struggle to work on the land. There was also the tough physical work involved in ploughing, sowing and harvesting. Coming from a city I always admired the fields of freshly cut stooks of hay in the surrounding countryside, when the sun was low and the shadows long. Of course, I didn't have the job of cutting the corn, tying the bundles and making the stooks. Nor did I have the job of picking them up again when strong winds blew them down. Then there was the job of building haystacks, which was an art in itself. A good haystack stood up to the wind and shed the water. One that was badly built would disintegrate in strong winds and rot as the dampness penetrated. My childhood memory of haystacks is climbing up and sliding down, causing the hay to be knocked down. Not even the best-built haystacks can withstand such abuse and my great-aunt, on whose farm the stacks were built, got very angry with me – and with good reason!

In 1924 Robert Nicholson with his wife and family moved to Skelpie to work as grieve on the farm. Robert had been badly injured on two occasions during the First World War and bore the scars for the rest of his life. His daughter Nell was only 2 when they arrived and much of this account of Skelpie comes from her at the age of 93 and her brother Will, who was born at Skelpie and worked there until he retired. In the 1920s and 30s the farmer at Skelpie was George Ostler. Mr Ostler took over the farm from Mr John Graham in 1910 and remained there until he died in 1945. It was in that year that the farm came into the tenancy of the Munro family and it has remained with them ever since.

The community between Skelpie and Burnturk has changed remarkably over the years. When the Nicholsons arrived there were 15 houses, including the community Nell referred to as West End (perhaps an alternative name for the village of Limehills). This lay at the top of the Priestfield road and consisted of six houses, three facing the road and three with their back to the road.

The lime works was served by nine pug engines which carried the lime down to Springfield and on to the markets around the country. The line crossed the Cults Brae, uphill from the farm. In 1935 Mr McGregor, gamekeeper at Crawford Priory, was killed by that engine as he lost control of his bike and landed beneath the wheels of a truck. There were many homeless travelling folk who would gather around the lime kilns in cold winter nights to get their warmth. One known to the Nicholsons was Sandy Stewart, who was given to sleeping rough at Paradise when it became a ruin. He called in to see Mr Munro every morning and received his breakfast there. Paradise had not always been a ruin; at one time it was home to the Witherspoon family. Mr Witherspoon was gamekeeper at Crawford Priory. He and his family decided to emigrate and Nell could remember a 'roup' being held in the garden to sell off their belongings as they could not take any with them. At the crossroads the home of the blacksmith, Mr Farquhar, and his family could be found. He came from the area around Fyvie in Aberdeenshire and when he first arrived he had to stay at Edenwood until his predecessor retired and his job became available.

In the days before World War II Skelpie employed nine men including four horsemen. The horses were cared for with great affection and when one died a great sense of loss was experienced by those who had cared for it. Among the occasional workers was Mr Sweeny and his five sons. They came from Ireland and arrived in spring every year, working until after the harvest was gathered, when they returned home for the winter. Life on the farm, although hard, was good and there was always a great sense of community and fun.

Sugar beet was an important crop feeding the factory in Cupar and, after the beet had been processed, the pulp was returned to the farm to be mixed with turnips to feed the cattle. Mr Ostler bought Canadian cattle at the Port of Glasgow and transported them by rail to Ladybank or Cupar. The beasts then had to be driven from the station along the road and up the hill to Skelpie. There they were fattened before being sold to the Co-operative butcher. Once the Munros took over it was sheep instead of cattle that had to be driven along the road and up the hill to Skelpie. They were reared at Bonar Bridge, Sutherland, and transported by train. By the time they arrived at Ladybank they were desperately hungry and the shepherds had a hard time keeping them out of private gardens because they went to eat any greenery they could find. Thirst too could be a problem and Will remembered seeing two thirsty lambs and a dog sharing the water from a trough.

Nell, Will and their brothers all attended Craigrothie School, walking there and back each day. When the weather was bad a trap was attached to a horse to carry the youngsters back home. Each year the farm workers had to make a settlement with the farmer to ensure they would be retained for another year. Every year Nell and Will hoped their father would have the opportunity to move to some place less remote. This was not to be. Mr Nicholson was a reliable and good worker and he received his half-crown annually, which acted as a retainer confirming that he was 'fee'd' for another year. Regular employment on the same farm was by no means ensured and it was only the best workers who found they were holding the same position year after year. This had a knock-on effect for Nell and Will because not only did they not get that longed-for home nearer a town or village, but they found themselves being expected to 'show the ropes' to the annual intake of new children at school.

While wages were low, the house, potatoes and meal were part of the wages of farm workers. As a result, they were saved from the worst effects of rationing during the Second World War. After 1945 many changes came about, some embraced willingly and others resisted. Mr Nicholson never really took to the tractor as it was not such good company as the horse, although it needed a great deal less attention. On the other hand, with the introduction of running water and getting a connection to the electricity in 1953, life became a great deal easier. Winters could still be hard, with 1947 being particularly memorable to Nell and Will. They were unable to get about for eight weeks and were glad of their stocks of tatties and meal to tide them over.

Skelpie remained home to Nell and Will until 1986 when they felt that it was sensible for them to move into Cupar. Nell had worked for only a few years because it was necessary for her to stay at home and care for her mother who suffered terribly from rheumatoid arthritis and needed a great deal of help. Will enjoyed his work on the farm and appreciated living in such a beautiful place.

Skelpie Law

On the hill behind Skelpie Farm is Skelpie Law with a tree that can be seen for miles. It was here that Will found a flint arrowhead, revealing that the history of this place is ancient with folk working the lands for generations. Skelpie or Skolpie is one of the most ancient farms in the parish, named on the oldest maps available. There are records in St Salvator's College bearing the name Alexander Schethum of Caskelpe [Skelpie] (Caskelpyr) granting to the college his lands of Weltoune and parts of his lands of Haltoune in Cults. This is dated 1524.[254]

One day in the 1990s I was taken on a trip into the past by a fellow elder of the Howe of Fife Parish Church. This was Willie Downie, who is sadly no longer with us. His story is well worth repeating here. It first appeared in the parish magazine and describes a community that no longer exists but is still alive in the memories of many residents of the Howe of Fife.

---

[254] University of St Andrews Chartulary B Call Number UYSS150/2

Back to Limehills with Willie Downie

It was a beautiful July afternoon as I set off to meet Willie. He suggested we start our walk into the past at the hairpin bend on the Cults–Bumturk road. The boundary between Cults and Kettle parishes is marked by a burn which rises just above this place and winds west and north through Pitlessie into the Eden. Right on the hairpin bend is a gate into a field and a track, now very overgrown, to Fronthill quarry. This was where the people of Limehill Cottages would often come, as a community, for summer picnics.

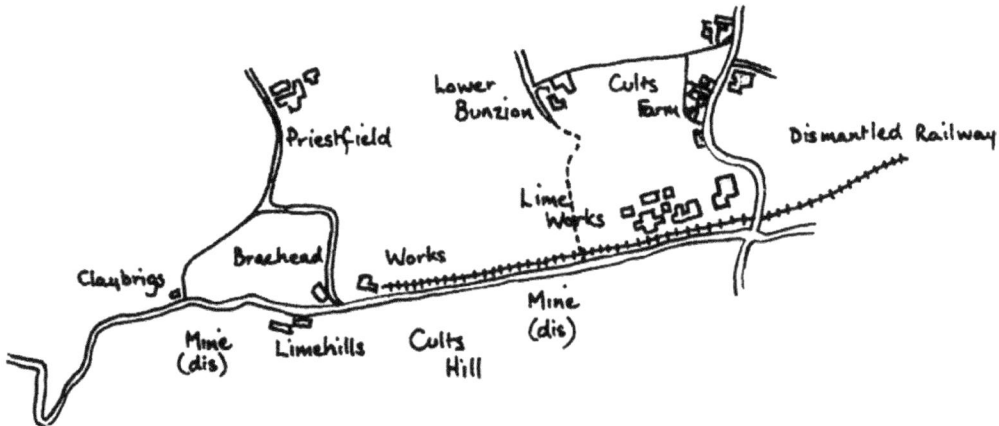

Fond Memories

Willie had many fond memories of this place. The road now bends round flat waste ground where once fir trees lined a deep gully. The banks around the area were covered with blackthorn, gooseberries and hawthorn and in spring a carpet of primroses. We did not investigate the brambles in the field known as Bugdales.

Claybrigs

Along the road towards Cults, we stopped at a clearing on the left. This, Willie said, was known as Claybrigs. On our right was an old quarry, once a source of stone used in manufacturing bricks at Aberhill. On our left there had been a house, a superior dwelling to those of Limehills but, like all houses in the area, lacking inside water and drainage. Next to the house a sawmill was built during the war. Many local fir trees were cut at that time. A steam engine drove the saw and the contractor was Brown of Buckhaven. Among the workers were Italian POWs. One married a local girl and spent the rest of his life in the Howe.

Braehead

A little further along the road we came to Braehead, from where there is a particularly magnificent view of the Howe. On fine sunny days the Downie family came here for picnics. Close by are the remains of open kilns. Although out of use since before Willie's grandfather's time, a few fire bricks are still visible in one kiln. Nearby was a mine which provided the lime. The coal came from Burnturk.

These were 'ingaun – een' or drift mines. Willie remembers clearly a worthy called Jimmy Duffy who took up residence in the disused Braehead mine between the wars. He had a curtain over the entrance and burned wood for cooking and heat. Today such conditions would be considered intolerable but there Jimmy lived and was eventually found dead.

Limehills

Our next stop was at the site of Limehills. While there is now no evidence of a settlement, Willie's recollections brought the whole place alive to me. There had been nine houses with a population of about 40. The houses were in two groups: one of six two-bedroom cottages with kitchen and scullery; the other three had one bedroom, kitchen and scullery.

The kitchen was the main room of the house, acting as living room and master bedroom with a double bed in a recess. Water ran from a tank in the woods behind the hamlet to a standpipe. In summer this source might dry up and water had to be carried from Braeside or Coaltown of Burnturk. Mr Smith of Priestfield supplied bins for carrying water and Willie remembers the family as good friends to the folk of Limehills. Electricity, of course, had not reached the community and the oil lamp was kept carefully trimmed to provide the only source of light. By the Second World War the friendly hiss of the Tilley lamp had become part of daily life. Sanitation was crude. Each cottage had a dry toilet and kitchen waste was carried across the road and thrown over the bank.

Also across the road there were wash houses and coal cellars and there was even a garage where one of the residents kept a round-nosed Morris. About a hundred yards through the woods towards Braehead was the 'Pooder Hoose'. Here explosives were locked in a brick building. At the eastern end of the village was the smiddy, an important and busy place in the life of the lime works. Willie's grandfather was the blacksmith's hammer man. They had access to Cults Church by rights of way that have now virtually disappeared. There was also Mr Howell, a piano tuner and evangelist from the Gospel Hall who came to the folk of Limehills on his bike. Services took place on the street corner and his concertina provided the music.

Life at Limehills

Life in Limehills was clearly not easy by modern standards but this was a close and caring community. They always welcomed strangers. The kitchens of each house were adjacent, with cupboard walls so thin that it was possible to have a conversation with the next-door neighbour. The women were avid knitters and often sat at the front door on a fine day. There were old folk as well as young and life would have been hard had the community not rallied round when needed. The able-bodied carried water for everyone when necessary and if someone was sick one of the children would take a note to Mrs Scott in Pitlessie, who would contact the doctor.

The postman was an important contact, walking from Pitlessie up to Limehills then on to Downfield and back by Skelpie and Paradise, the easternmost extremities of the parish. They were well served by baker's, grocer's and butcher's vans and the family diets were supplemented from the gardens. There were clearly compensations for the hardships of life at Limehills.

Willie spoke with great affection about his life there and the people he knew. The Downies moved to Kettle in 1954 to a house with all modern amenities. Willie remembers someone asking his mother if she would like to go back to Limehills. She said no because she appreciated all that was available to her in a modern house, especially running water and drainage.

The shop at Limehills

The Lime Works

The lime kilns

Returning to our walk, after a few yards we came to the main working of the lime works. The site was once occupied by Mr Robertson the woodman. The old kilns can still be seen. In 1937 a concrete face was built to prevent erosion of the bank. Recently this has become unstable and much of it has been removed. From the top we could see the kilns which are about 30 feet deep. The coal was carried in lorries which backed up to the edge of the kiln. The lime was mined across the road and a stationary engine pulled the trucks full of lime up from the mine and across a bridge to feed the kilns.

At the bottom of the kilns the men worked constantly shovelling the lime onto the trucks to be taken by the 'pug' each day to Springfield and the markets beyond. A derelict building by the side of the road marks the office and storeroom. Beyond is another derelict house once the home of Mr Rodger. Next to that stands the ruin of the manager's garage.

Rose Cottage, Where the Lorries were Kept

As we continued east we came to a road, now blocked, which went to Braeside of Cults, and opposite was the Kirk road. It was wide enough to take a 'horse-hearse'. Willie remembers using this road to go to church. By the time we reached Rose Cottage, where the lorries were kept, we were within sight of the present Cults Brickworks. Here too lime kilns once dominated the site. These gas kilns were enormous with great vents reaching into the sky. Coal, carried from Buckhaven by Mr Cuthbert in the Albion lorry, fuelled these gas kilns. There were also three Morris Commercials and a Fordson, which took the lime out to the markets. The drivers took a pride in their vehicles, which were always gleaming.

The End of the Road

Sadly, that took us to the end of our walk. For me this was a wonderful glimpse of the not-too-distant past. My enduring impression is of a warm community that embodied the Christian virtue of love for one's neighbour. It is good to know that many of those raised in this caring atmosphere are still in the community of the Howe of Fife today. While the above may well sound idyllic, life at Limehills was hard. The *Courier* records several fatal accidents over the years. One that stood out for me was the death of William Elder in 1892. He lived at Crossgates and worked at the lime works. A large piece of rock fell on the 50-year-old killing him and leaving a widow with seven or eight children.[255]

World War II

When, in 1939, the people of Cults were once again plunged into war, the young men followed in their fathers' footsteps to the battlefields of Europe. While it was very different from the 1914–18 war it was no less devastating for those involved, including the civilians being bombed. Once again young men went off to fight and there were those, whose names are recorded in the war memorial, who did not return.

Polish servicemen were billeted throughout the Howe of Fife. One young man found himself in the comfort of Pitlessie House. It is said that within a month of his arrival he married his landlady, and this engaged the local folk's thoughts and chatter for some time. After the war the brother of that Polish soldier joined them in Pitlessie.

As one would expect with a tight-knit community, Cults folk pulled together during these hard times. The WRI continued to hold regular meetings, frequently joining up

---

[255] *Dundee Courier* Thursday 28th January 1892

with Kettle or Springfield branches. During these years topics considered appropriate included 'Thrift' and 'Food Production in Wartime'.

At Cults Kirk a work party was organised to provide 'comforts' to local men serving in the forces. Events like whist drives and concerts raised funds. The WRI was also involved in this, but then I am sure it would have been difficult to differentiate between the work of one group and that of another. After all, it was the same folk who were involved. Apart from gifts supplied by the locals, these comforts often included knitted goods, and wool was collected and donated for this purpose.

Lady Cochrane, who had been president of the Fife Branch of the Red Cross during World War I, continued to have a strong interest in the provision of nursing care in the local community. As President of the Cults, Pitlessie and Springfield Nursing Association she encouraged fundraising to support this important service to the community. Those of us brought up under the umbrella of the National Health Service find it hard to appreciate the importance of such organisations prior to 1948. In 1941 Lady Cochrane, in her annual presidential address, intimated that the nurse paid for by this body had made a total of 3,270 visits in the previous year. These included medical, surgical and maternity cases as well as schoolchildren and school visits. Funding came from the small local groups running small events like the popular whist drives. Grand fetes at Crawford Priory were a major source of funds but, in 1941, with an income of just £189 and an expenditure of £259, there was quite a shortfall to bridge.[256]

The Cochranes: Thomas, Archibald and Ralph

Lady Cochrane's eldest son, Hon. Thomas Cochrane, Second Baron Cochrane, served as Lieutenant Colonel commanding the 2/7 Black Watch between 1914 and 1917 when he was transferred to the Scots Guards. His first son, Thomas George Fredrick, like his father also served in the Great War, being wounded three times and awarded the DSO, also three times.

The second son, Archibald, also had an illustrious record in the Great War. A submariner, he also received the DSO three times. At Gallipoli he was taken prisoner but

---

[256] *Dundee Courier* Saturday 18th January 1941

escaped from the Turks. With some others he had a long trek to the Mediterranean Sea where they stole a motor boat to escape. Eventually they found their way to London, arriving on Armistice Day feeling their achievement overtaken by events.

In civilian life Sir Archibald Douglas Cochrane served as MP for north-east Fife from 1924 and was Parliamentary Secretary to the Undersecretary of State for Scotland. During the 1930s he served as Governor of Burma. With the outbreak of World War II he rejoined the navy as Captain of a large Burma liner. He was serving in the Far East when the Japanese surrendered and it was arranged for their officers to submit their arms on his ship. As it happened he was the most junior officer present and was expected to stand at the top of the gangway as the Japanese boarded. He had decided that he would wear the uniform of the Governor General of Burma for this auspicious occasion. When the Japanese saw him attired in this impressive uniform complete with cocked hat, they assumed he was the senior officer and laid down their arms at his feet!

We cannot consider World War II without recalling the contribution of the youngest son of the First Baron Cochrane of Cults, Ralph Cochrane. As a young man he flew airships until it was recommended that he learn to fly aeroplanes. He soon mastered this and went on to assist in the creation of the Royal New Zealand Air Force in 1936, becoming its Chief of Staff in 1937. He promoted the skill of precision bombing during the war, which is specially remembered in the famous Dam Buster raid in May 1943 in which he played an important part. After the war he continued in the RAF with Transport Command. Here he was instrumental in reducing the high accident rate by encouraging greater training and the specialisation of pilots on specific types of aircraft. This is believed to have been a major factor in reducing the accident rate during the Berlin Airlift in 1948–49.

While air raids were not a major event in the area, blackout regulations were rigorously enforced. In the *Courier* of Wednesday 26th February 1941 Mr George Bryson, manager of the lime works, was fined 25*s.* because the flames of a lime kiln could be seen a long distance away.

The end of the war was welcomed by all and local folk became impatient to have their loved ones returned to them. Once again there were those who did not return and the names of Andrew Anderson, James Dallas and George Senior are inscribed on the war memorial.

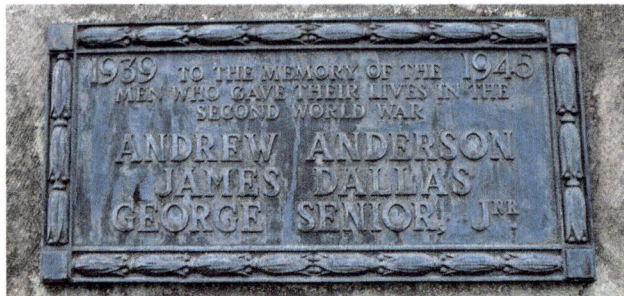

Celebrations at Crawford Priory

Pitlessie in the 1950s

By the early 1950s Pitlessie still looked much as it had done for at least 100 years. This picture was taken from the main road to Cupar. The view is along The Wynd. The house at the far end with dormer windows is still there and just beyond it is the property that was, until recently, the Post Office on the High Street. The buildings on the left were demolished in the 1950s and replaced with a large grassy area.

LORD AND LADY COCHRANE WED 70 YEARS

On Friday 1st December 1950 it was reported in the *Dundee Courier* that Lord and Lady Cochrane had reached their 70th wedding anniversary. We recorded the engagement and marriage of Lord and Lady Cochrane above, Lady Gertrude being the only daughter of Lord Glasgow.

Lord Cochrane had served in the 93rd Highlanders and the Black Watch. He had been a Member of Parliament for North Ayrshire and, from 1902 to 1905 was Undersecretary for the Home Department. He was also Parliamentary Private secretary to Joseph Chamberlain. For his public service he received his peerage in 1919. In addition to his service in politics and the Army Lord Cochrane was an innovative farmer and his 'model' dairy and farms were visited by people from around the world.

At the time this photograph was taken Lord Cochrane was aged 93 and Lady Cochrane was 91. Within a year Lady Cochrane would die, followed by her husband two years later.

The family continued to live at Crawford Priory into the 1960s. The costs of maintaining the old building were becoming daunting. There were many structural problems inherent in the building and the roof leaked badly. Dry rot infection was widespread and the sums required to bring the structure up to standard were unreasonable. Apart from structural problems it was a house of a different era requiring numbers of staff that few modern families could contemplate. In the end, the Cochrane family had no alternative but to build another house in the grounds and abandon Lady Mary's Gothic fantasy. The house had served its purpose for a bygone age and, however regrettable, it was time now to move on. Lord Cochrane has faced some criticism for this decision, which is unfortunate, for the old priory had been his childhood home and the home of his ancestors. No doubt the decision was most painful to him.

In 1968 Lord Cochrane died and was succeeded by his son Thomas Charles Anthony. Anthony chose to live near Elgin, while his younger brother Vere held the fort at Crawford Priory. The Third Baron Cochrane of Cults suffered from a disability all of his life. He did not marry and so when he died in 1990 the title was passed to his younger brother, Vere, who became Fourth Baron. Like his father, he took his place in the House of Lords. Unlike the Second Baron, he also spoke in the Upper House and was pleased to have been effective in initiating necessary changes in some legislation.

Mary Louden

Although Mary Louden grew up in Springfield rather than Pitlessie her connection with the parish goes back a long way.

Raised by her grandmother, who had to struggle to earn enough to care for Mary and herself, life was hard when she was a child. Tattie and berry picking earned money for winter clothes. Wash day was particularly busy and Mary would go to the pump to fill pails of water for the boiler. Although she never complained, Mary was sure that her grandmother did not need so much water for the washing! If anyone in the village had recently had a baby a pail of hot water was taken to them.

When leisure time came Mary and her friends had a favourite spot on the banks of the River Eden, in the grounds of Crawford Priory, where they loved to play. While changes have taken place to that spot, the photograph opposite shows it as Mary remembers it. Of course, they were not really allowed to play near the river, but children have always wanted to strike out for independence and this is how the youngsters in Springfield did it in the 1920s and 30s.

It was essential that Mary leave school and start earning money as soon as possible. At age 14 she found work at the lime works on Cults Hill. It was wartime and many men had joined the forces, leaving important industries short of staff. As a result, Mary found herself welcome at the lime works where she was expected to do the sort of work that had previously been reserved for men. One hundredweight bags of lime had to be lifted on to pallets, which were then transferred to lorries for transportation to the markets. Lime was then, as it is now, important in agriculture and in the building industry, so Mary and the other women were making a vital contribution by supporting an essential industry. At £1 2s. 6d. per week the pay was better than many women earned at the time, though less than a man would have expected. By the time she had made her contribution to her grandmother, Mary was left with 2s. 6d. to herself. One memory she has of her days at the lime works is of children suffering from bronchitis being taken to the kilns to inhale the fumes. It was believed this relieved the symptoms.

In time Mary left the lime works and went into service at a St Andrews hotel. Most of the clientele were RAF officers and it wasn't long before Mary wanted to be back home. Soon after that she went into domestic service with Hon. Vere and Mrs Cochrane (now Lord and Lady Cochrane) at Hospital Mill. At the Priory the staff included McGregor the butler, who lived at the lodge at Springfield. There was also a chauffeur and handyman. These were good days for Mary as she became a friend as well as an employee of the family. This happy relationship has continued over the years and she is always greeted as a friend by her former employers, while their younger son visits Mary with his family whenever he is in the area.

Mary's favourite spot on the River Eden

Saturday night was the time for fun and Mary would set off through the grounds of Crawford Priory for Pitlessie and dancing at the Wilkie Hall. The band was led by a fiddler named Adamson. Not only did they get the opportunity to enjoy dancing but the local girls and boys met there and it was here that Mary met her husband, William. Before long they were married and as William worked with the lime works they found a house in one of the wooden bungalows at Cults. In time the children came along and they moved to Pitlessie so that they would not have so far to walk to school.

At that time Pitlessie was a close, friendly and vibrant village. There were several shops including Nicol at the corner of the Priestfield road, which sold sweets and general groceries. The Co-op stood on the Cupar Road and there was a baker across from the Post Office on the High Street. Over the years the village has changed a great deal. Few inhabitants work in the area now, many travelling to the larger towns of Glenrothes, Kirkcaldy or Dundee. The ease of transport to Cupar and the supermarkets there have killed the small local shops that were once so important, not only for the produce sold but as gathering places for the local folk. It was often while shopping that news would be passed on about daily life in the community. Change is, as always, a feature of the passage of time. Our lives and communities slowly evolve to match the economic and social conditions of the time, which is inevitable. While this can bring with it great advantages, it may also be accompanied by a feeling of regret at what is lost forever.

Progress and Challenges

With the union, Cults benefited from access to the funds that were now being shared by all of the churches in the new Parish of the Howe of Fife. Maintenance of the Kirk remained a priority and, thanks to the dedication of members of the congregation and professional services of Elder Garland, necessary work was carried out to secure the future of the building.

In the 1990s the old ceiling showed signs of age and was in danger of falling down. Elder saw to it that a new ceiling was put in place and he cut a mould to match the existing cornice. The result was a fully restored ceiling identical to the original.

The union of 1983 was a difficult time, not only for the people of Cults, but for the congregations of all four churches. The general feeling was that Presbytery imposed the union on them, creating the largest parish in St Andrew's Presbytery. One of the main concerns was the ability of one minister to provide four services each Sunday as well as the necessary pastoral care. The unhappiness was to last for many years but in time it began to fade as friendships developed and new challenges, which were shared by all, demanded new solutions in the life of the Kirk and community.

CHAPTER FIVE: HOWE OF FIFE PARISH

The Howe of Fife
Parish Church:
We're All Together Now

~

February 23rd 1983 was a red letter day for the new Howe of Fife Parish Church, for this was the day of the induction of the **Rev. Iain Forbes**. Iain and his wife Ruth with their six children had travelled from Benbecula. Although in his early 40s Iain came with lots of experience, having served in Kenya from 1965–1970. On his return he spent five years at Church of Scotland HQ in Edinburgh in the Overseas Council before going to Benbecula in 1975.

Iain was born in Johnstone, Renfrewshire, but his family moved to Thurso when he was small, so that is where his early education took place. After leaving school he went to Aberdeen University to study Geology but no sooner had he graduated with a BSc than he decided to leave the ancient rocks behind and dedicate his life to the Rock of Ages. He went on to graduate with a BD. It was while in Aberdeen that he met Ruth, a midwife and daughter of the manse, her father being minister of St Machar's Cathedral. They were married in 1964.

Rev. Iain Forbes

It was when Iain was minister on Benbecula that he received a phone call from Hugh Munro, Session Clerk of the Howe of Fife, offering an invitation for an informal chat when Iain was next going to Edinburgh on business. When he arrived at Ladybank Iain was surprised to be taken into the church hall to face a full meeting with the Vacancy Committee. Happily this resulted in him being 'heard' at Auchtermuchty a few weeks later and then preaching as sole nominee.

The Forbes family came to the Howe of Fife at a difficult time. Many were unhappy and feeling the new union of the churches had been forced upon them. It was his task to soothe troubled souls and seek to bring a sense of unity among these folk who didn't want to be united. Iain saw it as his intention to generate among the elders, and so the parish as a whole, the feeling that the spiritual matters of the church belong to them so that they could be actively involved in developing the life of the church.

Iain, Ruth and family at the manse in 1987

The Basis of Union stated that ministerial assistance had to be available. This help came in the form of Rev. Johnston Titterington, a recently retired minister of Abdie and Dunbog Church. Mr Titterington was not only a man of great intellectual abilities but he was also very modest, bringing kindness and caring to the people of the parish during its formative years. There was about Mr Titterington an air of spirituality that made one feel in the presence of a truly holy man.

Iain too was a very hardworking and diligent minister. He aimed to encourage the folk of the parish in involvement in the life of the congregation. To this end a Worship Group was formed and also the Voyagers, for the teenagers. Activities included learning through watching videos, quizzes and games. For fun there was skating and stay-over trips to St Ninian's Centre in Crieff. There were monthly evening services at Kettle Church Hall and elders were encouraged to take 9 a.m. Sunday morning services during the summer months. With so much taking place it was necessary to find a replacement for Mr Titterington when he retired. It was then that Marion Paton began her long association with the Howe of Fife.

On Sunday 23rd May 1993 celebrations took place at Cults Kirk marking 200 years since the erection of the present building. A so-called 18th-century-style communion took place, though there was no catechising under tents, no communion tokens for different sittings and no long communion table. Everyone took communion together in the 'modern' way. The guest preacher was Rev. Professor James White and after the service the large congregation adjourned to the Wilkie Hall for lunch. Among those attending were Lord and Lady Cochrane with their guest the Earl of Elgin. They took their places in the 'Laird's Pew' and the 'Glasgow Silver' was used to dispense communion.

Later in the year the village of Pitlessie celebrated by having a 'Fair' almost like the one in Wilkie's famous picture. There were games, races and prizes for those with the best 19th-century costume. Iain again became involved and led worship from a cart in the middle of the village. A local artist made a large replica of *Pitlessie Fair*, which now hangs in the Wilkie Memorial Hall. Life-size characters copied from the original can be found at the back of the gallery in Cults Kirk.

Iain preaching from the cart at Pitlessie Fair

Throughout Iain's ministry Ruth was not only a support to him but very much part of the ministry team. A reader in the Church of Scotland, she has always had a keen interest in the Guild, and started a branch on Benbecula while there. She was also County Commissioner in the Western Isles for the Guides, reflecting her interest in the young, which she continued in the Howe of Fife by leading the Voyagers. Ruth saw her role as minister's wife as a unique position in the community allowing her ready access to people, and that brought her a great deal of pleasure. It also allowed her to become involved in the work of the Church nationally through the Women's Guild and the Board of National Mission and Unity. There is no doubt that, throughout the years of her marriage to Iain, Ruth has been very much a partner in his distinctive ministry.

In May 1993 after the General Assembly, a friend from the Kenya days came to stay with Iain and Ruth. He was Bernard Muindi, Moderator of the Presbyterian Church of East Africa. In conversation he told of the great need in Kenya and asked them to return. When Ian and Ruth approached the Church of Scotland's Africa Secretary, he suggested that they go to Mozambique instead where, he said, the need was even greater than in Kenya. On Sunday 24th October a special service was held to mark the conclusion of the ministry of Iain Forbes in the Howe of Fife. From Ladybank they soon found themselves off to Lisbon to learn Portuguese then on to Mozambique and new challenges.

In spite of the difficulty of the situation when Iain and Ruth arrived in the Howe, they made many friends while here. Evidence for this could be found in the Scots Night which was held in the Wilkie Hall at Easter in 1993 when Iain was presented with a new kilt jacket to mark his 10-year ministry in the Howe.

His ministry also inspired four parishioners to become ministers and, while it would be too much to claim unity in the parish, many elders had become used to leading worship and chairing meetings. This was evidence that Iain's desire that elders should take responsibility for spiritual matters was succeeding. So, as the congregation sang 'For my sake and the Gospel's go and tell redemption's story', Ian and Ruth left knowing their job had been well done and they had the prayers and good wishes of the congregation.

Iain being presented with a cake by Karen Garland at his farewell

Howe of Fife Parish Kirk Session 1993
Nisbet Stirling, Jack Semple, Jenny Williams, David Barclay, David Maillie, Ian Leslie, George Nicol, Franek Janeczko, John Anderson, John Stark, Angus Shaw.
Douglas McNeil, Alastair Milne, Alan Crawford, David Collins, Selina Donaldson, Hamish Mercer, Hugh Munro, Chris McCrone, Catherine Collins, Alastair Drummond, Ruth Forbes, Mae Richards.
David Scott, Avril Corbett, Bill Stewart, John Brand, Harry Mowbray, Iain Forbes, Marion Paton, Marjorie Whitson, Karen Garland,   Lena Scott, Jean Bradbury.

A period of vacancy followed when Rev. Andrew Stevenson was Moderator and the Associate Minister, Rev. Marion Paton, acted as locum. While it would be tempting to assume that the position of minister fell into Marion's lap because she was already on hand, that was very far from the case. A Vacancy Committee was established and advertisements posted. The preaching of ministers was listened to and interviews took place. Marion was, of course, a candidate, but she received no special dispensation because she was known in the parish. In the end she was chosen and so started a 13-year ministry. Marion has written her own contribution recalling her time in the Howe of Fife. I will allow her to tell her own story.

Memories of Howe of Fife 1994–2007 by Rev. Marion Paton

Having spent just over two years as Associate Minister of Howe of Fife working with the Rev. Iain Forbes, it was a great privilege to be called to be minister of this large and composite parish. Of course, it was a privilege that was not without its challenges, and from the beginning I was in a good position to appreciate just what would be involved. Four historic centres of worship, a scattered population, and long distances to travel to meetings, hospitals and the crematorium were just some of the practical difficulties that I knew I would encounter. However, the sense of call was very real, as I had not intended to apply for the position, but circumstance made it the right decision at the time.

Rev. Marion Paton

Howe of Fife at the time was blessed with some very fine and hardworking members and elders and I knew that there would be good support from these people. I was also assured that there would be an Associate Minister in place before too long. Sadly, this was not to be, and over the period of my 13-year tenure there was only part-time assistance for just over three years in total. This meant that I soon found myself running hither and thither around the parish, as I tried my best to serve the people in the name of Christ and, at the same time, keep up with Presbytery commitments.

Perhaps the greatest privilege of all was to stand, quite literally, in the footsteps of some of the great ministers of the Kirk, including at least one 'Father of the Kirk' who had served in the individual parishes in years gone by. Because the church buildings were so historic, there was always that sense that worship had been continuous on their sites for many centuries. To celebrate the sacraments using such historic vessels was very special, and I would often think of the hands that would have raised the cup before I had. To be a small link in that great golden chain of faith and service that had continued for so long was a great honour under God, as well as a huge responsibility, especially in my first full charge. It was also what made the whole experience of being minister of Howe of Fife so distinctive.

In order to keep it all going, I had an exercise book that I called the 'Masterplan', which had to have every service, and who was taking it, detailed three months in advance, just so that I could sleep at night! But I was always determined that there should be a service in every church every Sunday, for even though they may not have been all that well attended, I always thought it was important that each community had its own opportunity to worship together on a regular basis. It was also important that from time to time, as a union, the whole parish should come together for worship, and so these services were also entered in the Masterplan. I still have a record of every service I ever took in Howe of Fife, what the text was, what I said to the children, what we sang, and the numbers attending!

Wherever I was called to go, it was always a joy to come home, as the countryside of the parish was so beautiful. Driving over the hill from Kirkcaldy where the vista opened up in front of me, or visiting up in the hills on the other side of the parish, I was always filled with awe at the wonder of God's creation. People were often very generous when I visited them, and there was more than one house where I knew that a cup of tea would mean 'meat and two veg'! Of course, in the winter everything was much more difficult, and sometimes dangerous, especially in the snow, and on one occasion I never reached my destination because I was caught in a white-out, and on another I had to back out of the channel cut into the snow-drift by a tractor, when the height of the snow was over the roof of the car.

Of course, there were many memorable experiences. By far the saddest of these was the occasion when I was returning from visiting my assistant Carol, the night before she died, to be confronted by a diversion because of a road accident. It soon became clear that there had been four fatalities, four young people, all of whom I had known, all from the same village, who had lost their lives in a terrible tragedy. The next morning early found me in the village visiting parents and grandparents who were reeling from the shock and grief of what had happened, and trying to head off intrusive and insensitive reporters from national newspapers. The following week there were five funerals to deal with, four of them with roughly a thousand young people in attendance, and more than one of them televised. I'm not sure that village will ever recover from that trauma. Carol, in her wisdom, had decreed that I was not to take her funeral but to play the organ for it, because she felt that it would be too hard for me. It was at that time that I inherited her dogs, who became great companions and made sure that I at least got out for a walk every day.

However, life goes on, and there were also some very good experiences. Baptisms and weddings were great events, as also was the Golden Jubilee of Her Majesty Queen Elizabeth II. We celebrated this with a special service involving as many young people as possible in Kettle Church. Christmas and Easter too, besides being very busy times, were also happy times. The carol service at Collessie at 8 p.m. on Christmas Eve, with the huge Christmas tree with enormous numbers of lights, the smell of the paraffin lamplight, and the very large congregation from all over the county, the poetry, the traditional scripture readings and the enthusiastic singing, as well as emerging at the end into the frosty night, will live long in the memory. So too will the Good Friday musical meditation, and the early morning communion service in Cults Kirk on Easter morning, to be followed by two morning services, two afternoon services and a home communion. Exhaustion followed, but nonetheless these were special times.

Throughout my time in Howe of Fife I was blessed to have several very helpful organists. Mrs Komorowska at Kettle was a force to be reckoned with, once telling me when I chose a modern hymn that she was not going to play 'that boogie-woogie stuff'. I suggested that perhaps I might play that particular hymn, and she never complained to me again! Then there was John Walker at Collessie, a delightful gentleman who retired at the age of 90. He had begun to play at the age of 14, and had continued all his life, even when he had been interned in a prison camp in Burma, somehow managing to get hold of a harmonium, and organising services every Sunday. What a privilege to have known him. Then there was the choir, drawn from all four corners of the parish and offering an Advent carol service and a Good Friday meditation each year, sometimes Stainer's 'Crucifixion' or Maunder's 'Olivet to Calvary', always working very hard on a Tuesday evening in the manse, and at the same time having great fun as they learned the music.

I could go on and on as there are so many good experiences that I could share. But it would have been impossible to work on at that pace indefinitely, and the time eventually came when I knew it was right to move to pastures new. A call came to St David's High Kirk in Dundee and so off I went. However, I shall always be grateful for the opportunities to share the Gospel that Howe of Fife offered, as well as the friendships that are still cherished, and the faithful service that is still given. And on a Sunday morning as I shake hands with my congregation on the church steps in Dundee, I often look over to Fife, to the Lomond Hills, and think of the villages that nestle beneath them, of the churches where I served and, most of all, of the good and faithful people who continue the Christian work and service we all once shared.

To God be all the glory.

Time to Move on Again

Like the years Iain Forbes spent in the Howe, Marion's ministry was covering a period when the united Parish of the Howe of Fife was struggling to feel united. One of the main causes of fear for the people was the security of their church buildings. Folk were very aware that the cost of maintaining four churches, two church halls and the manse was stretching the finances to breaking point. It was during Marion's ministry, and with her encouragement, that Cults and Collessie churches each instituted 'Friends' to raise money for their upkeep. The idea was to find funding that would not be accessible to the church otherwise. This was to offset the cost of maintaining these historic places. In due course, Kettle too inaugurated a Friends group as they saw the advantages this brought to the church in question and the parish as a whole.

Because of the fears, uncertainty and lack of 'togetherness' in the parish, the Kirk Session decided that there was a need for a period of interim ministry to give the congregation time to reflect and refocus on its mission. That Interim Minister was **Rev. Dr Gordon McCracken**. Initially the appointment was for a period of two years, but in fact it lasted a little longer.

Rev. Gordon McCracken

Gordon came with one job in mind – unifying the parish – but finished up with another job regarding Ladybank Church. He soon decided that the pattern of worship in the parish had to change. Regular Sunday services would take place in Ladybank Church and services would be held in each of the other three churches on the first Sunday of each month. As Robert Burns said, 'The best laid schemes o' Mice an' Men gang aft agley'. Within weeks of this decision being made dry rot was discovered under the floor at Ladybank and it was no longer safe to hold services in that building. Soon carpets were lifted, pews moved to the side and the floorboards raised to reveal the awful truth about the extent of the problem. Very quickly it had to be decided to have regular services in Kettle Church with monthly services in Cults and Collessie.

Much time and effort was spent on deciding what to do. The general feeling was for a new building and a site was identified at the station. The congregation had to be consulted as it would mean closing Kettle Church and selling both it and Ladybank Church. People from all over the parish attended the meeting. The decision went against the new build by one vote. As a result of this it was agreed that the particular plan on the table should be dropped and Ladybank Church would be developed as a Parish Centre. This would be a flexible space open to the people of the parish for dances, films or whatever events were appropriate, as well as being a place of worship on Sunday.

Soon Gordon was called to another church and the Howe of Fife was once again without a minister. With Rev. Peter Neilson as Interim Moderator and a layman acting as locum the vacancy lasted for 18 months before the welcome arrival of **Rev. Bill Hunter**. Bill was attracted by the plans for a Parish Centre and felt that his experience elsewhere would stand us in good stead. He is a popular minister providing stimulating services and excellent pastoral care. He also has vision for our future and the ability to inspire others to share that vision.

Rev. Bill Hunter

This is vitally important as the Howe of Fife continues on the journey that was started around a thousand years ago or more.

A Rocky Path

It has taken time for the folk in each of the four parishes to come together and form the Howe of Fife Parish Church. But that is understandable when we remember that many people from one area found that those of another area were strangers to them. As a result, when the whole congregation gathered, folk tended to sit with those they knew. Those they knew were the folk from the same part of the parish. In time, of course, they have come to get to know one another from across the Howe of Fife and new friendships have been formed. The church has become stronger as a result. After all, it is fellowship that creates the church family, and that means knowing and caring for one another.

The things that have brought the church together, apart from Sunday worship, are the coffee mornings, Christmas fairs, the Burns Supper and the Parish Lunch, entertainment provided by CAMS (Cupar Amateur Musical Society), East Fife Male Voice Choir, more recently the church picnic, Harvest Lunch and other times when they have gathered socially as a family. What has been of concern is the future of buildings that have become more than places of worship. They are seen by many to be part of the identity of the communities in the parish and part of a sentimental past. They have also become a great financial burden.

The dilemma and difficulties this has caused have had the effect of bringing the people together. People from each of the four ancient parishes have come to recognise that the problem of the four churches and two halls is a shared problem that must be addressed by the modern parish. With occasional worship in Ladybank Church Hall but no worship in Ladybank Church since 2008, and fewer services in Cults and Collessie, some people have felt unable to join the congregation at Kettle Church where most services are currently held. Many, however, do go and they enjoy the fellowship of the larger, united congregation in worship.

The problem of financing all the buildings it has inherited has made it necessary for the church to look at its priorities. It must ask itself difficult questions about how effective it is at spreading the Good News of Jesus Christ in a world that many find difficult to comprehend. Society has changed from the 1950s and 60s. It is now the 21st century with all the distractions and technology that is in common usage.

Jesus taught people in the context which was meaningful to them in New Testament Israel 2,000 years ago. As the church has grown, developed and changed over the centuries it too has learned to address the people of each generation in a way that is meaningful to them. The churches rededicated by Bishop de Bernham were very different from the churches we are familiar with today. These 13th-century folk would not understand our worship and no doubt they would think we do strange things that they would disapprove of or not comprehend. In 800 years' time worship will be very different from what we recognise it to be today. The challenge for today is that we understand and address the needs of today's generation and speak to it in words and ways it understands.

This is also our duty as Christ's church in the world. Let us learn from the past, address the present and prepare for the future. If we fail in this we fail not only past generations but our children and their children. While their need for the grace of God will be as real as it is for the people of the past and each one of us in the present, they may not have a church to teach them about the grace that is given to all by a compassionate, loving God.

The value of history is that it teaches us about the changes that ordinary folk have had to make in their lives in order to cope with the reality of their time. As we look back through the history of the church in the Howe of Fife and the world, we see the changes that have taken place to allow an institution to endure. That institution may reflect the faith of many people in the world, but not all peoples. There are other institutions with other names trying to address the needs of people with different histories and cultures.

The great weakness in all institutions is that they are made and maintained by fallible people. The inspiration behind all faith is the one eternal, loving God who has allegiance to no particular faith and identifies with no particular nation. God is the loving Father of all people and, in the end, 'Thy will be done'– that is our only hope for the future.

Nec tamen consumebatur
And yet, it was not consumed

Appendices

∾

Chapter One

Timeline of Major Events in The History of the Church in Scotland

Circa 8000 BC	The first known settlements in Scotland
Circa 4000 BC	Evidence of the first farms
79 AD	The Romans built camps at St Andrews, Newburgh (Fife), Auchtermuchty and Boarhills – and elsewhere in Scotland
397	St Ninian founded the first Christian community north of Hadrian's Wall at Whithorn
500	AD Standing Stone at Collessie
Circa 6th–7th c	St Columba and the development of the Celtic Kirk throughout Scotland
664	Synod of Whitby
Circa 9th c	A church founded in St Andrews
1158	St Andrews Cathedral founded
1175	Records show the existence of Kirks at Collessie, Lathrisk and Quilts
1195	Founding of the Abbey of Lindores
1243	Bishop de Bernham rededicated Collessie, Lathrisk and Cults Churches
1318 – July	Consecration of St Andrews Cathedral
1517	Martin Luther nailed his 95 Thesis to the church door at Wittenburg setting in motion the events that were The Reformation across Europe
1528	Patrick Hamilton martyred at St Andrews
1541	Pitlessie made Burgh of Barony
1546	George Wishart martyred at St Andrews
1546	Murder of Cardinal Beaton at St Andrews Castle
1547	John Knox returned from Geneva
1560	Scotland became a Protestant country by Act of Parliament
	Kirk Sessions begin to appear
	The First Book of Discipline written by Knox setting out the organisation of church and national life

1562	Book of Common Order approved by the General Assembly
1563	Emergence of Moderators of the General Assembly
1567	James VI comes to the throne
1580	Presbyteries begin to appear
1584	The Black Acts are passed
1592	The Black Acts are rescinded and parts of the Second Book of Discipline reinstated
1600	Episcopacy reinstated in the Kirk
1605	The General Assembly discontinued and offending ministers punished
1618	Five Articles of Perth
1625	Death of James VI and succession of Charles I
1633	Charles I crowned in Edinburgh with an Episcopal ceremony; a committee of the Lords of the Articles that relied upon the King's bishops was elected
1635	A new Anglican Prayer Book is imposed upon the Kirk
1638	Signing of the National Covenant affirming the Scots commitment to Presbyterianism
1639	Pacification of Berwick
1642	Scots Presbyterians support the Roundheads in the Civil War
1643	The Covenant ensuring Presbyterianism in England as well as in Scotland
1649	Charles I is executed
	Act of Parliament granting freedom of General Assemblies and the abolition of patronage
1651	Charles II crowned at Scone
1660	Restoration of the monarchy
	All ministers appointed after 1649 required to make themselves available for reappointment by lay patrons of their parishes
1662	400 ministers expelled from parishes
1662–1685	Covenanters hold open-air conventicles
1679	Archbishop Sharp assassinated
1685	Death of Charles II
1688	Abdication of James VII and II and accession of William of Orange and Mary
1689	Claim of Right
1690	The Settlement of the Revolution – Scotland affirmed Presbyterian country
1707	Act of Union of the Scottish and English Parliaments
1712	Queen Anne repeals Act of Settlement returning the powers to patrons to select ministers
1732	Dissenters broke away from the General Assembly and formed the Associate Presbytery Church
1740	A group of ministers expelled from the General Assembly formed the Associate Presbytery, known as the Secession Church
1773	The Relief Synod is formed

1810	The United Presbyterian Church formed
1843	Disruption and the establishment of the Free Church of Scotland
1900	Union of the Free Church and the United Free Church forming the United Presbyterian Church
1921	Church of Scotland Act of Parliament granting the Kirk full independence on matters spiritual
1926	Parliament repeals the Act of 1712 and patrons would no longer choose the ministers
1930	The majority in the United Free Kirk reunite with the Established Church forming the Church of Scotland as we know it

Churches of Scotland timeline 1560–2000.
Author: Wikidwitch. This file is licensed under the
Creative Commons Attribution-Share Alike 3.0
Unported license.

Chapter Two Part One: Collessie

Ministers of Collessie Since the Reformation of 1560

1561	John Wobster (or Webster)
1574	John Kilgour
1576	Thomas Robertson
1578	Alexander Jarden
1580	Henry Balfour
1628	John Moncrieff
1641	John Littlejohn
1683	John Ogilvie
1696	William Pitcairn
1723	Thomas Robertson
1729	John Ballingall
1739	George Kay
1742	Hugh Blair
1744	John Mathie (or Matthew)
1757	James Ballingall
1760	William Walker
1772	Andrew Walker
1821	David Ogilvie
1833	John MacFarlane
1843	Robert Williamson
1883	John Henderson
1925	John Taylor
1968	Alexander Philp (union with Ladybank)
1975	Ian Wotherspoon
1983	See Howe of Fife Parish Church

Chapter Two Part Two: Ladybank

Ministers of Ladybank Parish Church Since 1881

1882	Robert Hagart Kerr
1925	John Douglas Glennie
1930	John Law Smith
1936	Angus Duncan
1947	Alexander Philp
1975	Ian Wotherspoon
1983	See Howe of Fife Parish Church

Chapter Three: Kettle

Ministers of Kettle Since the Reformation of 1560

1565	David Cuke
1574	John Balfour
1588	John Pitcairn
1589	William Cranston
1626	Robert Cranston
1633	John Ramsay
1667	John Barclay
1691	James Pitcairn
1717	James Munro
1731	Hugh Glass
1778	Peter Barclay
1842	William Reid
1878	Aeneas Gunn Gordon
1931	William Flint
1962	Angus Macaskill
1968	George McLean Henderson
1983	See Howe of Fife Parish Church

Wording of James Russel's Proclamation

A True and Exact Copy of a Prodigious and Traiterous Libel, Affixt upon the Church-door of Kettle, in Fife, the third of this instant, being Easter-day; written and subscribed by James Russel, one of those bloody and Sacrilegious Murtherers of the late Lord Primate of Scotland, his Grace.

Published by Authority, for the satisfaction and information of all His Majesties Loyal and dutiful Subjects

Edinburgh.

Printed by the Heir of *Andrew Anderson*, Printer to His Most Sacred Majesty, *Anno Dom.* 1681.

Edinburgh, *eighteenth day of* April, 1681.

Vera Copia collationed with the Original, (all written and signed by this execrable Murtherer his own Hand) which is kept among the Records of His Majesties Privy Council: and attested by

Will. Paterson, *Cl. Sec. Concilij.* Pat. Menzies. *Cl. Sti. Concilij.*

A True and Exact Copy of a Prodigious and Traiterous Libel, Affixt upon the Church-door of Kettle in Fife, &c.

Be in kind to all men, That whereas these who were once lawful Magistrats and Rulers, and were exercising their power, in opposition to all the Enemies of God and were a terrour to all evil doers are now become Tyrants and Land judgements, and Murderers of all these who departs from iniquity, and who are jeoparding their lives every day for maintaining and promoving of the Gospel of Christ and the true *Presbyterian Government*, which the three Kingdoms swore oftner nor once or twice to maintain with their lives and liberties, which Oaths they have all now broken, and have taken new Oaths contrair to the word of God, in opposition to their former Oaths and Ingagements, by which doing, they have overturned the whole Government, Civil and Ecclesiastick, and having made butcheries and havock of all the truly

Godly, and Loyal and true Subjects of the Land, and raised such Persecution, that I was forced to flee the Country; and I hearing tell that my Mother and others who medled with my Affairs, were still paying the Few-Duty (which properly belongs to the Crown of *Scotland*) and Sess [i.e. Cess Tax], which that Tyrant causes uplift for bearing down the Gospel of Christ, and for maintaining these Butcherers, Troopers and Souldiers, and with paying that Teind which properly belongs to the Ministers of the Gospel of Christ, to Mr *John Barkley*, who is both a thief and a robber; by paying of which, they acknowledge *Charles Stewart* to be a lawful Magistrate, and Mr *John Barkley* to be a Minister of Jesus Christ, which is blasphemy to say, as I shall prove afterwards; and after several times writing to my Mother, and some others who pretended kindness to me, shewing the great sin that we were involved in, by owning any of these Tyrants any manner of way, and earnestly desiring her to forbear and not to own them any manner of way directly or indirectly, but rather to suffer the outmost of hazard, than to sin against God by strengthening the hands of the stated and avowed enemies of our Lord

Jesus Christ, who is King, and alone Head of his Church; but my writing being to no purpose, and I being convinced of the greatness of this sin, and the heinous aggravations thereof, and the Judgements that would follow, if repentance prevented not, and being exercised for a long time, about what way to take for exoneration of my conscience before God and the World, and a testimony against all others who does go on in that sin, the clear conviction of the indispensibleness of this is my duty, I have now resolved through the grace of God, be the outward hazard whatsomever, to write thir two or three Lines, and cause put it on the Kirk-door of *Kettle*, being the most publick place, as my testimony against all the wrongs and injuries done to my sweet Lord Jesus Christ. As I do own and declare before God and the World, that Magistracie is an ordinance of God, so I disown and declare, that Tyranny is not of God, and so in opposition to God, and so against God, and therefor cannot be of God: and *Charles Stewart* being once made King of *Scotland*, upon condition that he should keep these Covenants, and rule according to these Covenants, and the Covenants being the Coronation Oath, which Oath he has broken, and caused burn these Covenants (which was the contract and Covenant betwixt him and the people) by the hands of the Hangman, by the burning of which Covenant, he has forfaulted his right of the Crown and Kingdom of *Scotland*, and is no more a King, but is become a Tyrant; therefore the people is loosed from all obligations and ties to him. [George] *Buchannan* acknowledges and sayes, *When the King breaks the Contract and Covenant that was betwixt Him and the people, and doth contrair to that He covenanted to do, whatever Right or Privileage did belong to Him by that Agreement & Covenant is then lost.* Likewise he saith, *When a King does those things which are directly for the dissolution of Society for the continuance whereof He was created, He is a Tyrant.* Other Loyalists acknowledge and say, *When a King overturns one of the Fundamental Laws, He is no more a King, but a Tyrant.* 2. They say, When a supream Magistrate maketh use of an absolute power, and so breaketh all Bonds for the good of the main Society, He is a Tyrant. 3. They say, *When He taketh from one or more members of the Commonwealth, free exercise of the Orthodox Clergie or Religion, He is a Tyrant.* 4. They say, *When a King doth not defend His Subjects from injuries, when he may, but suffereth them to be oppressed, He is no more a King, but a Tyrant:* (And much more when he oppresses them and murders them himself, as *Charles Stewart* does.) 5. They say, *When a King oppresses the Subjects by immoderate exactions, and hindereth the free sufferages of Members of Parliament, so that they dare not speak what they would, He is a Tyrant.* 6. They say, *When He taketh away from the people all power to resist His Tyrany as Arms, Strengths, and the chief men though innocent, he persecuteth and exhausts their goods without right or reason, He is a Tyrant.* 7. They say, *When a Magistrate for corrupting of youth, erects Stage playes, Whore-houses, and other Play-houses, and suffers the Colledges, and other Seminaries of Learning to be corrupted, they are unfit for any Office, therefore He must be a Tyrant.* Prov. 6.13. *Righteous lips are the delight of Kings, and they love him that speaketh right,* therefore *Charles Stewart* cannot be a King, because the unrighteous lips are his delight, and he loveth all them that doeth evil and speaketh against the truth, and therefore he must be a Tyrant: and seing that the least of all these forenamed particulars makes a King a Tyrant, surely without debate *Charles Stewart* must be one of the Monstruous and wildest of Tyrants, for he is guilty of all these, and has overturned the whole Fundamental Laws of the Land, by that Act *rescissory*, and has set up Lustful and Tyrannical Laws of his own, in opposition to the Laws of God; and if we believe *Buchannan* and other sound Writers, *A Tyrant has no just Authority over a People, neither is the People to own or obey him in any thing, for he is their enemy, and sayeth he, there is a just and lawful War with an Enemy;* much more with the enemy of all Mankind, that is Tyrant, of the which Tyrants *Charles Stewart* is one: and he saith, a lawful War being once undertaken with our Enemy, and for a just cause, *it is lawful not only for the whole People to kill that Enemy, but for every one of them.* I would speir That Question at these who are not of this Judgment, seing that Tyrants are reckoned in among the number of the most cruel bruits Beasts by all sound Writers; and Scripture, *Psal.*22.12. calls them *Bulls of Bashan*, of the which Bulls, *Charles Stewart* is one, and all his Associats are Bulls and Kine of *Bashan*: What would you judge to be your duty, if there were a wild and mad Bull running up and down all *Scotland*, killing and slaying all that were come in his way, man, wife, and bairn? would you not think it your duty and everyones duty to kill him, according to that Scripture, *Exod.* 21.28,29. [*If an ox gore a man or a woman, that they die: then the ox shall be surely stoned, and his flesh shall not be eaten; but the owner of the ox shall be quit. But if the ox were wont to push with his horn in time past, and it hath been testified to his owner, and he hath not kept him in, but that he hath killed a man or a woman; the ox shall be stoned, and his owner also shall be put to death.*] and if this is granted, as it cannot be denied, wherefore should any say, that it is not lawful to kill *Charles Stewart* or his Associats, that hath been these twenty years as it were, running up and down *Scotland*, killing and slaying all the true Subjects of the Land, and are still continuing, and killing all that are departing from iniquity, and are adhering to, and pursuing the ends of the *Covenants*, by desiring to bring all Malignants to condign punishment, according to the *Covenants*, which all the three Kingdoms did swear with lifted up hands to the most High God.

Therefore, I *James Russel* Portioner of Kettle, does reject *Charles Stewart* from being my King, or fromhaving any lawful authority over me; and I do declare before the world, that *I* will not own nor obey him any manner of way, either by paying the Few-Duty or any other thing which properly belongs to the Crown of *Scotland*, or that which they call Sess, which is falsely imposed upon the Kingdom, and lifted up for the banishing Christ and his Gospel out of the Land, yea, for upholding and maintaining ruffian Troopers and Souldiers, for no other thing but that they may Crucifie Christ in his members every day: and likewise I protest against *my Mother* and *James Dale*, who is labouring now on my Land, at my Mothers instance, against their paying of the Few-Duty, or any other thing which properly belongs to the Crown of *Scotland*, but not to a Tyrant, and therefore not to *Charles Stewart*; and against the paying of that which they call Sess. And likewise, I do protest against all these who take the name of Christians to themselves, who owns him or acknowledges him to have any lawful authority over them; and I do protest against the owning of any that has their authority and power flowing from him, either higher or lower Courts of Judicatures, for these who have no power themselves, cannot cloath others with power and authority: and *Charles Stewart* hath no power, therefore he cannot cloath any other with power and authority, for he cannot give others that which he hath not himself; therefore all these Courts and Judicatories that have their Power flowing only from *Charles Stewart*, have no lawful Power nor authority, more nor these who receives a commission from a Robber to go and kill and slay all that they meet with one the Highway; therefore cannot be owned, nor obediance given to them any manner of way, except they say that we must *obey the Devil, whose Viceregents they are*, and that will not be granted. And I do declare, that I look upon all who own that Tyrant or any under him to be lawful Magistrats, to be guilty of Blasphemy, and I prove it, Rom. 13.[1.] *For there is no power but of God and the powers that be, are ordained of God*; therefore that power that is exercised in opposition to God and godliness cannot be of God, for Rulers are not a terrour to good works, but to the evil, for he is the Minister of God to thee for good: Therefore *Charles Stewart's* power is not of God, for he exercises all his power in opposition to God and Godliness, and he is a terrour to good Works, and he gives praise and gifts to all these who do Evil; therefore *he is the Minister of the Devil*, to thee for Evil, for he executes Wrath on these who do Good, and therefore he hath no power of God; and therefore it must be acknowledged that it is the height of Blasphemy to say that he is a lawful Magistrate, seeing that he execises all his power in opposition to God; and therefore is no lawful Power, but an usurped tyrannical Power: Therefore, I would desire all that professe to be Christians to be at war of calling Charles Stewart a lawful Magistrat, or any whose power flows from him, to be lawfull Rulers, lest ye be found among the number of these Blasphemers, who say, that God in the Author of Sin; and ye may read the Blasphemers doom in *Lev.* 24.16. *And he blasphemeth the Name of the Lord, he shall surely be put to death, and all the Congregation shalt surely stone him*, &c. *Number* 15.30.31. I would desire all who are expectants of Heaven, as they would not have God to be their enemies, to bewar of doing anything that strengthens the enemies of Christs hands, if it were but to give them a leepy of Corn, or a bottle of Straw to their Horse, or Bread or Drink, or Lodging to themselves: for Christs enemies is another thing, nor our particular enemies. They will prepare a Table for the Troop, and furnish the Drink-offering for that number, they may read their sentence in Isa. 65.12. *Therefore will I number you to the sword, and ye shall bow down to the slaughter*, &c. and do it who will, when the Lord makes inquisition for the blood of his Saints, I am sure they will be found guilty, and to be more nor consenters to the Saints murdering, *Act*.25.20. *[And because I doubted of such manner of questions, I asked him whether he would go to Jerusalem, and there be judged of these matters.]* Yea, it is, as it were a burying of a sword & putting of it into a Robbers hand, to cut of all that's walking or trafficking in the Kings free road; yea it will be found to be a joyning Issue and interest with Gods stated and declared enemies, and they may expect to be ranked up amongst the number of these enemies (that our sweet Lord Jesus Christ, who is King and alone head of his Church,) will pass that Sentence against, if speedy Repentance prevent not, *Luk.*19.27. *But these mine enemies which would not that I should reign over them, bring hither and slay them before me.*

Likewise I do protest against the paying of Teind (which properly belongs to the Ministers of Christ) to Mr *John Barckley*, which is acknowledging him who is both a Thief and a Robber, to be a lawful Minister of Jesus Christ, according to that Scripture, *Joh.*10. *He that entereth not by the door into the sheepfold, but climbeth up some other way, the same is a thief and a robber*, which Theif and Robber Mr *John Barckley* is; for Christ is the door, ver.7. *I am the door of the sheep*, and not the Lordly Prelats, which was the entry that Mr *John Barckley* entered in, and all the rest both did, and doeth enter; therefore they are all Thieves and Robbers, *Mat.*20.25. *Ye know that the princes of the* Gentiles *exercised dominion over them*, &c. *ver.*26. *but it shall not be so among you, but whosoever will be great among you, let him be your Minister*, Luk.22.25,26,27. *But I am among you as he that serveth;* 1Pet. 5.3. *Neither being lords over Gods heritage, but being ensamples to the flock*: And Mr *John Barckley* was thrust in upon the flock against their wills by the Lordly Prelat, without so much as the Call of the least of all the Paroch; yea I was witness that day, that he was thrust in (to my shame I may tell this, and to the praise of his free Grace that has reclaimed me) and there was not one that would rise to take him by the hand, till they were threatened by the rest of the Hirelings; therefore he entred not by the door, but clim'd up another way, therefore he is both a Thief and a Robber, and a false Prophet, *Jer.* 23.21. *I have not sent these Prophets, yet they ran: I have not spoken unto them, yet they prophesied.* Mat.

7.15,16. *Beware of false Prophets, which come to you in sheeps clothing, but inwardly they are ravening Wolves, ye shall know them by their fruits*: 2Pet. 2.12. *But these are natural brute beasts*, &c. Jer. 10.21. *For the Pastors are become brutish, and have not sought the Lord; therefore they shall not prosper.* Ezek. 13.3. *Thus saith the Lord, wo unto the foolish Prophet*, ver.9. *Mine hand shall be upon the Prophets that see visions and divine lies, thay shall not be in the assembly of my people, neither shall they be written in the writings of the house of* Israel, *neither shall they enter into the land of* Israel, *and ye shall know that I am the Lord God, because, even because they have seduced my people, saying, peace, and there was no peace*, &c. to the 27. 2Cor. 11.15. *Therefore it is no great thing if these Ministers also be transformed as the Ministers of Righteousness, whose end shall be according to their works.* Ezek. 34.4. *Wo be to the shepherds of Israel that doth feed themselves*, &c. Ezek. 13.4. *And it shall come to pass in that day, that the Prophets shall be ashamed*, &c. Mal. 2.8. *But ye are departed out of the way, ye have caused many to stumble at the Law, ye have corrupted the covenant of* Levi, *saith the Lord: therefore have I also made you contemptible and base before all the people, &c. O ye dumb dogs, the blood of many souls will be found in your skirts, and in a little God will bring you to judgement, and will require the blood of all the souls in that congregation at your hands*, Ezek. 3.18. *The same wicked man shall die in his iniquity, but his blood will I require at thine hand*: I doubt nothing, but it would be acceptable service to God, to do with you all as *Elijah* did with *Baals* prophets, 1*King.* 18.40. *Take the Prophets of Baal, let not one escape, ye greedy dogs which can never have enough; come say ye, let us fill our selves with strong drink, and the morrow shall be as this day, and much more abundantly.*

Ye think your kingdoms will never be shaken, I doubt nothing but *Baals* Prophets thought so to, but they got a disappointment, and I doubt nothing but ye will meet with the like They cried to their God, but they were not heard: When any thing troubles you we may cry to your god, which is your belly, and to your King, which is King *Charles*, but rather that *Tyrant*, which you are all crying up so fast, and blessing him; it may be ye may get some kind of comfort, but I am sure that, the day will come, that both you and others that are crying him so fast up this day, will cry and not be heard, and will be made to curse your King and your God and look upward. It may be some will say, What needs all this hatred? I answer, *Psal.* 139.21[-22]. *Do not I hate them, O Lord, that hate thee? and am not I grieved with those that rise up against thee? I hate them with perfect hatred: I count them as mine enemies.* They'll may be say, I may hate them, and cry not out to let all the world know it. I answer, *Luk.* 19.40. *I tell you if these should hold their peace, the stones would immediately cry out.* I doubt not but some will say that I am mad to do that which will procure the hatred of all Ranks; I care not what perjured Apostats say, for my God hath said unto me, *fear not, for I am with you, be not dismayed, for I am your God, I will strengthen thee, yea, I will help thee, yea, I will uphold thee with the right hand of my righteousness.* I confesse if I would have sought counsel at flesh and blood, or yet at backsliding Ministers or Professors, I would not have ventured; but praise to the Name of my God, he hath advised me better in *Matth.* 18.28. *Fear not them which kill the body, but are not able to kill the soul, but rather fear him which is able to kill both soul and body in Hell.*

Written and subscribed with mine own hand, at --------- [Kettle?] the -------- [Third?] day of ----------- [the fourth month?] 1681.

Sic subscribitur, [James] Russel.

Certificate of Indenture

It is contracted, agreed and ended betwixt George Galloway, Shoemaker in Markinch on the one part and James Brown, sometime servant with James Mitchell, Nottingham in the parish of Kettle with the advice and consent of the Kirk Session of the parish of Kettle, in manner following, that is to say, The said James Brown with consent foresaid hath become and hereby becomes bound as Apprentice to the said George Galloway in the art and vocation of Shoemaking and that for the space of six years from and after the eleventh day of November Eighteen hundred and thirty seven years (being the term of his Entry on the said apprenticeship) during which space the said James Brown with consent foresaid, Binds and obliges himself to serve the said George Galloway honestly and faithfully and that he shall neither see nor conceal his skaith nor absent himself from the said George Galloway's work without leave asked and obtained for that effect; and if he do in the contrary, he shall serve two days after expiry of this present indenture for each day he shall be absent during the term hereof, For which causes and on the other part the said George Galloway Binds and obliges himself his heirs and successors not only to teach learn and instruct the said James Brown his apprentice in the haill points and articles of the said trade so far as he shall be capable to take up the same, but also to furnish the said James Brown in meat, clothing, bedding and washing, During the space aforesaid, and to give him a complete suit of clothes at the expiry of his said apprenticeship and both parties oblige themselves to perform their part of the present indenture hereunder to others, under the penalty of Forty Pounds Scots, by and attour performance, and farther the said George Galloway consents that execution shall pass against him and his friends at the instance of the Kirk Session of the parish of Kettle for the time being, for implement of his part of this present indenture and the said parties consent to the Registration hereof in the Books of Council and of Session or others competent, that letters of Horning on six days' charge and all other execution needful may pass hereon in form as effeirs, and thereto constitute

their Procurators &c. In witness whereof these presents (written by Robert Lyon, Schoolmaster in Kettle) are with another duplicate hereof subscribed by the said parties, as follows, viz? By the said George Galloway and James Brown at Markinch upon the twenty seventh day of December, Eighteen hundred and Thirty seven years, before these witnesses William Melville Weaver Markinch and James Johnston Shoemaker Markinch and by Peter Taylor spinner at Muirhead (as authorized by the Kirk Session of Kettle) at Muirhead upon the twenty eighth day of December in the said year before these witnesses William Melville and James Johnston

William Melville Witness } of the Subscription of { James Brown
James Johnston Witness } { George Galloway

William Melville Witness } of the Subscription of { Peter Taylor
James Johnston Witness }

James Brown certificate of indenture to George Galloway, shoemaker, Markinch

Amended Basis of Union

1930 – The Result of the Union of the Church of Scotland and the Free Kirk

AMENDED BASIS OF UNION (Min. 365) between KETTLE EAST, KETTLE WEST, and BALMALCOLM (KETTLE and CULTS) CONGREGATIONS.

Presbytery of Cupar.

Act of Union.—The Congregations of Kettle East, Kettle West, and Balmalcolm shall be united, under the name of Kettle, as from a date to be fixed by the Presbytery.

Transference of Property and Funds.—The property and funds belonging to each Congregation shall become the property and funds of the United Congregation, and shall be duly transferred.

Note.—Any bequests belonging to any Congregation for a particular purpose shall be used solely for that purpose, *e.g., :* In the case of the Campbell and the Arthur Bequests for the poor of Kettle West Congregation, preference shall be given to those of the West Congregation who are members or adherents at the time of union.

Place of Worship.—The Churches at present occupied and used by the Congregations of Kettle East and Kettle West shall be used as places of worship by the United Congregation at such hours and times as the united Kirk-Session shall determine. The Church at Balmalcolm shall be sold or let, subject to the titles on which it is held, and any money obtained therefrom shall be supplied to the Property Fund of the united Congregation.

Territorial Responsibility.—The bounds to be served by the united Charge shall be as the Presbytery shall determine.

Kirk-Session.—The Elders of the three Congregations shall be the Elders of the united Congregation, and form, with the Minister, the Kirk-Session of the united Congregation.

Note.—As the number of Elders in Kettle East is less than those in Kettle West before union is accomplished, an addition to the eldership should be made so that the number of Elders from Kettle East and Kettle West shall be equal.

Congregational Management.—The temporal affairs of the Congregation shall be administered by a Congregational Board, as detailed in Chapter II., Part III., of Manual of Practice and Procedure.

In the first instance, the Board shall consist of the Minister and all the present Elders and Deacons and Managers of the three Congregations.

Note.—That as Kettle East has no Deacons or Managers, before union is accomplished they shall elect members to serve on the Committee of Management, the number to be so elected to equal the number of Managers in Kettle West. The Board thus constructed shall hold office for one year, after which the ordinary provisions of the Congregational Board shall come into operation.

Minister.—The Rev. M. G. Gordon and the Rev. W. L. Craig shall retire on terms mutually arranged, and the united Congregation shall call a new Minister.

The Manse.—The Manse of Kettle West Congregation shall be recognised as the Manse of the united Congregation, and the Manse and Glebe of Kettle shall be sold, or let, or disposed of as the united Congregation shall subsequently determine, subject to the titles on which it is held.

The Manse at Balmalcolm shall be retained during the lifetime of the Rev. W. L. Craig, who shall have the liferent thereof on the same terms as he presently occupies it, and it shall afterwards be sold or let as the united Congregation shall determine, subject to the titles on which it is held. The united Congregation shall be responsible for the rates and taxes, and, so far as proprietors are liable, for the upkeep of the Manse. '

Ministerial Support.—The Stipend to be paid shall be the Stipend of the Parish, plus £40 contributed by the Congregation. In addition, the Congregation shah endeavour to contribute as generously as possible towards the Maintenance of the Ministry Fund, the terms to be adjusted on the Schedule of the Maintenance of the Ministry as in other vacancies.

Power to Readjust.—While these Articles and Terms shall form a Basis of Union for the three Congregations now uniting, the united Congregation shall be free, like other Congregations, to adjust arrangements under authority of the Presbytery as need may arise. In case of any difficulty arising, the minority shall have the right to appeal to the Presbytery.

Chapter Four: Cults

Ministers of Cults Since the Reformation of 1560

1560–1563	John Balfour
1563–1777	John Rutherford
1578–1595	Thomas Martin
1595–1608	Patrick Peat (Assistant)
1608–1635	Andrew Morton
1635	Edmond Cranstoun
1636–1641	James Martin
1641–1643	William Glasfurd
1643–1654	John Alexander
1656–1668	George Dishington (or Diston)
1673–1685	John Mathers
1685–1686	Alexander Skene
1686–1689	John Keir
1693–1697	Alexander Wilson
1699–1726	Thomas Birrell
1726–1762	Andrew Melvill
1762–1773	Andrew Hutton
1774–1812	David Wilkie
1813–1828	Thomas Gillespie
1829–1831	George Crawford
1832–1833	John Cook
1834–1838	Thomas Jackson Crawford
1839–1863	James Anderson
1864–1879	James Robert Chrystal
1879–1900	James Forbes
1900–1935	William Henry Porter
1936–1942	John William Goudie
1946–1952	Peter Lockhart
1952–1963	Archibald Bell
1964–1969	Angus Macaskill
1970–1983	George MacLean Henderson

Recommended Repairs to Cults Kirk Roof in 1762

1762 – West end of Cults Kirk roof:-

To Estimate of Tradesmen

	£	s.	d.
To taking down the roof	0	5	0
To 700 new slates at 6/8 per 100	2	6	8
To wood for 13 couples with Double Baulks	5	10	0
To Lath & Rigging & Easing Boards	1	17	6
To Lath Nails	0	10	0
To Garring nails	0	4	0
To 5 Balls Limestone for slating	0	5	10
To hair for plaster lime	0	2	0
To Two Windows and glass for them	1	2	2
To Slate Pins	0	5	0
To Wall Plates and Garring Nails			
For the feet of ye couples	0	6	0
To Wright work	1	13	0
To Three Roods of Slater Work	2	0	0
To mason work in building a pillar to Support the wall of the church west from east door, and pinning and harling the walls where needful on ye outside	1	0	0
The Whole Amount is	17	12	2 sterling

Chapter Five

Ministers of Howe of Fife Parish Church Since 1983

1983–1994	Iain Forbes
1994–2007	Marion Paton
2008–2011	Gordon McCracken
2011–	William Hunter

Draft Letter of Union

DRAFT LETTER

The Presbytery Clerk Presbytery of St Andrews

Dear Sir,

HOWE OF FIFE CHURCH - BASIS AND PLAN OF UNION

In his report following the quinquennial visitation to Howe of Fife Church, the convener of the visitation committee, Dr Porteous, referred to the concern expressed by the kirk Session that the Minister, because of the lack of continuing ministerial assistance, is unable, as he would like, to fulfil vital pastoral duties. Dr Porteous concluded that continuing ministerial assistance, which the Office - bearers believed to have been promised when the Howe of Fife Church was founded, is an urgent necessity.

At a recent meeting of the Presbytery's Unions arid readjustments committee, the concern of the Kirk Session about the lack of continuing ministerial assistance was again brought to the attention of the committee, together with the view that, in order to sustain the continuity of assistance, the provision of assistance should be written into the Basis and Plan of Union.

The Kirk Session was asked to write to the Presbytery Clerk, setting out the terms of the terms of a proposed revision of the Basis and Plan of Union and this we now do.

The Kirk Session of Howe of Fife Church, to ensure continuity and stability in the ministry to its people, submit the following clause to replace the existing clause seven of the basis and plan of union:

"7) MINISTER

The uniting Congregations shall proceed to the election of a Minister who shall be the Minister of Collessie and Ladybank in the first instance and then Minister of the united Congregation from the date of union.

The Minister so elected shall be under no obligation to conduct services in all four places of worship on any one Sunday.
To assist the Minister in the carrying out of the ordinances and to provide continuity and stability in the work of the Church in this very large Parish, an ordained assistant shall be appointed to the Parish as from 1st August 1991 for a period of five years, after which period the Kirk Session, with Presbytery, will review the situation. The funding of this new ministry shall be shared between the Department of Ministry and the Kirk Session in the proportions sixty per cent and forty per cent respectively.

Bibliography and Further Reading

❧

A Series of Original Portraits and Caricature Etchings by the Late John Kay, Miniature Painter, Edinburgh, vol. 1 (Edinburgh, Adam & Charles Black, 1877)

Brown, T. *Annals of the Disruption, with Extracts from the Narratives of Ministers Who Left the Scottish Establishment in 1843*, vol. II (MacNiven & Wallace, 1884)

Burleigh, J.H.S. *A Church History of Scotland* (Oxford University Press, 1961)

Calderwood, D. *History of the Kirk of Scotland*, vol. 6 (Edinburgh, printed for the Wodrow Society, 1842, p. 674)

Calley, G. *Collessie: A Parish Alphabet* (George Calley, 2000)

Collessie Public School Log Book (Extracts) 1874–1940

Collins C.P. Jr, *Royal Ancestors of Magna Charta Barons* (Dallas, Carr P. Collins Jr, 1959)

Croft Dickinson, W. *Scotland: From the Earliest Times to 1603*, rev. and ed. Archibald Duncan (Oxford, The Clarendon Press, 1977)

Cunningham, A. *The Life of Sir David Wilkie: With his Journals, Tours, and Critical Remarks on Works of Art and a Selection from his Correspondence*, vol. 1 (London, John Murray, 1843)

Dalrymple, D. *An Historical Account of the Senators of the College of Justice of Scotland from its Institution in 1532* (Edinburgh, James Stillie, 1849)

Divine, T.M. *The Scottish Nation 1700–2000* (Penguin Books, 2000)

Dowden, J. (ed.) 'Chartulary of the Abbey of Lindores' (Edinburgh University Press by T. and A. Constable for the Scottish History Society, 1903)

Dowden, J. *The Medieval Church in Scotland: Its Constitution, Organisation and Law* (Glasgow, James Maclehose, 1910)

Ecclesiastical Records: Selections from the Minutes of the Presbyteries of St Andrews and Cupar (Edinburgh, printed for the Abbotsford Club, 1837)

Fleming, D.H. (trans. and ed.) *Register of the Minister Elders and Deacons of the Christian Congregation of St Andrews 1559–1600* (Edinburgh University Press for the Scottish History Society, 1889)

Gillin, E.M., D. Toulmin and I.G. Wotherspoon, *A Short History of Collessie Parish* (John & Reid, 1979)

Goring, R. (ed.) *Scotland: The Autobiography* (Penguin, 2007)

Griffiths T. and G. Morton (eds) *A History of Everyday Life in Scotland, 1800 to 1900* (Edinburgh University Press, 2010)

Hammond, M. 'Charters of Ness son of William and his daughter Orabilis, lords of Leuchars, Fife', https://scottishmedievalcharters.files.wordpress.com/2014/02/ness-and-orabilis-for-web.pdf

Hammond, M. 'Women and the adoption of charters in Scotland north of the Forth, c. 1150–1286', *Innes Review*, 62(1) 2011, pp. 5–46, doi: 10.3366/inr.2011.0003

Haykin, M.A.G. 'Andrew Fuller and his Scottish Friends', *History Scotland*, vol. 15(6) 2015

Herman, A. *How the Scots Invented the Modern World* (New York, Three Rivers Press, 2002 p. 19)

Lang, A. *John Knox and the Reformation* (Project Gutenberg, 2004; original work published 1905), www.gutenberg.org/files/14016/14016-h/14016-h.htm

Leighton, J.M. *History of the County of Fife, From the Earliest Period to the Present Time*, vol. II (Glasgow, Joseph Swan, 1840)

Lewis, S. *A Topographical Dictionary of Scotland*, vol. 2 (London, 1846), www.british-history.ac.uk/topographical-dict/scotland

Lines, M. *The Traveller's Guide to Sacred Scotland: A Guide to Scotland's Ancient Sites and Sacred Places* (Somerset, Gothic Image Publications, 2014)

Lockhart, W. *The Church of Scotland in the Thirteenth Century: The Life and Times of David de Bernham of St Andrews (Bishop) AD 1239–1253* (Edinburgh and London, William Blackwood and Sons, 1899)

Lorimer, P. *John Knox and the Church of England: His Work in Her Pulpit and His Influence Upon Her Liturgy, Articles, and Parties* (London, Forgotten Books, 2013; original work published 1875)

Mallon, S. *Inside Verdict* (Scottish Christian Press, 2003)

Marshall, J.S. *The Story of Lathrisk House* (Glenrothes, J.S. Marshall, 1996)

Mathias, P. *The First Industrial Nation: An Economic History of Britain 1700–1914* (London, Methuen & Co Ltd, 1969)

McBeth, H.L. *The Baptist Heritage* (B&H Publishing Group, 1987)

Michie, C. *The Covenanters: The Historical Background to their Struggle* (Lochgoin and Fenwick Covenanters Trust, 1991)

Millar, A.H. *Fife: Pictorial and Historical, Its People, Burghs, Castles and Mansions*, vol. 1 (Cupar, A. Westwood & Son, 1885)

Miller, H. *The Cruise of the Betsey, with Rambles of a Geologist* (facsimile edition, National Museums of Scotland, 2003; original published 1856)

Mirabello, M.L. 'Dissent and the Church of Scotland 1660–1690 (PhD dissertation, University of Glasgow, January 1988)

Murch, J.D. *The Free Church: A Treatise on Church Polity with Special Relevance to Doctrine and Practice in Christian Churches and Churches of Christ* (Restoration Press, 1966)

O'Grady, O. 'Culdee Archaeology Project – lecture notes', Iona Workshop 11th April 2012, www.ionahistory.org.uk/iona-conf-ogrady-revised-2.pdf

O'Neill, A. QC 'Some Reflections on the Scottish Constitution and the Role of the UK Supreme Court', 21st September 2011, http://ukscblog.com/we-need-to-talk-about-the-referendum/

Porter, W. *Cults and its Ministers 1560–1843* (Cupar, J. & G. Innes, 1906)

Prebble, J. *The Lion in the North* (New York, Taylor & Francis, 1971)

Rae-Arnot, H. *Collessie Churchyard. To 31 Dec. 1911 (With a plan)* (Cupar, J. & G. Innes, 1912; part published by the Fife Family History Society in Publication 17, *Monumental Inscriptions*)

Reid, H. *Outside Verdict: An Old Kirk in a New Scotland* (Edinburgh, Saint Andrew Press, 2002)

Robertson, C. *The Origins of the Scottish Railway System 1722–1844* (Edinburgh, John Donald Publishers Ltd, 1983)

Robinson, M. (ed.) *The Concise Scots Dictionary* (Aberdeen University Press, 1985)

Royal Commission on the Ancient and Historical Monuments of Scotland, (n.d.) http://canmore.rcahms. gov.uk

Russel, J. 'A True and Exact Copy of a Prodigious and Traiterous Libel, affixt upon the Church-door of Kettle, in Fife' (Edinburgh, 1681)

Scott, H. *Fasti Ecclesiae Scoticanae, Volume 5: Synods of Fife and of Angus and Mearns: The Succession of Ministers in the Church of Scotland from the Reformation* (Edinburgh, Oliver & Boyd, 1925)

Sinclair, J. *The Statistical Account of Scotland* (Edinburgh, William Creech, 1791–99) ('the Old Statistical Account')

Sinclair, J. *The Statistical Account of Scotland* (Edinburgh, William Creech, 1834–45) ('the New Statistical Account')

Sinclair, J. *Statistical Accounts of Scotland*, vol. 2 (1791)

Small, R. *History of the Congregations of the United Presbyterian Church from 1733 to 1900* (Edinburgh, David M. Small, 1904)

Smiles, S. *Life of a Scotch Naturalist: Thomas Edward, Associate of the Linnean Society* (London, John Murray, 1877)

Smout, T.C. *A Century of the Scottish People 1830–1950* (Fontana Press, 2010)

Statutes of the Scottish Church 1225–1559, being a translation of 'Concilia Scotiae: Ecclesiae Scoticanae Statuta Tam Provincialia Quam Synodalia Quae Supersunt', ed. David Patrick, Scottish History Society, vol. 54 (Edinburgh, 1907)

Taylor, J.W. *Some Historical Antiquities, Chiefly Ecclesiastical, Connected with the North, the East and the Centre of Fife* (Cupar, William Robertson, 1868)

Taylor, S. and G. Markus *The Place-names of Fife*, vol. 2 (Donnington, Shaun Tyas, 2008)

Taylor, S. and G. Markus *The Place-names of Fife*, vol. 4 (Donnington, Shaun Tyas, 2010)

Testimony and Declaration of Principles of the Presbyterian Church Defence Association (Toronto, 3rd May 1881), https://archive.org/details/cihm_60227

Thomson, J. *General View of the Agriculture of the County of Fife, with Observations on the Means of its Improvement* (London, J. Moir, 1800)

Trades & Professions Directory for Fifeshire 1866

Walker, Rev. G.W. (ed.) *Church and Parish: Being Brief Historical Papers on the Parishes within the Presbytery of Cupar* (Cupar, J. & G. Innes, 1925)

Wodrow, R. *The History of the Sufferings of the Church of Scotland from the Restoration to the Revolution* (Glasgow, Blackie, Fullarton & Co., 1828)

Index

~

Lightning Source UK Ltd.
Milton Keynes UK
UKOW07n1151030716

277488UK00004B/64/P